AF657451

Counter Terrorism

Attention Authors

Manas Publications is fighting a war to tell the world that India can win the battle not only by the bullet but also by pen. We are converting fighters into writers. There is no dearth of intellectuals in our country, however, their knowledge is confined to them only. No sincere effort has been made by any other publisher to channelise their knowledge, which is why the talent of every intellectual remains latent. An author always presents the raw material in the shape of a manuscript and it is the job of the publisher to convert it to a finished product. Manas has been continually motivating intellectuals and publishing their manuscripts for more than two decades and would like to publish your manuscript too. If you or your colleagues have a manuscript ready for publication or are working on it, contact us with a detailed synopsis and list of contents. Manas will also suggest you a suitable title for writing related to your area of expertise. Manas is known for its publishing quality. We take utmost care in publishing and also give wide publicity to the book and its author through our national and international distribution network.

Counter Terrorism

US Department of State Publication

Manas Publications
(We Convert Fighters into Writers)
New Delhi-110002 (INDIA)

MANAS PUBLICATIONS

(Publishers, Library Suppliers, Importers & Exporters)

4402/5-A, Ansari Road (Opp. HDFC Bank)

Darya Ganj, New Delhi-110 002 (INDIA)

Off. © 23260783, 23265523, Res. © 23842660

Fax: 011-23272766

E-mail: manaspublications@gmail.com
manaspublications@vsnl.com

Website: www.manaspublications.in

US Department of State Publication

2011

ISBN 978-81-7049-395-2

Rs. 995

No part of this book can be reproduced, stored in a retrieval system, or transmitted in any form, by any means, including mechanical, electronic, photocopying, recording, or otherwise, without prior written permission of the publisher.

The views expressed in this book are those of the department and not at all of the publisher. The publisher is not responsible for the views of the department and authenticity of the data, in any way whatsoever.

Typeset at
Manas Publications

Printed in India at
RK Offset Process, Delhi
and published by Mrs Suman Lata for
Manas Publications, 4402/5-A, Ansari Road
(Opp. HDFC Bank),
Darya Ganj, New Delhi-110 002 (INDIA)

Contents

Introduction

Tracking and analyzing terrorist incidents can help us understand some important characteristics about terrorism, including the geographic distribution of attacks and information about the perpetrators, their victims, and other details.

In the last two decades, there have been more than a dozen attempts to build open source event data bases on terrorism. These data collections have traditionally excluded domestic terrorist attacks--even though analysts have long suspected that domestic attacks greatly outnumber international ones. Both the Worldwide Incidents Tracking System (WITS), collected by the National Counter-terrorism Center (NCTC), and the Global Terrorism Database (GTD), collected by the National Consortium for the Study of Terrorism and Responses to Terrorism (START) at the University of Maryland, have tackled this problem.

To have access to more comprehensive terrorism event databases, it is possible to think constructively about ways to further improve their quality. Following three ways have been recommended by Dr. Gary Lafree of the University of Maryland: validation studies, case control methods and geo-spatial analysis. First, as event data improves new avenues for validating it become feasible. For example, it is now possible to compare WITS to GTD and other event databases or to examine how media-related measures like newspapers per capita effect open source coverage. In some cases, it is also possible to compare event data to police or court data. Second, a limitation of event databases is that they include attacks that happened but provide no baseline for attacks that could have happened but did not. Advances here could be made by borrowing "case control methods" from medical research. For example, to understand suicide attacks it is useful to have information not only on the specific locations of attacks, but on case controls of similars locations that have not been targeted. And finally, the spatial dimensions of comprehensive event data bases like WITS and GTD have barely been explored. The NCTC should be applauded for substantially improving the government's publicly available data on terrorism and for seeking feedback from the research community.

CHAPTER – I

Strategic Assessment

AL-Qa'ida and Associated Trends: Al-Qa'ida (AQ) and associated networks continued to lose ground, both structurally and in the court of world public opinion, but remained the greatest terrorist threat to the United States and its partners in 2008. AQ has reconstituted some of its pre-9/11 operational capabilities through the exploitation of Pakistan's Federally Administered Tribal Areas (FATA), the replacement of captured or killed operational lieutenants, and the restoration of some central control by its top leadership, in particular Ayman al-Zawahiri. Worldwide efforts to counter terrorist financing have resulted in AQ appealing for money in its last few messages.

In the years since 9/11, AQ and its extremist allies have moved across the border to the remote areas of the Pakistani frontier, where they have used this terrain as a safe haven to hide, train terrorists, communicate with followers, plot attacks, and send fighters to support the insurgency in Afghanistan. Therefore, Pakistan's Federally Administered Tribal Areas (FATA) provided AQ many of the benefits it once derived from its base across the border in Afghanistan.

The threat from al-Qa'ida in Iraq (AQI) continued to diminish. While still dangerous, AQI experienced significant defections, lost key mobilization areas, suffered disruption of support infrastructure and funding, and was forced to change targeting priorities. Indeed, the pace of suicide bombings countrywide, a key indicator of AQI's operational capability, fell significantly during 2008. Initiatives to cooperate with tribal and local leaders in Iraq continued to encourage Sunni tribes and local citizens to reject AQI and its extremist ideology. The sustained growth and improved capabilities of the Iraqi forces increased their effectiveness in rooting out terrorist cells. In Baghdad, Anbar, Diyala Provinces, and elsewhere, local populations turned against AQI and cooperated with the Government of Iraq and Coalition Forces to defeat it.

The late 2006 Ethiopian incursion into Somalia forced AQ on the run in East Africa, but also served as a rallying point for anti-Ethiopian/anti-Government militia and al-Shabaab. After Ethiopian forces drove the Islamic Courts Council (ICC) out of power, al-Shabaab, the militant wing of the former ICC, and disparate clan militias launched a violent insurgency targeting the Ethiopian presence in Somalia, the Transitional Federal Government of Somalia (TFG), and the African Union Mission in Somalia peacekeepers.

Attacks against the Ethiopian and TFG forces continued in 2008, following the early 2007 call to action by AQ's Ayman al-Zawahiri, who urged all mujahedin to extend support to Somali Muslims in a holy war against Ethiopian forces. The subsequent security vacuum in parts of central and southern Somalia has led divergent factions to oppose al-Shabaab and its extremist ideology. However, hardcore al-Shabaab fighters, foreign fighters, and allied militias continued to conduct brazen attacks in Mogadishu and outlying environs, primarily in South/Central Somalia. AQ elements continued to benefit from safe haven in the regions of southern Somalia under al-Shabaab influence. After al-Shabaab's leaders publicly ordered their fighters to attack AU peace-keeping troops based in Mogadishu, a suicide vehicle bomber detonated near an AU base in the capital on January 24, 2008, killing an estimated 13 people.

Al-Qa'ida in Yemen (AQY) carried out several attacks against tourism and U.S and Yemeni government targets. The most notable was the September 17 attack against the U.S. Embassy in Sanaa that killed 18 people. A half a dozen other attacks occurred in Yemen in 2008 including a January attack that killed two Belgian tourists and two Yemeni drivers in the southern governorate of Hadramaut. Despite an August raid on an AQY cell that resulted in the death of its leader, the Government of Yemen has been unable to disrupt other AQY cells. Yemen continued to increase its maritime security capabilities, but land border security along the extensive frontier with Saudi Arabia remained a problem, despite increased Yemeni-Saudi cooperation on bilateral security issues.

Al-Qa'ida in the Islamic Maghreb (AQIM) maintained training camps and support networks in the isolated and remote areas of Algeria and the Sahel. AQIM continued to primarily target the Algerian government, but also made threats against what it termed "crusading" Westerners, particularly American and French citizens, although Russians, Danes, Austrians, Swiss, British, German, and Canadian citizens have been targeted as well, particularly in kidnappings for ransom. AQIM support cells have been discovered and/or dismantled in Spain, Italy, Morocco, Mauritania, Algeria, Tunisia, and Mali. In Algeria, there was a dramatic rise in terrorist attacks claimed by AQIM during the month of August, with at least 79 people killed in various incidents across the northeastern part of the country, many of them in suicide bombings.

AQ continued its propaganda efforts seeking to inspire support in Muslim populations, undermine Western confidence, and enhance the perception of a powerful worldwide movement. Terrorists consider information operations a principal part of their effort. Their use of the Internet for propaganda, recruiting, fundraising and, increasingly, training, has made the Internet a virtual safe haven. That said, bin Laden and Zawahiri appeared to be in the position of responding to events rather than driving them, particularly in the latter half of 2008.

Besides seeking to take advantage of international interventions in Iraq and Afghanistan as tools for radicalization and fundraising, AQ also sought to use the Israeli/Palestinian conflict, but lacked credibility in this regard. The international community has yet to muster a coordinated and effectively resourced program to counter extremist propaganda.

Taliban and other insurgent groups and criminal gangs: The Taliban and other insurgent groups and criminal gangs, some of whom were linked to AQ and terrorist sponsors outside the country, control parts of Afghanistan and Pakistan and threaten the stability of the region.

Attacks against our troops, NATO allies, and the Afghan government have risen steadily. Taliban insurgents murdered local leaders and attacked Pakistani government outposts in the FATA of Pakistan. Ideological allies of the Taliban conducted frequent attacks in Pakistan's Northwest Frontier Province (NWFP), particularly in the Swat Valley, and have extended operations in to the Punjab and the capital city of Islamabad. Suicide bombers are increasingly used to target Pakistanis, in addition to conducting cross-border raids on ISAF forces.

The Government of Afghanistan continued to strengthen its national institutions, and some polls indicated the majority of Afghans believed they were better off than they were under the Taliban. The terror-drug nexus and funding from the Gulf have increased the Taliban's ability to fight, and the Taliban's efforts to convince Afghanis that ISAF forces and corruption in the Afghanistan government are the source of Afghani pain has fueled the insurgency and curtailed legitimate efforts to influence Afghanis to reject violent extremism. The international community's assistance to the Afghan government to build counterinsurgency capabilities, ensure legitimate and effective governance, and counter the surge in narcotics cultivation is essential to the effort to defeat the Taliban and other insurgent groups and criminal gangs.

State Sponsors of Terrorism: State sponsorship of terrorism continued to undermine efforts to reduce terrorism. Iran remained the most significant state sponsor of terrorism. Iran has long employed terrorism to advance its key national security and foreign policy interests, which include regime survival, regional dominance, opposition to Arab-Israeli peace, and countering western influence, particularly in the Middle East. Iran continues to rely primarily on its Islamic Revolutionary Guard Corps-Qods Force to clandestinely cultivate and support terrorist and Islamic militant groups abroad, including: Lebanese Hizballah, Palestinian terrorist groups such as HAMAS and Palestinian Islamic Jihad, certain Iraqi Shia militant groups, and Islamic militants in Afghanistan, the Balkans, and elsewhere. Throughout 2008, the Qods force continued to provide weapons, training, and funding to Lebanese Hizballah to advance its anti-Israeli campaign and undermine the elected Government of Lebanon. Despite a dramatic decrease in attacks in Iraq since August 2008, security remains fragile, in part because the Qods Force continued to provide lethal support to select Iraqi militant groups that target U.S., Iraqi and Coalition forces. Iranian weapons transfers to select Taliban members in Afghanistan in 2008 continued to threaten Afghan and NATO troops operating under UN mandate and undermine stabilization efforts in that country. The Government of Iran also continued to pursue an expansion of its military ties during this period into the Western Hemisphere and parts of Africa, including through its IRGC-Qods Force.

DEFEATING AN AGILE TERRORIST ENEMY

The terrorist groups of greatest concern – because of their global reach – share many of the characteristics of a global insurgency: propaganda campaigns, grass roots support, transnational ideology, and political and territorial ambitions. Responding requires a comprehensive response that focuses on recruiters and their networks, potential recruits, the local population, and the ideology. An holistic approach incorporates efforts aimed at protecting and securing the population; politically and physically marginalizing insurgents; winning the support and cooperation of at-risk populations by targeted political and development measures; and conducting precise intelligence-led special operations to eliminate critical enemy elements with minimal risk to innocent civilians.

Significant achievements in this area were made this year against terrorist leadership targets, notably the capturing or killing of key terrorist leaders in Pakistan, Iraq, and Colombia. These efforts buy us time to carry out the non-lethal and longer term elements of a comprehensive counterterrorist strategy: disrupting terrorist operations, communications, propaganda, subversion efforts, planning and fundraising, and preventing radicalization before it takes root by addressing the grievances that terrorists exploit and discrediting the ideology that provides their legitimacy. Actions that advance these strategic objectives include building and strengthening networks among governments, multilateral cooperation, business organizations, and working within civil society. It is crucial to empower credible voices and provide alternatives to joining extremist organizations.

Working with allies and partners across the world, we have created a less permissive operating environment for terrorists, keeping terrorist leaders on the move or in hiding, and degrading their ability to plan and mount attacks. Canada, Australia, the United Kingdom, Germany, Spain, Jordan, the Philippines, Pakistan, Afghanistan, Iraq, and many other partners played major roles in this success. Dozens of countries have continued to pass counterterrorism legislation or strengthen pre-existing laws that provide their law enforcement and judicial authorities with new tools to bring terrorists to justice. The United States has expanded the number of foreign partners with which it shares terrorist screening information. This information serves as an important tool for disrupting and tracking travel of known and suspected terrorists. Saudi Arabia has implemented one of the first rehabilitation programs for returning extremists to turn them against violent extremism and to reintegrate them as peaceful citizens.

Through the Regional Strategic Initiative, the State Department and other United States agencies are working with U.S. ambassadors overseas in key terrorist theaters of operation to assess threats and devise collaborative strategies, action plans, and policy recommendations. We have made progress in organizing regional responses to terrorists who operate in ungoverned spaces or across national borders. This initiative has produced better intra-governmental coordination among United States government agencies, greater cooperation with and between regional partners, and improved strategic planning and prioritization, allowing us to use all tools of statecraft to establish long-term measures to marginalize terrorists. (*See Chapter 5, Terrorist Safe Havens (7120 Report) for further information on the Regional Strategic Initiative and on the tools we are using to address the conditions that terrorists exploit.*) 2008 witnessed improvement in capacity and cooperation on such key issues as de-radicalization, border controls, document security, interdiction of cash couriers, and biometrics and other travel data sharing. (*See Chapter 2, Country Reports, for further details on counterterrorism efforts taken by individual countries*).

Radicalization continued in immigrant populations, youth and alienated minorities in Europe, the Middle East, and Africa. A special focus on new approaches in Europe has been productive and has informed the way we understand government's role in combating radicalization. It is increasingly clear that radicalization does not occur by accident, or because such populations are innately prone to extremism. Rather, we saw increasing evidence of terrorists and extremists manipulating the grievances of alienated youth or immigrant populations, and then cynically exploiting those grievances to subvert legitimate authority and create unrest. We also note a self-radicalization process, through which youths reach out to extremists in order to become involved in the broader AQ fight.

Efforts to manipulate grievances represent a conveyor belt through which terrorists seek to convert alienated or aggrieved populations, by stages, to increasingly radicalized and extremist viewpoints, turning them into sympathizers, supporters, and ultimately, in some cases, members of terrorist networks. In some regions, this includes efforts by AQ and other terrorists to exploit insurgency and communal conflict as radicalization and recruitment tools, using the Internet to convey their message.

Counter-radicalization is a priority for the United States, particularly in Europe, given the potential for Europe-based violent extremism to threaten the United States and its key interests directly. The leaders of AQ and its affiliates are interested in recruiting terrorists from and deploying terrorists to Europe. They are especially interested in people familiar with Western cultures who can travel freely in the region and to the United States. However, countering such efforts requires that we treat immigrant and youth populations not as a threat to be defended against, but as a target of enemy subversion to be protected and supported. It requires that community leaders take responsibility for the actions of members within their communities and act to counteract extremist propaganda and subversion. It also requires governments to serve as facilitators, conveners, and intellectual partners to credible organizations/people who can do what governments cannot. Finally, bilateral, regional, and multilateral cooperation is essential.

We are also exploring how to harness the enormous potential of the private sector in the United States with its economic might and fast and flexible responses to market and security conditions. We need to find better ways to deploy this strength against terrorists. For its part, the private sector has a vested interest in partnering against violent extremists to secure its existing and future investments/economic opportunities. In addition, grassroots groups can play an important role in supporting immigrant and youth populations, strengthening their resistance to extremist approaches. Citizen diplomacy, cultural activity, person-to-person contact, economic cooperation and development, and the application of media and academic resources are major components of our response to the threat of violent extremism.

The commitment by governments to work with each other, the international community, private sector organizations, and their citizens and immigrant populations remains a key factor in coordinated efforts to confront violent extremism. Local communities and religious leaders are also a vital part of countering radicalization strategies.

This chapter sets the scene for the detailed analysis that follows. Significant achievements in border security, information sharing, transportation security, financial controls, and the killing or capture of numerous terrorist leaders have reduced the threat. But the threat remains, and state sponsorship, improved terrorist propaganda capabilities, the pursuit of weapons of mass destruction by some terrorist groups and state sponsors of terrorism, and terrorist exploitation of grievances represent ongoing challenges.

CHAPTER – 2

Country Reports

Africa Overview

The threat of terrorism - the senseless destruction of innocent lives and property, often times including oneself, beats every imagination. The world must unite to fight this scourge. No nation or person is protected against it. Those who feel so angry to carry out these dastardly acts defeat their own purposes because they end up killing those who may be ready to let the world hear their cases. They actually end up losing everything.

— Ellen Johnson Sirleaf, President of the Republic of Liberia
Statement to the 63rd Session of the UN General Assembly
September 23, 2008. New York City

A limited number of al-Qa'ida (AQ) operatives in East Africa and more numerous al-Shabaab militants in Somalia continued to pose the most serious threat to American and allied interests in the region. Somalia remained a permissive operating environment and emerged as a safe haven for both Somali and foreign terrorists. Its unsecured borders and continued political instability provided opportunities for terrorist transit and/or organization. Al-Shabaab and Islamic extremists in Somalia continue to disrupt peacemaking efforts, and desire to establish a harsh, abusive rule of law. A limited number of East Africa al-Qa'ida operatives in Somalia will continue to represent a long term threat to the international community. This threat has demonstrably increased; on October 29th, terrorists carried out five near-simultaneous suicide car bomb attacks against the United Nations Development Program and local government buildings across Puntland and Somaliland, killing at least 21. Al-Shabaab, which the United States designated as a terrorist group on March 19, 2008, has seized control of key parts of South and Central Somalia, including the port city of Kismayo and its environs.

In the North and West of the Continent, al-Qa'ida in the Islamic Maghreb (AQIM) expanded the scope of its terrorist operations in the Sahel, conducting terrorist operations in Mauritania and Mali. On February 1, the Israeli Embassy in Nouackchott, Mauritania and a nearby nightclub were attacked, which resulted in the wounding of one French civilian. In February, AQIM took two Austrian civilians hostage and released them eight months later after a ransom was paid. In September, AQIM murdered and beheaded eleven Mauritanian soldiers. According to Associated Press reports, AQIM kidnapped two Canadian UN diplomats on December 14, 2008 in Niger and held them hostage in Mali.

Many African governments improved their cooperation and strengthened their counterterrorism efforts. Both the African Union (AU) and African regional organizations continued initiatives to improve counterterrorism cooperation and information sharing. The Southern Africa Development Community (SADC) has publicly condemned all forms of terrorist activities and has expressed its readiness to work with the international community in the fight against terrorism. Despite its intentions, however, SADC's current capabilities and its efforts to date in fighting terrorism are limited.

The Financial Action Task Force (FATF), as the international standard-setting body to address threats of money laundering, terrorist financing and other relate crimes, established a network by which countries around the world can be included. These FATF-Style Regional Bodies (FSRBs) have the potential to serve both as a disciplinarian and as a resource. In sub-Saharan Africa, there are two such bodies recognized by the FATF: the Eastern and Southern Africa Anti-Money Laundering Group (ESAAMLG) and the Intergovernmental Action Group against Money Laundering and the Financing of Terrorist (GIABA). Like FATF and the other FSRBs, they conduct mutual evaluations, conduct typologies exercises, work on various issues with framework and implementation, and provide training for their members. Despite the existence and activities of these groups, Africa remains the single region in the world without FSRB coverage over wide swaths of its countries.

THE TRANS-SAHARA COUNTERTERRORISM PARTNERSHIP

The Trans-Sahara Counterterrorism Partnership (TSCTP) is a multi-faceted, multi-year strategy to combat violent extremism and defeat terrorist organizations by strengthening individual country and regional counterterrorism capabilities, enhancing and institutionalizing cooperation among the region's security and intelligence organizations, promoting democratic governance, and discrediting terrorist ideology. The overall goals are to enhance the indigenous capacities of governments in the pan-Sahel (Burkina Faso, Mauritania, Mali, Chad, and Niger, as well as Nigeria, and Senegal) to confront the challenge posed by terrorist organizations in the trans-Sahara, and to facilitate cooperation between those countries and U.S. Maghreb partners (Morocco, Algeria, and Tunisia).

TSCTP was developed as a follow-on to the Pan-Sahel Initiative, which focused solely on the Sahel. Ongoing concern that extremists continued to seek to create safe havens and support networks in the Maghreb and Sahel, as well as recognition that AQ and others were seeking to impose radical ideologies on traditionally moderate Muslim populations in the region, highlighted the urgency of creating an integrated approach to addressing current threats and preventing conditions that could foster persistent threats in the future.

TSCTP's main elements include:

- Continued specialized Antiterrorism Assistance Training (ATA), Terrorist Interdiction Program (TIP), and Counterterrorist Finance (CTF) activities in the trans-Sahara region and possible regional expansion of those programs;
- Public diplomacy/countering violent extremism programs that expand outreach efforts in the trans-Sahara region and seek to develop regional programming embracing the vast and diverse region. Emphasis is on preserving the traditional tolerance and moderation displayed in most African Muslim communities and countering the development of extremism, particularly in youth and rural populations;
- Democratic governance programs that strive, in particular, to provide adequate levels of USG support to build democratic institutions and address economic and social factors contributing to radicalism in the Maghreb and the Sahel, strengthening those states to withstand internal threats; and,
- Military programs intended to expand military-to-military cooperation, ensure adequate resources are available to train, advise, and assist regional forces, and establish institutions promoting better regional cooperation, communication, and intelligence sharing.

The African Union

The African Union (AU) has several counterterrorism legal instruments including a Convention on the Prevention and Combating of

Terrorism (1999), a 2002 Protocol to the Convention, and a 2004 Plan of Action. The Addis Ababa-based AU Commission provided guidance to its 53-member states and coordinated limited technical assistance to cover member states' counterterrorism capability gaps.

The AU worked with member states to eliminate redundancies between the Algiers-based African Center for Study and Research in Terrorism (ACSRT)[1] and the Committee on Intelligence and Security Services in Africa (CISSA), which was first established at the AU Summit in Abuja, Nigeria, in January 2005.

The Department of State and the Department of Defense's Africa Center for Strategic Studies (ACSS) have collaborated with the AU to run counterterrorism workshops. In December, ACSRT and ACSS jointly hosted an African Capacity Building Counterterrorism Workshop that focused on combating terrorist financing in North and West Africa. The workshop brought together approximately 50 African civilian and military officials from North and West African countries that are engaged in the Trans-Sahara Counterterrorism Partnership. ACSRT also held sub-regional counterterrorism seminars in Algeria in April, and in Congo in May, that examined the nature of terrorism threats in those regions, the capacity of countries in those regions to counter terrorism, and their needs for technical assistance to strengthen that capacity.

In 2005, with Danish funding, the AU hired a consultant to draft a counterterrorism Model Law to serve as a template to assist member states in drafting language to implement counterterrorism commitments. In December 2006, an AU-sponsored group of experts drafted counterterrorism language, which was in the process of being legislated. The group of experts decided to retain options for both broad and specific laws and determined that new legislation was needed to combat money laundering and other financial crimes. In August 2008, the AU Peace and Security Council requested that the AU Commission expedite the development of the African Counterterrorism Law.

Some AU member states maintained that Africa's colonial legacy made it difficult to accept a definition of terrorism that excluded an exception for "freedom fighters." Nonetheless, the AU is on record strongly condemning acts of terrorism. In August, the Peace and Security Council issued a statement condemning "unreservedly acts of terrorism, wherever they occur."

Although the AU Commission had the strong political will to act as an effective counterterrorism partner, AU staffing remained below requisite levels; consequently, capacity remained relatively weak. The AU created a counterterrorism unit at its Addis Ababa headquarters to coordinate and

---

[1]The Algiers-based African Center for Study and Research in Terrorism (ACSRT).

promote member state counterterrorism efforts more effectively. The AU welcomed technical and financial assistance from international partners and donors to bolster both AU headquarters and ACSRT activities approved by member states.

Angola

Angola's borders remained porous and vulnerable to movements of small arms, diamonds, and other possible sources of terrorist financing. Angola's high rate of dollar cash flow made its financial system an attractive site for money laundering, and the government's capacity to detect financial crimes remained limited. The government's limited law enforcement resources were directed towards border control and stemming the flow of illegal immigrants into the country, which increased exponentially since the 2002 peace treaty ending Angola's protracted civil war. Corruption, lack of infrastructure, and insufficient capacity continued to hinder Angola's border control and law enforcement capabilities. Angola recently reached out to engage the USG to support improving its maritime and airspace security.

Botswana

Terrorists could use Botswana as a transit point due to its porous borders, as evidenced by a 2006 report of organized smuggling of immigrants from Bangladesh and Pakistan, the large number of illegal Zimbabwean immigrants living in Botswana, and a 2007 report that suspected Islamic militant Haroon Rashid Aswad resided in Botswana in 2005 prior to his arrest in Zambia.

Botswana is a member of the Southern Africa Development Community (SADC), whose Organ on Politics, Defense, and Security is responsible for its counterterrorism efforts. The Government of Botswana established a National Counterterrorism Committee to address issues pertaining to terrorism and weapons of mass destruction. In April, newly-inaugurated President Ian Khama established Botswana's first intelligence agency, which is responsible for both domestic and foreign intelligence gathering. The Botswana Defense Force designated a squadron as its counterterrorist unit and sent several officers to IMET-sponsored counterterrorism training.

Terrorist financing is not criminalized as a specific offense in Botswana. However, acts of terrorism and related offenses, such as aiding and abetting, can be prosecuted under the Penal Code and under the Arms and Ammunitions Act. The Bank of Botswana circulates to financial institutions the names of suspected terrorists and terrorist organizations listed on the UN 1267 Sanctions Committee's consolidated list, the list of Specially Designated Global Terrorists designated by the United States pursuant to E.O. 13224, and the EU list. This circulation, however, is done on more of a voluntary, informational basis than a legal one because, as a World Bank assessment of the Botswana government's anti-money laundering and countering terrorism financing legislation noted, Botswana does not have a legal framework to implement UNSCR 1267 and 1373. There is no legal basis to freeze assets based on UNSCR 1267 lists. There is neither a legal framework to freeze assets based on a domestic or foreign designation of terrorists or terrorist organizations in the framework of UNSCR 1373. Although there is no Financial Intelligence Unit (FIU), the Directorate on Corruption and Economic Crimes has a dedicated unit investing suspicious transactions.

Burkina Faso

Burkina Faso continued to lack the resources necessary to protect its borders adequately and to monitor the movement of potential terrorists. There was no formal method for tracking the movement into and out of the country at border checkpoints, or at either of the country's two commercial airports. Burkina Faso has the potential of becoming a terrorist safe haven because of its close proximity to several countries in which terrorist groups currently operate and because its borders are porous, especially in the sparsely populated north.

Despite its lack of resources, Burkina Faso cooperated with the United States in its efforts to combat terrorism, where possible, and participated in training, seminars, and exercises, such as the regional Flintlock exercise held in Spain and Mali, and familiarization events offered by U.S. Africa Command (AFRICOM) and Special Operations Command Europe (SOCEUR). In September, SOCEUR initiated three projects in Burkina Faso to increase mutual understanding, improve tolerance, and combat extremist ideology by supporting non-violent conflict resolution and shared values.

The Government of Burkina Faso participated in regional efforts at combating terrorism with the Economic Community of West African States (ECOWAS), the African Union, and other international organizations.

Burundi

Burundi's counterterrorism efforts were hindered by domestic ethnic tension, the unsteadiness of a transitional period after more than a decade of civil war, a lack of mature governmental institutions, considerable corruption, and porous borders that enabled various rebel groups in Tanzania and Eastern Congo to freely enter Burundi. The government of Burundi has supplied troops to AU operations in Somalia; these deployed Burundian troops faced continued attack from al-Shabaab. Burundi's lack of capacity to regulate its financial system and investigate financial crime made it a likely location for money laundering or other terrorist financing. Burundian officials are nonetheless responsive to all offers of aid, assistance, and training.

Comoros

International terrorism concerns in Comoros focused on Comorian national Fazul Abdullah Mohammed (a.k.a. Harun Fazul), who is suspected of involvement in the 1998 bombings of the U.S. Embassies in Nairobi and Dar-es-Salaam. He was believed to have maintained contacts in the Comoros. The Comorian government's security forces had limited resources and training in counterterrorism and maritime security, so the country remained vulnerable to terrorist transit. Comorian police and security forces participated in U.S. antiterrorism assistance programs and cooperated with the Rewards for Justice Program.

Prior to 2008, the attempted secession of the island of Anjouan, and the establishment of hundreds of shell banks there, presented serious money laundering/terrorist financing vulnerabilities in that country. In 2008, Comoros made strides toward building an anti-money laundering/ counterterrorist finance (AML/CFT) regime. With assistance, the Union Government brought Anjouan back fully into the Union of the Comoros, and although lacking an AML/CFT law, made use of the tools it does have and began closing down the shell banks. Comoros also reached out internationally for legal and law enforcement assistance to build an effective AML/CFT regime and also to find and capture those responsible for the shell banks that were traced to Europe. Comoros applied for membership and was accepted as an observer to the Eastern and Southern Africa Anti-Money Laundering Group. At year's end, a draft AML law was in the Parliament.

President Sambi, democratically elected in May 2006, reconfirmed Comoros' rejection of terrorism, and with Comoros' religious leaders, publicly rejected religious extremism. President Sambi has sought close partnership with the United States to develop Comoros economically and to create opportunities for the country's youth. He visited Washington in July, and met with the Secretary of State. In September, Foreign Minister Jaffar led a Comoran delegation to the State Department for the second meeting of a joint committee to improve bilateral relations, which included counterterrorism cooperation.

Democratic Republic of Congo

The Democratic Republic of Congo's capacity to monitor and disrupt terrorist threats was extremely limited due to lack of resources and training, lack of governance, and unfamiliarity with the issue. The two principal foreign armed groups operating in the DRC and posing a threat to security and stability were the rebel group Democratic Forces for the Liberation of Rwanda (known by its French acronym FDLR) and the Lord's Resistance Army (LRA). The FDLR, which includes former soldiers and supporters of the regime that orchestrated the 1994 Rwanda genocide, continued to operate with relative impunity in parts of North and South Kivu provinces. The LRA, operating principally in northeastern Orientale province, arrived in the DRC in 2006 after a 20-year war against the government of Uganda.

Cote D'Ivoire

Cote d'Ivoire is recovering from a political-military crisis that essentially divided the country's territory in half. Instability and insecurity associated with the country's crisis has not been associated with any international terrorist organizations, and there was little evidence to indicate the existence of a terrorist threat. In an effort to improve border security, the Government of Cote d'Ivoire, in cooperation with the United States, implemented the Personal Identification Secure Comparison and Evaluation System, (PISCES), at its major airport and seaport. Cote d'Ivoire's Financial Intelligence Unit (FIU) became operational in 2008, allowing authorities to begin enforcing its reporting regime and enhance and target investigations. Members of the FIU, as well as Central Bank of West African States (BCEAO) examiners charged with anti-money laundering/ counterterrorist finance bank inspections, took part in financial regulatory training given by the United States in Washington, DC.

Djibouti

Djibouti hosted the only military base in Sub-Saharan Africa for the United States and Coalition Forces and was one of the most forward-leaning Arab League members supporting ongoing efforts against terrorism. President Ismail Omar Guelleh and many top leaders in Djibouti repeatedly expressed their country's full and unqualified support for the global campaign against terrorism. Although the government's capabilities were limited, Djiboutian counterparts were very proactive, and were highly receptive and responsive to United States requests for cooperation. The Djiboutian National Security Services and law enforcement agencies took extraordinary measures with their limited resources to ensure the safety and security of American citizens, the U.S. Embassy, and the U.S. military base at Camp Lemonier.

Eritrea

On May 14, the U.S. Department of State certified Eritrea "as a country that is not fully cooperating with U.S. antiterrorism efforts."[2] The lack of Eritrean cooperation has constrained the United States' ability to pursue terrorist suspects in East Africa, including al-Shabaab leaders linked to al-Qa'ida (AQ). In addition, the Government of Eritrea provided safe haven to Hassan Hahir Aweys, a Specially Designated Global Terrorist under U.S. Executive Order 13224 and UNSCR 1267 for his links to AQ.

The Eritrean government has linked broader cooperation on counterterrorism programs to the unresolved border dispute with Ethiopia and to a resolution of the ongoing conflict in Somalia.

Ethiopia

The Government of Ethiopia, facing a deteriorating security environment in Somalia that resulted in increased threats to its own security, and in support of the internationally recognized Transitional Federal Government of Somalia, battled insurgents and extremists that were formerly affiliated with the Council of Islamic Courts, including the al Qa'ida (AQ)-affiliated al-Shabaab factions. Until they announced their military withdrawal from Somalia in late 2008, Ethiopian forces provided critical support to the African Union Mission in Somalia (AMISOM) peacekeeping force, which was also targeted by extremist elements. In addition, Ethiopian forces countered individuals affiliated with organizations that attempted to conduct attacks inside Ethiopia.

Ethiopia's location within the Horn of Africa made it vulnerable to money laundering activities perpetrated by transnational criminal organizations, terrorists, and narcotics traffickers. However, the government has yet to establish an anti-money laundering/combating the financing of terrorism (AML/CFT) regime. Although passage of the AML/CFT regime stalled in 2007, the government pressed forward to pass an existing draft, and requested the participation of USG officials involved in prior technical assistance programs to work with Ethiopian central bank officials and local technical consultants in order to finalize the AML/CFT law before submission to parliament. In addition, the government requested that USG officials help draft AML/CFT training manuals for the Ethiopian banking sector. The manuals will be part of the establishment of a Financial Intelligence Unit at the National Bank of Ethiopia.

Ethiopia's National Intelligence and Security Service (NISS), with broad authority for intelligence, border security, and criminal investigation, was responsible for overall counterterrorism management. Federal and local police counterterrorism capabilities were primarily focused on responding to terrorist incidents. In November, the Ethiopian government's House of People's Representatives ratified the Protocol to the Organization

[2] As a result of this determination, Section 40A of the Arms Export Control Act, as amended (22 U.S.C. 2781), prohibits the sale or licensing for export of defense articles and defense services to Eritrea.

of African Union (OAU) Convention on the Prevention and Combating of Terrorism. Ethiopia was an active participant in African Union (AU) counterterrorism efforts, served as a focal point for the AU's Center for Study and Research on Terrorism, and participated in meetings of the Committee of Intelligence and Security Services of Africa (CISSA).

Ghana

Ghana's parliament passed, and President Kufuor signed, a Counterterrorism Act that made it an offense to commit or to provide financial or material assistance to a person or group which commits an act of terrorism. The Act also allows, with a court order, police to intercept communications, for the Director of Immigration to order the removal on non-citizens believed to be involved in the commission of a terrorist act, and for a national identification card program to be implemented. The cards will contain bio-metric data such as fingerprints and photos. AFRICOM provided the Ghanaian Navy with four 27-foot patrol boats to improve maritime interdiction capacity to help address Ghana's limited capacity to patrol its porous borders, including its maritime border. Ghana also passed an anti-money laundering law that provides for the establishment of a Financial Intelligence Unit (FIU); at year's end, the FIU had not yet been established.

Kenya

The escalating conflict in Somalia provided a permissive environment for terrorist groups such as al-Qa'ida (AQ) operatives and al-Shabaab. The most serious threat to Kenya came from AQ operatives such as Fazul Abdullah Mohammed (aka Harun Fazul), and Saleh Ali Saleh Nabhan, who were responsible for the 1998 U.S. embassy bombings. AQ also had a support network in the coastal region and in parts of Nairobi, such as the Eastleigh District. While the border with Somalia officially remained closed, some Kenyan officials characterized the closure as irrelevant given the ease of crossing in both directions.

Kenya lacked the counterterrorism legislation necessary to comply with the UN conventions it has signed. In addition, it remained difficult to detain terrorist suspects and prosecute them effectively under existing laws. For example, in September, an appeals court ordered Omar Said Omar, linked to the 2002 Kikambala Paradise Hotel bombing, released from custody due to a lack of useable evidence and improper police procedures. The issue of counterterrorism legislation remained highly controversial in Kenya with elements of the press, the human rights community, and Muslim leadership criticizing proposed legislation as anti-Muslim and as giving the government excessive power that could potentially be used to abuse human rights. In 2006, the Kenyan government submitted to Parliament a revised draft of the defeated 2003 "Suppression of Terrorism Bill," but critics sharply criticized the bill and it did not pass. The law was not reintroduced in the 2008 legislative session. Passage of legislation for combating money laundering and terrorist financing progressed slowly. The Proceeds of Crime and Money Laundering Bill went through two readings but did not pass before the end of the year's legislative session. Kenya is one of two countries in the Eastern and Southern Africa Anti-Money Laundering Group without an anti-money laundering law; in August Kenya assumed its presidency for a one-year term.

Supporters of AQ and other extremist groups were active in the East Africa region. As a result of the continuing conflict in Somalia, many members of these organizations have sought to relocate elsewhere in the region and some were believed to have travelled to Kenya. In August, police raided a house in the coastal town of Malindi searching for Harun Fazul, suspected of leading the plot to bomb the Embassy in 1998. Fazul escaped, but police said they seized two of his passports.

Kenyan security officials worked with the United States and other allies to seek to prevent terrorist infiltration into the country and apprehend suspected terrorists. The Kenyan Army worked to develop a Ranger Strike Force with assistance from the United States. The mandate for this unit includes operations against infiltrators and armed groups, including terrorists. The Kenyan Air Force procured additional F-5 fighter aircraft as being necessary to conduct maritime and counterterrorism surveillance and strike operations. The Kenyan Navy received training and equipment from the United States for maritime interdiction operations in territorial waters. The Maritime Police Unit and other agencies received equipment and training for coastal security from the State Department's Antiterrorism Assistance program (ATA). The U.S. military's Combined Joint Task Force-Horn of Africa (CJTF-HOA) collaborated with ATA on maritime operations training, and was in the formative stages of creating a Regional Maritime Center of Excellence designed to deal with terrorism and other maritime security issues. At year's end, CJTF-HOA was in the process of installing a Maritime Security and Safety Information System (MSSIS) in key positions along the coast.

Liberia

Despite limited resources, inadequately trained personnel, and a weak judicial system, products of 14 years of civil war, the Government of Liberia demonstrated a willingness to cooperate with the United States and the international community to combat terrorism. Through rule of law and security sector reform assistance programs, the United States supported a number of initiatives that addressed Liberia's vulnerabilities, which included porous borders, rampant identification document fraud, lax immigration controls, wide-scale corruption, and underpaid law enforcement, security, and customs personnel.

There have never been any acts of transnational terrorism in Liberia. of concern, however, were reports that during the Charles Taylor-era, hundreds of Middle Eastern businessmen purchased legitimately issued but fraudulently obtained Liberian diplomatic passports from Ministry of Foreign Affairs (MFA) officials. These documents would permit free movement between the Middle East and West Africa. The government took steps to stop this practice by requiring that diplomatic passports be issued only by the Ministry of Foreign Affairs in Monrovia. New restrictions on who qualifies for Liberian diplomatic or official passports were implemented by the Foreign Ministry's passport office.

Liberia's indigenous, war-weary, and predominantly Sunni Muslim community, which represents between 15-20 percent of the country's population, has demonstrated no interest in religious extremism to date. That said, outstanding land disputes negatively affecting large numbers of Muslim land owners in Nimba and other counties could fan ethnic and religious tensions with the predominantly Christian central government.

Madagascar

International terrorism was a concern in Madagascar because of the island nation's inadequately monitored 3,000 mile coastline. Malagasy police, military, intelligence, and security forces have not had much training in counterterrorism and maritime surveillance. Despite these limitations, there was little evidence to indicate any terrorist threat.

Despite limited resources, government officials were willing to cooperate with the United States and the international community. Madagascar volunteered to be chosen by the UN as a pilot country for counterterrorism efforts, and received a UN evaluation mission in October. The UN team will draft a report of recommendations for the Government of Madagascar on how to better implement UN Resolution 1373, likely focusing on improved coordination between the intelligence services, police, and the gendarmerie.

To combat terrorist threats, the government has created the Central Counterterrorism Service within the Ministry of Interior to work with INTERPOL and to provide information within the framework of regional and international cooperation. It also created a special counterterrorism branch within the Central Intelligence Service. In June, the Financial Intelligence Unit (SAMIFIN) was officially launched, and was charged with combating money laundering, including terrorist finance.

The Malagasy government took steps to create a coast guard to improve maritime security and border control. The government improved customs methods and equipment and adopted a biometric passport. It installed an information system to track arrivals and departures, x-ray machines, UV lamps, and magnetometers at the international airports. Judges, prosecutors, and judicial police were trained on international counterterrorism cooperation in January and parliament drafted a bill encompassing the universal counterterrorism instruments, including the requirements of UN Security Council Resolution 1373. Despite this progress, political unrest and limited resources constrained Madagascar's ability to confront a potential terrorist threat. The Malagasy authorities still lacked the capacity to effectively monitor suspect organizations, control suspicious financial transactions, identify terrorist suspects, and control the movement of people and goods across its borders.

Mali

Disparate Tuareg rebel groups in northern Mali attacked Malian military forces on several occasions, but none of these incidents were related to terrorist activities. Al-Qa'ida in the Islamic Maghreb (AQIM) used isolated and remote areas of northern Mali as a safe haven and held two Canadian UN officials, but did not focus attacks within Mali. Mali's extremely long and porous northern border, together with severe resource constraints stemming from Mali's status as one of the poorest countries in the world, hampered the Malian government's ability to prevent AQIM from seeking refuge within northern Mali. An active and engaged member of the Trans-Sahara Counterterrorism Partnership (TSCTP), Mali worked with the United States and other regional partners to address the threat posed by AQIM. Mali was also an active participant in U.S. programs including bilateral and regional military training and the Antiterrorism Assistance program. On October 31, AQIM released two Austrian tourists who were kidnapped in February in southern Tunisia to government authorities in northern Mali after a ransom was paid.

Mali worked to combat terrorism and responded on terrorist financing issues. In May, Mali's National Section for the Processing of Financial Information (CENTIF) began operations. The CENTIF, which reports to the Ministry of Finance, is responsible for processing information on money laundering and terrorist financing. In July, the Malian National Assembly ratified a new counterterrorism law that classified terrorist financing as an act of terrorism. Mali also created an inter-agency counterterrorism commission composed of senior level officials from the Ministries of Foreign Affairs, Finance, Interior Security, Defense, Territorial Administration, and Justice. A member of the Intergovernmental Anti-Money Laundering Group in Africa, Mali's mutual evaluation report was discussed and adopted by the plenary body in November 2008.

Mauritania

Al-Qa'ida in the Islamic Maghreb (AQIM) represented the primary terrorist threat to Mauritania. After two fatal attacks in late December 2007, AQIM significantly increased its level of activity and severity of attacks. In 2008:

- On February 1, six gunmen attacked the Israeli embassy and an adjacent nightclub in Nouakchott. No one was killed, but three foreigners were injured. AQIM claimed responsibility for the attack, and all of the perpetrators were later arrested by Mauritanian security forces.
- In April, one of the suspects in an attack on French tourists in December 2007 escaped from the main Nouakchott courthouse. This led to an intensive manhunt that culminated in a pitched gun battle between Mauritanian security forces and several suspected terrorists holed up in a house. A police inspector and two suspects were killed in the shootout, and several were wounded. The remaining suspects managed to escape, though several were later arrested, including the suspect who had escaped from the courthouse. Based on these arrests and other ongoing investigations, Mauritanian security forces discovered a villa in Nouakchott stocked with weapons and explosives.
- On September 15, an ambush on a military convoy near the remote northern village of Tourine resulted in the deaths of 11 soldiers and a civilian guide. The attack was particularly gruesome, with the attackers decapitating the soldiers and mining their bodies with explosives. AQIM claimed responsibility for the attack.

On August 6, General Mohamed Ould Abdel Aziz's bloodless coup against democratically-elected President Sidi Mohamed Ould Cheikh Abdallahi resulted in U.S. government suspension of all non-humanitarian assistance, including most military cooperation and counterterrorism training to the junta-led Mauritanian government.

The lawless eastern and northern regions of Mauritania were a haven for smugglers and terrorists. The porous borders with Algeria, Mali, and Western Sahara posed ongoing challenges for the ill-equipped and poorly funded Mauritanian security services. A new counterterrorism force that received U.S. government training and assistance before the coup was rushed into deployment in October, in an attempt to bolster Mauritania's northern defenses in the wake of the Tourine attack. This new counterterrorism force was untested in combat at year's end. The Mauritanian government arrested approximately 90 terrorist suspects during 2007 and 2008 combined. Approximately 60 of these suspects were arrested in April 2008 during the massive manhunt for the escaped suspect in the attack on French tourists. All suspects from that attack were arrested or rearrested, and remained in custody at year's end.

Mauritius

In November, Mauritian Prime Minister Ramgoulam announced before Parliament a series of planned security upgrades to ports and airports in an unprecedented push to prevent terrorism in Mauritius. The airport measures will include upgrades of the existing x-ray machines and the installation of two new units, a 100 percent screening of hold baggage at the airport, the installation of an Advanced Passenger Information (API) system, and the linking of Customs, Passport, and Immigration Services databases. Mauritius is also developing an Alert Color Code System in accordance with international practices.

As a result of limited available resources to cover its shores and waterways, Mauritius has traditionally had problems controlling land access, especially by small boats. To address this challenge, Mauritius has fortified its port security measures by strengthening access controls through an enhanced identification system, updated Closed Circuit Television Systems, and an increased number of police and customs officers.

Mauritius' Customs Mutual Assistance Agreement with the United States coupled with its goal of being a port where 100 percent of entering cargo is scanned have prompted progress on the Mauritian Cargo Community System (CCS) project. The CCS project aims to collect, organize, and provide advance electronic information on cargo and container shipments to ensure adequate risk assessment. Progress on this project has led to a continuous increase in the percentage of containers scanned.

Mauritius has a comprehensive and growing antiterrorism legislative framework based on "The Prevention of Terrorism Act of 2002," which criminalized terrorist financing and gave the government the power to track and investigate terrorist-related assets. The Government of Mauritius is well aware that organizations that accept charity funds could be susceptible to terrorist financing, and monitors these types of activities accordingly.

In November, Mauritius established a counterterrorism unit that includes the Commissioner of Police, the Commander of the National Guard, and the Head of the Interior Affairs Ministry.

In December, Mauritius implemented a new Border Control System that enables more effective controls over travel documents. Before the implementation of the new system, Mauritian Customs officials had caught

20 travelers using false passports. While most of these individuals were released in November, customs officials caught six Iraqis on their way to Australia using false Danish passports. The Iraqis were being held at year's end until the Mauritian authorities could verify their identities.

Mauritius is one of three countries in sub-Saharan Africa whose Financial Intelligence Unit is an Egmont Group[3] member. In 2008, Mauritius underwent a discussion of its mutual evaluation by the Eastern and Southern Africa Anti-Money Laundering Group plenary, and the report of the evaluation was adopted by the plenary body.

Namibia

In 2008, the Government of Namibia enacted the 2007 Financial Intelligence Act, which serves as the cornerstone of Namibia's anti-money laundering and counterterrorist financing efforts in concert with the Prevention of Organized Crime Act (2004), the Anti-Corruption Act (2003), the Drug Control Bill, and the Antiterrorism Bill (the latter two were not yet enacted at year's end).

This legislative package calls for reporting of the following acts: suspicious transactions, large cash transactions, electronic funds transfers, and cross-border conveyances of currency. It also strengthened the government's ability to investigate and prosecute money-laundering crimes. With the support of the United States, Namibia's Financial Intelligence Unit has been established and is operational.

Nigeria

The Government of Nigeria took steps regarding counterterrorism legislation. The National Focal Point on Terrorism, an interagency task force formed in February 2007, composed of the State Security Service (SSS), the Nigerian Customs Service, the Ministry of Foreign Affairs, Immigration, and other relevant authorities, met periodically throughout the year. In October, in an effort to improve coordination and communication between the legislative and executive branches, the UN Office on Drugs and Crime sponsored a workshop on counterterrorism legislation for Focal Point participants and members of relevant committees in the National Assembly.

A Senate bill based on the Commonwealth Secretariat's Model Legislative Provisions on Measures to Combat Terrorism passed its second

[3] The Egmont Group consists of 108 financial intelligence units (FIUs) from across the world. FIUs are an essential component of the international fight against money laundering, the financing of terrorism, and related crime. Their ability to transform data into financial intelligence is a key element in the fight against money laundering and the financing of terrorism.

reading on September 17, and was referred to the Senate Committees on National Security and Intelligence and the Judiciary for further review.

The Nigerian government approved the installation of U.S.-funded body scanners in all four international airports to detect explosives and drugs on passengers. The scanners were installed in March, May, and June. The Nigerian and U.S. governments also cos-ponsored a conference on aviation security in Abuja from November 17-18. Despite repeated requests from the U.S. government, however, the Nigerian government has not yet approved the use of U.S. Federal Air Marshals on direct flights between Nigeria and the United States.

On May 5 in Abuja, President Yar'Adua, in a message delivered by Vice President Goodluck Jonathan to open a conference of the Committee of Intelligence and Security Services in Africa (CISSA), charged the assembled heads of intelligence and security services with developing strategies to check the spread of extremist ideologies in West Africa by external elements, and called for increased regional and global networking to meet the threat. Ambassador Emmanuel Imohe, Director General of Nigeria's National Intelligence Agency (NIA), also took a leadership role at the meeting, calling for greater cooperation and intelligence sharing, particularly given the region's porous borders.

On May 14, the Nigeria Police Force announced the deployment of units from its newly created Antiterrorism Squad (ATS) to Lagos, Abuja, Port Harcourt, and Kano, reportedly as a result of an alleged terrorist threat.

On May 27, Malam Kasimu Umar, leader of an extremist Shia group in Sokoto, and 112 members of his sect, were sentenced by the Sokoto Upper Sharia Court to eight years imprisonment on weapons charges, resisting arrest, public incitement, and inciting contempt of religious creed, in connection with violence in the aftermath of the July 2007 assassination of a renowned Islamic preacher Malam Umaru Dan Maishiyya, a crime whose motive has never been determined.

From September 8-12, members of the Nigerian Armed Forces, as well as authorities from customs and immigration and other relevant civilian agencies, participated in a USG security seminar on protecting the maritime domain. During the September 17-22 visit of the USS Elrod, under the auspices of the Africa Partnership Station, a joint exercise was successfully conducted with the newly operational Regional Maritime Awareness Capability (RMAC) system in Lagos. Progress continued on the establishment of an additional RMAC station in the east. Nigerian military personnel attended operational and strategic counterterrorism training in the United States and Germany under the auspices of the Trans-Sahara Counterterrorism Partnership. Twelve Nigerians attended a U.S.-sponsored Post-Blast Investigation Training course in August, while

20 participated in a Maritime Port and Harbor Security Management course in September.

On November 2, the Nigerian Police Force announced the deployment of ATS units to strategic locations in the Federal Capital Territory, as well as Rivers, Lagos, and Kano States. On November 7, the Nigerian Federal Government elevated its threat level over potential sabotage of national infrastructure in a confidential memo that was subsequently leaked to the *Nigerian Tribune* newspaper.

A member of the Intergovernmental Anti-Money Laundering Group in Africa, Nigeria's mutual evaluation report was discussed and adopted by the plenary body in May 2008. Nigeria's Financial Intelligence Unit (FIU) is the only Egmont member in the sub-region, and has volunteered to sponsor four additional FIUs in the sub-region for membership. Actions taken by the Nigerian authorities in 2008 regarding the Economic and Financial Crimes Commission have led to concerns about the effectiveness of this institution and its continued sustainability.

Rwanda

The Government of Rwanda reinforced border control measures to identify potential terrorists and to prevent the entry into Rwanda of armed groups operating in the Democratic Republic of the Congo. Rwanda's intergovernmental counterterrorism committee and a counterterrorism reaction team in the police intelligence service were operational. In June, a U.S. Coast Guard team trained Rwanda Defense Force marines on border control operations on Lake Kivu (bordering the Congo), including harbor security, interdiction of illegal traffic in goods and persons, the law of naval warfare, anti-narcotrafficking, and counterterrorism drills and procedures.

Rwandan officials (particularly in the Central Bank and Ministry of Finance) cooperated on terrorist financing issues. Parliament approved new comprehensive legislation supporting the prevention and suppression of money laundering and financing of terrorism. The legislation, awaiting signature by the president, included provisions to enhance the transparency of financial transactions, establish a Financial Investigations Unit (FIU), and authorize the freezing of assets of individuals and organizations involved in illicit or terrorism-related activities. Rwanda officially committed itself to locating and freezing terrorist assets identified by the international community.

Rwanda participated in regional initiatives on international counterterrorism cooperation, including the East Africa Standby Brigade. In October, Rwanda hosted a meeting of African Union Attorney Generals and Ministers of Justice, which considered a broad range of law enforcement issues, including counterterrorism cooperation and legislation. Rwanda also hosted several extensive training courses for senior police commanders on counterterrorism and other issues in cooperation with the United Kingdom.

Besides reinforcing border security and refining counterterrorism legislation and intelligence sharing, the Government of Rwanda developed counterterrorism response strategies. The Rwandan national tourist office continued its development of a communications network to alert embassies should their citizens be harmed in Rwanda's national parks. Work continued as well on increased disaster preparedness. The national Civil Aviation Authority, working in conjunction with the U.S. Federal Aviation Administration and the Department of Transportation, reviewed East African Community security measures for airports and airlines in Rwanda, focusing in particular on security and disaster response at Kigali International Airport.

This year was the first that Rwanda sent National Police officers to the International Law Enforcement Academy for a range of criminal investigation courses with counterterrorism applications.

Senegal

The Government of Senegal cooperated with the United States to identify terrorist groups operating in Senegalese territory. More work remained to be done, however, to develop first responder services, to facilitate the quick sharing of information between agencies, and to control porous borders where police and security services were undermanned and ill-equipped to prevent illicit cross-border trafficking. Although al-Qa'ida in the Islamic Maghreb did not launch attacks or secure safe haven in Senegal, it attempted to set up transit points and facilitation networks in the country. The Government of Senegal affirmed its commitment to USG-assisted efforts to augment its border security. Senegal recognized that some groups of concern have attempted to engage in fundraising and propaganda activities and participated in regional efforts to combat terrorist finance. Senegal lacked specific counterterrorism legislation and current laws made it difficult to prosecute terrorist suspects. Senegalese government officials participated in Antiterrorism Assistance programs. One of the first Financial Intelligence Units (FIUs) in the sub-region, Senegal's FIU, known as CENTIF, has been active in sponsoring and holding implementation, consciousness-raising and awareness workshops on anti-money laundering/terrorist finance issues for its own stakeholders as well as for counterparts from around the sub-region. A member of the Intergovernmental Anti-Money Laundering Group in Africa, Senegal's mutual evaluation report was discussed and adopted by the plenary body in May 2008.

Somalia

Somalia's fragile transitional federal government, protracted state of violent instability, its long, unguarded coastline, porous borders, and proximity to the Arabian Peninsula, made the country an attractive location for international terrorists seeking a transit or launching point for operations in Somalia or elsewhere. On October 29, awareness of the technology, methodology, and magnitude of the Somali terrorism threat increased dramatically when unknown suicide terrorists detonated five near-simultaneous vehicle bombs against UN, Ethiopian diplomatic, and government offices in Bossaso and Hargeisa. Authorities suspected southern Somali extremists with ties to al Qa'ida (AQ) were responsible. There were other high profile terrorist attacks:

- On January 18, three international aid workers were killed by a roadside bomb in Kismayo.
- In February, two bombs killed 20 and injured over 100 in Bossaso.

On March 10, a moderate Somali cleric and peace activist was murdered as he left a Mogadishu mosque.

- On March 12, a police chief was kidnapped and beheaded.

On June 1, President Abdullahi Yusuf's convoy was ambushed by gunmen.

- On July 6, an assassin killed the Director of the United Nation Development Program in Mogadishu.
- On August 3, a roadside bomb killed 20 female street sweepers in Mogadishu.
- On November 9, Somali militants crossed the Kenyan border to kidnap two Italian nuns.

Despite on-going peace negotiations between the Transitional Federal Government (TFG) and moderate opposition, the Alliance for the Re-Liberation of Somalia, the terrorist group al-Shabaab (The Youth) militarily captured much of southern Somalia in the second half of the year. By year's end, the TFG was confined to parts of Mogadishu. Al-Shabaab, whose leaders are affiliated with AQ, consists of a disparate grouping of armed extremist militia, many of whom do not adhere to the jihadist ideology that is shared among the leaders of the group. Several senior leaders are believed to have trained and fought with AQ in Afghanistan. Al-Shabaab and other extremists also conducted remote-controlled roadside bombings, kidnappings, and assassinations of government officials, journalists, humanitarian workers, and civil society leaders. Al-Shabaab threatened agencies and their staff and expelled U.S. humanitarian aid agency CARE from southern Somalia. The African Union Mission in

Somalia (AMISOM), securing the air and sea ports and presidential compound, lost three soldiers to extremist attacks during the year. Among the foreign AQ operatives al-Shabaab is sheltering are individuals wanted for the 1998 embassy bombings in Kenya and Tanzania and a 2002 hotel bombing in Kenya, including Fazul Abdullah Mohammed (aka Harun Fazul), and Saleh Ali Saleh Nabhan. The capability of the TFG and other Somali local and regional authorities to carry out counterterrorism activities was extremely limited.

Somalia-based piracy remains a significant threat in the Gulf of Aden and the Somali basin. The international community is responding with naval assets but the nature of the threat and the vastness of the area make stopping piracy nearly impossible without a shore-based strategy to address piracy. While there is no clear nexus with terrorism, such a link remains possible.

South Africa

South Africa supported efforts to counter international terrorism and shared financial, law enforcement, and limited intelligence information with the United States. Some analysts believe that elements and support systems for al-Qa'ida (AQ) and/or other extremist groups have a presence within South Africa's generally moderate Muslim community, but it was unclear to what extent foreign terrorist groups have a presence in South Africa. In 2007, the Department of the Treasury designated South African nationals Farhad and Junaid Dockrat as AQ financiers and facilitators, subjecting them to U.S. sanctions.

Border security challenges, socio-cultural attitudes, and document fraud negatively affected the government's ability and efforts to pursue and intervene in counterterrorism initiatives. South African identity and travel documents generally included good security measures, but because of poor administration, lack of institutional capacity, and corruption within the Department of Home Affairs, which is responsible for immigration services, thousands of bona fide South African identity cards, passports, and work/residence permits were fraudulently issued.

South Africa is the only Financial Action Task Force member in Africa and has one of the three Egmont-member Financial Intelligence Units in the region. It is also a member of Eastern and Southern Africa Anti-Money Laundering Group (ESAAMLG) and as such, has served as a resource for other ESAAMLG members.

Tanzania

Tanzania remained vulnerable to international terrorism, as the terrorist network responsible for the 1998 U.S. Embassy bombing remained active in the region. Tanzania established a National Counterterrorism Center in late 2007 and continued its participation in several multi-year programs to strengthen its law enforcement and military capacity, improve aviation and border security, and combat money laundering and terrorist financing. Tanzania's Anti-Money Laundering Act, which created a Financial Intelligence Unit as an extra-ministerial department of the Ministry of Finance, was signed into law in July 2007, with implementing regulations published in September 2007.

Uganda

Uganda, situated in a region rife with insecurity, was working to find a permanent solution to two domestic insurgencies while also addressing a regional terrorist threat from al Qa'ida (AQ) and al-Shabaab in neighboring countries. Extremists moving between the Horn of Africa and North Africa and Europe used Uganda as a transit point. While in transit, their members were believed to have illegally purchased government documents and engaged in recruitment activities. In response, the Government of Uganda continued efforts to track, capture, and hold individuals with suspected links to terrorist organizations. In October, the government put Kampala on high alert and increased security at government installations, popular shopping centers, and other soft targets. Somalia-based al-Shabaab has never conducted an attack in Uganda, but identified Uganda as a potential target as retribution for its participation in the AU-led peacekeeping mission in Somalia. While the Ugandan government was a strong advocate for cross-border solutions to persistent problems in the Great Lakes Region, resource limitations and corruption hampered more effective counterterrorism measures. Uganda is one of two members of Eastern and Southern Africa Anti-Money Laundering Group with no anti-money laundering/terrorism finance legislation. On December 14, 2008, Uganda commenced a joint operation with the Democratic Republic of the Congo (DROC) against the Ugandan terrorist group Lord's Resistance Army resident in DROC.

Zambia

In 2007, the Zambian Government passed an antiterrorism bill, which criminalized acts of terrorism, including terrorist training and incitement, and granted the government significant authority to investigate, prevent, and prosecute acts of terrorism. However, inadequate resources and training impeded Zambia's law enforcement agencies' counterterrorism capabilities. Zambia's borders are long and porous, often cutting across ethno-linguistic lines, and were not effectively monitored or controlled. Its points of entry are vulnerable to human trafficking and international crime. Instability in Zimbabwe resulted in an increase in migrants during 2008. Despite assistance from the United States Treasury, the Zambian government does not have an internationally-compliant anti-money laundering or counterterrorist financing regime.

Zimbabwe

Zimbabwean government agencies routinely provided assistance by conducting investigative inquiries, traces, and border checks of individuals thought to be threats to U.S. government facilities or personnel. Zimbabwe's continued economic decline, however, has had a detrimental impact on local law enforcement and national security elements responsible for implementing and coordinating counterterrorism efforts. The Suppression of Foreign and International Terrorism Bill, enacted in August 2007 to combat terrorism and mercenary activities in Zimbabwe, has been redirected to suppress the political opposition.

EAST ASIA AND PACIFIC OVERVIEW

Extremist terrorism must not be allowed to undermine our racial and religious harmony. Singaporeans understand that terrorism is a threat to all of us.

— Lee Hsien Loong, Prime Minister of Singapore
New Year Day's Message
December 31, 2008

Since 2001, the sustained commitment to counter terrorism by the governments in Southeast Asia and their citizens has significantly weakened Jemaah Islamiya (JI) and other regional terrorist groups. The efforts of law enforcement, intelligence, and prosecutors have been bolstered by increased regional security cooperation and committed support from the United States and other international partners. The interdiction of a small, semi-autonomous terrorist cell in Palembang, South Sumatra by Indonesian security forces in July, however, demonstrated the possible reemergence of groups that espouse violent extremist ideologies. Six years after the 2002 Bali attacks, which killed over 200 people, elements of a seriously fractured JI and their adherents retained the intent to destabilize regional security and attack Western and U.S. interests in Southeast Asia. Additionally, the unresolved conflict in the Southern Philippines between the Government of the Philippines and the Moro Islamic Liberation Front (MILF) boiled over late in the year when a carefully-negotiated peace accord failed to win approval from the Philippine Supreme Court. This led to a renewal of violence in Mindanao as MILF insurgents perpetrated bombings, assassinations, and kidnappings aimed at government forces and in some cases the general civilian population.

In November, the Government of Indonesia executed three of the 2002 Bali bombers: Amrozi bin Nurhasym, Imam Samudra, and Ali Gufron (aka Mukhlas). The executions provoked no serious security incidents despite calls by JI co-founder Abu Bakar Ba'asyir for retaliatory attacks. Additionally, in January, the Government of Indonesia formally charged the ten suspected members of the Palembang Cell, who were arrested in July. Such trials of suspected violators of terrorism laws in Indonesia have demonstrated Indonesia's commitment to due process in all stages of the criminal justice process and have increased the credibility of Indonesia's counterterrorism policies.

The U.S. dual strategy of politically supporting the peace process between the Government of the Philippines and the MILF while providing developmental assistance in areas at risk for terrorist recruitment continued to marginalize the few remaining ASG and JI terrorists in the southern Philippines. Philippine military and law enforcement agencies conducted intensive civil-military and internal security operations to eliminate terrorist safe havens in the Sulu Archipelago and central Mindanao. JI bomber Umar Patek and several ASG operatives remained on the run, probably on Jolo Island.

In February, Mas Selemat Kastari, the former leader of a JI cell in Singapore, escaped from Singaporean detention. Despite a massive manhunt, Singaporean authorities failed to locate and re-capture Kastari. Other prominent terrorists, such as key JI operatives Noordin Mohammad Top, Dulmatin, and Umar Patek, also remained at large in the region.

Malaysia continued to use the Internal Security Act (ISA) to detain terrorist suspects without bringing them to trial. At year's end, Malaysian authorities held 16 terrorist suspects linked to JI and 13 linked to Darul Islam – some of whom were undergoing a program of rehabilitation – under ISA detention. On average, the Malaysian government has held suspected terrorists and suspected terrorist supporters in ISA detention for two to six years. Over the past year, the government released 32

[4] The ethno-nationalist separatist insurgency in Thailand's extreme southern provinces of Songkhla, Pattani, Narathiwat, and Yala continued through 2008. Some 3400 people have been killed in the conflict since the violence escalated in 2004 in assassinations, beheadings, and coordinated bombings using improvised explosive devices. This region has experienced episodic, separatist-related violence for decades between the predominantly ethnic Malay-Muslim population and the Thai government. Thai press reports and security forces attributed nearly all the attacks in the South to militant separatists; it is unclear, however, how much of the violence was also attributable to crime and political disputes.

detainees, including 13 terrorist suspects linked to JI and six linked to Darui Islam.

Thai and USG officials have long expressed concern that transnational terrorist groups could establish links with southern Thailand-based separatist groups[4]. However, there were no indications that transnational terrorist groups were directly involved in the violence in the south, and there was no evidence of direct operational links between southern Thai separatist groups and regional terrorist networks.

Despite a series of violent incidents – none of which have been tied to terrorists – and threats leading up to the Beijing Olympics, the Games were held successfully without episodes of terrorism. Starting in June, representatives of a group calling itself the Turkistan Islamic Party (TIP) posted videos on the Internet taking credit for violent incidents in China and threatening to strike the Olympic Games. TIP is believed to be another name for the Eastern Turkistan Islamic Movement (ETIM), a UN-listed terrorist organization.

On October 11, the United States rescinded the designation of the Democratic People's Republic of Korea (DPRK) as a state sponsor of terrorism in accordance with criteria set forth in U.S. law, including a certification that the Government of North Korea had not provided any support for international terrorism during the preceding six-month period and the provision by the government of assurances that it will not support acts of international terrorism in the future.

As in 2007, institutes like the United States-Thailand International Law Enforcement Academy (ILEA) in Bangkok, the Australian-Indonesian Jakarta Center for Law Enforcement Cooperation (JCLEC), and the Southeast Asia Regional Center for Counterterrorism (SEARCCT) in Malaysia sought to expand their efforts to provide effective counterterrorism training to law enforcement officers throughout the region. Multilateral fora, including the UN Security Council's Counterterrorism Committee (UNCTC), the G8's Roma-Lyon Group and Counterterrorism Action Group (CTAG), the Asia-Pacific Economic Cooperation (APEC) forum, the Association of Southeast Asian Nations (ASEAN), and the ASEAN Regional Forum (ARF), also promoted regional counterterrorism cooperation.

Australia maintained its position as a regional leader in the fight against terrorism and worked to strengthen the Asia-Pacific region's counterterrorism capacity through a range of bilateral and regional initiatives in fora such as APEC, ASEAN ARF, and the Pacific Island Forum. Japan also continued to assist counterterrorism capacity building in developing countries through seminars, workshops, and training. In October, the United States, Japan, and Australia convened for the fourth annual session of the Trilateral Strategic Dialogue Counterterrorism Consultations in Washington.

Australia

Australia maintained a leading position in regional counterterrorism efforts. Along with Japan and the U.S., Australia worked to strengthen regional cooperation on border, transport, and maritime security. In April and May, Australia conducted trilateral regional workshops to identify and disrupt terrorist cash courier operations and to respond to bioterrorism. These events were capped by the annual U.S.-Australia-Japan Trilateral Counterterrorism Strategic Dialogue in October. In September, the Government of Australia announced the appointment of William (Bill) Paterson as the country's new Ambassador for Counterterrorism. In 2008, the Australian government appointed a National Security Adviser (NSA) to help the Prime Minister on a range of policy matters, including countering terrorism and overseeing the implementation of national security policy arrangements. The National Intelligence Coordination Committee (NICC) chaired by the NSA will ensure that national intelligence efforts are fully and effectively integrated across governmental agencies. In February, the Lombok Treaty between Australia and Indonesia came into full force, providing a framework for bilateral law enforcement cooperation, particularly against human trafficking, trade in illicit drugs, and terrorism. The treaty marked a continuation of Australian efforts to build Indonesian police capacity, such as the Jakarta Centre for Law Enforcement Cooperation (JCLEC), which plays an important role in fostering cooperation among Southeast Asian agencies involved in counterterrorism, the commencement of joint legal training programs in July, the renewal of the counterterrorism Memorandum of Understanding (MOU), and inaugural counterterrorism consultations that were held in May 2008. The treaty marked increased bilateral cooperation in law enforcement, border control, maritime and transport security, legal assistance, financial monitoring, defense, and management of chemical, biological, radiological, and nuclear terrorist threats.

In May, Australia and the Philippines held high-level counterterrorism consultations, which reviewed capacity building and operational collaboration, and agreed on broad priorities and directions for future cooperation. In June, Australia extended for a further six months the assignment of an Australian official to Cambodia to assist the Cambodian Government on counterterrorism capabilities. Also in June, Australia expanded its bilateral counterterrorism talks to include first round talks with Russia. In December, Australia signed a counterterrorism MOU with Bangladesh, the 14th such bilateral agreement concluded by Australia.

Following the September bombing of the Marriott Hotel in Islamabad, Australia announced plans to expand its counterterrorism efforts with Pakistan, including possible provision of law enforcement assistance, counter-insurgency training, and technical assistance.

Australian multilateral engagement continued in forums such as the United Nations, the Association of Southeast Asian Nations (ASEAN), the ASEAN Regional Forum, Asia Pacific Economic Cooperation, the Pacific Island Forum and the G8 Counterterrorism Action Group.

The Australian Federal Police (AFP) received further funding to expand its investigative and specialist training, currently delivered to regional law enforcement partners through facilities like JCLEC. Funding was targeted toward:

- conducting offshore exercises and training with regional partners,
- increasing the number of counterterrorism advisers working in AFP's international liaison officer network,
- introducing to high priority locations a custom-built Case Management and Information System developed for use in overseas jurisdictions, and
- enhancing specialist forensic and technical training for law enforcement agencies in the region and in theaters of war, such as Iraq and Afghanistan.

The AFP's International Deployment Group deploys numerous officers overseas in counterterrorism technical assistance and operational/liaison roles. The AFP Operational Response Group was designed to respond on short notice to emerging law and order issues and to conduct stabilization operations to head off lawless situations that terrorists could exploit. Australia continued to provide legal drafting assistance to regional states seeking to adopt international conventions and protocols against terrorism.

The Australian Security Intelligence Organization (ASIO) reported that, within Australia, a small but significant minority of the Islamic community holds or has held extremist views. An even smaller minority was prepared to act in support of them, including by advocating violence, providing logistic or propaganda support to extremists, or traveling abroad to train with terrorist groups or participate in violent activities. Under Australia's Criminal Code, 18 groups are on the Listing of Terrorist Organizations. The Attorney General reaffirmed three in November: the Abu Sayyaf Group (ASG), Jamiat ul-Ansar (JuA), and al-Qa'ida in Iraq (AQI).

During 2007-08, legal proceedings commenced against a number of individuals charged with terrorism offences, and in one trial, convictions were handed down by a jury in Melbourne. Yet, the nation has also required that the government review its 2005 terrorist legislation in 2010 in light of a need for protection of guaranteed rights. Because of the deportation of an innocent relative of a terrorist, there was felt a need to insure that the unwarranted deportation of the innocent would not occur again.

The Australian Transaction Reports Analysis Centre (AUSTRAC), which monitored financial transactions, served as the national Anti-Money Laundering and Combating Terrorist Financing (AML/CTF) regulator, with supervisory, monitoring, and enforcement functions over a diverse range of industry sectors. A new set of regulatory reforms, introduced in draft legislation made public in August 2007, was heading for legislative enactment. These included new regulations regarding real estate, precious gems and stones, and specified legal accounting and trust services. AUSTRAC continued to seek and fund additional staff and technical capabilities, and establish identity security strike teams to investigate and prosecute people and syndicates involved in manufacturing false identities.

Australia supported a range of activities promoting tolerance and mutual understanding, and countering extremist ideology and propaganda, among communities in the region. In June, the New South Wales (NSW) Department of Corrective Services provided targeted training in Australia for a range of senior Indonesian corrections officials. Australia also conducted research in Indonesia on Indonesian popular attitudes toward democracy, politically motivated violence, extremist ideology, and pluralism. Australian authorities also facilitated meetings with Southeast Asian academics, journalists, and community leaders to discuss these issues.

Australia exchanged information with the United States on terrorists using the Terrorist Screening Centre as the operational hub for encounter management, as well as in APEC's Regional Movement Alert System. Both programs enhanced our joint ability to disrupt travel by known and suspected terrorists.

The Australian Defense Force has deployed 1,090 personnel to Afghanistan and 120 troops to Iraq.

Burma

Bilateral relations between Burma and the United States remained strained. The government defined almost all anti-regime activities as "acts of terrorism," making little distinction between peaceful political dissent and violent attacks by insurgents or criminals. The Burmese government was quick to link dissident groups with terrorist organizations to justify scrutiny and disruption of their activities.

The Burmese government characterized a series of bomb blasts in Rangoon and other parts of Burma as subversive acts, "committed by a group of insurgent destructive elements who wanted to disturb and destroy stability of the state." However, authorities have not presented credible evidence to support these accusations. Requests by the U.S. Embassy to view either the scenes of the blasts or fragments of the explosive devices were consistently denied. There is no evidence of any terrorist groups targeting American interests in the country.

Cambodia

Cambodia's political leadership demonstrated a strong commitment to aggressive legal action against terrorists and to increase its counterterrorism investigative capability, but its ability to investigate potential terrorist activities was limited by a lack of training and resources. Despite this shortfall, the Royal Government of Cambodia to date has fully cooperated with U.S. counterterrorism efforts.

Conditions in Cambodia – such as porous borders, endemic corruption, massive poverty, high unemployment, a poor education system, and disaffected elements within the Cham Muslim population, which makes up approximately five percent of the population – are conditions that terrorists could exploit. Although the Cham were not generally politically active, the Cambodian government was aware of the possibility that foreign terrorists might use Cham areas as safe havens. For example, Hambali, a senior Jemaah Islamiya and al-Qa'ida operative accused of involvement in the 2002 Bali nightclub bombings, took refuge in a Muslim school in Cambodia in 2002-2003.

Despite these challenges, Cambodia remained committed to strengthening its counterterrorism capability. Cambodia's National Counterterrorism Center, a policy-level decision making body established in 2005 and chaired by the prime minister, continued to improve cooperation and information sharing among Cambodia's security agencies. In January, the Cambodian Government established five departments under the secretariat of its proposed National Counterterrorism Committee (NCTC) to coordinate counterterrorism efforts. The Ministry of the Interior imposed strict controls on the use of weapons, explosive devices, chemical substances, and radioactive materials in Cambodia.

The Cambodian government made notable progress in strengthening its counterterrorist finance regime. In May, the Governor of the National Bank of Cambodia (NBC) signed an announcement of a Prakas[5] of the Law on Anti Money-Laundering and Combating the Financing of Terrorism

[5] The Prakas is a key implementing regulation of the law.

(AML/CFT), promulgated in June 2007. The AML/CFT legal regime included the January 29 establishment of a Financial Intelligence Unit (FIU), which operated within the framework of the National Bank of Cambodia (NBC). The FIU monitors suspicious transactions and interfaces with the Ministry of Interior's Financial Crimes Investigation Unit. Initial efforts to develop the AML/CFT regime focused on the banking sector, and the NBC issued Circulars and Prakas to regulate the financial sector. The 2007 Law on Counterterrorism and the AML/CFT Law introduced a comprehensive asset-freezing system. Implementation began in 2008.

With U.S. assistance, Cambodian authorities monitored computerized border control systems at Phnom Penh and Siem Reap airports, and at the land border crossing of Poipet and Koh Kong. U.S. officials also provided training to Cambodian authorities on crime scene investigation and methods for countering money laundering.

The Cambodian Government also cooperated with other regional governments on counterterrorism issues. Australia conducted a one-week work workshop on dissemination and implementation of counterterrorism law, as well as a workshop on implementing money laundering law. Officials from the Cambodian government attended workshops in China, India, Malaysia, and Singapore dealing with cross-border crimes and terrorism.

In May, the UN Counterterrorism Committee's Executive Directorate (CTED) conducted an on-site visit to Cambodia to monitor Cambodia's implementation of Security Council Resolution 1373. The committee's comprehensive final report included recommendations for improvements, and outlined Cambodia's technical assistance requirements to meet or exceed its counterterrorism commitments and goals.

China

China increased counterterrorism cooperation with the United States and other nations both leading up to and following the August Olympic Games in Beijing. In March, China hosted the U.S.-China Counterterrorism Dialogue aimed at increasing cooperation on counterterrorism. China also held counterterrorism exercises with neighboring countries, including Thailand and India. As a founding member of the Shanghai Cooperation Organization (SCO), China has made counterterrorism one of the SCO's main objectives. China continued to participate in the Container Security Initiative (CSI) with U.S. Customs and Border Protection inspectors stationed at the ports of Shanghai and Shenzhen.

In October, the U.S. and China marked the ten year anniversary of the Joint Liaison Group (JLG) on Law Enforcement Cooperation with a plenary meeting in Washington, DC. The seven working groups of the

JLG are aimed at increasing policy dialogue and improving cooperation writ large between U.S. and Chinese law enforcement agencies.

Although implementation of the Yangshan Deep Water Megaports project was underway by the U.S. Department of Energy (DOE), the General Administration of China Customs (GACC) told DOE that it would increase the number of scanners used in the project. In October, GACC told DOE that contacts on Megaports would be suspended until further notice due to unrelated issues. The status of implementation of the Yangshan Megaports project was unknown at year's end.

China's cash-based economy and robust cross-border trade contributed to a high volume of difficult-to-track cash transactions. Though mechanisms were in place for tracking financial transactions in the formal banking sector, the large size of the informal economy, prevalence of counterfeit identity documents, and large numbers of underground banks presented major obstacles to law enforcement authorities. According to International Monetary Fund statistics, money laundering in China may account for as much as $24 billion per year.

Terrorist financing is a criminal offense in China, and the government has the authority to identify, freeze, and seize terrorist financial assets, but laws defining terrorist financing were not yet consistent with international standards, according to reporting by the Financial Action Task Force. China's Financial Intelligence Unit (FIU), housed within the People's Bank of China (PBOC), worked closely with the Financial Crimes Enforcement Network (FINCEN) in the United States to develop its capabilities. In addition to its domestic collection and analysis activities, the FIU exchanged information with foreign FIUs on a case-by-case basis. Coordination in this area could be further enhanced through China's membership in the Egmont Group, an umbrella body that coordinates the activities of over 100 FIUs worldwide. Though China has applied for membership in the Egmont Group, domestic political concerns about Taiwan's participation in the organization have reportedly hampered membership discussions.

China expanded its role in international efforts to combat terrorist finance and money laundering by becoming a full member of the Financial Action Task Force (FATF) in June 2007. Since 2004, China has also been a member of the Eurasian Group (EAG), a FATF-style regional grouping that includes China, Russia, and several Central Asian countries.

Despite a series of violent incidents and threats leading up to the Beijing Olympics, the Games were held successfully without terrorist incidents. Starting in June, representatives of a group calling itself the Turkistan Islamic Party (TIP) posted videos on the Internet taking credit for violent incidents in China and threatening to strike the Olympic Games. TIP is believed to be an another name for the Eastern Turkistan Islamic Party (ETIP), also known as the Eastern Turkistan Islamic Movement (ETIM), which was added by UN 1267 Committee to its Consolidated List of individuals/entities associated with Usama bin Laden, al-Qa'ida, or the Taliban on September 11, 2002. Among the incidents TIP took credit for was a series of bus bombings in Kunming, Yunnan Province that killed two people in July. In March, the Chinese government claimed that flight attendants foiled a plot to detonate a homemade explosive on a flight from Urumqi, Xinjiang to Beijing by subduing a female passenger.

Human rights organizations have accused China of using counterterrorism as a pretext to suppress Uighurs, a predominantly Muslim ethnic group which makes up the majority of the population within the Xinjiang Uighur Autonomous Region (XUAR) of western China. In the lead up to the Olympics, China tightened security in Xinjiang, instituting road checkpoints and arresting people it suspected of being linked to terrorism. In July, the Urumqi, XUAR Public Security Bureau in Urumqi declared that it detained 82 terrorists during the first six months of the year while police in Kashgar claimed to have rounded up 12 terrorist groups.

Security forces maintained a high-level of vigilance both in Xinjiang and throughout the country during the Olympics. In spite of this, a series of violent incidents did occur in Xinjiang during the Olympics which the Chinese government has blamed on terrorist organizations. In the most violent reported incident, 17 People's Armed Police Border Guards were killed on August 4 when assailants attacked them with a vehicle, homemade bombs, and knives. Formally established in 2002, the FBI Legal Attaché Office in Beijing bolstered U.S.-China cooperation on counterterrorism investigations. China provided substantive intelligence in some cases, but more work remained to be done in terms of the depth and overall responsiveness to U.S. requests. Another incident in Xinjiang seven days later resulted in two deaths when a series of homemade bombs were detonated in the remote Xinjiang town of Kuqa.

Hong Kong

Hong Kong's position as a major transit point for cargo, finances, and people and its open trade and financial regime made it a potential site for money laundering and terrorist financing activities. The high level of cooperation and the successful implementation of the Container Security Initiative (CSI) by Hong Kong Customs officials received continued praise from visiting USG delegations, which described it as a model for CSI implementation. The Hong Kong government extended the Strategic Freight

Initiative (SFI) pilot project, originally scheduled to run through April 2008 for an additional year.

Hong Kong law enforcement agencies provided full support and cooperation to their overseas counterparts in tracing financial transactions suspected of being linked to terrorist activities.

Hong Kong actively participated in various anti-money laundering and counterterrorist financing initiatives, including the Financial Action Task Force (FATF) and the Asia/Pacific Group (APG) on Money Laundering. Hong Kong is a member of the Egmont Group, reporting through its Joint Financial Intelligence Unit (JFIU), operated by Hong Kong Police and the Customs and Excise Department. The results of Hong Kong's 2007 FATF and APG mutual evaluation were announced in June 2008. In response to recommendations in the report, Hong Kong authorities are expected to propose legislation to increase supervision of money changers and remittance agents, but have made no plans to establish reporting requirements for cross-border currency movements.

Macau

The Macau Special Administrative Region is a member of the Asia Pacific Group (APG) and completed a mutual evaluation of its Anti-Money Laundering Regime in 2007. In response to recommendations contained in the report, Macau authorities have taken steps to improve compliance with suspicious transactions reporting requirements in banks and casinos, but the threshold reporting limits remain well above international norms. Macau's Financial Intelligence Office (FIO) remained a temporary body, although its staffing continued to increase. Macau has not proposed establishing reporting requirements for cross-border currency movements.

The Government of Macau continued to exchange information with the Hong Kong Special Administrative Region and counterparts in mainland China. Additionally, Macau cooperated internationally in counterterrorism efforts, through INTERPOL and other security-focused organizations within the Asia Pacific Region, and considered information sharing mechanisms that would enable it to join the Egmont Group.

Indonesia

Indonesia experienced its third consecutive year without a major terrorist attack while the Government of Indonesia continued to build a legal and law enforcement environment conducive to fighting terrorism within its borders. The Indonesian government's counterterrorism efforts across law enforcement and judicial sectors drastically reduced the ability of terrorist groups, such as Jemaah Islamiya (JI), to plan and carry out attacks. Arrests in South Sumatra and Jakarta demonstrated that JI-affiliated individuals and groups, as well as other radical institutions, such as the Komite Aksi Penanggulangan Akibat Krisis (the Crisis Management Committee (KOMPAK)), remained a security threat, but with reduced ability to carry out attacks.

The Indonesian National Police (INP) used information gained from suspects arrested last year to maintain tight surveillance over suspected militant strongholds. In July, the INP raided a home in Palembang, South Sumatra, capturing ten suspected terrorists and a small cache of explosives. At the time of the arrests, the men were allegedly plotting an attack on a cafe frequented by non-Muslims in a resort town in Sumatra. Members of the group have also been accused of killing an Indonesian teacher in 2007 and of attempting to kill a Catholic priest in 2005.

In October, a raid on a house in Kelapa Gading, North Jakarta, led to the capture of five suspects and another small cache of explosives. The Jakarta suspects were connected to KOMPAK, which in the past had provoked militancy in Poso, Sulawesi, and to Darul Islam, a long-standing extremist Islamic group with some militant strains. Both raids demonstrated INP successes in interdicting terrorist operations. The United States worked to build the investigative support for and forensic capabilities of the INP through numerous developmental programs.

The Antiterrorism Assistance Program (ATA) continued to provide tactical and investigative training, equipment and technical assistance to the INP's elite counterterrorism units, Detachment 88. Regional Detachment 88s, working with other specialized factions of the INP, have participated in operations that lead to the arrest and successful prosecution of terrorist suspects in the past few years. As a result of ATA's train-the-trainer initiative, INP instructors now have the instructional skill sets necessary to conduct all Detachment 88 tactical training.

The Attorney General's Task Force on Terrorism and Transnational Crime successfully prosecuted terrorists, and the U.S. Department of Justice worked with Indonesian prosecutors to enhance the prosecutorial capacity of the task force. In April, acting JI Emir Ustad Syahroni (aka Zarkasih) and senior JI operative Abu Dujana (aka Ainul Bahri), were sentenced to 15 years in prison each for violating the 2003 counterterrorism law. Zarkasih, as acting JI Emir, was one of the most senior JI leaders ever arrested. Dujana, also an Afghanistan-veteran and JI military leader, had been involved in several JI attacks. In addition to handing down the sentences, the judges said JI was a terrorist organization, laying the legal basis for the Indonesian government to ban JI in the future. In November, Abu Dujana testified on behalf of the prosecution in the terrorist trials of Dr. Argus Purwantoro and Abu Husna. Additionally, the Task Force successfully prosecuted 12 other JI members. The court sentenced five

JI members for aiding and abetting Abu Dujana and Zarkasih to between seven and eight years of prison each. The court sentenced six other members of JI's military wing to eight to ten years each in prison. The Government of Indonesia formally charged the ten suspected terrorists who were arrested in July. The Attorney General's Terrorism and Transnational Crime Task Force led the prosecutions in the trials, which were being held in the Central Jakarta District Court. The AGO Task Force on Terrorism and Transnational Crime has successfully prosecuted 43 terrorists, including 26 JI members, since September 2006.

Other Indonesian legal institutions took a hard line against terrorists. In October, the Constitutional Court rejected a last-ditch appeal by the Bali bombers of their death sentences and upheld that death by firing squad was constitutional. Also in October, the Ministry of Law and Human Rights did not include sentence remissions for convicted terrorists in its annual Eid holiday remissions list.

In November, the Government of Indonesia executed three of the 2002 Bali bombers, Amrozi bin Nurhasym, Imam Samudra, and Ali Gufron (aka Mukhlas). The three had been convicted for planning and carrying out the October 2002 bombings in Bali, which killed over 200 people. There were no serious incidents following the executions, and the public reaction was calm, despite public calls by JI co-founder Abu Bakar Ba'asyir for retaliatory attacks.

The Indonesian government made genuine efforts to develop an effective anti-money laundering system for investigations and prosecutions in compliance with certain provisions in UNSCR 1267 and 1373. Indonesian police froze terrorists' financial assets uncovered during investigations. However, the Government of Indonesia had yet to demonstrate the political will to implement all requirements under UNSCR 1267. The Financial Action Task Force (FATF) Mutual Evaluation Report released in July noted that although Indonesia made significant progress in recent years with its implementation of anti-money laundering measures, relatively little implementation of countering terrorist finance measures has occurred.

USAID promoted capacity-building to the Financial Crimes Transaction and Analysis Center (PPATK) and related governmental agencies through its Financial Crimes Prevention Project (FCPP), a multi-year program, now concluded, which provided technical advisors and policy support to develop an effective and credible anti-money laundering and terrorist finance regime. FCPP assistance included the drafting of a National Anti-Money Laundering Strategy adopted by the President in 2007, to develop a comprehensive asset forfeiture law (that remained in progress), and certification of Indonesian government officials as anti-money-laundering specialists and fraud examiners. The number of

Suspicious Transaction Reports received increased from 10 per month in 2002 to over 811 per month in 2008 (through October); these reports led to 19 prosecutions during the period. One had a terrorist component, and the strengthened financial oversight improved the tracking of potential terrorist financial transactions.

The INP continued its program to de-radicalize convicted terrorists. The program identified individuals who might be open to more moderate teachings and focused on providing spiritual support to the men and on providing modest financial support to their families. The program aimed to reduce terrorist recruitment inside prisons. Based on the success of the INP de-radicalization program, the Indonesian Department of Corrections also decided to undertake a prisoner de-radicalization program. The Directorate General for prisons proposed that the creation of a set of guidelines for the handling of terrorist prisoners would improve security and surveillance of the prisoners and encourage prisoners to not resort to violence to carry out their religious beliefs.

Though Indonesia's counterterrorism efforts have been impressive and its capacity to fight terrorism within its borders has improved steadily, continued vigilance is needed. The arrests in Palembang and North Jakarta demonstrated that militant networks remained partially intact and that groups continued to stockpile explosives for potential operations. Malaysian JI operative and recruiter Noordin Mohammed Top, who is suspected of involvement in every anti-Western terrorist attack in Indonesia since 2002, remained at large.

Japan

Japan bolstered its border security and enhanced national counterterrorism measures in coordination with the United States. Japanese immigration officials strengthened their capability to identify suspicious travelers upon entry into Narita International Airport through fingerprinting and facial recognition technology. Using the Biometric Immigration Control System, officials denied entry to roughly 860 travelers during the year for offenses such as prior deportation and fake passports. In July, the Japanese Foreign Ministry's International Counterterrorism Cooperation Division extended the pilot Immigration Advisory Program with the U.S. Department of Homeland Security (DHS) for one additional year. The program, which embeds DHS officers at Narita, was viewed by the Japanese government as an effective way to prevent improperly documented air passengers from boarding U.S.-bound flights. Tokyo also worked to ensure the integrity of Japanese travel documents to reduce the risk of travelers using fake passports under the expanded VISA Waiver Program.

Japanese authorities collaborated with U.S. officials to increase U.S. access to database records and fingerprints of known or suspected terrorists. As a VISA Waiver Program country, Japan held discussions with U.S. counterparts to widen database and biometric record exchanges on known and suspected terrorists under Homeland Security Presidential Directive (HSPD)-6. The Japanese Government also educated travelers on the Electronic System for Travel Authorization through media spots and briefings to major domestic travel agencies.

Japan likewise took steps to strengthen port and shipping security. Under the Container Security Initiative, Japanese authorities worked with U.S. officials embedded at Japanese ports to review ship manifests and to screen suspicious containers. Japan and the United States agreed in July to launch a pilot project under the Megaports Initiative Program, which provides for scanning of containers to detect radiological material. Japan was in the process of procuring necessary equipment, such as radiation portal monitors. Japan also continued collaboration with the U.S. on science and technology for homeland security through the U.S.-Japan Framework Initiative for a Safe and Secure Society.

Inside Japan, the NPA and the Public Security Intelligence Agency (PSIA) continued to monitor the activities of Aum Shinrikyo, renamed Aleph, and its splinter group, Hikari no Wa. In December, PSIA filed a request with the Public Security Examination Commission, a Justice Ministry-affiliated decision-making board, to maintain surveillance of Aleph and Hikari no Wa for an additional three years. PSIA has monitored Aum since 2000 under the Organization. Control Law, a measure that allows the Agency to conduct on-site facility inspections and to obtain quarterly operational reports from the group. Both groups continued to perpetuate the ideology of Aum founder and sarin gas attack planner Chizuo Matsumoto, aka Shoko Asahara. PSIA inspections revealed that many original Aum members continued to hold leadership positions in the groups, and that Aum facilities maintained portrait photos and video teachings of Asahara.

Japan also reached beyond its borders to fight terrorism. Japan is the second largest contributor to Iraq reconstruction, with $1.5 billion in grants, $3.5 billion in concessionary loans, and $6.9 billion in debt relief. Japanese Air Self Defense Force transport aircraft operated out of Kuwait in support of Operation Iraqi Freedom but ended its mission in December. Japan remained an active partner in Operation Enduring Freedom (OEF) and a key international contributor to Afghan stabilization and reconstruction. Japan has pledged more than $2 billion in reconstruction aid since 2002 and continued construction on the 114 kilometer stretch of the southern ring road between Kandahar and Herat. The Maritime Self Defense

Force continued to conduct refueling operations in support of OEF in the Indian Ocean and has provided more than $150 million of fuel to U.S. and coalition vessels since 2003.

In October, Japan participated in the fourth annual U.S.-Japan-Australia trilateral strategic dialogue on counterterrorism, as part of the Trilateral Strategic Dialogue, which aimed to coordinate regional activities. Japanese officials chaired a specialist working group on border security and took part in discussions on Chemical, Biological, Radiological, and Nuclear weapons (CBRN), law enforcement capacity building, and counter-radicalization.

Japan assisted counterterrorism capacity building in developing countries through seminars, workshops, and training. In January, Japan hosted the Seminar on Promotion of Accession to International Counterterrorism Conventions and Protocols for the fifth consecutive year. Tokyo promoted information sharing and provided implementation guidance to participants including Fiji, Papua New Guinea, and several members of the Association of Southeast Asian Nations (ASEAN). In May, Japan joined the United States, Australia, and the Southeast Asia Regional Centre for Counterterrorism at the Southeast Asian Bioterrorism Workshop in Kuala Lumpur to augment the crisis management and counter-CBRN capabilities of several ASEAN participants. Japan also assisted third country law enforcement personnel by dispatching experts and accepting trainees. The Japanese Coast Guard (JCG), for example, provided capacity building services and training seminars to authorities from states that border the Strait of Malacca. Since 2002, Japan has offered technical assistance to support local police in Indonesia and has provided training to coast guard counterparts from the Philippines. Beyond Southeast Asia, Japan dispatched three JCG members to Oman and Yemen in December to assist local officials in addressing piracy concerns in waters off the Horn of Africa.

Japan contributed to counterterrorism capacity building through membership in multilateral fora. In April, Japan participated in the Sixth Asia-Europe Meeting (ASEM) Counterterrorism Conference, where members shared threat assessments and discussed ways to increase counterterrorism capacity-building. During the ASEM Summit in October, Japan joined other members in condemning terrorism and reaffirming commitment to the UN Global Counterterrorism Strategy. Under Japan's G8 presidency, Japan issued calls to improve information sharing, strengthen the security of land, sea, and air transportation and maintain momentum on the G8 Counterterrorism Action Group. Also under Japan's stewardship, participants held the G8 Bioterrorism Experts Group workshop in the United States (May) and in Germany (June).

Japan undertook measures to combat terrorist financing. Under the Law for Prevention of Transfer of Criminal Proceeds, Japan expanded the scope of businesses and professions under the previous law's jurisdiction. Under the Foreign Exchange and Foreign Trade Law, Japanese financial institutions must confirm the identity of customers sending 100,000 yen or more overseas. For domestic remittances, financial institutions must identify the originators of wire transfers over 100,000 yen. To help stem the flow of terrorist financing to al-Qa'ida and the Taliban, Japan also took steps to freeze assets of individuals and entities listed under UN Security Council Resolution 1267.

Japan became the 22nd country to undergo a comprehensive Financial Action Task Force (FATF) Mutual Evaluation; it had difficulty meeting FATF recommendations specific to financial institutions. FATF made a number of findings regarding Japan's illicit finance practices, including the low number of money laundering prosecutions (225 in 2006). It noted that Japan's established mechanism for freezing terrorist assets did not cover the potential use of domestic funds or other means of support for listed terrorist entities and did not allow Japan to freeze terrorist funds expeditiously. FATF also found that Japanese law had no requirements for financial institutions to establish and maintain procedures, policies, and internal controls to prevent illicit finance.

Republic of Korea

The Republic of Korea (South Korea) demonstrated excellent law enforcement and intelligence capabilities to combat terrorism. South Korean immigration and law enforcement agencies had an excellent record of tracking suspicious individuals entering their territory and reacting quickly to thwart potential terrorist acts. In August, the South Korean Government started issuing e-passports to ordinary citizens to further protect the identities of lawful travelers and to help prevent terrorists from using counterfeit passports. South Korea agreed on a mechanism to exchange terrorist screening information with the United States as part of Seoul's successful effort to join the Visa Waiver Program. Seoul reviewed and strengthened its emergency response plan and also further tightened its legislative framework and administrative procedures to combat terrorist financing.

South Korea supported U.S. counterterrorism goals in Afghanistan, maintained a military contingent in Iraq through December, and led a Coalition Provincial Reconstruction Team in Irbil Province. In October, South Korea's Ambassador for Counterterrorism visited Washington to meet with U.S. counterterrorism officials to discuss means of further strengthening bilateral cooperation. In addition, South Korea worked closely with other foreign partners and played a constructive role in improving regional counterterrorism capabilities. Seoul continued to participate in the counterterrorism activities of the Asia-Pacific Economic Cooperation forum, the ASEAN Regional Forum, and the Asia-Europe Meeting. The Korea Overseas International Cooperation Agency hosted counterterrorism training and capacity-building programs for regional partners in forensic science, prevention of money laundering, and cyber security.

North Korea (DPRK)

The Democratic People's Republic of Korea (DPRK) was not known to have sponsored any terrorist acts since the bombing of a Korean Airlines flight in 1987. On October 11, the United States rescinded the designation of the DPRK as a state sponsor of terrorism in accordance with criteria set forth in U.S. law, including a certification that the government of North Korea had not provided any support for international terrorism during the preceding six-month period and the provision by the government of assurances that it will not support acts of international terrorism in the future.

Four Japanese Red Army (JRA) members who participated in a jet hijacking in 1970 continued to live in the DPRK. On June 13, the Government of Japan announced that the DPRK had agreed to cooperate in handing over the remaining members of the JRA involved in the hijacking.

The Japanese government continued to seek a full accounting of the fate of 12 Japanese nationals believed to have been abducted by DPRK state entities. The DPRK admitted to abducting eight of these individuals but claimed they have since died; the DPRK denied having abducted the other four individuals. On August 12, Japan and the DPRK agreed on steps towards the eventual resolution to this issue. The DPRK has not yet implemented its commitment to reopen its investigations into the abductions, however. Since 2002, five other abductees have been repatriated to Japan.

Laos

Since 2002, the Government of Laos has consistently denounced international terrorism and expressed a willingness to cooperate with the international community on counterterrorism. While domestic opposition elements have in the past employed terrorist tactics, such as ambushing civilian buses as recently as 2003 and bombing civilian targets as recently as 2004, Lao officials at many levels saw international terrorism as an issue of only marginal relevance to Laos. They believed that Laos, as a small and neutral country, would not be targeted or exploited by international terrorists.

Laos does not have a separate counterterrorism law, but the Lao judicial system was equipped to prosecute acts of terrorism as crimes under the Lao criminal code, and Laotian officials have amended the criminal code to strengthen counterterrorism sanctions. Still, a 2006 UN-sponsored counterterrorism workshop illustrated shortcomings and vagaries in the theoretical application of the Lao criminal code to deal with terrorism-related crimes, so successful prosecution under these laws is not assured. These shortcomings remained unresolved.

Laos' border security was weak; border officials could not effectively control access to the country at any of the country's border checkpoints. Border crossing along the Mekong River into Burma, Thailand, and Cambodia could be accomplished easily and without detection. Border delineation remained poor in more remote sections of the country, especially along its land borders with Vietnam and China; it was likely that unmonitored border crossings by locals occurred on a daily basis. Since September 11, 2001, Lao authorities have strengthened airport security, and airport security forces have participated in U.S.-supported security seminars to raise their standards, but security procedures at land immigration points remained lax compared with those of most other countries in the region. In addition, official Lao identity documents, including passports and ID cards, were easy to obtain.

In accordance with its obligations under UNSCR 1373, the Bank of Laos vetted government and commercial bank holdings for possible terrorist assets, as identified by U.S.-provided lists of terrorist organizations and individuals, and issued freeze orders for assets of organizations and individuals named on these lists. However, the Bank has yet to require the freezing of assets of individuals and entities included on the UN 1267 Sanctions Committee consolidated list.

Lao authorities issued orders limiting the amount of cash that could be withdrawn from local banks or carried into or out of the country and strengthened reporting requirements of state and privately owned commercial banks. Banking regulation remained extremely weak, however, and the banking system was vulnerable to money laundering and other illegal transactions.

Malaysia

The police forces in Malaysia, who fall under the authority of the Malaysian Home Ministry, conducted all of the country's counterterrorist investigations and operations. Amendments to five different pieces of legislation – the Anti-Money Laundering Act, the Penal Code, the Subordinate Courts Act, the Courts of Judicature Act, and the Criminal Procedure Code – enabled Malaysia to accede to the UN International

Convention for the Suppression of the Financing of Terrorism in 2007. To date, however, Malaysia has not initiated prosecution of any terrorist suspects using these amended laws, instead relying on its Internal Security Act (ISA) to detain terrorist suspects without bringing them to trial.

As of December 2008, Malaysian authorities held 16 terrorist suspects linked to Jemaah Islamiya (JI) and 13 linked to Darul Islam (DI), some of whom were undergoing a program of rehabilitation, in ISA detention. On average, the Malaysian government has held suspected terrorists and suspected terrorist supporters in ISA detention for two to six years. However, allegations that the Malaysian government has used the ISA to detain some persons for political reasons, rather than security concerns, placed pressure on Kuala Lumpur to amend or abolish the ISA. In 2008 the Malaysian government released 32 ISA detainees, including 13 terrorist suspects linked to JI and six linked to DI. Home Minister Syed Hamid Albar, in confirming the most recent release of the detainees, was quoted in the press as stating that they were no "longer a threat."

The Malaysian Government engaged with its neighbors on issues related to counterterrorism and transnational crime, and continued to operate the Southeast Asian Regional Center for Counterterrorism (SEARCCT). The Center has facilitated the training of Malaysian security officials, but has done less to identify forward-looking or regional counterterrorism priorities. SEARCCT is seeking to expand its mission portfolio to include youth outreach and prison rehabilitation.

Malaysian mediators continued to work in the southern Philippines to help end the conflict between the Philippine government and the separatist Moro Islamic Liberation Front (MILF), although on November 30, Malaysia withdrew its remaining participants from the International Monitoring Team (IMT) that monitors the ceasefire between the government and the MILF. Malaysia, along with Singapore and Indonesia, invited Thailand to join the "Eyes in the Sky" program designed to provide enhanced security to the Strait of Malacca, the world's busiest shipping lane. Malaysia has actively contributed to counter-piracy efforts off the coast of Somalia and sent several naval vessels to the Gulf of Aden following the pirating of two Malaysian commercial vessels there. Malaysia's naval vessels will remain off the coast of Somalia until February 2009. The pirated ships were released upon the payment of significant ransom fees to the pirates.

Malaysia's central bank signed memoranda of understanding on the sharing of financial intelligence with the FIUs of seventeen nations, including the United States. Malaysia is an active member of the Asia/Pacific Group Donor & Provider Group for Technical Assistance and has worked with the World Bank, International Monetary Fund, Asian Development Bank, United Nation Counterterrorism Committee Executive Directorate,

United Nations Office on Drugs and Crime, and the Australian FIU (AUSTRAC) to provide technical assistance in various ASEAN member countries.

Micronesia, Federated States of

Law enforcement efforts against terrorism, limited as they are given the region's lack of capacity, fall within the purview of the Transnational Crime Unit (TCU). Reliant on American funding and Australian supervision since its opening in April, the TCU brought officers from other Pacific island nations to Palikir, the Micronesian capital, to share information on such issues as narcotics, human trafficking, and terrorism. The TCU also exchanged information with the FBI and the Australian Federal Police, making it the recipient of any terrorist-related intelligence.

Mongolia

Although there were no known terrorist groups operating in Mongolia and no known bases of support, Mongolian government officials cited more than 6,000 kilometers of porous borders, easy entry for foreign travelers, and poverty as conditions that terrorists could exploit, and moved to increase awareness of terrorism and to consider new laws. In November, Mongolia's State Specialized Inspection Agency, Border Protection Agency, and Customs Authority; in partnership with the Second Line of Defense program of the U.S. Department of Energy's National Nuclear Security Administration, installed and began using portals to detect the movement of nuclear and radiological devices and materials at the northern and southern rail border crossings, and at Chinggis Khaan International Airport in Ulaanbaatar. The Mongolian police, the Ministry of Justice, and the General Intelligence Agency's counterterrorism branch cooperated with their U.S. counterparts on counterterrorism issues. As a result of resource and technical limitations, however, Mongolian counterterrorism law enforcement capacities remained modest.

Internationally, Mongolia deployed a total of ten rotations of 100 Mongolian soldiers to Iraq in support of Operation Iraqi Freedom. These rotations ended in September, with the downsizing of the Multi-National Forces Iraq contingent strength. Mongolia also supported Operation Enduring Freedom through the provision of teams of Mongolian soldiers to Afghanistan to train the Afghan National Army.

New Zealand

The New Zealand government continued to assist Pacific Island Countries' (PICs) compliance with international counterterrorism efforts and focused on legislative and operational capacity-building projects in the region through its Pacific Security Fund. New Zealand convened and chaired the annual Pacific Islands Forum Working Group on Counterterrorism (WGCT), which provided an opportunity for PICs to receive up-to-date information and to coordinate technical assistance projects to assist their compliance with UN Security Council reporting obligations. At the June 2 meeting of the WGCT, New Zealand offered assistance with UN reporting. Similarly, New Zealand used its Asia Security Fund to promote counterterrorism capacity building and a range of partnered regional security initiatives. To address radicalization and terrorist recruitment in the Asia-Pacific region, New Zealand continued to participate in interfaith and inter-cultural initiatives such as the Asia-Pacific Regional Interfaith Dialogue and the UN-led Alliance of Civilizations initiative.

A member of the Proliferation Security Initiative's (PSI) Operational Experts Group since 2004, New Zealand attended and presented at PSI meetings throughout the year. In June, New Zealand provided a PSI presentation to the Pacific Islands Forum Working Group on Counterterrorism and raised PSI at the Pacific Islands Forum Regional Security Meeting in Suva. New Zealand's bilateral PSI outreach included Indonesia, Laos, Chile, Brazil, Thailand, Cambodia, Egypt, Republic of Korea, and Pacific Island countries.

In October 2007, New Zealand police arrested and detained 17 people and seized a sizable weapons cache, including semi-automatic weapons and petrol bombs. Amid evidence that some detainees were possibly involved in the planning of terrorist acts against the state, 12 of the 17 were later referred for possible prosecution under the Terrorism Suppression Act (TSA), the first time the Act was invoked since it became law in 2002. New Zealand's Solicitor-General, however, declined TSA prosecution but nonetheless prosecuted the 17 arrested under the Firearms Act. In October 2008, the courts acquitted one of the 17 initially arrested in the 2007 raids because of insufficient evidence. The 16 remaining arrestees were on bail pending a future court date. In a related event, the Solicitor-General filed contempt of court proceedings against Fairfax Media and the editor of the *Dominion Post* newspaper for publishing 13 extracts in November 2007 from conversations recorded during police surveillance of those 17 people detained under possible terrorism charges. The matter remained before the courts at year's end.

In December, the New Zealand Police requested U.S. funding to enable officers of the elite Special Tactics Group (STG) to provide covert in-flight security on 2.5 percent of all flights to or over the United States. New Zealand law already allows armed police on flights to meet international aviation security standards, though the government said none had yet been deployed.

New Zealand remained active in Operation Enduring Freedom in Afghanistan and worked with coalition partners in undertaking maritime security operations in the Persian Gulf. New Zealand commanded the Provincial Reconstruction Team (PRT) in Afghanistan's Bamyan Province, with up to 140 PRT personnel. Three New Zealand Police were based in Bamyan working with the European Police Mission in Afghanistan.

Papua New Guinea, Solomon Islands, or Vanuatu Pacific Island nations, in general, are at a crossroads in development which has left a large, younger generation with fewer options for education and employment than is required for healthy growth. Without sustained social and economic development the growing youth population could be more vulnerable to extremist influences. None of these countries' governments maintained strong counterterrorism or intelligence gathering programs and therefore might be unable to detect highly organized and trained terrorists in their territories, nor have they taken any type of specific, proactive action to detect, disrupt, or deter terrorist activity.

Philippines

As in recent years, terrorist groups active in the Philippines included the Abu Sayyaf Group (ASG), Jemaah Islamiya (JI), the New People's Army (NPA), and the Rajah Solaiman Movement (RSM). U.S. intelligence, reconnaissance, and surveillance supported Armed Forces of the Philippines' operations against terrorist elements in the southern Philippines, while U.S. Department of Justice criminal-investigation and antiterrorism programs trained approximately 5,000 police and other security personnel. Implementation of the Coastwatch South program continued to move forward; its radar stations and sea-surface and aerial assets will dramatically improve the government's oversight of the "Terrorist Transit Triangle" region bordered by the Philippines, Malaysia, and Indonesia. The Department of Homeland Security Immigration and Customs Enforcement's newly-developed Philippine Biometric Initiative has provided Philippine National Police with fingerprints, photographs, and other information on 130 suspected terrorists.

Philippine security forces continued to make progress against terrorist groups, killing 35 terrorists and capturing another 16 during the first half of the year. Those apprehended included an RSM cofounder and two bomb makers in Mindanao.

The U.S. counterterrorism strategy of offering development opportunities in areas at risk for terrorist recruitment continued to marginalize the small remaining numbers of ASG and JI terrorists from Muslim insurgents in the southern Philippines. While the 5,000-strong

NPA continued to disrupt public security and business operations with intermittent attacks on communication and transportation infrastructure throughout the Philippines, it continued to decline in personnel and effectiveness. However, the NPA remained steadfast in its refusal to accept President Arroyo's broad amnesty overtures, turning down offers to negotiate unless its U.S. and international designations as a terrorist organization were rescinded. RSM maintained close links to ASG and JI, and was alleged to have been responsible for multiple attacks in the Philippines. In early 2008, RSM was included on the UN 1267 Committee sanctions list. This led to the freezing of RSM bank accounts and real estate.

Philippine military and law enforcement agencies conducted intensive civil-military and internal security operations to eliminate terrorist safe havens in the Sulu Archipelago and central Mindanao. In July, Ruben Pestano Lavilla, Jr., a leader and founding member of the RSM, was arrested in Bahrain and deported to the Philippines. In December, the Court of Appeals ordered the trial of RSM founder Hiliarion "Ahmad" Santos and other suspected RSM members for their alleged involvement in multiple bombings and kidnappings in the Philippines during 2005 and 2006.

The 2007 passage of the Human Security Act (HSA) was an important step in the modernization of tools available to Philippine law enforcement for use against terrorists. The Act permits wiretapping of members of judicially-designated terrorist organizations, and financial investigations of individuals connected to terrorist organizations. However, the law's tight restrictions have limited its actual application. The key difficulty in implementing the law is that stiff fines will be imposed on the law enforcement agency for violating a suspect's rights if the accused is later acquitted or the case is dismissed (fines are approximately USD 10,000 per day for the entire period of detention). The Act did, however, provide for the establishment of an Antiterrorism Council to effectively implement counterterrorism efforts in the country and ensure interagency cooperation. The Council focused its first year's efforts in building the organizational and administrative infrastructure necessary to facilitate closer cooperation between Council members and supporting agencies.

The United States had excellent cooperation from Philippine law enforcement officials in obtaining access to terrorist detainees and witnesses for FBI interviews, and access to criminal, immigration, financial, and biographic records via the mechanisms established in the U.S. - Philippine Mutual Legal Assistance Treaty (MLAT). The Philippine Security Engagement Board was the primary mechanism for the planning and coordination of nontraditional security issues, including counterterrorism and maritime security. Throughout the year, the Embassy continued to achieve significant progress in supporting the counterterrorism efforts of the Philippine government, including well-coordinated Embassy programs aimed at strengthening security forces and promoting peace and development in Mindanao. This pro-active partnership with the Philippine government has yielded solid results in combating terrorist elements, including ASG, JI, and the NPA.

The Antiterrorism Assistance (ATA) Program continued to increase the capabilities of Philippine law enforcement agencies to detect, deter, counter, and investigate terrorist activities in the Philippines through carefully-targeted and sequenced delivery of training courses and equipment grants. During 2008, ATA increased its focus on Mindanao by providing valuable training in a wide range of areas including Interdicting Terrorist Activity, Explosive Incident Countermeasures, Post-Blast Investigation, Advanced Computer Forensics, and Cellphone Forensics. ATA instituted a K-9 program of bomb-detection dogs with the Philippine National Police (PNP) by funding U.S.-trained dogs, their handlers, veterinarians, and kennel facilities. ATA assistance has also focused on training in response mechanisms to chemical, biological, radiological and nuclear (CBRN) terrorism. On the prevention end of the spectrum, U.S. assistance under the Biosecurity Engagement Program (BEP) has received strong cooperation from the GRP in securing laboratory infrastructure, dangerous pathogen collections, and raising awareness on biological threats in order to prevent bioterrorism in the Philippines, a place where burgeoning biotechnology, infectious diseases, and transnational terrorist threats coexist.

The U.S. Department of Justice/International Criminal Investigative Training Assistance Program (DOJ/ICITAP) trained 4,197 police personnel and pursued police development primarily through the Model Police Station Program, which trained PNP personnel at 10 stations in 15 critical subjects; the Maritime Police Project, which when completed will equip maritime police in Palawan Province with special patrol boats to monitor the western Sulu Sea bordering Malaysia; and the Southern Philippines Law Enforcement Development Project, which entailed training PNP personnel in basic police operations and investigation techniques in Sulu Province.

Other programs have included the DHS Immigration and Customs Enforcement (DHS/ICE) development of the Philippine Biometrics Initiative, whereby fingerprints, photographs, and other information on suspected terrorists were collected and provided to the appropriate Philippine authorities. The Coastwatch South program will dramatically improve oversight of the tri-border "Terrorist Transit Triangle" with the use of 12-17 coastal radar sites connected by a string of air, ocean, and ground surveillance and interdiction assets, including Forward-Looking Infrared Radar (FLIR) pods for Philippine Navy aircraft and 10 rigid-hull inflatable boats (RHIBs).

The Philippine Department of Foreign Affairs (DFA) issued digitized, machine-readable passports at all its locations.

Singapore

Singaporean officials took strong measures to enhance maritime security in nearby waters, especially the Strait of Malacca, including countering terrorist threats, piracy, and other criminal attacks. The three littoral states – Indonesia, Malaysia, and Singapore – continued their surface, naval, and air patrols in and over the Strait of Malacca. The Republic of Singapore Navy (RSN) continued construction of the Changi C2 Centre, which will house a multi-agency Port Operations and Control Centre, a Multinational Operations and Exercises Centre, and an Information Fusion Centre, the latter to be staffed with International Liaison Officers. The Regional Cooperation Agreement on Combating Piracy and Armed Robbery against Ships in Asia (ReCAAP) Information Sharing Centre (ISC) continued its operations, connecting 14 governments in Asia to enhance piracy-related information sharing.

The RSN participated in the annual bilateral exercise "Cooperation Afloat Readiness and Training" with the U.S. Navy and U.S. Coast Guard, and the multilateral "South East Asia Cooperation Against Terrorism" (SEACAT) exercise. Singapore conducted its own internal, annual exercise, *APEX*, which tested the government's interagency response to a maritime terrorism incident.

As of December, Singapore-held detainees included members of JI who in 2001 and 2002 had plotted to carry out attacks in Singapore, and members of the Moro Islamic Liberation Front (MILF). Under detention orders, the detainees were required to undergo a program of religious counseling with a group of volunteer religious counselors. Singapore enlisted the support of religious teachers and scholars to study JI's ideology, develop teachings to counter the group's spread within Singapore's Muslim community, and provide counseling to detainees. One JI detainee was released on a Restriction Order (RO) in February; and five JI members were released on ROs in September. Singapore authorities determined that the released detainees had cooperated in Singaporean security investigations and responded positively to rehabilitation, including religious counseling. One person with links to terrorist groups was newly detained in 2008. The recidivism rates among detainees released in Singapore is unknown.

In February, Mas Selemat Kastari, the Singapore leader of JI, escaped from detention. Despite a massive manhunt, the Singapore authorities failed to locate and re-capture Kastari, who had reportedly escaped by climbing out of a restroom window located in a meeting area of the detention center.

In February, the Financial Action Task Force (FATF) published the results of its review of Singapore's anti-money laundering and counterterrorism financing regime, finding it compliant or largely compliant with most of the FATF's recommendations. The evaluation noted that Singapore had improved feedback to financial institutions, enhanced supervisory oversight and stepped up training. However, concerns remained over the effectiveness of Singapore's money laundering regulations and new system for declaring cross-border transactions. In December, the government amended the Terrorism (Suppression of Financing) Act to allow the government to respond to requests for extradition from Parties to the International Convention for the Suppression of the Financing of Terrorism, even in the absence of an extradition treaty, for all terrorism financing offenses.

In September, Singapore cooperated with U.S. authorities to investigate and subsequently apprehend a Singapore suspect who had allegedly sent terrorist threats by e-mail to several airlines and embassies around the world.

In June, the United States and Singapore signed a Memorandum of Cooperation to strengthen ongoing collaboration on aviation security. In August, the United States and Singapore signed a host country Memorandum of Understanding concerning challenge inspections under the Chemical Weapons Convention (CWC). Singapore has been a signatory to the CWC since 1997.

Taiwan

Taiwan is not a member of the United Nations and, therefore, is not subject to UNSC Resolutions and cannot join UN conventions and protocols related to terrorist financing. Nonetheless, Taiwan sought to implement, to the maximum extent possible, all UN resolutions related to combating terrorism and terrorist finance issues. Taiwan continued to provide rapid and thorough responses on terrorism financing issues to the American Institute in Taiwan (AIT). In 2006, Taiwan's Executive Yuan submitted an "Antiterrorist Action Law" to the Legislative Yuan. This bill was still awaiting action by the legislature. If passed, it will empower the Financial Supervisory Commission to seize assets of entities involved in terrorist activities, and employ a package of trade, travel, and financial sanctions against North Korea in response to UNSCR 1718.

The cabinet-level Counterterrorism Office (CTO) conducted several large-scale training exercises. In January, Taiwan law enforcement participated in an AIT sponsored Digital Video Conference with security organizers from the Salt Lake Olympics Games. In November, the CTO conducted an inter-ministerial exercise that covered natural disaster and counterterrorist responses. Taiwan engaged in seeking ways to harden and protect its critical infrastructure, in order to maintain continuity of operations and government in the event of an attack or a disaster.

Thailand

Counterterrorism cooperation with the Government of Thailand remained strong despite considerable internal political turmoil and the Thai government's concern with domestic political issues. Thai and USG officials have long expressed concern that transnational terrorist groups could establish links with southern Thailand-based separatist groups. However, there were no indications that transnational terrorist groups were directly involved in the violence in the south, and there was no evidence of direct operational links between southern Thai separatist groups and regional terroristnetworks.

The ethno-nationalist separatist insurgency in Thailand's extreme southern provinces of Songkhla, Pattani, Narathiwat, and Yala continued through 2008. Some 3400 people have been killed in the conflict since the violence escalated in 2004 in assassinations, beheadings, and coordinated bombings using improvised explosive devices. This region has experienced episodic, separatist-related violence for decades between the predominantly ethnic Malay-Muslim population and the Thai government. Thai press reports and security forces attributed nearly all the attacks in the South to militant separatists; it is unclear, however, how much of the violence was also attributable to crime and political disputes.

The porous nature of Thailand's southern border with Malaysia remained an issue of concern because of the difficulty both Thailand and Malaysia have in controlling it. In a March meeting with Malaysian Prime Minister Abdullah Badawi, then Thai Prime Minister Samak Sundaravej agreed to continue cooperation on measures to improve security in the border area through discussions on issues of dual nationality, sharing information, and joint patrols by Thai and Malaysian security forces. In September, Thailand agreed to conduct joint sea and air patrols of the Malacca Strait with Indonesia, Malaysia, and Singapore. Thailand joined the Malacca Strait Patrols agreement which includes Eyes in the Sky and intelligence exchange programs.

Legal mechanisms to counter the Southern Thai insurgency lagged behind security efforts. Government prosecutors struggled to develop cases that could stand up in court and relied chiefly on confessions to bring prosecutions. Police forensics and ballistics work often failed to produce evidence that led to arrests following separatist attacks. Because of the difficulties in bringing cases to court, security forces engaging in operations to arrest militants relied instead on their powers under martial law and the 2005 Emergency Decree to detain suspects, who can be held for 37 days without being charged with a crime.

Thai security forces cooperated with the United States and with other countries to deny safe haven to terrorists within their borders. In the past, Thailand has served as a transit point for regional terrorists, as evidenced by the 2003 capture in central Thailand of Nurjaman Riduan bin Isomuddin (a.k.a. Hambali), JI's operations chief and the architect behind the 2002 Bali bombings.

Thai police and security officials participated in a series of U.S. training programs sponsored through the Antiterrorism Assistance (ATA) program, the Force Protection Detachment (FPD), and the International Law Enforcement Academy (ILEA) in Bangkok. Training modules included post-blast and crime scene investigation courses, and the Antiterrorism Executive Forum. U.S. and Thai militaries cooperated in a series of training events designed to build counterterrorism capacity to respond to terrorist acts. These events culminated around the Cobra Gold 2008 Joint-Combined Military Training Exercises, in which peacekeeping, humanitarian assistance, and disaster relief were for the first time combined to respond to the changing nature of the security environment in Southeast Asia.

Thailand has been an active and cooperative partner in combating WMD terrorism, and is a participant in the Container Security Initiative (CSI) and the Megaports Initiative. Working through the Embassy's Export Control and Border Security (EXBS) program, Thailand participated in port and border security programs, and programs to strengthen Thailand's controls on the export of munitions, dual use goods, and related technologies. The Thai government participated in EXBS assistance assessments at the ports of Laem Chabang, Bangkok, and Chiang Saen; a border crossing assessment at Mae Sai; and a Seaport Interdiction Training at Laem Chabang. Thai officials participated in workshops on Strategic Trade Controls and attended a conference on international transshipment issues held in Tangier, Morocco. he Thai government, led by the Ministry of Commerce, stood up an Export Control Working Group in March and began examining better ways to automate its strategic trade licensing system.

The Thai Anti-Money Laundering Office (AMLO) was the center for interdicting terrorist finance, and is Thailand's official Financial Intelligence Unit. Thailand has been a member of the Financial Action Task Force's Egmont Group since June 2001. AMLO, the Bank of Thailand (the central bank), and the Securities and Exchange Commission, are empowered to supervise and examine financial institutions for compliance with anti-money laundering/counterterrorist financial laws and regulations.

In October 2007, the Ministry of Finance issued new regulations governing cross border cash carrying, bringing Thailand into line with the Financial Action Task Force Special Recommendation on Terrorist Financing. In January 2008, it issued a regulation stipulating that persons traveling in and out of the country carrying more than USD 20,000 must declare the amount to Thai customs. In August, the Bank of Thailand reissued instructions to financial institutions (Thai and foreign commercial banks, finance companies, and asset management companies) to adopt know your customer and customer due diligence procedures in order to comply with FATF recommendations on Anti-Money Laundering and Combating the Financing of Terrorism.

The Thai government cooperated on the extradition of international arms dealer Victor Bout, who is under federal indictment in New York for conspiring to sell millions of dollars worth of weapons to the Revolutionary Armed Forces of Colombia (FARC). Bout was arrested in Bangkok in March, and his extradition proceedings remained ongoing. U.S. and Thai authorities have cooperated extensively throughout the investigation and extradition proceedings.

Thailand participated actively in international counterterrorism efforts through the Asia Pacific Economic Cooperation (APEC), the Association of Southeast Asian Nations (ASEAN), the ASEAN Regional Forum (ARF), and other fora. In January 2007, Thailand became a signatory to the ASEAN Convention on Counterterrorism; the Thai Cabinet approved the convention's ratification, and it was ratified by the Foreign Minister in February 2008.

Europe and Eurasia Overview

So, the question is how - at one and the same time - we can ensure we give no quarter to terrorism and organized crime, while still advancing the liberties our society is founded upon...

The British way cannot be a head-in-the-sand approach that ignores the fact that the world has changed with the advent of terrorism, which aims for civilian casualties on a massive scale and which respects not only no law, but also no recognizable moral framework. Instead, it must be an approach that is prepared to make the difficult decisions to protect our security – not by ignoring the demands of liberty but always at the same time doing everything we can to protect the individual from unfair or arbitrary treatment.

—Gordon Brown, Prime Minister of the United Kingdom
Speech on Security and Liberty
June 17, 2008

European countries improved their capabilities to counter the terrorist threat, foiled several significant terrorist plots, and prosecuted and jailed terrorist suspects. European governments were increasingly concerned and sought greater understanding of the process of "radicalization" and how to prevent it. Toward that end, European governments continued their efforts at outreach to domestic Muslim communities and made attempts to gain support from those communities to counter the appeal of violent extremist ideology.

European nations continued to work in close partnership with the United States against a terrorist threat characterized by both external and, increasingly, internal components. The contributions of European countries in sharing intelligence, arresting members of terrorist cells, interdicting terrorist financing, and logistics were vital elements in the global effort to combat terrorism and violent extremism.

The United States and European Union continued to cooperate closely to counter terrorism. At the June 2004 U.S.-EU Summit, the sides agreed on a Declaration on Combating Terrorism that renewed the transatlantic commitment to develop measures to maximize capacities to detect, investigate, and prosecute terrorists; prevent terrorist attacks; prevent access by terrorists to financial and other economic resources; enhance information sharing and cooperation among law enforcement agencies; and improve the effectiveness of border information systems. These commitments were reaffirmed at the 2008 Summit, and work continued on the implementation, and, in particular, the ratification of mutual legal assistance treaties intended to advance transatlantic cooperation.

European nations were active participants in a variety of multilateral organizations that contribute to counterterrorist efforts, including the G8, NATO, the Financial Action Task Force, the Global Initiative to Combat Nuclear Terrorism, the Organization for Security and Cooperation in Europe (OSCE), the International Maritime Organization, and the International Civil Aviation Organization. The United States worked with its international partners through multilateral organizations to establish and implement best practices, build the counterterrorism capabilities of "weak but willing" states, and help counter terrorism globally. OSCE members committed themselves to becoming parties to the 13 international terrorism conventions and protocols, to work together to modernize travel documents and shipping container security, to prevent and suppress the financing of terrorist organizations, and to implement UNSC Resolution 1540 to counter WMD (related materials and the means of delivery) proliferation.

Terrorist activity and the presence of terrorist support networks in Europe remained a source of serious concern. Efforts to combat the threat in Europe were sometimes slowed by legal protections that made it difficult to take firm judicial action against suspected terrorists, the absence of adequate legislation, or standards of evidence that limited the use of classified information in holding terrorist suspects. Terrorists also sought to take advantage of the ease of travel among Schengen countries. At times, some European states have not been able to prosecute successfully or hold some of the suspected terrorists brought before their courts – a product, in part, of insufficient measures to use intelligence information in judicial proceedings. The EU as a whole remained reluctant to take steps to block the assets of charities associated with HAMAS and Hizballah.

No major terrorist attacks took place in Europe in 2008, but arrests in Italy, Spain, France, Belgium, the UK, Turkey and other countries brought home the scope of the challenge facing European governments and security forces. The level of threat in Western Europe remained high, particularly in the Netherlands, Denmark, Germany, France, and Belgium. The deaths of Swedish extremists in Somalia and Iraq and the first-ever German-born suicide bomber in Afghanistan highlighted the global nature of the threat and the ease with which extremists can travel to conflict areas.

Cooperation with and among European law enforcement agencies remained vital for counterterrorism successes, and judicial proceedings in countries across Europe resulted in the successful convictions of several terrorist suspects. France and Spain continued to cooperate effectively against Basque Fatherland and Liberty (ETA), scoring major successes including the arrests of ETA alleged political and military chiefs. Germany and other European countries continued to maintain pressure on the militant Kurdish nationalist group Kurdistan Workers' Party (PKK), which raised funds, often through illicit activity, to support violence in Turkey. Cooperation between France and Belgium led in December to the arrests to 23 persons allegedly connected to al-Qa'ida (AQ). German courts also convicted suspects for activities connected to organizations ranging from AQ and the Islamic Jihad Union, to the PKK. A Danish court convicted Hammad Khurshid, a Pakistani-born Danish citizen, and an accomplice for conspiring to commit terrorism. Italian authorities addressed similarly broad challenges, arresting, charging, and convicting suspects linked to Islamic extremism, the Tamil Tigers, and violent left and right-wing fringe groups. Recent court decisions have called into question the European Council's regulations for implementing asset freezes against terrorists and supporters of terrorism, including those who have been designated by the UN. Trials in Belgium in the case of Bilal Soughir and five other men suspected of having recruited and trained terrorists for suicide attacks in Iraq resulted in convictions with sentences between ten and two years; all of the sentences were later reduced on appeal. There were also other appeals - an appeals court in The Netherlands acquitted the seven members of the Hofstad terrorist group of participating in a criminal and terrorist organization, though the convictions of three terrorists were upheld, and the prosecution appealed the acquittals to the Supreme Court. In Spain, the Supreme Court acquitted on appeal four of the 21 convicted defendants in the Madrid train bombings trial who had been sentenced in October 2007.

Albania

Albania pledged to increase its contribution of troops to Afghanistan, froze bank accounts related to money laundering and terrorist financing, and aggressively worked with the United States and other countries to combat terrorism. Albania made progress in identifying vulnerabilities at land and sea borders, but the government and police forces continued to face challenges to enforce border security fully and combat organized crime and corruption.

On January 14, the criminal trial began against Hamzeh Abu Rayyan, the suspected administrator for UNSCR 1267 Committee-designated terrorist financier Yassin Al-Kadi, who is charged with hiding funds used to finance terrorism. This marked the first ever criminal terrorist finance-related trial in Albania; the trial was ongoing at year's end. A civil suit filed by al-Kadi to release his assets from seizure was dismissed, was then refiled in July, and again was dismissed by the court in September. Al-Kadi's company, Loxhall, also filed a lawsuit in April, aimed at annulling the Council of Ministers' decision as well as the two orders of the Ministry of Finance related to the administration of seized terrorism assets.

Although no new groups' assets were frozen this year under Albania's Terrorism Financing Freeze law, as of October, the Ministry of Finance claimed that it maintained asset freezes against six individuals and 14 foundations and companies on the UNSCR 1267 list. Despite this progress, the effectiveness of the government's counterterrorist financing effort was undermined by a lack of data-processing infrastructure and an inadequate capability to track and manage cases properly.

Armenia

Armenia's counterterrorism partnership with the United States included granting blanket over-flight clearance and ad hoc landing rights to U.S. military aircraft, deployment of a peacekeeping contingent to Iraq in support of Operation Iraqi Freedom (OIF), and participation in bilateral assistance programs that strengthened the government's capacity to monitor illicit financial flows and confront trafficking in hazardous substances.

Widespread corruption, however, continued to hamper full implementation and enforcement of laws that would improve Armenia's counterterrorism posture and response capability.

In response to a Government of Iraq notice that it would not require the same level of international security assistance in 2009, the Armenian 46-man peacekeeping contingent re-deployed in October after successfully completing its assigned missions. Since then, the Armenian Ministry of Defense has expressed active interest in sending a peacekeeping contingent to Afghanistan in support of the International Security Assistance Force.

Armenia was an active participant in several bilateral and multilateral assistance, security, and training initiatives targeted at strengthening its ability to combat terrorist financing and the smuggling of illicit and hazardous materials. These initiatives included: the Global Initiative to Combat Nuclear Terrorism, the Nuclear Smuggling Outreach Initiative, the Biological Threat Reduction Program, and related training programs sponsored by the resident offices of Export Control and Border Security and the Organization for Security and Cooperation in Europe (OSCE). By December, Armenia had achieved measured progress in implementing border security and anti-trafficking measures. These measures included: the installation of Radiation Portal Alarms at all land ports of entry and at its main airport; the installation of sensors for and increased monitoring of Armenia's green border with Georgia; and the Armenian Border Guard Service expected to have full connectivity of its automated Border Management Information System (BMIS) with all points of entry, which would reduce the possibility of passport and visa fraud. (Note: The BMIS contains criminal and terrorist watchlists as updated by the Republic of Armenia's Police and National Security Service.)

In May, Armenia revised its law on Combating Money Laundering and Terrorism Financing. This revision significantly expanded the range of reporting entities required to report suspicious transactions to the Financial Monitoring Center (FMC), a specialized intelligence unit within the Central Bank that is responsible for combating money laundering and terrorism financing. The FMC continued to share information internationally with other FIUs through its membership in the Egmont Group. To date, no transactions involving watchlist designees or other suspected terrorist financing cases have been uncovered.

Armenia continued to demonstrate interest in strengthening its ties with Iran. In May, Armenia declared support for expanding joint projects in the energy and transportation sectors. This was followed by the visits of at least two cabinet-level officials to Tehran in the fall to discuss cooperation in security, political, economic, and cultural spheres. In a reciprocal visit, Armenia hosted the Deputy Secretary of Iran's Security

Council in December to discuss bilateral cooperation further. As a result of the increased diplomatic activity, Armenia continued to be reluctant to participate in international efforts that criticized or placed pressure on Iran for its non-compliance on issues related to nuclear proliferation and terrorist financing.

Austria

Sympathizers of jailed Kurdistan Workers' Party (PKK) leader Abdullah Ocalan were believed to have been behind the October arson attacks against the Turkish consulate in Salzburg and Turkish associations in Vienna and Graz. In a separate incident, also in October, Kurdish demonstrators unsuccessfully tried to force their way onto the UN premises in Vienna. In March, a wanted PKK activist and Ocalan confidante, Ayfer Kaya, transited Austria and was subsequently arrested in Bavaria.

Austria fulfilled its obligations to freeze assets, pursuant to UN Security Council sanctions and EU Clearinghouse designations, but did not initiate any freezing actions independently. At the end of 2007, in order to implement the EU's Third Money Laundering Directive, the Austrian Parliament approved amendments to the Stock Exchange Act, the Securities Supervision Act, the Insurance Act, the Business Code, and Austrian laws governing lawyers and notaries. In the first half of 2008, it made amendments to the Gambling Act and the law governing accounting professionals. These introduced stricter regulations regarding customer identification procedures, including requiring customer identification for all transactions of more than USD 21,400 for customers without a permanent business relationship, as well as examining businesses suspected of money laundering, terrorist financing, and non-face-to-face transactions.

On August 28, Austria's Supreme Court ordered the case of Muhammad Shawqi, to be re-tried because the prosecutor did not present arguments to the jury in as clear a language as required by law. On March 13, a Vienna court had sentenced Shawqi and his wife to prison for belonging to a terrorist organization with links to al-Qa'ida and of trying to blackmail the Austrian government. Shawqi allegedly sent email threats to the Austrian and German Governments demanding they withdraw their forces from Afghanistan or face unspecified terrorist attacks.

In November, the Vienna public prosecutor suspended criminal investigations against representatives of the Palestinian Association in Austria, an organization on the U.S. Treasury Department's Office of Foreign Assets Control's Specially Designated Nationals list. The prosecutor stated that he was unable to establish proof of terrorist financing or membership in a terrorist organization. In August, a Vienna court ruled that the government should unfreeze about USD eight million from a bank account belonging to the Abu Nidal terrorist group. The court determined there was insufficient evidence that the money was connected to terrorism or would be used to support terrorism. The ruling was under appeal at year's end.

Austria's Bureau for the Protection of the Constitution and Counterterrorism expressed concern about radicalization and singled out a handful of suspected extremist mosques in Vienna for monitoring. The Bureau also continued to monitor the Egyptian Islamic Jihad movement, certain radicalized converts to Islam, and suspected Afghan extremists entering Austria as asylum seekers. Media sites monitored by the BVT include the Global Islamic Media Front and the as-Sahab Foundation for Islamic Media Publications.

The Austrian government worked to implement the Pruem Treaty, which involves the exchange of DNA, fingerprint, and vehicle data between government agencies, and was designed, in part, to identify terrorism suspects.

The Government of Austria convened a number of international conferences under its Dialogue Between Cultures and Religions program, which were attended by government and religious leaders from around the world. In December, an international group of women activists founded Sisters Against Violent Extremism (SAVE), an antiterrorism organization headquartered in Vienna that seeks to develop a network of women who have been victims of terrorism.

As a country participating in the Visa Waiver Program (VWP), Austria continued to comply with requirements in the VWP law related to information sharing and other law enforcement and counterterrorism cooperation. This cooperation was further enhanced by the Implementing Recommendations of the 9/11 Commission Act of 2007.

Azerbaijan

Azerbaijan and the United States have a strong record of cooperation on counterterrorism issues that predates the September 11, 2001 attacks. Azerbaijan, located on the crucial air route to Afghanistan, has granted blanket overflight clearance, engaged in information sharing and law-enforcement cooperation, and approved numerous landings and refueling operations at Baku's civilian airport in support of U.S. and Coalition military operations. Azerbaijan supported peacekeeping operations in Iraq from August 2003 to November 2008 with an infantry company of approximately 150 soldiers stationed at the Haditha dam. A platoon of Azerbaijani soldiers has served in Afghanistan since November 2002 and Azerbaijan is preparing to increase its contingent to 90 personnel, including medical and civil affairs specialists. Through tailored Export Control and Related Border Security and Cooperative Threat Reduction programs,

Azerbaijan cooperates with the United States to strengthen its capacity to secure its land and maritime frontiers against terrorist exploitation for the movement of people and materiel.

Azerbaijan is a logical route for extremists with ties to terrorist organizations, including several organizations which have been inspired or directed by Iran. These groups have sought to move people, money, and materiel through the Caucasus, but the government has actively opposed them and has had some success in reducing their presence and hampering their activities. Azerbaijan has taken steps to combat terrorist financing and identify possible terrorist-related funding by distributing lists of suspected terrorist groups and individuals to local banks. The Council of Europe, however, has issued a negative assessment of Azerbaijan's anti-money laundering reform effort thus far through its Committee of Experts on the Evaluation of Anti-Money Laundering Measures and the Financing of Terrorism mechanism. The government's draft law on money laundering, with the objective of creating an anti-money laundering and counterterrorist finance regime, including reporting requirements, a Financial Intelligence Unit, and other components as defined by international standards, was in an advanced stage of the legislative process at year's end. In anticipation of future adoption of this law, the USG has trained prosecutors, investigators, and judges on implementing anti-money laundering and counterterrorism financing law enforcement techniques.

On August 17, an unknown assailant or assailants attacked Baku's main Sunni mosque with grenades, killing three and wounding eight. The government closed the mosque after the attack. In late October, a Baku court ordered the mosque reopened, but soon reversed itself. The government detained thirteen suspects in late August and early September in connection with the attack. In its September 2 public statement on the attack, the Ministry of National Security alleged that Ilgar Mollachiyev, an Azerbaijani citizen associated with extremist activities in Russian region of Dagestan, and his brother-in-law Samir Mehtiyev had masterminded the attack. Mollachiyev was killed by Russian security forces in Dagestan in September. The mosque remained closed and the investigation into the attack is ongoing.

Belgium

Belgium continued to strengthen its capacity to respond to the threat of terrorism, developing new institutions over the past several years to coordinate the Belgian government's effort to use and share information to combat terrorism, maintain vigilance of persons and groups of concern, and actively work to prevent terrorist financing. In December, a major operation leading to the arrest of 15 suspected terrorists demonstrated the

Belgian government's will and capacity to take effective action.

In October 2007, hearings began in the case of Bilal Soughir and five other men suspected of recruiting and training terrorists for suicide attacks in Iraq, including Muriel Degauque, a Belgian national who, in 2005, blew herself up in a failed bomb attack in Iraq. Federal authorities planned ongoing reviews of court rulings to gauge what acts and groups could be prosecuted successfully under the 2003 legislation and what types of sentences could be imposed. On January 10, 2008, the verdicts ranged between 10 years for the leader, Bilal Soughir, five years for three of his accomplices, and lesser sentences for two others. All of the verdicts were later reduced on appeal to roughly half of the original sentences.

Belgian police and security agencies have used legislation enacted in recent years to improve information collection on alleged extremists and suspected terrorists. Belgium's Coordinating Body for Threat Analysis (OCAM/OCAD) was on its way to becoming fully operational. OCAM operates under the joint authority of the Justice and Interior Ministers and includes representatives from the external and internal services, the Federal Police, Customs, and the Ministries of Transport, Finance, and Foreign Affairs. It facilitates the exchange of information among all governmental counterterrorism bodies and develops common threat analyses on the basis of such information exchanges.

Belgian authorities have the ability to create a national list of terrorist entities, separate from UN and EU lists, coordinated by OCAM, including financiers and suspected financiers of terrorism. This information allowed Belgian authorities to develop and apply a national capacity to freeze assets, in addition to UN- and EU-mandated asset freezes that Belgium already implements. Belgian cooperation on security programs such as the Container Security Initiative, Megaports, and export controls was excellent.

Belgian authorities reviewed and updated emergency action plans to prepare for and respond to potential attacks, including bioterrorism. On a local level, authorities instituted drills of rapid alert systems and reviewed critical infrastructure support, civil protection, and medical assistance procedures. Federal and local authorities participated in a U.S. European Command (EUCOM) Weapons of Mass Destruction Consequence Management exercise, furthering U.S.-Belgian cooperation in this area. Police and private sector working groups targeted terrorists, the financing of terrorism, and terrorist use of the Internet.

Belgium increased its significant military contribution to the International Security Assistance Force in Afghanistan, where it deployed a force of about 400 troops. The main force protected Kabul airport and some personnel were deployed at the German-led Provisional Reconstruction Team in Kunduz. Belgium contributed approximately USD 47 million toward Afghan reconstruction and promised to boost its support for reconstruction and development, totaling approximately USD 65 million to be disbursed over the next four years. Assistance to Iraq included expanded participation in the Jordan International Police Training Center in Amman (which subsequently closed in September), training for Iraqi diplomats and magistrates in Belgium, and training for Iraqi servicemen in Abu Dhabi, in cooperation with Germany.

Belgian authorities remained concerned about potential terrorist activities involving groups from Algeria and North Africa and have investigated groups such as the Moroccan Islamic Combatant Group; the People's Revolutionary Liberation Party Front (DHKP/C), a far right group with links to neo-Nazi groups; and a cell suspected of training members for attacks in Iraq. The PKK is a known presence with television production studios in Denderleeuw, Belgium. Belgium fined the studios, made several arrests, and effectively shut them down.

Belgium continued to take action in response to EU and UN Security Council actions to freeze suspected terrorist assets and examined steps to improve its ability to combat and control terrorist financing.

In December 2007, Belgian officials arrested and quickly released 15 persons who had reportedly threatened to attack unspecified Belgian targets, which led to an increased level of alert and the closing of trash cans at major tourist locations. While Belgian media and public opinion were quite critical of the perceived over-reaction, the subsequent year-long investigation led to the December 2008 arrest of 15 suspected terrorists.

As a country participating in the Visa Waiver Program (VWP), Belgium continued to comply with requirements in the VWP law related to information sharing and other law enforcement and counterterrorism cooperation. This cooperation was further enhanced by the Implementing Recommendations of the 9/11 Commission Act of 2007.

Bosnia and Herzegovina

Despite ethnic polarization and disputes among Bosnian political leaders that hindered the functioning of state government, Bosnia and Herzegovina's law enforcement organizations cooperated with the United States on international counterterrorism issues. Bosnia remained a weak, decentralized state with poor interagency communication and competing security structures. Efforts by Republika Srpska officials to undermine state-level institutions slowed efforts to improve operational capabilities to combat terrorism and terrorist financing. These factors, combined with political interference in law enforcement, resulted in Bosnia being vulnerable to exploitation as a potential staging ground for terrorist operations in Europe.

The State Investigation and Protection Agency (SIPA) is the state-level Bosnian law enforcement agency with primary responsibility for counterterrorism operations, but SIPA's capacity was limited. The government filled the position of SIPA Director in December 2007 after a vacancy that lasted almost a year.

The issue of terrorism in Bosnia, including terrorism threat analysis and counterterrorism operations, continued to be politicized. Consequently, Bosnian capabilities and potential for independent action at the state level did not improve as much as hoped. However, the state-level intelligence service provided excellent cooperation and Bosnian authorities were generally responsive to U.S. counterterrorism cooperation requests.

Some former members of the mujahedin brigade[6], whose citizenship was revoked by the Citizenship Review Commission, have pursued appeals of these decisions that remained unresolved. In the case of Abu Hamza al-Suri (Imad al-Husayn), the Bosnian Constitutional Court issued a ruling that upheld lower court decisions stripping him of his Bosnian citizenship. The Constitutional Court did, however, return one portion of Hamza's appeal to the State Court to consider whether deportation and possible resulting family separation would violate his human rights. The court had not adjudicated this case as of December 2008.

In March, a group of five individuals with alleged ties to extremists, led by Rijad Rustempasic, was arrested for possession of arms and explosives. For reasons that remain unknown, charges against the defendants were dropped in May and the defendants were released from custody. Investigation of this case continues.

The Bosnian organization Aktivna Islamska Omladina (Active Islamic Youth, or AIO) experienced fractures among its leaders and is no longer an officially registered organization in Bosnia. However some former members continued to spread extremist doctrine. These former members maintained links with extremists in Western Europe and the United States.

In December, Bosnia successfully concluded its mission in Iraq with the redeployment to Bosnia of its Emergency Ordnance Disposal (EOD) team and infantry platoon for fixed site security. Through eight rotations to Iraq, the EOD team reduced the threat of unexploded ordnance and excess ammunition.

---

[6] Bosnian mujahedin brigade were foreign Muslim volunteers who fought on the Bosnian government side during the 1992-1995 Bosnian war.

Bulgaria

In November, the Bulgarian Council of Ministers approved a National Action Plan against terrorism to prevent terrorist acts within Bulgaria and against Bulgarian citizens, against installations and contingents abroad, and to counter possible terrorist activities among the Bulgarian population. The new Counterterrorism Coordination Centre at the State Agency for National Security (DANS) will be the national hub for the suppression of international terrorism and coordinates interaction among Bulgarian ministries and with relevant counterterrorism structures of the EU and NATO.

Bulgaria's religious leaders, including the leaders of the nation's Muslim community, spoke out strongly against extremism and terrorism.

During the year, a total of 20 Bulgarian officials attended Department of Defense counterterrorism training in the United States or in Bulgaria's neighboring countries through the Embassy's Office of Defense Cooperation under the Counterterrorism Fellowship Program (CTFP). CTFP training focuses on counterterrorism issues taught in residential courses in the United States or through Mobile Training Teams in Europe. The officials included military officers and civilians from the Ministry of Defense, the Ministry of the Interior, and DANS. The CTFP program total for FY 2008, including both direct allocation and EUCOM discretionary funding, amounted to $252,417.

At the request of the Government of Iraq, Bulgaria concluded its participation in Operation Iraqi Freedom (OIF) on December 17. Its 2008 OIF contribution consisted of a 153-soldier contingent, initially at Camp Ashraf but transferred to Camp Cropper in April. Bulgaria also contributed two officers to the NATO Training Mission in Iraq. In Afghanistan, Bulgaria continued to increase participation in the International Security Assistance Force, where it deployed an additional 50 soldiers to take responsibility for one of the Entry Control Points to Kandahar Airfield, bringing its total, in country, to 470 with the bulk in Regional Command–South. Bulgaria had an infantry company and an infantry platoon in Kabul, an infantry company at Kandahar Airfield, one medical team in Kabul and two in Herat, and two officers serving with the Hungarian Provincial Reconstruction Team in Pol-e Khomri.

In 2008, Bulgaria signed and ratified the counter-WMD Agreement to permit the U.S. Defense Threat Reduction Agency to provide training and equipment for law enforcement entities to enhance customs and border guards' ability to detect, interdict, identify, investigate, and respond to the illicit trafficking of WMD and related materials. The Government of Bulgaria also signed and ratified the Second Line of Defense Agreement to permit the U.S. Department of Energy to install radioactivity detectors at Bulgarian seaports, airports, and border crossings.

DANS came into force on January 1, 2008 and combined the National Security Service, the State Agency for Protection of Classified Information, the Military Counterintelligence organization, and the Financial Intelligence Agency (now the Financial Intelligence Directorate). In addition to its primary mandate of counterterrorism and counterintelligence, DANS is also charged with fighting organized crime, money laundering, and high-level corruption. After a promising start at the beginning of 2008, DANS's reputation rapidly declined and hit a low in September and October following a series of scandals and the apparent politicization of high-profile disputes that led to the dismissal and resignation of several senior intelligence professionals.

The DANS law limited the Financial Intelligence Directorate's (FID) effectiveness and autonomy of FID by changing its status from an independent agency within the Ministry of Finance to a directorate within the DANS. Some of the FID's previous authorities were removed from the law and included only in regulations, further diminishing the FID's status; other authority was assigned to the Director of DANS, but not expressly to the FID, thereby de facto limiting its ability to compel de jure compliance by banks. In addition, discrepancies between the Law on Measures against Money Laundering (LMML) and the law creating DANS created uncertainty regarding the FID's inspections and sanctioning authorities, including its ability to perform anti-money laundering on-site inspections. The anti-money laundering and anti-terrorist financing activities of FID-DANS were suspended from January 1 to May 1 because of legislative changes in the national legal framework.

Internal reorganizations notwithstanding, FID remained vigilant against terrorist financing and continued to cooperate with the USG on identifying and investigating terrorist assets. The FID reliably distributed lists of individuals and organization linked to terrorism to all of the banks in Bulgaria, the Ministry of Interior, Customs, and the Border Police. The FID has been responsive to all mandated UNSCR-designated terrorist organizations, and has also been very supportive and cooperative on USG designated individuals and organizations. The FID has advised the banking sector to use the Department of Treasury Office of Foreign Assets Control (OFAC) website as a reliable information resource for individuals and organizations associated with terrorism. FID also continued to provide feedback, including information on the response level of Bulgaria's banks, to the U. S. Treasury Department's Financial Crimes Enforcement Network.

Croatia

In December, Croatia passed a new national strategy for the prevention of terrorism which will enhance Croatia's ability to cooperate in international counterterrorism efforts. Also in December, Croatia, in its

Presidency of the UN Security Council, chaired an open debate on "Threats to International Peace and Security Caused by Terrorism," which resulted in a UN Presidency Statement condemning terrorist acts and advocating the advancement of international efforts to combat terrorism.

Croatia was in the initial phases of introducing biometric passports, but border security remained a challenge. Border patrol forces were limited by a lack of personnel and training to cover a 750 mile border with Serbia, Montenegro, and Bosnia. Monitoring the country's 6,000 miles of coastline posed similar problems. As Croatia prepared to join the European Union it was engaged in ongoing reforms of its judiciary to enhance the government's ability to arrest and prosecute criminals of all varieties, including terrorists.

Croatian law-enforcement institutions cooperated well with U.S. counterterrorism initiatives and participated in training from the International Law Enforcement Academy in Budapest, Hungary; the Antiterrorism Assistance program; and U.S. Marshals. The Croatian government has increased its contribution to the International Security Assistance Force in Afghanistan from 200 to 300 soldiers. These troops serve as military police, medical support, force security, and in liaison and training roles.

Cyprus

Cyprus took a clear stand against international terrorism and generally supported U.S. counterterrorism efforts. The government continued to allow blanket overflight and landing rights to U.S. military aircraft supporting operations in Iraq and Afghanistan. Cyprus was responsive to efforts to block and freeze terrorist assets, implemented Financial Action Task Force (FATF) recommendations, and conformed to European Union counterterrorism directives. On August 9, Cypriot authorities arrested Aslan Tayfun Ozkok, a wanted People's Revolutionary Liberation Party Front (DHKP-C, formerly Dev-Sol) member, who was transiting Cyprus from and Syria. Ozkok, whom Turkey had placed on red Interpol notice for high crimes committed on behalf of DHKP-C, was subsequently sentenced to eight months in prison in Cyprus for traveling on false documentation.

Cyprus's legal framework for investigating and prosecuting terrorist-related activity remained relatively weak. The United States and Cyprus cooperated closely on terrorist financing and money laundering issues. The Cypriot Anti-Money Laundering Authority (MOKAS) implemented new UNSCR 1267 and 1373 Committee decisions immediately and informally tracked suspect names listed under U.S. executive orders.

While Cypriot agencies responsible for nonproliferation assess only a small risk of illicit materials moving through transit cargo, the United

States continued to push for increased maritime cooperation. The Embassy organized and executed training programs to assist Cyprus to create a stronger export control regime and to pursue more proactive nonproliferation enforcement.

The de facto division of Cyprus since 1974 into Greek Cypriot- and Turkish Cypriot-dominated sectors has precluded counterterrorism cooperation between law enforcement authorities in both communities, and between Cyprus and Turkey. The largely porous, lightly-patrolled green line separating the two sides is routinely exploited for trafficking people, narcotics, and other illicit goods, and is vulnerable to penetration by terrorist groups. Regular ferry service that began in October 2007 between Latakia, Syria, and Famagusta, in the area administered by Turkish Cypriots, continued to facilitate increased illegal migration into Cyprus and the wider EU.

In the Turkish Cypriot-administered area, issues of status and recognition inevitably restricted the ability of authorities to cooperate on counterterrorism. Turkish Cypriots cannot sign treaties, UN conventions, or other international agreements, and lack the legal and institutional framework necessary to combat money-laundering and terrorist financing effectively. Within these limitations, Turkish Cypriots cooperated in pursuing specific counterterrorism objectives. They regularly alerted the USG to apparent money-laundering efforts through Turkish Cypriot banks by US citizens and in June froze a wire transfer and opened an investigation into the suspect transaction.

In February, pressure from the international community culminated in the Turkish Cypriot-administered area being included as a jurisdiction susceptible to money-laundering by FATF, the global anti-money laundering (AML) body. This designation galvanized Turkish Cypriot authorities and bankers, who quickly passed updated AML laws bringing offshore banks under the authority of the Central Bank. A financial investigation unit-equivalent was created and began operations, and a new law that would better regulate casinos was pending at year's end. Commercial bankers upgraded their systems for identifying and reporting suspicious transactions and held seminars for other industries on methods to identify possible money-laundering activities. In October, FATF welcomed significant progress made in the northern part of Cyprus in substantially addressing identified AML deficiencies.

Ethnic Kurdish communities exist on both sides of the island. The Kurdistan Workers' Party has a presence in Cyprus. Its activities generally were fundraising and transit en route to third countries. Authorities on both sides believed there was little risk the group would conduct operations on the island.

Czech Republic

Czech authorities continued to cooperate with the United States across a wide spectrum of security, law enforcement, and military matters as part of its counterterrorism efforts. Whether protecting the Prague headquarters of Radio Free Europe/Radio Liberty and other U.S. facilities, providing critical military assistance in Iraq and Afghanistan, or cooperating in criminal investigations, the Czech Republic remained a steadfast U.S. ally. While intelligence services continued to do their job well, an ongoing manpower shortage in the police force raised some concern about the government's ability to effectively respond to a terrorist incident.

The Czech Republic made significant contributions in support of coalition efforts in Afghanistan: the Czechs deployed a new Provincial Reconstruction Team to Logar and a new Special Operations task force in support of Operation Enduring Freedom (OEF). They also provided security to the Dutch PRT in Uruzgan, deployed an Operational Mentoring and Liaison Team to work alongside the Afghanistan National Air Corps, and continued the deployment of a 100-person military field hospital based at the Kabul International Airport. The Czechs also took part in the U.S. efforts to equip the Afghanistan National Air Corps by donating 12 newly reconditioned Mi-family helicopters. The Czechs deployed over 500 soldiers to Afghanistan in support of OEF and International Security Assistance Force, which represented a 100 percent increase from 2007. In Iraq, Czech forces successfully transitioned from providing security in Basra to helping train the Iraqi Armored Corps in Tadji. In Iraq, the Czech forces completed their mission at year's end, leaving only a small presence at the NATO Training Mission.

On the information sharing front, the Czech Interior Ministry signed a cooperative treaty with the United States on October 15, establishing the National Contact Point for Terrorism (NCPT) in Prague. The NCPT is intended as a specialized and centralized analytical and information gathering unit of the Czech police for combating terrorism. The NCPT will monitor and evaluate terrorist threats and will cooperate with other law enforcement agencies to detect and prevent terrorist acts. Within the next three years, the Police Presidium plans to establish a Passenger Information Unit within NCPT and a National Criminal Bureau that would be partner with NCPT, with a long term goal of bringing other emergency, law enforcement, and intelligence agencies under the NCPT umbrella.

A continued shortage of manpower in the police force raised some concern about the government's ability to effectively respond in the event of a terrorist incident. Since the end of 2007, the police Combating Terrorism and Organized Crime Unit has recruited 40 top level professionals and provided training, including language training for the new officers. Eighty more officers are still needed, however.

As a country participating in the Visa Waiver Program (VWP), the Czech Republic continued to comply with requirements in the VWP law related to information sharing and other law enforcement and counterterrorism cooperation. This cooperation was further enhanced by the Implementing Recommendations of the 9/11 Commission Act of 2007.

Denmark

The Center for Terror Analysis of the Danish Security and Intelligence Service (PET) assessed that there is a general terrorist threat against Denmark, both from groups and individuals in Denmark as well as a threat against Danes and Danish interests abroad. The threat comes primarily from networks, groups, and individuals who adhere to various forms of militant Islamic ideology, including al-Qa'ida (AQ)-related groups and networks. The February reprinting of controversial cartoons of the Prophet Mohammed led to increased threats.

While there were no terrorist attacks in Denmark in 2008, a plot to assassinate a leading journalist was disrupted and several judicial proceedings resulted in convictions of terrorist suspects. Denmark continued to strengthen its response to the threat of terrorism, fashioning new institutions in its security services and ministries, improving internal coordination among antiterrorism offices and promulgating new regulations to deal with terrorism more aggressively.

In 2008, Denmark passed a regulation restricting the sale of hydrogen peroxide. In April, the Ministry of Refugee, Immigration and Integration Affairs created an office to address the prevention of extremism. The Cohesion and Prevention of Radicalization Office coordinated with other ministries.

Denmark worked closely with the United States on UN and other multilateral counterterrorism efforts, including the Financial Action Task Force, and in international nonproliferation groups, such as the Proliferation Security Initiative (PSI) and the Global Initiative to Combat Nuclear Terrorism. Denmark cooperated closely with EU partners and institutions within the field of counter-radicalization. We note however, that Roj-TV, a Kurdistan Workers' Party (PKK)- affiliated media outlet, continued to operate in Denmark.

On February 12, the Danish police arrested two Tunisian nationals on charges of allegedly plotting to assassinate Mohammed cartoonist Kurt Westergaard. One suspect remained in custody until August 21, when he voluntarily left the country after PET recommended his deportation. The second suspect was detained until October 20, when the Supreme Court decided that there was insufficient evidence to uphold his detainment. The Refugee Appeals Board blocked his deportation on grounds of possible prosecution in his home country. Danish security services continued to monitor his whereabouts. In April, the Refugee Board ruled that Denmark could not deport Muhammad Ezzedine Hamid and Amer Ihsan Namik Saeed, two Iraqis suspected of facilitating foreign fighters into Iraq, because the Iraqi government could not guarantee their safety if repatriated.

Multiple individuals were prosecuted under terrorist legislation on charges of incitement to terrorism:

- On October 21, a Danish court sentenced Hammad Khurshid, a Pakistani-born Danish citizen, to 12 years for conspiring to commit terrorism; and his accomplice, Abdoulghani Tokhi, an Afghani citizen living in Denmark, to seven years followed by deportation. Khürshid was found guilty of bringing bomb manuals to Denmark from an AQ training camp in Pakistan. Together with Abdoulghani Tokhi, he was filmed manufacturing a triacetone triperoxide bomb in 2007.
- On November 18, the Glostrup District Court found a third suspect in the so-called Glasvej case not guilty of allegedly inciting Muslims abroad to kidnap Danish soldiers and nationals in order to pressure Danish authorities to release Khurshid and Tokhi.
- On September 18, the Danish High Court convicted six individuals of supporting terrorism by transferring a portion of the proceeds of the sale of T-shirts to the Popular Front for the Liberation of Palestine and the Revolutionary Armed Forces of Colombia. In 2007, a Danish court acquitted the suspects in the group but the acquittal was overturned in 2008. Two suspects received six-month sentences, two received four-month suspended sentences and two received 60-day suspended sentences.

The Danish government increased its troop deployment to Afghanistan, raising its forces to more than 700 as part of the International Security Assistance Force. Most of these are engaged in NATO's Helmand Province in southern Afghanistan.

As a country participating in the Visa Waiver Program (VWP), Denmark continued to comply with requirements in the VWP law related to information sharing and other law enforcement and counterterrorism cooperation. This cooperation was further enhanced by the Implementing Recommendations of the 9/11 Commission Act of 2007.

Estonia

As a member of the International Security Assistance Force in Afghanistan, Estonia contributed one motorized infantry company plus staff officers (140 soldiers) to the U.K.-led provincial reconstruction team in the Helmand Province. Estonia has maintained a constant presence in

Iraq since 2003, to include one infantry platoon consisting of 35 soldiers to participate in combat operations in Iraq in 2008. In addition, three staff officers served in the NATO-led training mission in Iraq.

Estonia actively enforced all EU laws regarding counterterrorism and cooperated fully with the United States in law enforcement matters.

The Government of Estonia installed radiation monitors at Narva, on its eastern border with Russia. New Estonian passports issued since May 2007 (including alien passports issued to stateless residents of Estonia) have the latest in biometric security features, including an embedded computer chip containing biometric information.

The Government of Estonia's antiterrorism council is responsible for its counterterrorism policy's basic principles and action plan. The council consists of representatives from the Ministries of Defense, Justice, Foreign Affairs, Economic Affairs and Communication, Internal Affairs (which include Security Police and Central Criminal Police) and the State Chancery's National Security Coordination Office. The Ministry of Internal Affairs heads the council. On January 28, the new Money Laundering and Terrorism Financing Prevention Act (MLTFPA) came into force. The new legislation maintains the principles of the money laundering and terrorist financing regime provided for by the 1999 Money Laundering Prevention Act (MLPA), and the amendments made to it from 2000 to 2007. The new legislation also harmonizes Estonian law with EU standards and brought Estonia's money laundering regime into total compliance with the Financial Action Task Force recommendations.

As a country participating in the Visa Waiver Program (VWP), Estonia continued to comply with requirements in the VWP law related to information sharing and other law enforcement and counterterrorism cooperation. This cooperation was further enhanced by the Implementing Recommendations of the 9/11 Commission Act of 2007.

Finland

The Government of Finland focused on economic, social, and development aid projects aimed at addressing the conditions that terrorists exploit. Finland maintained its annual contribution of approximately $15 million in development assistance to Afghanistan, synchronizing reconstruction support in Afghanistan with other donors and announcing new Rule of Law (particularly police), governance, humanitarian, and counternarcotics assistance initiatives.

Finnish and American officials shared counterterrorism information effectively, including a wide range of information on threat assessments, terrorist networks, and government responses to both. The Finnish government continued to participate actively in ongoing EU efforts to remove institutional barriers to counterterrorism cooperation.

During Finland's 2008 OSCE Chairmanship, it supported UN activities and sought ways to intensify international co-operation in combating terrorism within the OSCE. It used legislative and regulatory mechanisms to keep a close watch over potential terrorist cells or financial support operations and to interdict their activities within the country. In May, Finland tightened its terrorism prevention law, criminalizing planning and support for terrorism. Finland upgraded port and border security to monitor more traffic. In cases when another government presented a legal request for action or when an individual or organization was suspected of having committed an offense within Finland's borders, Finland had available regulations that allowed it to freeze assets without prior UN or EU action.

Finland engaged in significant efforts to mitigate the social and economic factors that might lead members of the country's small (less than 2 percent) population of foreign-born residents to adopt extremist ideologies. It carried out programs to help immigrants find jobs and integrate into Finnish society, and it encouraged religious and ethnic tolerance through a variety of legislation, government-funded social programs, and ombudsmen's offices.

Finland provided approximately 100 troops in Afghanistan in support of ongoing NATO/International Security Assistance Force operations.

As a country participating in the Visa Waiver Program (VWP), Finland continued to comply with requirements in the VWP law related to information sharing and other law enforcement and counterterrorism cooperation. This cooperation was further enhanced by the Implementing Recommendations of the 9/11 Commission Act of 2007.

France

France was one of a number of major European countries combating terrorism at home and abroad, although it has not suffered a significant terrorist incident in recent years. Local Corsican separatists, Basque Fatherland and Liberty (ETA) members, and ultra-left anarchist factions have been responsible for the majority of recent incidents French authorities have classified as terrorism. The number and violence of ETA and Corsican attacks in France have continued their downward trend, but France remained a target for al-Qa'ida in the Islamic Maghreb (AQIM), which posed a considerable threat to French interests, underscored in statements made by al-Qa'ida (AQ) senior leadership or AQIM itself, and Kurdistan Workers' party (PKK) affiliates. France remained on high alert and recognized its continuing status as a target of AQIM and of other extremist groups in France and abroad.

French casualties from terrorism included one citizen killed June 8 in an attack in Algeria and two French citizens killed November 26 in the Mumbai attacks. On December 16, French police recovered fives sticks of dynamite, placed without fuses, in a major department store located in central Paris. A previously unknown group, the Afghan Revolutionary Front, claimed responsibility, but French authorities have since raised doubts about the group's authenticity and motives. Cohesion within the French counterterrorism agencies and rapid reaction to contingencies is a key strength of French counterterrorism and was a hallmark of the French approach in 2008.

On December 11, one day before the European summit in Brussels, a joint Belgian and French counterterrorism operation arrested 17 Islamic extremists with alleged ties to AQ. Fourteen suspects were arrested in Belgium and nine were arrested and held in France. French authorities arrested and extradited to Switzerland three Iranian members of the criminal extremist group Mujahedin-e-Khalq on charges of involvement in terrorist finance. In December, the French government passed legislation that allowed the Ministry of Interior to freeze terrorist assets for six-month periods that may be successively renewed in consultation with the Ministry of Justice.

French authorities detained and prosecuted a number of other people with ties to various terrorist organizations, including Corsican separatists (46 convictions), ETA members (24 convictions), Islamic terrorists (19 convictions), ultra-left anarchist factions (17 convictions), the Liberation Tigers of Tamil Ealam (two convictions), and Kurds with links to the PKK (14 convictions).

The French government undertook several counterterrorism operations with other countries including the UK, Belgium, Germany, Italy, Spain, and Portugal. Two prominent examples were the May and November capture, respectively, of ETA's senior commander, Javier Lopez Pena, and ETA's military head, Mikel Garikoitz Aspiazu Rubian, alias Txeroki. In addition to undertaking operations to arrest and prosecute terrorists, France continued programs to address radicalization and extremism through the use of social and economic incentives to reduce the susceptibility of at-risk populations. To further combat radicalization, France took judicial and administrative action against people who incited violence or hatred. French law allows for the expulsion from French territory of non-citizens who incite hatred or violence. The French government is very concerned about Islamic radicalization in the French prison system and has commissioned a study to identify key indicators of radicalization and to generate proposals on its prevention and suppression.

France's most recent CT legislation was adopted in 2006. Three articles in that legislation, preemptive identification checks on cross-border trains, access to phone and internet connection data, and access to certain administrative records, were adopted as provisional measures and extended by the National Assembly on November 20 through 2012. Preliminary detention for terrorists in France is limited to six days, although the French state may thereafter place suspects under pre-trial detention for up to four years in view of compelling evidence or when the suspect is considered to present an imminent threat. In conjunction with local government, the national government has continued to increase video surveillance in major cities. French law also allows for asset seizure, video and telephone surveillance, monitoring of public transport records, and provides other broad powers for official access to connection data held by internet cafes and to various personal data. The sentence for a convicted terrorist can be up to 30 years for leading or organizing an attack and from 10 to 20 years for assisting a terrorist organization or operation. Notably, French nationality may be revoked, leading to expulsion from French territory, if the person in question was naturalized in the preceding 15 years.

On the military front, France had over 3,000 troops actively participating in operations in Afghanistan and Operation Enduring Freedom. The French commitment included ground troops and air assets. On August 18, 10 French soldiers were killed in an ambush in the Uzbin valley. Subsequently, the prime minister announced on September 22 that France would increase its military commitments in Afghanistan, to include air mobility assets, intelligence officers, support personnel, helicopters, drones, and additional ground troops.

As a country participating in the Visa Waiver Program (VWP), France continued to comply with requirements in the VWP law related to information sharing and other law enforcement and counterterrorism cooperation. This cooperation was further enhanced by the Implementing Recommendations of the 9/11 Commission Act of 2007.

Georgia

Georgia has granted blanket overflight clearance to all U.S. military aircraft engaged in operations in Afghanistan and Iraq. Georgia contributed over 2,000 troops to counterterrorism efforts in Iraq and became a contributing nation to the International Security Assistance Force in Afghanistan. Georgia withdrew its troops from Iraq during the August war with Russia to provide for homeland defense.

The Georgian government continued to improve border security operations and worked to eliminate corruption at border checkpoints, focusing its efforts on stopping the smuggling of contraband, including money, illegal drugs, and weapons (chemical, nuclear, and biological) that could support terrorism. Through a combination of the Department of Energy's Second Line of Defense Program, the Department of Homeland Security's Georgia Border Security and Law Enforcement program, and the State Department's Export Control and Related Border Security program, there was a significant improvement in infrastructure, equipment, and enforcement training at most major border crossing checkpoints, including rail and seaport ports of entry. All three programs trained individuals in the Georgian Border Police, Georgian Coast Guard, Customs, Revenue Service, the Nuclear Radiation Safety Service, Patrol Police, and the Institute of Physics, thus enhancing the Government of Georgia's radioactive material detection capabilities. The Department of Justice conducted a bulk cash smuggling seminar with the Office of Prosecutor General, Border Police, Ministry of Interior, and Customs.

Border crossings into Russia from the separatist regions of Abkhazia and South Ossetia continued, but were not under the control of the Government of Georgia. This situation allowed for the unrestricted and unidentified flow of people, goods, and other items from Russia into these regions. Since the Russian invasion in August, the Administrative Boundary Lines between Georgia and the conflict regions have been heavily militarized and movements across the boundary were controlled, although no formal customs checks or procedures existed.

Germany

Germany investigated, arrested, and prosecuted numerous terrorism suspects and disrupted terrorist-related groups within its borders with connections to international Islamist, Kurdish nationalist, and Marxist-Leninist terrorist organizations. Germany provided leadership in the areas of border and transportation security, countering terrorist financing, and international efforts in Afghanistan. Germany also strengthened programs to promote integration of the country's Muslim communities and to counter violent extremism.

Although there were no terrorist attacks in Germany, on March 3, Cüneyt Ciftci, a German resident with Turkish citizenship, carried out a suicide bombing in Khost, Afghanistan that resulted in the deaths of two U.S. soldiers. Ciftci was associated with the Islamic Jihad Union (IJU), formerly known as the Islamic Jihad Group, which is a Specially Designated Global Terrorist pursuant to E.O. 13224.

During the year, German law enforcement authorities arrested a number of individuals suspected of involvement in terrorism. Prominent new actions and arrests included:

- On February 14, Germany's Federal Prosecutor charged German citizen Aleem Nasir with six counts of supporting al-Qa'ida (AQ). He was accused of financially supporting AQ, assisting recruiting efforts, and procuring military-relevant equipment.
- On June 19, Germany banned the Kurdistan Workers' Party (PKK)-affiliated Roj TV, a Denmark-based television station with offices in Germany.
- In September, Germany banned a Kurdish youth website on grounds that it distributed PKK propaganda.
- In a series of arrests in July and August, German authorities arrested a number of Turkish citizens with Kurdish ethnicity on suspicion of holding leadership roles within the PKK in Germany.
- On September 12, authorities arrested Ömer Özdemir, a Turkish national, on suspicion of recruiting fighters, and procuring donations and equipment for AQ.
- On September 18, authorities arrested Omid Shirkhani, a German citizen of Afghan descent; and Hüseyin Özgun, a Turkish citizen; on suspicion of supporting the IJU.
- On November 6, three Turkish nationals were arrested on suspicion of membership in the banned Revolutionary People's Liberation Party-Front (DHKP-C), a Marxist-Leninist terrorist group that seeks to topple the Turkish government.

German courts also began trials or reached verdicts in some notable counterterrorism cases:

- The Schleswig-Holstein Higher Regional Court found three individuals guilty of founding a terrorist organization (in Sudan) and assisting terrorist organization al-Qa'ida in Iraq (AQI). On January 24, German-Moroccan national Redouane El-Habhab received a five year and nine month prison term; on February 21, Jordanian Thaer Alhalah was sentenced to two years in jail; and on September 24, Moroccan national Abdelali Miftah was sentenced to four years in jail.
- On June 19, the Celle Higher Regional Court found Iraqi national Ibrahim Rashid guilty of promoting membership in, and support of, AQ and AQI. He was sentenced to three years imprisonment.
- On July 15, the Stuttgart Higher Regional Court found three Iraqi nationals guilty of belonging to the Ansar al-Islam terrorist organization and attempting to assassinate former Iraqi Prime Minister Allawi during his 2004 visit to Berlin. The three received prison sentences between seven and ten years.

- On November 5, Dusseldorf's Higher Regional Court imposed a two-year suspended sentence for membership in the PKK terrorist organization on Ahmet A., a Turkish citizen of Kurdish origin.
- On December 9, the Dusseldorf Higher Regional Court sentenced Lebanese national Youssef Mohammad El-Hajdib to life imprisonment for attempted murder in connection with the failed terrorist bombing of two commuter trains in July 2006.
- On December 19, convicted Red Army Faction terrorist Christian Klar was released after serving 26 years in prison. Klar was convicted of involvement in a number of high-profile RAF assassinations and attacks in the late 1970s, including the failed assassination of U.S. four-star General Frederick Kroesen, who commanded the Seventh Army in Heidelberg at the time.
- On October 22, authorities arrested Turkish citizen Burhan Yilmaz, who is the brother of one of the three IJU suspects arrested in September 2007 for allegedly plotting terrorist attacks directed at U.S. interests. Yilmaz is suspected of supporting the IJU with money and equipment transfers.
- In November, Turkey extradited German citizen Attila Selek who stands accused of being an associate of the three IJU suspects and having assisted in procuring detonators for them.

Germany remained a strong advocate of the UNSCR 1267 sanctions regime.

Germany was the third largest troop contributor to the International Security Assistance Force (ISAF) in Afghanistan, with nearly 3,500 troops deployed. Germany led the ISAF Provincial Reconstruction Teams (PRT) in Kunduz and Feyzabad, provided a forward support base in Mazar-e-Sharif, and commanded ISAF's northern region, which encompassed nine provinces and five PRTs. Germany is a major contributor to civilian police training efforts in Afghanistan and supported the creation of a police training academy in Mazar-e-Sharif, pledged $50 million in project funding, and agreed to participate in the U.S.-led Focused District Development police training program. Germany is the top European contributor to the EU police training mission in Afghanistan, EUPOL.

On December 19, the Bundesrat (upper parliamentary chamber) approved new legislation that broadened the powers of the Federal Office of Criminal Investigation (BKA) in counterterrorism investigations. The law provided the BKA with preventative investigatory powers and gave the BKA lead responsibility in terrorism investigations where the threat extends across multiple federal states, where state-level competence is unclear, or where state officials request federal assistance.

The German government strengthened its outreach and engagement with Muslim communities to promote integration and tolerance. The Ministry of Interior continued the German Islam Conference initiative that it began in 2006. The conference is made up of several working groups that meet on a regular basis to discuss issues relevant to Muslims living in Germany such as education, religious instruction, separation of church and state, mosque construction, and strengthening relations between Muslim communities and the media and business sectors. One forum within the Conference focuses on improving cooperation between security authorities and the Muslim community in order to address radicalization and extremism.

In October, a landmark bilateral agreement was signed to enhance fingerprint and DNA information sharing to combat terrorism and serious crime. The U.S. Embassy's Law Enforcement Working Group continued its ongoing engagement of state-level law enforcement contacts by organizing four security conferences throughout Germany in which the topic of Islamic terrorism featured prominently. Germany participated in the Department of Homeland Security (DHS) Customs and Border Protection's Container Security Initiative in the ports of Hamburg and Bremerhaven. The DHS Transportation Security Administration's presence in Frankfurt, together with U.S. and German air marshals, formed key parts of bilateral efforts to provide air transport security for the seven German airports with flights to the United States.

As a country participating in the Visa Waiver Program (VWP), Germany continued to comply with requirements in the VWP law related to information sharing and other law enforcement and counterterrorism cooperation. This cooperation was further enhanced by the Implementing Recommendations of the 9/11 Commission Act of 2007.

Greece

Greece and the United States have a strong record of counterterrorism cooperation. Greece is increasingly an EU entry point for illegal immigrants coming from the Middle East and South Asia, and there was concern that it could be used as a transit route for terrorists traveling to Europe and the United States. The number of illegal immigrants entering Greece through the Aegean Sea increased dramatically in 2008 and about 100,000 illegal immigrants were arrested. Greek authorities participated in the Container Security Initiative and cooperated with U.S. officials on information sharing, as well as the training of Greek security and customs officials, and judicial personnel. Greece sustained its participation in the International Security Assistance Force in Afghanistan by providing engineers and other support officers. Greek forces operated in the Kabul region. Convicted November 17 (N17) members have continued to make extremist public statements from prison, for example, Dimitrios Koufodinas released a statement in a Greek newspaper in November extolling "direct action" that would "strike blows to the capitalist system." Revolutionary Struggle (RS), a radical leftist group aligned with the ideology of N17, claimed responsibility for the December 23 shooting of a bus carrying riot police in the Athens district of Goudi and for placing a bomb, subsequently detonated by police on October 24, outside the Athens headquarters of the oil company Shell. For further information on N17, see Chapter 6, *Terrorist Organizations*.)

Throughout the year, self-styled "anarchists" attacked banks, police stations, and other "imperialist-capitalist targets" with tools such as firebombs and Molotov cocktails. Since these attacks usually occurred at night, few persons were seriously injured and there were no deaths. Several U.S. businesses were targeted. Police officials pursued a more proactive approach to deterring these attacks and arrested perpetrators. In December, rioting broke out following the death of a young student at the hands of the police. In the ensuing days, anarchists and students attacked and destroyed police stations and businesses. No damage to the Embassy or injuries to personnel was noted.

Hungary

Hungary remained a consistent and reliable counterterrorism partner militarily, economically, and politically. The Hungarian military continued its leadership of a Provincial Reconstruction Team in Afghanistan. The Hungarian government fully implemented legislation supporting both USG and EU efforts to counter terrorist organizations, including terrorist financing and money laundering activities. The Hungarian government closely monitored potential extremists, including Hungarian nationals. While there were no known terrorist groups openly operating in Hungary, Hungarian officials have expressed concern regarding a recent increase in the frequency and the sophistication of violence targeting domestic political figures and minority communities. Hungary worked to manage its role as the eastern-most border in the Schengen zone, including the increased entry of foreigners seeking asylum. The Hungarian government shifted security forces to the east to improve its ability to apprehend individuals attempting illegal entry, and intensified use of stationary nuclear material detection systems and mobile units to enhance identification and control of dangerous materials. Additionally, Hungary signed a bilateral, criminal data-sharing agreement and HSPD-6 with the U.S. in 2008. While the agreement allows Hungarian citizens the right to travel to the U.S. under the Visa Waiver Program as of November 17, it will provide the USG additional information, when needed, on individuals requesting entrance into the United States. As a country participating in the Visa Waiver

Program (VWP), Hungary continued to comply with requirements in the VWP law related to information sharing and other law enforcement and counterterrorism cooperation. This cooperation was further enhanced by the Implementing Recommendations of the 9/11 Commission Act of 2007.

Iceland

The Government of Iceland worked to strengthen domestic border security and counterterrorism capabilities. The Icelandic Coast Guard (ICG) strengthened ties with neighboring states and took over as Chair of the North Atlantic Coast Guard Forum in October. In June, the government established the Icelandic Defense Agency under the Ministry of Foreign Affairs. The IDA has responsibility for operational ties with NATO and other allied states, including intelligence exchanges.

In July, the Minister of Justice presented a threat assessment prepared by the National Police Commissioner to the government. The assessment focused on the threat to Iceland from domestic and international terrorism and organized crime, and it was the first to be ever prepared in Iceland. It concluded that, although the likelihood of terrorist incidents in Iceland is low, the potential consequences are severe enough to merit a high level of vigilance.

In October, the ICG hosted NORTHERN CHALLENGE 2008, a NATO-supported exercise focusing on Explosive Ordnance Disposal and counterterrorism scenarios.

Also in October, the ICG and the U.S. Coast Guard signed a cooperative agreement based on the bilateral Joint Understanding from October 2006 and its provisions on increasing bilateral security cooperation between civil institutions. In May, the United States and Iceland held the second annual round of high level security dialogue talks as specified in the Joint Understanding.

The Icelandic government supported multilateral counterterrorism efforts. Iceland continued its deployment of personnel at Kabul International Airport and International Security Assistance Force (ISAF) Headquarters in Afghanistan in support of NATO operations there, and made funding contributions to several key NATO/ISAF trust funds.

As a country participating in the Visa Waiver Program (VWP), Iceland continued to comply with requirements in the VWP law related to information sharing and other law enforcement and counterterrorism cooperation. This cooperation was further enhanced by the Implementing Recommendations of the 9/11 Commission Act of 2007.

Ireland

Counterterrorism measures implemented in previous years were sustained and relations between USG and Irish law enforcement officials were positive. The Irish government permitted the transit of U.S. military personnel and material though Irish airspace and airports for deployment to theaters in Iraq and elsewhere. Ireland continued a modest troop commitment to the International Security Assistance Force in Afghanistan.

As a country participating in the Visa Waiver Program (VWP), Ireland continued to comply with requirements in the VWP law related to information sharing and other law enforcement and counterterrorism cooperation. This cooperation was further enhanced by the Implementing Recommendations of the 9/11 Commission Act of 2007.

Italy

Italy aggressively investigated and prosecuted terrorism suspects, dismantled terrorist-related cells within its borders, and maintained high-level professional cooperation with its international partners. Italy's law enforcement and judicial authorities had several noteworthy cases in 2008.

In May, authorities arrested 19 foreigners (mostly Tunisians) in Milan and Pisa and filed new charges against four others already in jail for alleged drug trafficking and terrorism offenses. Prosecutors believe that the suspects may have used the proceeds from drug sales to support terrorist activity abroad and terrorist recruitment in Italy. One of the suspects is Maher Bouyahia, who was sentenced to six years imprisonment in 2007 for recruiting extremists.

In June and July, authorities arrested around three dozen suspected Tamil Tiger members (all of Sri Lankan origin), including 28 in Naples, in operations to dismantle groups allegedly dedicated to financing the Sri Lankan terrorist group. Related arrests were also made in Palermo, Bologna, Genoa, Rome, and other cities.

In August, authorities arrested five alleged Islamic fundamentalists in and near Bologna who were accused of raising funds and preparing to send individuals to fight in Iraq and Afghanistan, according to reports. The five North Africans, four Tunisians, and one Moroccan, were under investigation for three years. They have been accused of international terrorism but have not yet been formally charged. Officials alleged the cell sent tens of thousands of dollars to Bosnian groups linked to terrorist organizations in Iraq and Afghanistan.

Also in August, police again arrested Abdelmajid Zergout, a Moroccan imam in the northern city of Varese, in response to a provisional arrest warrant from Morocco for his extradition. Zergout had already been arrested in 2005 and was tried for having raised funds and recruited for the Moroccan Islamic Combatant Group, but he was acquitted by a Milan court in 2007.

In November, police searched the homes and cultural meeting places of members and sympathizers of Morocco's banned Islamist group al Adl Wa Ihassan (Justice and Charity) in several regions of northern Italy and Tuscany, which resulted in eleven persons formally under investigation on terrorism and international terrorism charges.

Also in November, the Milan court of appeals confirmed the prison term of three years and eight months for Abu Imad, Egyptian Imam of a mosque in Milan, on charges of organizing and funding terrorism attacks in Afghanistan and Iraq. For the other ten defendants in the same trial, from Egypt, Morocco, and Algeria, the court confirmed six sentences and reduced four.

In December, Italian authorities arrested two Moroccan nationals outside Milan on terrorism charges for their plans to attack targets in and around Milan. According to press reports, the alleged terrorists were planning attacks against the main cathedral in Milan, a Carabinieri station, an immigration office, and Standa department stores. The reports also indicated that they were AQ sympathizers angry about Italy's role in Afghanistan.

Domestic anarchist-inspired and extreme-left terrorist groups presented a continued (albeit small-scale) threat despite Italian authorities' continued efforts to dismantle their organizations. In April, Italian police caught domestic terrorist Roberto Sandalo attempting to set fire to a mosque near Milan. Sandalo is thought to be the leader of the Christian Combatant Front, which was linked to two 2007 attacks in February and April against Muslim institutions. In November, Sandalo was sentenced to a prison term of nine years and nine months. During the 1970s, Sandalo was the leader of the Front Line, a small anti-western, leftist terrorist group similar in ideology and tactics to the Red Brigades. It was known for robbing banks to finance terrorist attacks. It is unclear how large the Christian Combatant Front is and how many of the ten attacks on Muslim institutions in the past year were their responsibility.

The Italian government continued to make use of reinforced counterterrorism legislation enacted in 2005, which facilitated the detention of suspects, mandated arrest for crimes involving terrorism, and expedited procedures for the deportation of persons who may be involved in terrorist activities.

The European Court of Human Rights (ECHR) is reviewing the Italian government's policy of expulsions and deportations without judicial review. On February 28, the ECHR ruled against an expulsion order signed by former Minister of the Interior Giuliano Amato regarding Tunisian national Nassim Saadi, 34. The order called for Saadi to be returned to Tunisia, his country of origin. Saadi was convicted on charges of international terrorism in both Italy and Tunisia, where he was previously sentenced to 20 years in prison. According to the ECHR, deporting Saadi would violate article three of the European Convention on Human Rights, which prohibits torture and inhumane or degrading treatment even in cases of serious threat to the community. Amato's expulsion decree was based on a July 2005 law authorizing measures to combat international terrorism. In June, Italian authorities expelled Sami Ben Khemais Essid to Tunisia. Following this act, the ECHR sent the Italian government a letter reminding it of its obligation to allow the court prior to deportation to examine Ben Khemais's claim that he faced the risk of torture or prohibited ill-treatment upon return to Tunisia.

Italian authorities have stated publicly that many radical Islamist groups in Italy are inspired by or connected to al-Qa'ida in the Islamic Maghreb (AQIM) and other extremist groups and use Italy as a logistical and financial base. Organizations affiliated with the Kurdish nationalist group Kurdistan Workers' Party did not have a major presence in Italy but were thought to have links with charitable organizations that maintained Italian branches.

With respect to financial aspects of fighting terrorism, Italy aggressively identified and blocked financial resources destined for suspected terrorist individuals and groups. Italy worked closely with the United States on money laundering matters and information sharing; and cooperated with other foreign governments as an active member of the Financial Action Task Force (FATF) and the Egmont Group. As a non-permanent member of the UN Security Council, Italy advocated multilateral cooperation in countering terrorism.

Italy was a leading financial contributor to the United Nations Office on Drugs and Crime (UNODC) Counterterrorism Prevention Branch. Within the G8, Italy played an active role in the Rome-Lyon Group and the Counterterrorism Action Group (CTAG), within which Italy leads an initiative to enhance counterterrorism security measures in airports in the western Balkans.

Italy is an important partner in the Proliferation Security Initiative and the Container Security Initiative. As a country participating in the Visa Waiver Program (VWP), Italy continued to comply with requirements in the VWP law related to information sharing and other law enforcement and counterterrorism cooperation. This cooperation was further enhanced by the Implementing Recommendations of the 9/11 Commission Act of 2007. In May 2006, the U.S. and Italy signed a new treaty on extradition and mutual legal assistance, which will allow for joint investigative teams, easier asset freezing, and faster sharing of financial information. The U.S. Senate has already ratified the treaties. On the Italian side, the treaties were approved by the Council of Ministers in November 2008, but were pending a final vote of approval in Parliament at year's end.

Italy participated in NATO's Active Endeavour naval mission against terrorism in the Mediterranean, and contributed to international military missions in, Afghanistan, where it held Regional Command-West; and Iraq, where it played a lead role in the NATO Training Mission, among others.

Italy contributed training personnel to various regional counterterrorism training centers such as the South East Asia Regional Centre on Counterterrorism in Malaysia, the Joint Centre on Law Enforcement Cooperation in Indonesia, and the African Union's Antiterrorism Centre in Algeria.

Kosovo

The UN Interim Administrative Mission in Kosovo (UNMIK) administered Kosovo under the authority of UN Security Council (UNSC) Resolution 1244 of 1999 until June 15, when Kosovo's constitution came into effect. With the promulgation of the Kosovo constitution in June, the Kosovo Government assumed growing responsibility for the country's civil administration and law enforcement, including counterterrorism. The EU's Rule-of-Law Mission in Kosovo (EULEX) started operating on December 9 and replaced UNMIK Police throughout the country. EULEX's primary role is to provide advice and mentoring to Kosovo rule-of-law institutions.

The Kosovo government and UNMIK continued to monitor suspected terrorist activity throughout the year. The Ministry of Internal Affairs (MoIA) suspected that a few of the more than 1,000 NGOs operating in Kosovo were involved in suspicious activities and sought to prevent extremists from using non-governmental organizations to gain a foothold in Kosovo. Some NGOs used public facilities for religious gatherings but Kosovo authorities and municipalities attempted to prevent misuse of facilities for events that had no consent from the relevant religious community.

The Kosovo Police (KP) and UNMIK Police Counterterrorism Units (CTUs) were primarily responsible for Kosovo's counterterrorism efforts but were small and lacked resources. In December, the UNMIK CTU transferred its responsibilities to EULEX. Prior to that, the UNMIK Police CTU monitored, mentored, and advised its KP CTU counterparts. While UNMIK possessed executive authority over the KP, in practice it was not exercised. The KP and UNMIK received information and analysis support from the UNMIK Central Intelligence Unit (CIU) and the KP CTU's intelligence, surveillance, and investigations units. The KP CTU, currently manned at half its intended strength, continued to focus on building up its unit, training and equipping its officers, and collecting information on potential terrorist threats.

Porous boundaries that were easily crossed by individuals trafficking in persons, weapons, and narcotics hampered Kosovo's counterterrorism efforts. Traffickers took advantage of numerous roads and trails leading into Kosovo that lacked border controls. Poorly paid border and customs officials were susceptible to corruption. The lack of full customs enforcement on two northern posts along the Kosovo-Serbia border hampered counterterrorism efforts further. These two posts were destroyed by Serb hardliners following Kosovo's February 17 independence declaration. For security reasons, UNMIK and EULEX have not acted to re-establish customs enforcement at these posts.

The Kosovo Police with UNMIK's Department of Justice continued its Witness Protection Task Force to ensure that witness intimidation did not resurface as a problem in other areas. The Task Force completed constructing its safe house, encouraged the use of video conferencing equipment in Kosovo's district courts, and increased its efforts to secure relocation agreements with other jurisdictions.

One incident of suspected terrorism occurred during the year. On November 14, an explosive device detonated in front of the headquarters of the International Civilian Organization (ICO), the institution charged with supervising Kosovo's independence. There were no injuries. Kosovo Police continued to investigate the incident at year's end. There was one unverified claim of responsibility from a previously unknown group, but Kosovo authorities had insufficient evidence to bring charges against any perpetrators.

The UNMIK Department of Justice (DOJ) conducted additional terrorism investigations independent of Kosovo authorities. During the year, the UNMIK DOJ obtained two terrorism-related convictions. International prosecutors and the Kosovo Special Prosecutor's Office (KSPO) also initiated four terrorism-related investigations. One trial, handled by the KSPO before a panel of local judges, and two cases handled by International Prosecutors were pending trial at year's end. The Government of Kosovo with UNMIK DOJ made no indictments in terrorism cases during 2008.

The Albanian National Army (AKSH), which UNMIK designated as a terrorist organization in 2003, continued to intimidate Kosovo citizens. On January 26, three men were arrested for shooting at a KP police officer in Pristina. After their arrest, the three claimed AKSH membership, as did a fourth, who was arrested on April 25. In a separate incident on September 17 in the town of Vushtrri/Vucitrn, a bus carrying people to work at the KEK Power Plant was stopped at a checkpoint manned by 12 to 13 men wearing AKSH insignia and carrying weapons. The men examined the identification of all present and then released the workers. The case remained under investigation at year's end with no arrests made.

Latvia

Latvia's Financial Intelligence Unit maintained a terrorist financing database that it shared with local banks. Since the May 2005 U.S. Treasury designation of two Latvian banks as institutions of "primary money laundering concern" under Section 311 of the Patriot Act, Latvian government and regulatory agencies have worked very closely with the United States to enhance their legislative and regulatory framework. There have been no further sanctions on Latvian banks. In 2006, Treasury lifted the proposed sanction against one bank. In the case of the second institution, the issue is specific to the bank and its ownership structure, and does not reflect Latvian regulatory efforts.

On September 4, the Counterterrorism Center of the Latvian Security Police and the Freeport of Riga Authority organized the counterterrorism exercise "RiverJack" in Riga harbor. The scenario was a hostage situation on a hijacked passenger ferry, which included a fire during the hostage release operation. Representatives from the State Police (including the Counterterrorism Unit "OMEGA' and the Mobile Team "Alfa"), State Border Guards, State Fire and Rescue Service, Center of Emergency and Disaster Medicine, Mobile Team of the National Armed Forces, Navy Coast Guard Unit, Maritime Administration and the Prosecutor's General Office participated. The exercise was part of the counterterrorism plan "Ship", developed by the Counterterrorism Center. Latvia contributed 150 soldiers to support the International Security Assistance Force in Afghanistan, including deploying its first ever Operational Mentoring and Liaison Team (OMLT). Latvia completed its participation in Iraq; the last three officers returned in November.

As a country participating in the Visa Waiver Program (VWP), Latvia continued to comply with requirements in the VWP law related to information sharing and other law enforcement and counterterrorism cooperation. This cooperation was further enhanced by the Implementing Recommendations of the 9/11 Commission Act of 2007.

Lithuania

A new domestic law on Money Laundering and Terrorist Financing Prevention came into force in January. This legislation and associated legal acts codified and amended existing Lithuanian laws to bring them in line with a number of EU directives and regulations on money laundering and terrorist financing. As a country participating in the Visa Waiver Program (VWP), Lithuania continued to comply with requirements in the VWP law related to information sharing and other law enforcement and counterterrorism cooperation. This cooperation was further enhanced by the Implementing Recommendations of the 9/11 Commission Act of 2007.

In October, an Agreement for the Prevention and Combating of Serious Crimes was signed, which will require Parliament ratification. Also in October, the Association of Lithuanian Banks and the U.S. Department of the Treasury held a two day U.S.-Baltic Banking Conference on Combating Money Laundering and Terrorist Financing in Vilnius. The conference brought together government and financial sector representatives to facilitate the exchange of information and promote strong anti-money laundering and counterterrorist financing practices in the region.

The Lithuanian military was an active participant in multinational operations against terrorist and insurgent elements. In Iraq, Lithuania had an infantry platoon serving in Multinational Division Center (MND-C) near Al Kut until July, and four trainers serving in the NATO Training Mission-Iraq (NTM-I). In Afghanistan, Lithuania led a provincial reconstruction team in Ghor Province. This consisted of approximately 140 Lithuanian troops and civilians responsible for maintaining a stable environment throughout the province and coordinating reconstruction efforts. Lithuania also contributed approximately 60 Special Forces troops to NATO's International Security Assistance Force in Southern Afghanistan.

Macedonia

The Government of Macedonia continued its close coordination with the United States on counterterrorism matters, which included intelligence sharing on potential terrorist groups operating in or transiting the country. The government also cooperated with its regional and European Union partners, and worked closely with INTERPOL and other international law enforcement agencies.

Macedonia provided adequate security for weapons generally sought by terrorists with annual inventories and worked to improve security on its weapons facilities. The Macedonian Ministry of Defense provided support to the Ministry of Interior for actions against domestic and regional terrorist groups.

Macedonia passed legislation on nuclear security and terrorism, chemical weapons, and entered into bilateral law enforcement, security, and extradition agreements. Macedonia continued to provide supported troop rotations to Afghanistan and Iraq. Macedonia's troop presence in Iraq ended in December, coinciding with the expiration of the Status of Forces Agreement between Iraq and the United States. The government trained several hundred police and military personnel in counterterrorism techniques, technologies, and methods.

Macedonia continued to cooperate closely on preventing terrorist financing and money laundering through close coordination with the Embassy and in partnership with the banking sector.

Malta

Malta's location between the African and European continents and its large Search and Rescue area brought many immigrants to Malta's shores. Since 2002, some 11,646 migrants, most from East Africa, have been rescued at sea by the Armed Forces of Malta. Upon arrival in Malta, the immigrants were screened by the Maltese Immigration Police and transferred to closed centers. Most of then applied for asylum. They can be held up to 12 months pending resolution of the application, or up to 18 months if the claim is rejected. The Government of Malta engaged in dialogue with leaders of the migrant community, and provided training to detention center personnel, with the goal of checking possible extremist threats. The Maltese government continued to freeze the assets of those organizations on the UN consolidated list of designated terrorist organizations. Malta actively participates in the EU Clearing House and cooperates with other Member States and third states to defeat terrorist activities and by extension, to prevent terrorist financing, to deny safe havens to terrorists, and to exchange information to stop the commission of terrorist acts. The Maltese government has historically supported sharing information with the USG on matters relate to terrorism, and has demonstrated a commitment to interdiction operations and compliance with international requests. The Maltese criminal code includes several specific provisions on terrorism. The law addresses "acts of terror" and "terrorism" and enumerates the actions constituting the offense. Malta criminalized terrorist financing through the Prevention of Money Laundering Act, which was expanded to include provisions for the funding of terrorism. Additionally, the Act expanded the powers of the Maltese Financial Intelligence Unit (the investigative arm) to include terrorist financing. Since 2006, the Prevention of Money Laundering Regulations have been extended to terrorist financing and include controls that require proper record keeping, specific reporting requirements, and relevant training.

As a country participating in the Visa Waiver Program (VWP), Malta continued to comply with requirements in the VWP law related to information sharing and other law enforcement and counterterrorism cooperation. This cooperation was further enhanced by the Implementing Recommendations of the 9/11 Commission Act of 2007.

Moldova

The Moldovan government managed its counterterrorism strategy based on Moldova's 2003-2008 National Action Plan on Combating Terrorism and worked on implementation of its obligations under UNSCR 1373, Executive Order 13224, and other provisions related to terrorist financing. Moldova joined the Egmont Group of financial intelligence units on May 20. The Moldovan government openly welcomed information regarding terrorist financing from the USG and other bodies, as well as actively applied such information in its monitoring efforts through its Center for Combating Economic Crimes and Corruption (CCECC). The CCECC issued a decree regarding actions to be taken to enforce the provisions of the Law on Preventing and Combating Money Laundering and Terrorism. The CCECC decree listed entities worthy of particular focus due to possible money laundering and/or terrorist financing concerns. These entities included countries that do not have legal provisions against terrorist financing, and persons, groups, and entities identified as participating in terrorist activities. The decree was developed on the basis of Moldova's national interests and from U.S. and UN lists of designated terrorists.

On December 5, the Moldovan parliament ratified a blueprint on cooperation with the Commonwealth of Independent States (CIS) states in combating terrorism. This document was originally signed in August 2005 and provides for joint measures aimed at the prevention and countering of terrorism and extremism. The document allows for the exchange of information on combating terrorism between CIS states, and provides for the extradition of persons suspected of financing or committing terrorist actions. The Moldovan parliament also ratified the specific program on CIS member states' cooperation in combating terrorism and extremism for 2008-2010. This three-year program reflects the activities that were included in the blueprint.

The separatist-controlled Transnistria region of Moldova remained a potential area of concern. Moldovan law enforcement worked hard to track the whereabouts and activities of individuals moving in and out of Transnistria, an area where central-government police and security services are rarely able to operate. Some of the individuals moving in and out of Transnistria were foreign students who remained in Moldova illegally, as the government lacked the resources to deport them when their visas expired. Corruption was endemic, and it was not difficult to obtain false travel documents in both Transnistria and Moldova. The United States has not obtained any information about known terrorist organizations or terrorists operating from or within the Transnistrian region.

The primary investigative body in counterterrorism cases is the Information and Security Service, Moldova's intelligence service. U.S. law enforcement assistance programs aided Moldovan efforts to impede the ability of terrorists and other citizens without proper documents to cross national borders. The programs also facilitated automation at ports of entry to ensure greater security of passports and travel documents.

Montenegro

The Ministry of Interior, through the Police Directorate and the Agency for National Security (ANB), is primarily responsible for counterterrorism operations. In 2008, the Ministry of Interior began work on a National Counterterrorism Strategy, which will foster better counterterrorism cooperation among the different institutions. Montenegrin legislation on terrorism has been harmonized with EU standards and UN conventions. Criminal acts of terrorism are defined by Montenegrin Criminal Code Article 365 as, "anyone who, with the intention of endangering the constitutional order and security of Montenegro causes an explosion or fire or undertakes other dangerous measures or kidnaps a person, or commits another act of violence or threatens to undertake some dangerous action or to use nuclear, chemical, biological, or other dangerous substance and whereby may cause fear or feeling of insecurity of citizens shall be punished by imprisonment for a term of three to fifteen years."

In 2007, the Parliament of Montenegro passed the Law on the Prevention of Money Laundering and Terrorist Financing, and during the same year the government's Agency for the Prevention of Money Laundering and Terrorist Financing (also known as the Financial Intelligence Unit, or FIU) accepted the Financial Action Task Force on Money Laundering (FATF) Special Recommendations on Terrorist Financing. The FIU also publishes an international list of terrorists and terrorist organizations established pursuant to Security Council resolution 1483.

Montenegro ratified the Council of Europe's Convention on the Prevention of Terrorism, and Convention on the Laundering, Search, Seizure, and Confiscation of the Proceeds from Crime and on the Financing of Terrorism. In addition, Montenegro has signed bilateral agreements and memoranda on police cooperation in counterterrorism with almost all regional countries including Serbia, Croatia, Bosnia and Herzegovina, Slovenia, and Albania, as well as with Belgium, Turkey, Bulgaria, Romania, and Austria.

In September 2006, in what is known as the "Eagle's Flight" case, seventeen ethnic Albanians, four of whom are U.S. citizens, were arrested and charged with planning terrorist acts to incite an ethnic Albanian rebellion. In August 2008, after a lengthy trial, the Higher Court in Podgorica convicted the defendants of plotting to disturb the constitutional order and security of Montenegro. Sentences ranged from three months to six years and six months in prison. The defendants have filed appeals.

Although Montenegro is not a known safe haven for terrorists, the Montenegrin authorities are focused on potential threats stemming from Islamic extremists in neighboring countries and the activities of very small groups of local extremists. Montenegrin police forces, including the Special Antiterrorism Unit, have received international and U.S. training and equipment. For example, the Department of Justice ICITAP program conducted a regional international terrorism workshop and provided training for the police organized crime unit, which is responsible for conducting terrorism investigations. Despite significant training and equipment from outside donors, Montenegrin law enforcement and security agencies required additional assistance to attain international standards.

The Netherlands

The Dutch continued their response to the global terrorist threat with leadership and energy in the areas of border and transportation security, terrorist financing, bilateral counterterrorism cooperation, and Coalition efforts in Afghanistan. The Netherlands continued operations with 1,650 troops in Afghanistan as part of the International Security Assistance Force. The Dutch led a Provincial Reconstruction team in Uruzgan province, took command in Kandahar of NATO's efforts in southern Afghanistan for a year beginning in November, and contributed approximately USD 100 million in development aid for Afghanistan. The Netherlands deployed eight trainers in support of the NATO Training Mission in Iraq, two officials for the EU rule of law mission in Iraq, contributed USD 15 million for Iraqi programs, and made the final commercial debt relief forgiveness of USD 72 million.

In a March quarterly terrorism threat analysis, the Dutch National Counterterrorism Coordinator (NCTb) raised the domestic threat level from "limited", where it had been since April 2007 to "substantial," meaning there was a real chance of an attack in the Netherlands. (The Netherlands has four threat levels: minimum, limited, substantial and critical.) The level was raised primarily because of the Netherlands' high international profile and increased activities of terrorist groups like al-Qa'ida. In the September threat assessment, the NCTb cited Dutch MP Geert Wilders' controversial film *Fitna*, and the increasing number of reports about Western extremists at training camps along the Afghanistan/Pakistan border as the rationale for maintaining the level at "substantial." The NCTb noted that the Netherlands was specifically mentioned on international terrorists' websites. According to the September assessment, little activity was observed within local autonomous networks in the Netherlands, though some militants expressed a desire to join the terrorists in Afghanistan and Iraq.

The NCTb also cited growing resistance among the Muslim community in the Netherlands to radicalization noting that extremists also became more wary about expressing radical views because resulting negative publicity might undermine their cause. The NCTb concluded that the government's integration efforts, including educating imams in the Dutch language and culture, are proving effective. According to the 2008 Trend Analysis on Polarization and Radicalization, which Interior Minister Ter Horst submitted to Parliament in December, the Netherlands has 2,500 to 3,000 potential radicals.

According to a November NCTb poll, the Dutch population worried more about the economy than about terrorism. Only 13 percent of people queried feared a terrorist attack while 85 percent did not. The NCTb attributed this to the absence of concrete threats and attacks in the Netherlands. The poll also showed that the number of Dutch worried about radicalization dropped from 21 percent in 2007 to eight percent in 2008.

The Justice Ministry's *Netherlands against Terrorism* campaign continued, with a particular focus on prevention of radicalization. The government's terrorist alert system, which became operational in June 2005, now includes 14 economic sectors: the financial sector, seaports, airports, drinking water, railway, natural gas, oil, electricity, nuclear, chemical, municipal and regional transport, hotels, public events, and tunnels and flood defense systems. In March, the Dutch tested the alert system for the nuclear sector. In August, the National Forensic Investigation Team staged an international exercise for forensic experts to improve international cooperation in terrorist attacks. In November, Dutch security services published a brochure warning traveling businessmen, civil servants, politicians, and other people having access to certain military, technological, or economic data, that they could be targets of espionage.

According to an October Justice Ministry progress report on the border control action plan, major steps have been taken to improve security along external borders and at Schiphol airport to counter terrorist activities, including intensified cooperation between the border police, the port police, and the customs service. In February, Schiphol closed three staff access passages and introduced 100 percent physical controls of personnel and carry-on goods.

There were two major terrorism-related appeal cases this year. In January, the appeals court in The Hague acquitted the seven members of the Hofstad terrorist group of participating in a criminal and terrorist organization, because "there was no question of a lasting and structured form of cooperation, nor of a commonly shared ideology." The appeals court upheld only the conviction of Jason Walters (a dual U.S.-Dutch national), sentenced to 15 years' imprisonment for having thrown a hand grenade at police officers in November 2004, and for possession of hand grenades. However, the court did not consider the throwing of a hand grenade a terrorist act. The sentence of Walters' accomplice, Ismael Aknikh, was reduced to a 15-month prison term (from 13 years) for possession of hand grenades. In February, the public prosecutor's office in The Hague filed an appeal with the Supreme Court.

In April, six members of the Hofstad group were removed from the EU terrorist list. The Hofstad group itself, as well as "important" members of the group, remained on the list.

In December 2006, the Rotterdam district court convicted four members of the "Piranha" terrorist group of participating in a terrorist organization. One defendant was acquitted and the sentences handed down were much shorter than prosecutors had sought. The public prosecutor therefore appealed the cases and sentences to the appeals court in The Hague, and in October 2008, the four guilty verdicts were upheld and longer prison sentences were imposed. A fifth defendant originally acquitted was convicted. All of the "Piranha" terrorist group defendants were found guilty of "participating in an organization with terrorist intent." The appeals court ruled that there was sufficient evidence the group had planned to attack Dutch politicians and a building of the general intelligence service (AIVD). The court sentenced Samir Azzouz to nine years' imprisonment, Nouredine El Fatmi to eight years, Mohammed Chentouf to six and a half years, El Fatmi's former wife Soumaya Sahla to four years, and Mohammed Hamdi received three months. Defense attorneys appealed the verdict to the Supreme Court.

In March, the Rotterdam court sentenced two former associates of Azzouz to three years' imprisonment for participating in a terrorist organization, preparing attacks and possessing dangerous firearms. The two had testified against Azzouz and his co-defendants and were subsequently tried separately on similar charges in the "Piranha II" case. Defense attorneys have appealed the verdict.

In May, the public prosecutor's office in Rotterdam dropped charges against three Rotterdam terrorist suspects arrested in late 2007 for lack of evidence that they were planning a terrorist attack. In October, the Maastricht district court threw out the public prosecutor's case against 16 alleged Kurdistan Workers' Party fighters arrested in late 2004 on charges of participating in a criminal organization with terrorist intent. The case was dismissed because the Turkish Justice Minister rejected a legal assistance request allowing Dutch attorneys to hear witnesses in Turkey. The court ruled that, as a result of this rejection, there could not be a fair trial. In April, the Netherlands extradited a Pakistani terrorist suspect to Spain. The man, who was arrested in March, is believed to be a member of a terrorist organization that was planning attacks on Spain and other European countries. In November, the National Crime Squad arrested a man in The Hague who may have been involved in preparing terrorist attacks. Following the arrest of a Dutch woman in the UK in October, on suspicion of involvement in terrorist activities, the AIVD put the woman's two brothers on the watch list.

The Dutch government remained committed to active cooperation with the United States in designating known terrorist organizations, and interdicting and freezing their assets, and supported the continued exchange of information on financial transactions. Dutch officials continued to play a constructive role within the Financial Action Task force to combat terrorist financing. In August, the Prevention of Money Laundering and Financing of Terrorism Act became effective. The Act incorporated the EU's third Money Laundering Directive into Dutch national law. The Dutch government worked with the United States to emphasize the importance of balancing security and the effectiveness of the financial system.

No new counterterrorism laws were adopted in 2008. A bill making participation and cooperation in a terrorist training camp a serious punishable offense, even if the training takes place outside the Netherlands, was awaiting action by the lower house of Parliament at year's end. The Bill on Administrative National Security Measures, which allows the Interior Minister to issue restraining orders to prohibit a terrorist suspect's physical proximity to specific locations or persons, was still awaiting action by the upper house of Parliament at year's end.

In July, the government set up a committee, which is to provide the Cabinet with recommendations concerning issues warranting special attention, for example, the compatibility and consistency of various antiterrorism laws, and the identification of remaining gaps in the Dutch counterterrorism legal regime. The committee's recommendations should contribute to the ongoing assessment of counterterrorism legislation.

In May, the Netherlands and the United States signed a joint statement enabling the start of the International Expedited Traveler Initiative between Schiphol Airport in Amsterdam and JFK in New York. In July, the Dutch Parliament ratified the U.S.-EU Extradition and Mutual Legal Assistance treaties. In November, the Dutch National Police hosted a bilateral "experts meeting" on terrorism with FBI officials, fulfilling one of the action items agreed at the 2007 U.S.-Dutch bilateral law enforcement "Next Steps" consultations.

As a country participating in the Visa Waiver Program (VWP), the Netherlands continued to comply with requirements in the VWP law related to information sharing and other law enforcement and counterterrorism cooperation. This cooperation was further enhanced by the Implementing Recommendations of the 9/11 Commission Act of 2007.

Norway

Norwegian authorities considered the threat of terrorist attacks in Norway low and the widespread belief among the general public was that Norway was not in danger of attack. In December, the parliament revised its counterterrorism laws in order to be able to ratify the Council of Europe Convention on the Prevention of Terrorism. These revisions allowed incitement, recruiting, and training for terrorist acts to become punishable offenses independent of whether an attack is actually carried out. They also, however, require specific "intent" to commit an act that causes terrorism, whereas the prior standard had been "willfulness" to commit the act.

In February, Norwegian police arrested three suspects of Somali descent for financing terrorism by collecting money for al-Shabaab. (Three others were arrested in Sweden.) Charges against five were eventually dropped; only one suspect remained under investigation in Norway, although he is not in custody and retained his passport. Members of the Norwegian press criticized Norway's failure to maintain a separate terrorist organization list, on the grounds that, absent such a list, people cannot know which organizations are illegal to contribute to.

In May a court convicted Afran Bhatti of conspiracy to commit "serious vandalism" in connection with gunshots fired at the Oslo synagogue in 2006, but acquitted Bhatti of the charge of terrorism in connection with the shooting and plots to attack the United States and Israeli embassies. The court sentenced Bhatti to eight years' imprisonment for attempted murder and threatening behavior, separate charges unrelated to the synagogue shooting and embassy plots, with the possibility of additional detention based upon review of his danger to society. Bhatti remained in custody pending his appeal of the attempted murder conviction.

Norway contributed more than 500 troops to International Security Assistance Force efforts in Afghanistan.

As a country participating in the Visa Waiver Program (VWP), Norway continued to comply with requirements in the VWP law related to information sharing and other law enforcement and counterterrorism cooperation. This cooperation was further enhanced by the Implementing Recommendations of the 9/11 Commission Act of 2007.

Poland

Poland continued to support international counterterrorism efforts with heightened participation in Afghanistan. Poland increased its contribution to the International Security Assistance Force to 1,600 troops. Poland also took independent military responsibility for Ghazni Province and began planning for its own associated Provincial Reconstruction Team. Poland turned over command of the Multinational Division Center-South to Iraqi authorities and withdrew the last of its combat forces. Poland maintained about 20 soldiers as part of the NATO Training Mission Iraq.

Through participation in initiatives including the Proliferation Security Initiative and the Global Initiative to Combat Nuclear Terrorism, Poland remained an active participant in various international undertakings to combat terrorist threats. One year after integration into the Schengen zone, Poland maintained a close and growing collaboration with its European neighbors on counterterrorism. During the year, Poland also established an inter-agency 24-7 Counterterrorism Center to coordinate terrorist threat assessments.

The bilateral Counterterrorism Working Group (CTWG), formed in 2005 to further U.S.-Polish collaboration on counterterrorism by synchronizing counterterrorism policy and training counterterrorism specialists, continued to hold regular meetings. The CTWG identified specific areas of mutual interest, including critical infrastructure and terrorist financing, and developed further plans for training and cooperation. The Polish and U.S. militaries reached consensus on a Bilateral Agreement on cooperation in combating cyberterrorism. In 2008, the Illinois State Partnership Program initiated a five-year program to expand cooperation between the Illinois National Guard and various Polish ministries on consequence management.

Portugal

Portugal worked proactively with other nations on programs to combat terrorism and disrupt funding for terrorist groups. Portugal does not have any indigenous terrorist groups, therefore the legal system and law enforcement focus is on dissuading international groups from establishing operations on its soil.

Portuguese and American officials shared counterterrorism information effectively, including information on threat assessments and terrorist operative activities. In cooperation with other European Union partners, the Portuguese government continued to participate actively in ongoing EU efforts to remove institutional barriers to cooperation on counterterrorism.

In September, the Government of Portugal created a new Secretary General for Internal Security, a move designed to facilitate communication between the Judicial Police (FBI-equivalent), Public Security Police (national uniformed police), and the National Republican Guard (paramilitary police force). As a result, the distinct law enforcement agencies were able to share information about terrorism investigations more effectively.

Portugal contributed approximately 130 Portuguese troops that were deployed in Afghanistan in support of ongoing International Security Assistance Force and NATO operations, and maintained its annual contribution of 6.6 million Euros (USD 8.4 million) in development assistance to Afghanistan.

As a country participating in the Visa Waiver Program (VWP), Portugal continued to comply with requirements in the VWP law related to information sharing and other law enforcement and counterterrorism cooperation. This cooperation was further enhanced by the Implementing Recommendations of the 9/11 Commission Act of 2007.

Romania

The Romanian Government had strong comprehensive internal mechanisms to combat terrorism, including a *National Antiterrorism Strategy* and guidelines to prevent the use of Romanian financial institutions, including its banking system, to finance terrorist-related activities. In 2008, the Supreme Council for National Defense updated the General Protocol for the National System for Preventing and Countering Terrorism.[7]

Romania made its airspace, ground infrastructure, and naval facilities available to U.S. and NATO forces. Approximately 500 Romanian troops were serving in Iraq and 820 in Afghanistan as part of coalition and NATO Alliance efforts to combat terrorism and promote peace and stability. The Romanian troops in Afghanistan represented a 300-plus increase over 2007. In June, the Supreme Council for National Defense confirmed Romania's commitment of troops deployed in Iraq and Afghanistan through 2009.

Romanian also ratified the European Convention on the Suppression of Terrorism, the Protocol amending the European Convention on the

[7] The General Protocol for the National System for Preventing and Countering Terrorism (NSPCT) was adapted in 2002. The Protocol empowered the Romanian Intelligence Service (SRI) as the national authority in the counter-terrorist field and the technical coordinator of the NSPCT.

Suppression of Terrorism, the Council of Europe Convention on the Prevention of Terrorism, and the Council of Europe Convention on laundering, search, seizure, and confiscation of the proceeds from crime and on the financing of terrorism.

The Romanian Intelligence Service (SRI) operated as the technical coordinator for 11 Ministries of the Romanian Government; three other special Services (the Foreign Intelligence Service, the Protection and Guard Service, and Special Telecommunications Service); three other governmental agencies (the National Agency for Export Controls, the National Committee for Control of Nuclear Activities, and the National Office for Prevention and Control of Money Laundering); the National Bank of Romania; and the Prosecutor's Office attached to the High Court of Cassation and Justice. There were 54 prosecutors assigned to the Directorate to Investigate International Criminal Organizations and Terrorism.

Bucharest is also the headquarters for the Southeast European Cooperation Initiative (SECI) Regional Center for Combating Transborder Crime (SECI Center), a regional center that provided law enforcement training and intelligence sharing on transborder criminal activities, including terrorist-related activities, for the 12 member countries in South Eastern and Central Europe, including Romania. Romania participated in the SECI Center's Antiterrorism task force, which Turkey chaired.

In February, the High Court of Cassation of Justice reconfirmed the 20-year prison sentence for Omar Hayssam who was convicted of terrorism in the 2004 kidnapping case of four Romanian journalists in Iraq (the Syrian-born Romanian citizen Hayssam fled Romania following his conviction and remained at large).

On May 15, Romania ratified the September 2007 Bucharest Protocol to the May 1999 U.S.-Romania Mutual Legal Assistance Treaty. The Protocol enhanced mutual assistance on the identification of banking information regarding money laundering and terrorism activities, as well as other criminal activities on which the United States and Romania subsequently agree. Notable cases of U.S.-Romania law enforcement cooperation in this area included the extradition of Tareq Al Ghazi and Luis Moreno to the United States to stand trial on terrorism and money laundering charges related to their efforts to sell weapons to the Revolutionary Armed Forces of Colombia (FARC); significant assistance related to Viktor Bout, the renowned international arms trafficker known as the "Merchant of Death" who agreed to sell weapons to the FARC; and the case of Yeyha Ali Zeiter, who was arrested on drug-related terrorism charges.

On June 4, the government issued Executive Order 594/2008 which approved the rules to enforce the provisions of the law 656/2002 in conformity with EU regulations on preventing and sanctioning money laundering, as well as on establishing some measures to prevent and counter the financing of terrorist activities.

On June 25, the National Securities Commission issued Order 83/2008, to institute measures to prevent and fight money laundering and terrorism financing via the capital market. The order was published in the Official Gazette 525 on July 11.

The National Bank of Romania issued its own internal regulations regarding customer due diligence procedures in order to prevent money laundering and terrorism financing. The regulations were published in the Official Gazette on July 14.

The Financial Intelligence Unit submitted a restructuring program in order to implement more effectively the provisions of the Governmental Emergency Ordinance no. 53/2008 and the Governmental Decision no. 594/2008, to check against possible terrorist-related financing activities, including a new cooperation protocol for the National Office for Prevention and Combating of Money Laundering and the National Agency of Exports Control, as well as law enforcement and intelligence services, which enhances intra-governmental cooperation within the National System for Prevention and Combating of Terrorism.

The Romanian Government's Emergency Decision no. 202/2008, which was published in the Official Gazette on December 8, provides a mechanism for the implementation of international sanctions to prevent and counter terrorism, including empowering the National Office for Prevention and Control of Money Laundering, reporting on suspicious transactions, blocking funds, and obliging institutions to conduct due diligence in establishing the bona fides of clients.

December 31marked the official implementation of the new electronic passport protocols under Government Decision no. 557/2006 and in accordance with the provisions of the EC Regulation no. 2252/2004 on the standards for integrating security and biometric elements in passports and travel documents.

Russia

Violence and terrorism continued to roil the North Caucasus, where the decline in incidents in Chechnya was replaced by an increase in terrorism in Dagestan, Ingushetia, and North Ossetia. Other violent acts took place in Moscow and St. Petersburg, but did not match the level of terrorist violence in Russia's south and were difficult to differentiate from criminal acts. The Russian government continued to view counterterrorism as a top priority, and considered cooperation in this field with the United States a pillar of bilateral relations. Russia did not pass significant new counterterrorism legislation in 2008, but President Medvedev signed a decree reorganizing the Ministry of the Interior's counterterrorism efforts by combining assets from counter-narcotics and anti-organized crime sections into new units to counter extremism. Russia did not offer safe haven to terrorists, but there was evidence of a foreign terrorist presence in the North Caucasus with international financial and ideological ties. As in 2007, there were no high-profile terrorist incidents in Russia involving a large number of civilian casualties.

In October, Director of Federal Security Services (FSB) Aleksandr Bortnikov announced that Russia had disrupted 69 terrorist acts planned by terrorist cells in the Volga region, the Urals, the North Caucasus, and Siberia. Among them, the FSB claimed to have disrupted a plot to bomb tourist sites in Sochi in July and August using improvised explosive devices.

Throughout the North Caucasus, groups have moved away from mass attacks on civilians in favor of targeted attacks on policemen, local interior ministry officials, and departments responsible for fighting the insurgency. As violence has declined in Chechnya, it has increased substantially in the surrounding region, although it was often difficult to characterize whether it was the result of terrorism, political violence, or criminal activities. In 2008, terrorists killed three colonels heading the Anti-organized Crime Units (UBOPs) in North Ossetia, Kabardino-Balkaria, and Karachay-Cherkessia. These units lead antiterrorist operations within their regions for the Interior Ministry. In one of the deadliest attacks in Russia since the September 2004 school seizure in Beslan, a female suicide bomber struck a minibus in the North Ossetian regional capital of Vladikavkaz on November 6. The attack killed 12 and injured as many as 41 civilians, most of whom were students at local colleges.

The 1998 federal law On Fighting Terrorism" and the 2006 federal law On Countering Terrorism remained the main counterterrorism legal authorities. The National Antiterrorism Committee, organized in 2006, is the main government body coordinating the Russian government's response to the terrorist threat. On September 6, President Medvedev signed a decree reorganizing the federal and regional Ministry of Interior organized crime units, which were increasingly handling counterterrorism duties, into new units tasked with fighting extremism.

The United States and Russian Counterterrorism Coordinators met in June to advance cooperation within the context of the United States-Russia Counterterrorism Working Group. Cooperation continued on a broad range of counterterrorism issues. Russian law enforcement agencies also cooperated closely with U.S. agencies, including participation in the September 2008 Counterterrorism Working Group-Intelligence Sub Group meeting in Washington, D.C. with representatives from the CIA, FBI,

Russian Federal Security Service, and Foreign Intelligence Service (SVR). The U.S. and Russian law enforcement agencies shared substantive, concrete terrorism intelligence at this meeting. Past cooperation led to the release of a hostage victim and the conviction of a U.S.-based subject attempting to purchase shoulder-to-air missiles.

Regulating and investigating terrorist websites was a major concern with numerous requests to the United States for assistance from both the Federal Security Service and the Cybercrime Directorate. At the St. Petersburg G8 Summit in July 2006, the United States and Russia jointly announced the Global Initiative to Combat Nuclear Terrorism and invited other nations to join. The Initiative demonstrated Russia's effort to take a leadership role in establishing a partnership among nations to accelerate efforts to combat nuclear terrorism. The fourth meeting of the Initiative took place in Spain in June. (See Chapter 4, The Global Challenge of Nuclear Terrorism, for further information on the Global Initiative to Combat Nuclear Terrorism.)

In March, Russia hosted the Seventh International Meeting of the Heads of special services, security agencies, and law-enforcement organizations, which FBI, CIA, DOE, and NCTC attended. Russia continued to work with regional groups to address terrorism. It sent representatives to September's OSCE Public-Private Partnership Counterterrorism Conference, which focused on partnerships between state authorities, civil society, and the business community in combating terrorism. Russia joined with other members of the Shanghai Cooperation Organization (SCO), at its annual summit, in a commitment to work with the UN to develop a Comprehensive Counterterrorism Charter and to continue to conduct exercises like Peace Mission 2007, which Russia hosted. The Collective Security Treaty Organization (CSTO) elected not to hold its annual International Antiterrorism Forum.

Russia is a member of the Financial Action Task Force on Money Laundering and Terrorist Financing (FATF) and is a leading member, chair, and primary funding source of the FATF-style body known as The Eurasian Group on Money Laundering (EAG). EAG members include Russia, China, Belarus, Kazakhstan, Kyrgyzstan, Uzbekistan, and Tajikistan. Russia, through EAG, provided technical assistance and funding towards establishing legislative and regulatory frameworks and operational capabilities.

Serbia

Serbia's law enforcement and security agencies, particularly the Customs Administration, Criminal Police, Border Police, Security Information Agency, and other security services, greatly increased bilateral counterterrorism cooperation since the July formation of the new government. Intra-governmental cooperation between these agencies also improved, increasing their effectiveness. Serbia had two police organizations that operated as counterterrorism tactical response units, the Special Antiterrorist Unit and the Counterterrorist Unit. In addition, the government created a Criminal Investigative Unit for Counterterrorist Investigation within the Interior Ministry's Criminal Investigation Directorate.

The United States provided counterterrorism training and assistance to the Serbian government. In May, the Department of Justice International Criminal Investigative Assistance Training Program's Organized Crime Advisor (ICITAP) conducted a counterterrorism workshop for Serbian and Montenegrin police officers in Montenegro. The workshop covered trends in international terrorism, the formation of a Joint Terrorist Task Force, investigative techniques, vulnerability assessments, crime scene management, case studies, and practical exercise problems. ICITAP also conducted two informant development courses for Serbian counterterrorism police officers in January and November. In January, ICITAP donated a special forces boat to the Special Antiterrorism Unit. In June and November, the Defense Threat Reduction Agency conducted two multi-agency counterterrorism courses. The Export Control and Border Security Program (EXBS) provided weapons of mass destruction detection equipment and training, as well as training in detecting illicit radioactive materials and chemical trafficking, to the Border Police, Customs, and prosecutorial and licensing authority agencies. In conjunction with the Departments of Homeland Security and Energy, EXBS provided other courses in undercover operations, export control, and dual use commodity identification to Border Police, Customs, and police investigative, prosecutorial, and licensing authority agencies.

A bill on terrorist financing, now pending Parliamentary approval, will apply all provisions of the Anti-Money Laundering Law to terrorist financing. It will require reporting of transactions suspected to be terrorist financing and will create mechanisms for freezing, seizing, and confiscating suspected terrorist assets.

A trial of 14 Islamic fundamentalists charged with conspiracy to commit unconstitutional activity, terrorism, illegal possession of firearms, and attempted murder commenced in April. Authorities found evidence that the group was planning attacks on infrastructure in the city of Novi Pazar, a local religious leader, and several sites in Belgrade, including the U.S. Embassy. Authorities charged an additional four persons with planning an attack on Novi Pazar police in March.

Slovakia

The primary police unit responsible for investigating criminal offenses related to terrorism is the Counterterrorism Unit (CTU) of the Organized Crime Bureau. The CTU is authorized to carry out criminal investigations and make arrests of suspected terrorist or extremists within the country. It also has the mandate to develop Slovakia's counterterrorism strategy. The most recent version, approved in October 2007, focuses on developing the legislative and institutional framework to combat terrorism, as well as strengthening the coordination, collaboration, and exchange of information among key institutional actors. The Financial Intelligence Unit (FIU) of the Organized Crime Bureau and the Slovak Information Service also have counterterrorism responsibilities.

One suspected terrorist, Mustapha Labsi, has been held in Slovak custody since May 2007. In November 2007, the Bratislava Regional Court approved a Slovak government request to extradite him to Algeria where he has been convicted in absentia to life in prison. In January 2008, the Supreme Court confirmed this decision. In June, the Constitutional Court ruled that the Supreme Court must verify that Labsi will not face torture upon extradition. In December, the Migration Office again denied Labsi's request for asylum in Slovakia, which he appealed.

Slovakia cooperated closely with a range of international partners in numerous fora. For example, Slovak police participated in the Police Working Group on Terrorism, a consortium of EU member states, Norway, and Switzerland. The Slovak Information Service is engaged in the Club de Berne, which facilitates exchange of police and intelligence information on terrorism. It also participated in the EU's Joint Situation Center.

Cooperative ties with other EU member states, as well as with the United States, have strengthened as a result of Slovakia's accession to Europe's border-free Schengen zone on December 21, 2007, and entry into the U.S. Visa Waiver Program on November 17, 2008. As a country participating in the Visa Waiver Program (VWP), Slovakia continued to comply with requirements in the VWP law related to information sharing and other law enforcement and counterterrorism cooperation. This cooperation was further enhanced by the Implementing Recommendations of the 9/11 Commission Act of 2007.

In August, at the request of the Slovak Customs, U.S. Customs and Border protection held a five-day anti-corruption and integrity enhancement course in Bratislava. Thirty-two Slovak participants, including investigators, prosecutors, and analysts in the Customs Service, Alien and Border Police, Police Presidium, Ministries of Interior and Justice, and Special Court, took part in the five-day course taught by four trainers from Washington D.C.

In 2008, Slovakia increased the level of its permanent deployment to the International Security Assistance Force in Afghanistan to 176, more than doubling its contingent.

Slovenia

In January 2008, Slovenia's 2007-enacted Act on the Prevention of Money Laundering and Financing of Terrorism became applicable. During Slovenia's Presidency of the EU Council, Slovenia chaired an EU troika meeting with the United States on the external aspects of fighting against terrorism, as well as international terrorist financing. Slovenia also chaired an EU-U.S. workshop on financial sanctions. In September, Slovenia's Ministry of Defense held a regional counterterrorism conference, sponsored by the Counterterrorism Fellowship Program. The Conference included 90 military and civilian personnel from Slovenia and six western Balkan countries. Slovenia continued to provide two instructors as part of the NATO training mission in Iraq and 15 support personnel to the NATO mission in Chad. Slovenia also contributed 66 troops to International Security Assistance Force efforts in Afghanistan. As a country participating in the Visa Waiver Program (VWP), Slovenia continued to comply with requirements in the VWP law related to information sharing and other law enforcement and counterterrorism cooperation. This cooperation was further enhanced by the Implementing Recommendations of the 9/11 Commission Act of 2007.

Spain

The Government of Spain and its citizens were concerned that their country remained a principal target of domestic terrorism and Islamic extremism. On the international front, al-Qa'ida (AQ) deputy Ayman al-Zawahiri and the leaders of al-Qa'ida in the Islamic Maghreb (AQIM) routinely called for the recapture of the former Muslim-controlled region in the Iberian Peninsula they still call *al-Andalus*. As the fifth anniversary of the March 11, 2004 Madrid train bombings approached, the Spanish government remained in a constant state of heightened alert and took pride in the fact that there have been no further deaths in Spain at the hands of international terrorists since 2004. Spain cooperated closely with the United States to investigate and prosecute acts of terrorism and to prevent future attacks, and worked hard to disrupt terrorist acts that possibly were directed against U.S. interests. Spain remained an important transit and logistical base for terrorist organizations operating in Western Europe. Its geographical location, large population of immigrants from North Africa, and the ease of travel to other countries in Europe, made Spain a strategic crossroads for international terrorist groups.

Spain continued to aggressively target terrorist recruiters and facilitators. The Ministry of Interior detained 65 suspected Islamist terrorists. Many of these individuals were believed to be supporters of terrorist groups such as AQ, AQIM, and the Moroccan Islamic Combat Group (GICM).

The Spanish government began 2008 with the January 19 arrest of 14 suspected radical Islamists, primarily Pakistanis, in Barcelona, who allegedly were plotting to attack the city's transportation system. The Tehrik-e-Taliban Pakistan terrorist group, which has links to AQ, claimed that those arrested were part of its organization and that the attacks had been planned to retaliate against the Spanish military presence in Afghanistan. In June, Spanish police arrested eight Algerian nationals on charges of suspicious activities with links to terrorist cells, including recruiting and indoctrination, as well as providing financial and logistical support to Islamic terrorist organizations. In October, security services arrested a dozen radical Islamist suspects, all Moroccan nationals, accused of financing terrorism and of sending recruits to Iraq. Some members of the cell were also accused of helping some of the suspects in the Madrid train bombings flee the country. All were subsequently set free, except for four individuals already in prison on other charges.

The domestic terrorist group Basque Fatherland and Liberty (ETA), whose aim is to create an independent Basque state, waged its deadliest year since 2004:

- On March 7, on the eve of Spain's national election, ETA gunmen murdered a former town councilman in Mondragon.
- On May 14, an ETA truck bomb detonated at a barracks in Legutiano killed a Civil Guard.
- On September 22, a car bomb detonated at a military academy in Santona, killing a corporal in the Spanish army.
- On December 3, the fourth victim, a Basque businessman, was shot by ETA gunmen.

Nevertheless, Spain's intensified cooperation with the French government put considerable pressure on ETA. Joint operations in France resulted in, among other successes, the detention of ETA's alleged political leader in May, and its alleged military chief who reportedly was also the number-one authority in ETA, in November. On December 9, a joint operation resulted in the arrest of the alleged replacement military chief. All three arrests occurred in France with the participation of Spanish security forces. As of mid December, security services had arrested 158 alleged ETA members or associates, including 33 in France.

In the judicial arena, the Spanish Supreme Court overturned the convictions of several radical Islamists from two previous, high-profile cases.

- In July the Spanish Supreme Court announced the acquittal on appeal of four of the 21 convicted defendants in the Madrid train bombings trial who had been sentenced in October 2007. The four had been sentenced to between five and 12 years for smuggling explosives and membership in a terrorist organization.

- The Supreme Court also upheld the lower court's acquittal of the suspected mastermind of the attacks, agreeing with the lower court's decision that he be acquitted of belonging to a terrorist organization because he had already been sentenced in Italy and could not be tried for the same crime twice.
- In October,the Supreme Court overturned 14 of the 20 convictions of a cell sentenced in February for plotting to truck bomb the National Court and reduced the sentences of another four of those convicted in the plot.

Spain participated in the Megaports and Container Security Initiatives, and worked hard to deny terrorists access to Spanish financial institutions. Spain maintained a robust law enforcement and intelligence posture against terrorist financing. Spain was a member of the G8 Counterterrorism Action Group and provided technical assistance to other countries to help build their institutions to counter terrorist financing. Spain is a longtime member of the intergovernmental Financial Action Task Force and its efforts to combat money laundering were considered comprehensive and effective. However, Spain has not frozen the assets of or designated as a terrorist Imad Eddin Barakat Yarkas, the convicted and jailed leader of the Madrid-based AQ-affiliated cell who was detained shortly after 9/11.

Spain played an active role in the Global Initiative to Combat Nuclear Terrorism; it hosted a table-top exercise in May, a plenary meeting in June, and a field training exercise in October. These events developed Spain's own expertise in disaster preparedness and contingency planning and served to build the capacity of fellow Global Initiative partner nations.

Spain also signed numerous multilateral agreements to strengthen counterterrorism cooperation on a political level. In May, the Ministers of Interior from Spain, France, Portugal, Italy, Malta, Algeria, Libya, Morocco, Mauritania and Tunisia agreed to strengthen their exchange of information to prevent anybody accused of a terrorist crime from finding shelter in those countries.

On a bilateral level, Spain signed agreements with Morocco and Algeria. In June, the Spanish and Moroccan General Prosecutors Offices signed an International Protocol of Cooperation to fight terrorism and organized crime. Also in June, Spain and Algeria signed a bilateral Agreement on Security to Fight Terrorism, Illegal Immigration, and Organized Crime, which includes the exchange of information.

Spain contributed more than 750 troops to the International Security Assistance Force in Afghanistan.

As a country participating in the Visa Waiver Program (VWP), Spain continued to comply with requirements in the VWP law related to information sharing and other law enforcement and counterterrorism cooperation. This cooperation was further enhanced by the Implementing Recommendations of the 9/11 Commission Act of 2007.

Sweden

The Government of Sweden placed a high priority on increasing international cooperation against terrorism. Swedish authorities considered the threat of terrorist attacks inside Sweden to be low, but they monitored a number of known terrorists and terrorist organizations within their borders, including al-Qa'ida (AQ), Al-Shabaab, Ansar al-Islam/Sunna, the Revolutionary Armed Forces of Colombia (FARC), Hizb Al-Tahrir, Hizballah, Islamic Jihad, and the Kurdistan Workers' Party (PKK). These groups provided logistical and financial support to their respective organizations abroad.

The Government of Sweden did not provide safe haven to terrorists or terrorist organizations. Terrorist organizations exploited Sweden's considerable legal protections of personal freedoms and civil liberties to maintain a presence in the country, however. Sweden's political asylum policy attracted individuals from areas of conflict.

According to Swedish terrorism experts, members of terrorist groups, such as Ansar al-Islam, Ansar al-Sunna, and Hizballah, used funds earned in Sweden to finance terrorist activities elsewhere. In 2007, the Swedish government shut down the al-Aqsa Foundation in Malmo when it was suspected of facilitating such activity for Hizballah. On December 22, its deputy chairman, Khaled al-Yousef, was charged with financing terrorism in Israel; he has not been sentenced.

Swedish law does not provide the government independent national authority to freeze or seize assets, unless in connection with an ongoing criminal investigation. However, once the EU takes action, the government can and does freeze assets of entities and persons listed on the UN 1267 Sanctions Committee list. This procedure is managed through the Sanctions Act (1995). Sweden can also take action against entities designated by the EU clearinghouse process, although Sweden has not yet proposed individuals or entities for inclusion on such lists.

Sweden played an active role in EU deliberations to develop legal instruments for the listing and de-listing of terrorist organizations and an appeals process after the freezing of financial assets. Without a designation by the UN or EU, Swedish authorities only have the right to seize assets once a criminal investigation has been initiated. Efforts to create a national authority and address existing shortcomings are underway.

Terrorism-related cases in Sweden included:

- On May 8, Ahmad Hamad, a Swedish resident born in Iraq, was arrested and placed in detention by U.S. forces in Iraq. Hamad remained in detention.
- In the spring, three Swedish residents of Somali origin were released from prison after being held for three months on suspicion of funneling funds to terrorist organizations in Somalia. (Three others were arrested in Norway.)
- On October 5, Abu Qaswarah, a Swedish citizen, died in a firefight with Iraqi and U.S. forces in Iraq. He allegedly was the second in command of AQ and was the senior leader of AQ in northern Iraq. A Moroccan native, Qaswarah had historic ties to AQ in Iraq founder Abu Musab al-Zarqawi and senior AQ leaders in Afghanistan and Pakistan. According to the Swedish Security Service, Qaswarah was known for his activities in violent Islamist circles in Sweden and was listed on the UN and EU terrorist lists in December 2006.
- In 2005, the Swedish Court of Appeal found Ali Berzengi and Ferman Abdullah, Iraqi citizens with Swedish residency permits, guilty of financially supporting Ansar al-Sunna terrorist actions in Irbil, Iraq. They remained in custody awaiting a government decision on deportation.
- On August 4, a Moroccan, Abderazzak Jabri, was extradited from Sweden to Morocco. He first arrived in Sweden via Spain in 2002 and applied for asylum. He moved into the mosque in Brandbergen, where he shared rooms with Abu Qaswarah (see above). The mosque was under surveillance by Swedish authorities, who in March 2004 arrested several suspects, including Jabri. Afterwards Jabri was seen as a security threat," resulting in the rejection of his asylum case. Jabri disappeared but turned up in Vienna two years later (2006) with a fake passport and tickets to Syria. Jabri claimed he was on his way to Spain to apply for amnesty as an illegal immigrant. He was then held by Swedish authorities until his extradition to Morocco in August 2008.

The Swedish government also agreed to pay damages to two Egyptian nationals, Ahmed Agiza and Muhammed Alzery/al-Zari. The men claimed they had been deported by Sweden to Egypt, where they had been tortured. An asylum request to return to Sweden was subsequently denied by Swedish authorities; both men have appealed and remained in Egypt, where Agiza is incarcerated.

Through the European Common Foreign and Security Policy, Sweden continued to contribute to capacity-building projects in Morocco, Algeria, and Indonesia. Sweden participated in EUROPOL and EUROJUST, European law enforcement institutions that coordinated member states' counterterrorism cooperation and activities. Additionally, it participated in the Nordic Council of Ministers Regional Forum for Nordic Governmental Cooperation. Sweden contributed over USD 1,000,000 to the Terrorism Prevention Branch of the UN Office on Drugs and Crime. In December, Sweden's Parliament voted to raise its troop contribution to the International Security Assistance Force in Afghanistan from 350 to 500.

As a country participating in the Visa Waiver Program (VWP), Sweden continued to comply with requirements in the VWP law related to information sharing and other law enforcement and counterterrorism cooperation. This cooperation was further enhanced by the Implementing Recommendations of the 9/11 Commission Act of 2007.

Switzerland

The United States worked closely with the Swiss government, the Swiss Bankers' Association, the Swiss Interagency Counterterrorism Task Force, and cantonal law enforcement authorities. Swiss security services continued to monitor activities of terrorist groups with a presence in Switzerland and to coordinate with appropriate USG officials, though the scope of the coordination was limited. Swiss law severely restricted the level of information-sharing possible on banking issues.

On December 5, the Government of Switzerland extended, for the second time, its ban against al-Qa'ida (AQ) and its associate organizations for three years. The ban includes not only all activities by the organization itself, but also all activities in support of the organization. Approximately $16.6 million (SFr 20 million) in AQ and Taliban assets in 35 separate accounts remained frozen.

The Swiss government maintained a list of individuals and organizations connected with international terrorism or terrorist financing, in accordance with UN lists. On December 4, 2007, Switzerland proposed to the UN General Assembly a new process intended to enable better coordination in global counterterrorism efforts. Pursuant to this initiative, Switzerland and the other four countries have held a series of workshops and made recommendations for better coordinating the activities of the various UN bodies involved in the fight against terrorism. The recommendations were included in a resolution that the General Assembly adopted during the review of the UN counterterrorism strategy on September 4-5.

Along with the U.S. and UN lists, the Swiss Economic and Finance Ministries have drawn up their own internal list of individuals and entities connected with international terrorism or its financing. Swiss authorities have thus far blocked about 48 accounts totaling approximately USD 20.6 million from individuals or companies linked to individuals or entities listed pursuant to relevant UN resolutions. The Swiss Attorney General also separately froze 41 accounts representing about approximately USD 23 million on the grounds that they were related to terrorist financing, but the extent to which these funds overlap with the UN consolidated list has yet to be determined. As far as Taliban and AQ assets are concerned, on October 24, SECO wrote that 35 bank accounts totaling approximately USD 19 million were still frozen.

Counterterrorism activities were carried out by several police units: The Federal Criminal Police's Counterterrorism Unit focuses on AQ-related cases and employed 21 officials — 11 working on terrorism, nine working on terrorist financing, and a unit chief. Of the 130 employees who work in the Department for Analysis and Prevention in the Federal Office for Police, approximately twelve concentrate on counterterrorism matters, in addition to the roughly 85 cantonal policemen focusing on counterterrorism activities.

In practice, the Swiss government does not compile lists of prohibited organizations. The sole recent exception has been AQ, which is banned on the basis of UN Security Council decisions. Due in part to increased antiterrorism activities in neighboring EU countries, several terrorist organizations, including the Liberation Tigers of Tamil Eelam, Kurdistan Workers' Party (PKK), and the Revolutionary Armed Forces of Colombia (FARC), have a presence in Switzerland. Existing Swiss law and practice prevent the government from listing these entities as terrorist organizations.

The Government of Switzerland estimated there are 4,000 well-organized sympathizers of the PKK, in Switzerland and approximately 100 individuals in the PKK's central coordinating cadre. PKK's headquarters is located in Basel, but their activities also covered the Zurich area. Most of its activities in Switzerland consisted of media relations, training of management staff, and fundraising. In 2007, a group of about twenty Kurdish people raided the premises of various newspapers, radio and television stations in Basel, Bern, Biel, and Zurich, and an Amnesty International office. One year later, in October 2008, other Kurdish activists were strongly suspected by the Federal Office of Police (FEDPOL) of raiding a dozen Turkish cafes, travel agencies and other buildings in several Swiss-German cantons. FEDPOL managed to track several PKK-related messages claiming responsibility that were sent to Switzerland and abroad. Judicial investigations were ongoing at year's end. The Government banned fundraising events during Kurdish celebrations in November, such as the 30th anniversary of the founding of the PKK. It also applied a more restrictive policy on permits, including demonstration permits, residence permits, and Swiss citizenship applications.

In late September, French and Swiss police forces reportedly arrested twelve people belonging to the Mujahadin-e Khalq. They were involved in the financing of a terrorist organization linked to money laundering. Several persons were detained for judgment. In addition to not designating the FARC as a terrorist organization, Switzerland designated Jean-Pierre Gontard, a Swiss professor, to act as Switzerland's designated mediator for the FARC over the past several years. Colombia expressed strong criticism against Jean-Pierre Gontard following Columbia's successful military operation on July 2, 2008, which released 15 hostages including former presidential candidate Ingrid Betancourt and three American defense contractors. Colombian officials accused Jean-Pierre Gontard of exceeding his authority and of being a money courier for FARC based on documents found at the FARC camp and have since cut off all Swiss mediation efforts. The Swiss government defended Gontard, stating that his work was "strictly humanitarian."

In practice, Switzerland does not extradite persons based solely on their membership in a "terrorist" organization. However, terrorism and membership in a terrorist organization are illegal and subject to criminal penalties. Article 260 of the Swiss penal code defines a terrorist as someone who takes part in an organization that keeps its structure and membership secret and that has the purpose of committing violent crimes or of enriching itself by criminal means. Anyone who supports such an organization or participates in its criminal activities can be punished with up to five years in prison. The penal code also provides for punishment of those who commit criminal acts outside of Switzerland if their organization conducts its criminal activities partly within Swiss boundaries or plans to do so.

Switzerland, in conjunction with Liechtenstein, commissioned a study in November on the financing of terrorism.

In late June 2007, the U.S. Securities and Exchange Commission put Credit Suisse (CS), ABB, and Syngenta on its "black list" of companies suspected of indirectly sponsoring terrorist countries. Credit Suisse said that it was conducting a controlled withdrawal of its business from Cuba, North Korea, Syria, Iran, and Sudan. ABB said that it no longer had dealings with North Korea, Burma, or Sudan and would review its business dealings with Iran if the U.S. sanction procedures changed.

As a country participating in the Visa Waiver Program (VWP), Switzerland continued to comply with requirements in the VWP law related to information sharing and other law enforcement and counterterrorism cooperation. This cooperation was further enhanced by the Implementing Recommendations of the 9/11 Commission Act of 2007.

Turkey

Counterterrorism cooperation is a key element of our strategic partnership with Turkey. Domestic and transnational terrorist groups have targeted Turkish nationals and foreigners in Turkey, including, on occasion, USG personnel, for more than 40 years. Terrorist groups that operated in Turkey have included Kurdish nationalists, al-Qa'ida (AQ), Marxist-Leninist, and pro-Chechen groups.

Turkish terrorism law defines terrorism as attacks against Turkish citizens and the Turkish state; this definition may hamper Turkey's ability to interdict, arrest, and prosecute those who plan and facilitate terrorist acts to be committed outside of Turkey.

AQ-inspired terrorists continued to target U.S. and foreign personnel in Turkey. On July 9, three gunmen attacked the U.S. consulate in Istanbul, killing three police officers. The Turkish government arrested four alleged associates of the attackers in the following days and believe that the gunmen were AQ-inspired terrorists. Earlier in the year, the Turkish National Police (TNP) and the National Intelligence Organization (MIT) conducted a successful series of raids against suspected AQ-affiliated terrorists. In January, police raids in Gaziantep against an alleged AQ cell ended in firefights, leading to the deaths of four suspects and the arrests of another 18. Follow-on raids in April led to the detention of an additional 35 people; 24 were indicted for various offenses. In mid-December, the Turks arrested another 60 suspected Islamic extremists in Istanbul, Izmir, and Manisa.

Most prominent among terrorist groups in Turkey is the Kurdistan Workers' Party (PKK). Composed primarily of Kurds with a nationalist agenda, the PKK operated from bases in northern Iraq and directed its forces to target mainly Turkish security forces. In 2006, 2007, and 2008, PKK violence claimed hundreds of Turkish lives. The Kurdistan Freedom Falcons (TAK), a group designated under E.O. 13224, is affiliated with the PKK and has claimed responsibility for a series of deadly attacks in Turkish cities in recent years.

On February 19, TAK announced it would engage in a renewed campaign of violence in Turkey. On July 27, two bombs exploded in the Istanbul working-class neighborhood Gungoren, killing 17 and injuring more than 150. No group claimed responsibility, but Turkish authorities blamed the PKK. On August 19, both TAK and the PKK claimed responsibility for an August 19 car bomb at a Mersin police checkpoint and for an August 23 car bomb in a residential area of Izmir. The PKK also claimed responsibility for a car bomb in Diyarbakir on January 3, which killed six civilians and wounded 70; it apologized for this attack, claiming that the attackers were PKK members acting independently of orders.

The Turkish military and the PKK engaged in constant skirmishes in the Southeast throughout the year, the largest of which was an October 4 attack against a military outpost at Aktutun, in which 15 soldiers were reported killed. On October 17, 2007, in the midst of weeks of violence, during which PKK attacks claimed scores of killed or wounded Turkish soldiers and citizens, the Turkish parliament overwhelmingly passed a motion authorizing cross-border military operations against PKK targets in northern Iraq, which it renewed in October 2008. U.S. information sharing, begun in November 2007, helps ensure these Turkish actions hit terrorist rather than civilian targets. Turkish forces carried out extensive operations along the Turkey-Iraq border in the latter part of the year and continued to carry out strikes along the Turkey-Iraq border throughout 2008. In February, the Turks launched ground operations into northern Iraq, targeting PKK locations, and then disengaged by the end of the month. The Turkish government claimed that 657 PKK members were killed, 161 were captured, and 161 had surrendered in skirmishes throughout the year. In addition, 120 PKK members turned themselves over to Turkish authorities under the terms of a repentance law passed in 2005.

Other prominent terrorist groups in Turkey included the Revolutionary People's Liberation Party/Front, a militant Marxist-Leninist group with anti-U.S. and anti-NATO views that seeks the violent overthrow of the Turkish state; and Turkish Hizballah (not affiliated with Lebanese Hizballah), an organization of Sunni Kurds with a violent history. The Great Eastern Islamic Raiders Front is a decentralized Islamic revivalist group that was particularly active in the 1990s; it claimed ties with al-Qa'ida (AQ). A previously unknown terrorist organization, Revolutionary Headquarters (Devrimci Karargah), an apparently Marxist organization espousing an anti-imperialist, anti-Zionist agenda, claimed responsibility for two attacks in Istanbul against political and military targets. Investigations into an organization named Ergenekon, allegedly composed of former military officials, bureaucrats, politicians, journalists, and underworld figures, began in 2007, leading to arrests in the summer of 2008. Alleged members of Ergenekon were on trial for a number of crimes including terrorism charges; the details of the case were murky, however, and Ergenekon's status as a terrorist organization remained under debate at year's end.

In November 2008, Turkish customs officials at the Port of Mersin seized a suspicious Iranian shipment bound for Venezuela which contained 22 shipping containers of barrels of nitrate and sulfite chemicals, commonly used for bombs, along with dismantled laboratory equipment. Customs officials detected the equipment during a search of 22 containers manifested as "tractor parts." They were being transshipped to Port of Mersin by trucks from Iran. In December, customs officials asked Turkish Atomic Energy Authority and military experts to examine the seized material. At year's end, disposition of the shipment remained undecided.

The Turkish government has proposed a number of reforms to its counterterrorism and intelligence structure including increasing civilian control of counterterrorism operations and improving civil-military cooperation in CT efforts. The reform proposals predated 2008, but were given a sharper focus following the October 4 Aktutun attack. The proposals were still in the formative stage at year's end.

Turkey has consistently supported Coalition efforts in Afghanistan. Turkey has over 800 troops as well as a military training team in Kabul, a civilian Provincial Reconstruction Team in Wardak Province, and has undertaken training of Afghan police officials, politicians, and bureaucrats in Turkey. It has pledged a total of $200 million to reconstruction efforts in Afghanistan. Turkey has provided significant logistical support to Coalition operations in Afghanistan and Iraq, authorizing the use of Incirlik Air Base as an air-refueling hub for Operation Enduring Freedom and Operation Iraqi Freedom, and as a cargo hub to transport non-lethal cargo to U.S. troops in Afghanistan and Iraq. Almost 60 percent of air cargo for U.S. troops in Iraq transits Incirlik. Establishment of this hub allows six C-17 aircraft to transport the amount of goods it took nine to ten aircraft to move from Germany, and saves the United States almost $160 million per year. Between one-third and two-thirds of the fuel destined for the Iraqi people and more than 25 percent of fuel for Coalition Forces transits from Turkey into Iraq via the Habur Gate border crossing. Turkey was active in reconstruction efforts, including providing electricity to Iraq. Turkey contributed headquarters personnel to the NATO Training Mission in Iraq (NTM-I) and completed military leadership training in Turkey for 89 Iraqi officers as a further contribution to the NATO NTM-I.

Pursuant to its obligations under UNSCR 1267 and subsequent resolutions, Turkish officials continued to circulate UN and U.S.-designated names of terrorists to all law enforcement and intelligence agencies, and to financial institutions. Only UN-listed names, however, were subjected to asset freezes enforced through a Council of Ministers decree. This legal mechanism for enforcing sanctions under UNSCR 1267 was challenged in Turkish courts by UN-designated terrorist financier Yasin al-Kadi, whose assets had been frozen by the state. Following a series of legal actions, the decree freezing his assets has been successfully challenged but was still in effect pending appeal.

Ukraine

Ukraine suffered no domestic terrorism incidents, although law enforcement authorities sometimes labeled ordinary criminal activity as terrorist acts. The Ukrainian State Committee for Financial Monitoring

(SCFM) and the Professional Association of Managers of Financial Companies signed an agreement to include real estate financial transactions in data reported to the SCFM. The agreement was intended to counteract the ability of criminal and terrorist organizations to launder money through real estate transactions.

From October 30-31, the SBU hosted a seminar on "The Prevention of Terrorism: International Experience and its Relevance for Ukraine" in Kyiv that brought together senior government officials with international experts to discuss how Ukraine can learn from the experience of its European counterparts. On November 13-14, government counterterrorism officials also participated in OSCE-sponsored training on incorporating international counterterrorism laws into Ukrainian legislation. Ukraine continued to contribute to stabilization efforts in both Iraq and Afghanistan.

United Kingdom

In December, a jury at Woolwich Crown Court in south London convicted Bilal Abdulla, a doctor who had been practicing medicine in Scotland, of conspiracy to murder and conspiring to cause explosions in the June 30, 2007 car bomb attack at Glasgow International Airport and in failed car bomb attacks in London a day earlier. He was sentenced to life in prison and is expected to serve at least 32 years before being eligible for release. Abdulla was accused of planning two attacks in London and Glasgow[8] just days after Prime Minister Gordon Brown took office.

In December, Manchester Crown Court convicted Rangzieb Ahmed of being a member of al-Qa'ida (AQ) and directing a terrorist organization in Britain. He was sentenced to life in prison and is expected to serve a minimum of ten years. A co-defendant, Habib Ahmed, was also found guilty of belonging to AQ. Rangzieb was accused of leading a three-man terrorist cell that was planning a terrorist attack overseas, and his conviction marked the first of its kind in the United Kingdom since directing terrorism became an offense under the Terrorism Act of 2000. The prosecution

---

[8]A paramedic became suspicious of the contents of one of the vehicles, (the other had already been towed away for parking illegally), which led to the discovery of the plot. Neither vehicle detonated as police managed to defuse them. The following day, two terrorist suspects, Abdulla and Kafeel Ahmed, believed to have fled from London, attempted to drive a vehicle filled with gas cylinders into an entrance of Glasgow airport. The vehicle caught fire and did limited damage to the building. The driver, Ahmed, died later as a result of injuries sustained at the scene, while an airport employee apprehended Abdulla as he exited the vehicle. Abdulla, who is of Iraqi origin, had associated with a Sunni terrorist cell in Baghdad before returning to Britain to plan the 2007 attacks.

presented evidence that Rangzieb was in contact with senior AQ members. Both men's arrest and the disruption of their cell was the result of a three-year international investigation by police.

In November, Parliament passed the Counterterrorism Act 2008. The act lays out and refines government powers to pursue and prosecute suspected terrorists, and focuses mainly on rules of evidence and information gathering, search and seizure, terrorist finance, jurisdiction, questioning suspects, and forfeiture of assets. The government was forced to throw out one provision of the Act which would have extended the detention period for terrorist suspects before being charged to 42 days. A heavy defeat in the House of Lords voted down the controversial measure 309 to 118 in October. In the wake of defeat in the House of Lords, Home Secretary Jacqui Smith indicated that new legislation would be brought forward to allow the director of public prosecutions to apply to the courts for the right to question terrorist suspects for up to 42 days if necessary.

On November 8, police re-arrested radical cleric and terrorist suspect Abu Qatada at his home in west London after a Special Immigration Appeals Commission revoked his bail over concerns that he was a flight risk and was in danger of breaching his bail conditions. Suspected of being Osama bin Ladin's "right-hand man in the UK" and an AQ recruiter in Europe, Qatada had been released from prison to house arrest in June after successfully contesting UK plans to deport him to Jordan where he was convicted in absentia of planning terrorist attacks. Between his release in June and his re-arrest in November, Qatada had been living under strict bail conditions, including a 22-hour per day curfew and a ban from using mobile telephones or the Internet. The Home Office continued attempts to secure his deportation to Jordan.

Abdelbasset al-Megrahi, a Libyan citizen, continued to pursue a second appeal of his conviction by a Scottish court in connection with the 1988 terrorist bombing of Pan Am flight 103 over Lockerbie, Scotland, which killed 270 people. Following his diagnosis of incurable cancer by doctors in Scotland in September, Megrahi applied for bail (he qualified to make the bail application because of his pending appeal). The Scottish High Court of Justiciary denied Megrahi's bail request on November 14, indicating that Meghrai's declining health had not reached a stage at which early release would be appropriate. Megrahi is serving a life sentence in Scottish prison.

The government continued to hone its response to terrorism under its "CONTEST" Counterterrorism Strategy. The CONTEST strategy divides government resources under four thematic response areas: Prevent, Pursue, Protect, and Prepare. In December the government hosted its second annual "Prevent" conference, drawing together over 700 participants from national and local government, community and civil society organizations, law enforcement agencies, and social service providers to review progress in the government's counter-radicalization efforts at the local level. The conference was an opportunity for stakeholders to take stock of efforts to develop and implement local government-funded programs aimed at countering extremism in communities throughout the United Kingdom. Participants shared information on best practices and discussed programs as varied as cultural and sports workshops, discussion forums, and joint police-social service partnerships focused on identifying young people vulnerable to messages of extremism. The Home Secretary opened the conference by calling on participants to confront radical ideology that contends that being British and being Muslim are incompatible.

In October, the Home Secretary announced new measures aimed at strengthening the government's power to exclude foreign extremists from entering Britain. The so-called "preachers of hate" rules are expected to extend to anyone suspected of advocating illegal activity to stir tensions in the UK. The new rules will give the Home Office new powers to "name and shame" extremists blocked from entering Britain and to share their details with other countries. The rules, which could apply equally to radical clerics as well as animal-rights protesters and far-right groups, are expected to see an increase in the number of people banned from entering Britain and will shift the burden of proof from the government to suspected individuals, by demanding that they refute accusations made against them by publicly denouncing or retracting their reported views. By year's end, it was not clear whether the measures had been applied to anyone, nor was it clear whether the measures would survive a court challenge.

In testimony to the House of Commons Defense Committee in October, government Security Minister Lord West warned that Britain faced a 30-year struggle to counter radicalization among extremist elements of the country's young Muslims. West praised the government's efforts to open dialogue with young British Muslims, insisting that engagement was beginning to pay dividends, but cautioned that there was still a long way to go, and that it would take decades to win the battle of ideas against terrorism and extremism. Lord West's testimony before the committee investigating Britain's preparedness to defend itself against terrorism drew strong reaction when West, a former Royal Navy admiral and First Sea Lord, raised concern over the UK's ability to monitor all the vessels entering British waters and to patrol the 11,000 miles of British coast effectively. UK media reported that committee members expressed concern that management of the UK's national security apparatus remained fragmented between various ministries and Whitehall departments.

In October, the Secretary of State for Schools announced plans to issue guidance to UK primary and secondary schools requiring teachers and school administrators to play a key role in getting young people to reject extremism. The goal was to empower young people to expose and refute extremist ideology through classroom discussions, short courses, and anti-hate seminars. The guidance would require teachers to report students to the police if there is suspicion of them being drawn to violent extremism. Similarly, in November, the Home Office requested in November that universities monitor the attendance and movements of international students in an attempt to counter student visa scams.

In early 2008, UK authorities also detained and expelled a PKK representative in Britain, and in December they conducted raids against a group of individuals suspected of providing support to the PKK.

As a country participating in the Visa Waiver Program (VWP), the United Kingdom continued to comply with requirements in the VWP law related to information sharing and other law enforcement and counterterrorism cooperation. This cooperation was further enhanced by the Implementing Recommendations of the 9/11 Commission Act of 2007.

Northern Ireland

Since May 2007, Northern Ireland has been governed by a power-sharing agreement led by the Democratic Unionist Party (DUP) and Sinn Fein, the political wing of the IRA. Activities by dissident republican groups opposed to Sinn Fein's participation in the peace process and the current power sharing government were the main source of concern. In June, the Secretary of State for Northern Ireland Shaun Woodward stated that dissident republican activity was at its highest level in five years. Later in the year, police raised concerns that a five-month impasse between Sinn Fein and the DUP over devolution of policing and justice could embolden dissident groups. The impasse was resolved in November, however, and the parties were working together toward devolution. Unionists raised concerns about devolution occurring while the IRA Army Council was still active. At the request of the British and Irish governments, the Independent Monitoring Commission (IMC) looked into the Army Council's operations and determined there was no evidence that it was operational.

The Independent Monitoring Commission (IMC), a four-person body established by the Irish and British governments in 2004, regularly releases reports on paramilitary activity in Northern Ireland and Ireland. In a 2008 report, the IMC stated that it had not observed a material increase in the number of dissident activists or an increase in their access to weapons. The IMC did note that the targeting by dissident groups of Northern Ireland police officers remained a serious concern. Various dissident republican groups, including the Continuity IRA and the Real IRA, were involved in attacks on police throughout the year.

In December, the British government announced that loyalist paramilitary groups had until February 2010 to decommission their weapons or face prosecution for illegal possession of illegal arms. The International Commission on Decommissioning (IICD) continued to work with the Ulster Defense Association (UDA) and Ulster Volunteer Force (UVF) to complete this process.

Middle East and North Africa Overview

Terrorism and criminality are the enemies of every religion and every civilization. They would not have appeared except for the absence of the principle of tolerance.

—King Abdullah bin Abdulaziz of Saudi Arabia
The United Nations, New York City
November 13, 2008

Most governments in the region cooperated with the United States in counterterrorist activities and undertook efforts to strengthen their capabilities to counter terrorism effectively. These efforts included participation in USG-sponsored antiterrorism assistance (ATA) programs and taking steps to bolster banking and legal regimes to combat terrorist financing.

The Iraqi government, in coordination with the Coalition, made significant progress in combating AQI and affiliated terrorist organizations. There was a notable reduction in the number of security incidents throughout much of Iraq, including a decrease in civilian casualties, enemy attacks, and improvised explosive device (IED) attacks in the last quarter of the year. Terrorist organizations and insurgent groups continued their attacks on Coalition and Iraqi security forces using IEDs, vehicle-borne improvised explosive devices (VBIEDs), and suicide bombers. The Iraqi government continued to emphasize national reconciliation and made progress in passing key pieces of reconciliation-related legislation. There were also practical steps taken that helped to advance reconciliation at the provincial and local level. The United States continued its focused efforts to mitigate the threat posed by foreign fighters in Iraq. State sponsors of terrorism, Iran and Syria, continued to play destabilizing roles in the region. [See Chapter 3, *State Sponsors of Terrorism*.]

The Expanded Neighbors Process continued to provide a forum for Iraq and its neighbors to address the political and security challenges facing Iraq and the region. In November, the Iraqi government sent representatives to Syria to participate in the second Neighbors Process working group on border security where the group sought new ways to limit the flow of foreign terrorists into Iraq.

Israel responded to the terrorist threat as it has in recent years, with operations targeted at terrorist leaders, terrorist infrastructure, and active terrorist activities such as rocket launching groups. Israel Defense Forces (IDF) and Israel Security Services (ISA) continued incursions into the West Bank to conduct roundups and other military operations designed to increase pressure on Palestinian terrorist organizations and their supporters. The Israeli security services also imposed strict and widespread closures and curfews in Palestinian areas. The regular and indiscriminate rocket attacks on Israel from Gaza were met by retaliatory fire by the IDF. Israel also maintained its targeted assassinations policy in Gaza. While there continued to be an overall decrease in the number of successfully perpetrated terrorist attacks in comparison to previous years, Israeli security officials maintained that the decrease was not for lack of terrorists' efforts, but because the security services were able to keep terrorist planners and operators off balance and foil acts before they were carried out. The Israeli Air Force increasingly launched airstrikes against launch teams in November and December following escalations in rocket and mortar attacks. Israel launched Operation Cast Lead in Gaza on December 27 in response to these rocket attacks.

In Lebanon, a campaign of domestic political intimidation continued, including several attacks against members of the Lebanese army and Internal Security Forces. In May, Lebanese Hizballah initiated armed confrontations against Lebanese government and other Sunni and Christian elements in the country following the government's efforts to shut down Hizballah's independent telecommunications network, in addition to the removal of the Hizballah-affiliated head of airport security. A Hizballah official suspected in several bombings against U.S. citizens, Imad Mughniyeh, was killed in Damascus, Syria in February. No one has taken responsibility for his death.

Attacks in Algeria in August killed nearly 80 people. These attacks were indicative of the shifts in strategy made by al-Qa'ida in the Islamic Maghreb (AQIM) towards attacks employing suicide tactics and improvised explosive devices (IEDs), and the targeting of Western interests as well as Algerian government officials and civilians.

On March 10, AQIM claimed responsibility for kidnapping two Austrian tourists near the Tunisia-Algeria border. The hostages were released on October 31 after a ransom was paid. In February, the Tunisian courts handed down guilty verdicts on eight of 30 Tunisians convicted in a December 2007/January 2008 plot targeting U.S. and UK interests in Tunisia.

The security situation in Yemen deteriorated significantly over the past year as al-Qa'ida in Yemen increased its attacks against Western and Yemeni government institutions. On January 17, suspected al-Qa'ida operatives ambushed a tourist convoy in the eastern Hadramout Governorate, killing two Belgians. The U.S. Embassy was attacked on September 17; fatalities included several Yemeni security personnel and citizens, as well as an American citizen.

Algeria

The security situation in Algeria was marked by a decrease in the number of high profile terrorist attacks throughout the country compared with 2007, although the overall number of attacks did not decline and ongoing low-level terrorist activities continued in the countryside. In the first half of the year there was a lull in attacks by terrorist groups as security forces stepped up their operations following the December 2007 bombing of the UN headquarters in Algiers. There was a dramatic rise in terrorist attacks during the month of August, however, with at least 79 people killed in various incidents across northeastern Algeria, most of them in suicide bombings. The targets included police stations, a coast guard outpost, and a bus transporting Algerian workers for a Canadian company. Previously, the Salafist Group for Preaching and Combat (GSPC), now al-Qa'ida in the Islamic Maghreb (AQIM), focused on targeting Algerian government interests and had been more averse to suicide attacks and civilian casualties. Although Algerian government interests remained the primary focus of AQIM, the attack on the bus and an attack against French railroad workers confirmed AQIM's intention to act on its public threats against foreigners. AQIM continued to diversify its tactics by importing tactics used in Iraq and Afghanistan.

National reconciliation remained a contentious issue for many Algerians, who are still divided over whether amnesty and re-integration or a more aggressive, unforgiving approach to terrorism is the best way to address the continuing threat. Although the Charter for Peace and National Reconciliation has officially expired, its terms may still be applied on a case by case basis at the exclusive discretion of the president.

Following the 2006 announcement of affiliation with al-Qa'ida (AQ), AQIM began to increase the threats against what it termed "crusading" Westerners, particularly American and French citizens, although Russians, Danes, Austrians, and now Canadians have been targeted as well. AQIM support cells have been discovered and dismantled in Spain, Italy, Morocco, Mauritania, and Mali, with AQIM-maintained training camps and support networks in northern Mali.

The year was punctuated in the month of August with several high-profile terrorist attacks:

- On August 3, a police station in Tizi Ouzou, the capital of the Kabylie region, was damaged in a suicide bomb attack, leaving over twenty people injured.
- On August 9, eight people, all civilians, were killed in an attack on a police station in Zemmouri al-Bahri, a seaside town to the east of Algiers.
- On August 10, three policemen were killed in a bomb attack on the nearby beach of Tigzirt.
- On August 19, the heaviest casualties from the August spate of attacks occurred when a suicide bomber exploded his vehicle outside a gendarmerie training college in Issers where prospective new recruits were waiting for the gates to open. The Algerian government reported that 43 people were killed and 45 injured.
- On August 20, there were two car bomb explosions in the nearby town of Bouira. The first, outside a military building, left four soldiers lightly wounded, according to the official Algerian Press Service. The second exploded outside of a hotel and killed 11 people. It was reported that the hotel was being used to house foreigners working on the nearby Koudiet Acerdoune dam project, run by a Canadian company. During the attack, the driver of the suicide vehicle rammed a bus carrying workers of the company and detonated the bomb.

The police and army response to the August attacks was energetic, and public disapproval of the large number of civilians killed in the attacks increased the number of tips phoned in, which may account for the historically low number of attacks that occurred during the subsequent Ramadan holiday in September. A noticeable increase in the visible security presence in major cities may have also contributed to the low number of terrorist incidents during Ramadan.

The majority of attacks have occurred in rural and suburban areas. The terrorists were very careful to establish remote bases, communicate sparingly, and planned and carried out attacks meticulously. AQIM appeared aware of the need to avoid civilian casualties, but this has been difficult to accomplish as its police and military targets often operated among civilians. Roadside bombs and ambushes persisted despite the efforts of the security forces. In some cases, however, approaching terrorists were intercepted before they could successfully complete their attacks. The combination of a population weary of civilian casualties from over a decade of Islamic terrorist violence, and the growing availability and use of cell phones has made the terrorists more vulnerable to detection and attack by the police.

AQIM's strategy in Algeria appeared to be influenced by AQ's experience in Iraq. AQIM has issued directions to avoid civilian deaths and attacks have been concentrated on military, police, and foreign targets. AQIM sought to disrupt business and commercial activity and probably used such attacks to discourage foreign investment. The overall civilian death toll due to terrorist attacks has declined in recent years.

It was estimated that the Algerian security services killed, wounded or arrested 1,000 terrorists in 2008, compared to an estimated combined figure of about 1,100 for 2007. Although the total number of attacks rose in 2008 to 295 compared to 218 in 2007, the number of civilian casualties decreased. The counterterrorism successes of the Algerian services, combined with the public rejection of terrorists, possibly reduced AQIM's overall effectiveness. One of the most effective counterterrorism operations took place in August when 12 terrorists were killed in the forests of Ouacif and Ain Elhamam, in the wilaya of Tizi Ouzou. The surge in terrorist activity in late August may have been revenge attacks for this operation. In addition, over 300 terrorists were sentenced (often in absentia, with sentences never carried out) to capital punishment during the year, of which 257 were sentenced by the court of Boumerdes alone. The Government of Algeria instituted a program to hire 100,000 new police and gendarme officers, reinforce the borders, augment security at airports, and increase the overall security presence in the city of Algiers. The initiative was effective in reducing the impact of terrorist incidents during the year and also demonstrated the government's determination to fight terrorism.

AQIM, thanks in part to high unemployment among Algerian youth, was partially successful in replenishing its numbers after the arrests, surrender, or death of an estimated 1,000 terrorists. Those remaining appeared to be more hard-line and resistant to the government's amnesty offer. Despite the upsurge of AQIM activity in August, the overall security situation remained greatly improved from the situation of the late 1990s. The Algerian military and security forces were often criticized as slow to adapt to AQIM's changing tactics as well as slow to accept that they faced a better organized international threat in the form of AQIM rather than a purely internal threat.

Bahrain

The Government of Bahrain actively monitored terrorist suspects, but domestic legal constraints at times hampered its ability to detain and prosecute such suspects. The trial of five men accused of membership in a terrorist organization, undergoing terrorist training, facilitating the travel of others abroad to receive terrorist training, and financing terrorism ended with their conviction on January 16. The court sentenced the five to six months imprisonment with credit for time served. The case represented the first use of the new 2006 counterterrorism law.[9]

Security forces monitored the activities of two other Bahraini citizens and arrested them on June 9. Prosecutors charged the men with maintaining links to al-Qa'ida and financing terrorism. Their trial began on August 24 and was ongoing at year's end.

Bahrain continued its cooperation with U.S. authorities on counterterrorist finance. Its Financial Information Unit (FIU) resides in the Central Bank of Bahrain (CBB). The CBB, FIU, and local banks worked cooperatively on counterterrorist finance and anti-money laundering issues. The government expressed its desire to host a conference in conjunction with the U.S. Department of the Treasury on the regulation of Islamic charities. In addition, Bahrain hosts the Middle East and North Africa Financial Action Task Force secretariat.

Egypt

While there were no attacks by foreign terrorist groups in Egypt, the smuggling of humans, weapons, and other contraband through the Sinai into Israel and the Gaza Strip has created criminal networks that may be associated with terrorist groups in the region. The apparent radicalization of some Sinai Bedouin may possibly be linked in part to these smuggling networks and Egyptian efforts to dismantle them.

The Egyptian and U.S. governments maintained a strong dialogue and shared information on a broad range of counterterrorism and law enforcement issues. In 2008, Egypt hosted the fourth annual session of the U.S.-Egypt Counterterrorism Joint Working Group.

In the past six years, Egypt has tightened its terrorist finance regulations in keeping with relevant UN Security Council resolutions. Egypt strengthened its anti-money laundering legislation by specifically adding terrorism financing to the list of punishable crimes. The Government of Egypt also maintained open lines of communication with U.S. officials concerning terrorist finance information. The Egyptian government regularly

[9] The 2006 counterterrorism law was the first of its kind in Bahrain to specifically criminalize terrorism. It enumerated the types of crimes considered to be terrorism and established punishments, ranging up to and including the death penalty. The law also criminalized conspiracy to carry out an act of terrorism and outlawed membership in proscribed groups, including al-Qa'ida. Bahrain enacted amendments to an existing anti-money laundering law in 2006 that criminalized the undeclared transfer of money across international borders.

informed its own financial institutions of any individuals or entities that are designated by any of the UN sanctions committees. A team from the UN Counterterrorism Committee Executive Directorate visited Egypt to review efforts to implement UN Security Council resolutions on counterterrorism.

Egypt maintained its strengthened airport security measures and security for the Suez Canal, and continued to institute more stringent port security measures.

The Egyptian judicial system does not allow plea bargaining, and terrorists have historically been prosecuted to the full extent of the law. Terrorism defendants may be tried in military tribunals or emergency courts. Many of the Egyptian president's far-reaching powers in the realm of counterterrorism come from Egypt's Emergency Law, which has been in force since 1981, and was renewed by Parliament for two years in June. President Mubarak has pledged to lift the Emergency Law and has called for new counterterrorism legislation to replace the Emergency Law, noting that Egypt should follow the example of other countries that have recently passed comprehensive laws to combat terrorism. Such legislation reportedly has been drafted but not yet submitted to Egypt's Parliament.

The imprisoned former leader of Egyptian Islamic Jihad, Sayid Imam al-Sharif, issued a sequel to his 2007 critique of violent jihad. His critique, while not a rejection of the concept of violent jihad, attempted to establish "rules of engagement" and also suggested non-violent alternatives.

Iraq

Iraq remained a committed partner in counterterrorism efforts. The Iraqi government, with support from Coalition Forces, continued to make significant progress in combating al-Qa'ida in Iraq (AQI) and affiliated terrorist organizations, as well as Shiite militia elements engaged in terrorism. The significant reduction in the number of security incidents throughout much of Iraq, beginning in the last half of 2007, continued in 2008, with an even further decrease in civilian casualties, enemy attacks, and improvised explosive device (IED) attacks.

Terrorist organizations and insurgent groups continued attacks on Coalition and Iraqi security forces using IEDs, including vehicle-borne improvised explosive devices, and suicide bombers. Beginning in November 2007 and through July 2008, improvised rocket-assisted mortars were used in attacks on Coalition Forces resulting in both military and civilian casualties. AQI and its Sunni extremist partners also increasingly used Iraqi nationals and females as suicide bombers. Coalition Forces conducted a full spectrum of operations to defeat the adaptive threats employed by AQI, by, with, and through Iraqi forces.

Iraqi and Coalition Forces tactically defeated many AQI cells in Baghdad and Anbar, and AQI elements consolidated into Ninewa and Diyala provinces. Despite being limited to smaller safe havens within Iraq, AQI retained pockets of extremists in and around Baghdad and in Anbar. In Ninewa, Coalition Forces focused operations against AQI and like-minded Sunni extremists by capturing or killing senior leaders. On October 5, U.S. troops killed Abu Qaswarah, AQI's Emir of the North and second-in-command. AQI continued primarily to target the Iraqi security forces, SOI (Sons of Iraq) groups, and tribal awakening movement members. Despite the improved security environment, AQI still possessed the means to launch high-profile attacks against Iraqi civilians and infrastructure and their focus seemed to have shifted to such attacks. In addition to countering AQI and Sunni extremists, Iraq is making progress in defeating terrorists with alternative motivations.

Foreign terrorists from North Africa and other Middle Eastern countries who were sympathetic to Sunni extremists continued to flow into Iraq, predominantly through Syria. Their numbers, however, were significantly fewer than in the previous year. Terrorism committed by illegal armed groups receiving weapons and training from Iran continued to endanger the security and stability of Iraq, however incidents of such violence were markedly lower than in the previous year. Many of the groups receiving ideological and logistical support from Iran were based in Shia communities in Central and Southern Iraq. Iraqi government officials continued to strongly condemn terrorists from all quarters. On November 19, Iraq, Turkey, and the United States renewed its formal trilateral security dialogue as one element of ongoing cooperative efforts to counter the militant Kurdish nationalist group, Kurdistan Workers' Party (PKK). Iraqi leaders, including those from the Kurdistan Regional Government continued to publicly state that the PKK was a terrorist organization and would not be tolerated in Iraq. The Trilateral discussions continued through the end of the year.

The Iraqi government increased its bilateral and multilateral efforts to garner regional and international support against the common threat of terrorism. The Expanded Neighbors Process continued to provide a forum in which Iraq and its neighbors could address the political and security challenges facing Iraq and the region. In November, the government sent representatives to Syria to participate in the second Neighbors Process working group on border security where the group sought new ways to limit the flow of foreign terrorists into Iraq. Also on the diplomatic front, ambassadors from Jordan, Bahrain, Syria, United Arab Emirates, Kuwait, and the Arab League all presented their credentials in 2008.

The Iraqi government pressed senior Iranian leaders to end support for lethal aid to Iraqi militias, and the Iraqi army defeated extremists trained and equipped by Iran in Basra, Baghdad, and other areas. For example, in the Charge of the Knights operation in April in Basra, Prime Minister Maliki ordered Iraqi security forces to combat extralegal Iranian-supported militias. Iraqi forces arrested violent extremists, confiscated arms, and helped to reestablish the rule of law in Basra. The operation was Iraqi-led, while small British and American Military Transition Teams were in place to provide Iraqi leaders with advice, access to surveillance, and the ability to call for additional resources as needed.

On April 19, in published comments in response to the operations, Muqtada al-Sadr threatened to wage open war until liberation against the Iraqi government unless it agreed to stop targeting Mahdi Army members. Attacks by Mahdi Army members increased in Baghdad's Sadr City neighborhood after Sadr's statement. However, Iraqi Foreign Minister Hoshiyar Zebari vowed, in response, that the Iraqi government would continue to pursue militias. Although attacks by militants have since sharply decreased, Shia militant groups' ties to Iran remained a challenge and threat to Iraq's long term stability.

The Government of Iraq attributed security gains to both the Coalition troop surge and the purported decisions by some elements affiliated with Muqtada al-Sadr's Jaysh al-Mahdi Army to forego armed action in favor of political activity. Improved Iraqi Security Forces proficiency and increasing popular support for the actions of Iraqi Forces against AQI and other extremist groups also illustrated security progress. SOI groups provided Coalition and Iraqi forces with valuable information that helped disrupt terrorist operations and exposed large weapons caches. The SOI began integration into Iraqi Security Forces in October. Sunni tribal awakening movements formed alliances with the coalition against AQI and extremist groups. Ethno-sectarian related violence continued to decline, although reports late in the year that Christians were targeted for assassination in Mosul indicated that AQI still sought to sow fear and instability by promoting inter-ethnic and inter-religious animosity.

The Iraqi security forces continued to build tactical and operational momentum and assumed responsibility for security in all of Iraq's 18 provinces. On November 17, the Governments of Iraq and the United States signed a Security Agreement that provided the legal basis for continued security cooperation, which will help Iraq build its capacity to fight terrorist organizations, and established formal mechanisms for ensuring that future security operations are conducted in accord with the Security Agreement. Continued international support will be critical for the Iraqi government to continue building its capacity to fight terrorist organizations. Iraq's intelligence services continued to improve in both competency and confidence, but will require ongoing support before they will be able to adequately identify and respond to internal and external terrorist threats.

Israel, West Bank, and Gaza

Twenty-seven Israeli civilians were killed in at least 10 separate terrorist attacks during the year, up from six attacks in 2007. Israel continued to experience terrorist threats emanating from the West Bank and Gaza. Rocket and even more accurate mortar fire emanating from the Gaza Strip were Palestinian terrorist organizations' preferred form of attack, while incidents of Palestinian suicide bombings continued to decline relative to previous years.

Israel responded to the terrorist threat as it has in recent years, with operations targeted at terrorist leaders, terrorist infrastructure, and active terrorist activities such as rocket launching groups. Israel Defense Forces (IDF) and Israel Security Services (ISA) incursions into the West Bank continued to conduct roundups and other military operations designed to increase pressure on Palestinian terrorist organizations and their supporters. The Israeli security services also imposed strict and widespread closures and curfews in Palestinian areas. By some reports, Israeli military operations in 2008 killed an estimated 782 Palestinians in the West Bank and Gaza, including at least 315 by year's end as a result of Israeli Air Force (IAF) airstrikes.

Radical groups used Gaza casualties for propaganda purposes. Due to budgetary constraints, construction on an extensive security barrier in the West Bank and Jerusalem was sporadic in 2008. Israeli officials believed the separation barrier played an important role in making terrorist attacks more difficult to undertake.

Terrorist attacks in Israel and the West Bank included the following:

- On February 4, a Palestinian suicide bomber struck a shopping mall in the southern town of Dimona, killing one person and injuring nine others. Israeli police killed a second attacker before he was able to detonate his bomb belt. Two terrorist groups, the al-Aqsa Martyrs' Brigade (AAMB) and the Popular Front for the Liberation of Palestine (PFLP), claimed joint responsibility for the attack.

- On March 6, a Palestinian resident of East Jerusalem shot and killed eight students and wounded 11 others at the prominent Mercaz Harav Kook Yeshiva (Jewish religious school) in West Jerusalem. An off-duty soldier entered the yeshiva and killed the assailant.

- On April 25, a terrorist operating on behalf of HAMAS and the Palestinian Islamic Jihad (PIJ) infiltrated Israel from the West Bank and shot to death two civilian security guards at an industrial park near the village of Qalansuwa.

- On June 1 and 20, Israeli settlers fired three rockets toward the Palestinian town of Burin. In late July, settlers threw a Molotov cocktail into a home in Burin as well. No injuries were reported from either attack.
- On July 2, a Palestinian resident of East Jerusalem killed three people and wounded at least 18 others with a bulldozer in West Jerusalem before being shot and killed by an off-duty soldier. The government defined the incident as a terrorist attack, but police were unable to determine a clear motive.
- On July 22, a Palestinian resident of East Jerusalem wounded at least 16 people with a bulldozer on a busy West Jerusalem street before being killed by police. The attack was widely viewed as a copycat of the July 2 attack.
- On September 25, a prominent Hebrew University professor and critic of Jewish settlements in the West Bank was wounded when a pipe bomb, allegedly planted by radical members of the settlement movement, exploded as he opened the door of his home in West Jerusalem. After the attack, police found flyers near the academic's home calling for the establishment of a new state in the West Bank based on Jewish religious law. The flyers, signed by a Jewish extremist group called the Army of the State Liberators, also offered USD 314,000 to anyone who killed a member of the non-governmental organization, Peace Now. Israeli Security Services continued to investigate the attack.
- During the year, rocket, mortar, and sniper fire from the Gaza Strip killed eight Israeli civilians and one Ecuadorian kibbutz volunteer.

Throughout the year, Israel's security services were able to keep terrorist planners and operators off balance, reporting multiple foiled attempts:

- On January 16, IDF, Civil Administration, and police forces intercepted a truck containing 800 kg of potassium/nitrate at the Eliyahu border crossing south of Qalqiliya, West Bank. Potassium nitrate is a banned substance in Gaza and the West Bank due to its use in the manufacturing of explosive devices and Qassam rockets.
- On November 4, IDF and security forces discovered a tunnel situated 250 meters from the Gaza security fence that they believed would be used for the abduction of IDF soldiers. Israeli forces killed several militants during an ensuing firefight.

- On November 12, IDF forces killed four armed militants in Gaza that were attempting to place an explosive device near the Gaza security fence.
- On November 28, IDF forces identified another attempt by militants to lay an explosive device at the Gaza security fence near Khan Yunis. In an ensuing firefight, IDF forces killed one terrorist and wounded four others.

The smuggling of commodities, arms, explosives, and funds in support of terrorist groups such as HAMAS through tunnels along the Philadelphi Route between the Gaza Strip and Egypt remained problematic. On January 23, HAMAS terrorists blew up several sections of the border fence separating the Gaza Strip from the Egyptian town of Rafah. According to the Israeli Ministry of Foreign Affairs (MFA), HAMAS used this opportunity to smuggle explosives, anti-tank, and anti-aircraft weapons into the Gaza Strip.

Despite the fact that the IDF thwarted the above-mentioned attacks, terrorist groups conducted mortar attacks against the Israeli-manned crossings between Gaza and Israel, and Qassam rocket launches from Gaza that terrorized Israeli communities abutting Gaza. Palestinian terrorists routinely fired rockets and mortars at Israeli civilians from the Gaza Strip despite an Egyptian-negotiated truce or cease fire between Israel and HAMAS that began on June 19. According to the Israeli MFA, Palestinian terrorist groups fired approximately 1,750 rockets and 1,528 mortars into Israel in 2008, up from 896 rockets and 749 mortars in 2007. Rocket and mortar attacks began to escalate toward the end of the year; the MFA estimated that Palestinian terrorist groups fired 213 rockets and 126 mortars at Israel from November 4 to December 18 in the lead up to the end of the ceasefire. On December 17, the press reported that terrorist groups in Gaza fired 25 Qassam rockets at Israel. On December 18, HAMAS leadership announced the end of the ceasefire. In total, 361 rockets were launched on Israel from Gaza during the month of December. Targeted Israeli towns included Sderot and Ashkelon, as well as a number of nearby agricultural collectives (kibbutzim) and IDF bases. Palestinian terrorist groups increasingly used 122 mm Grad missiles, which landed in or near Ashkelon. While there were no fatalities resulting from rocket and mortar attacks between the June 19 ceasefire and December 18, these attacks resulted in numerous cases of shock and property damage, and disrupted daily life.

The reliance on rockets reflected technological advancements that allowed groups to manufacture the rockets cheaply, stockpile them, and launch them greater distances. As the rockets' ranges continued to increase, Israeli authorities in the port city of Ashdod initiated emergency response training in anticipation of eventual rocket attacks in their city. Mortars were used mainly against Israeli targets within or on the edge of the Gaza Strip, to include crossings, which had the effect of closing the crossings to the detriment of Gaza's residents.

From February 29 to March 1, the IDF conducted Operation Warm Winter against terrorist targets in Gaza. Following the November 4 tunnel discovery along the Gaza security fence, Israel undertook small-scale military operations and airstrikes against suspected launch teams and sites in Gaza. The Israeli Air Force increasingly launched airstrikes against launch teams in November and December following escalations in rocket and mortar attacks. Israel launched Operation Cast Lead in Gaza on December 27 in response to these rocket attacks. In the first few days of the operation, the Israeli air force and navy conducted a heavy bombardment of HAMAS targets in the Gaza Strip, including bases, training camps, and suspected weapons caches. These actions caused civilian casualties and some international observers alleged that the Israeli response was disproportionate.

Israel's security establishment remained concerned about the terrorist threat posed to Israel in the north by Hizballah and its Iranian and Syrian sponsors. Israeli security officials said Hizballah continued to provide support to select Palestinian groups to augment their capacity to conduct attacks against Israel. Throughout the year, Israeli officials claimed publicly that Hizballah had completely replenished its ranks, possessed more short and medium-range rockets than it had before the 2006 war, had moved arms back to southern Lebanon, and was providing training to HAMAS operatives from Gaza. While Israel's northern border remained comparatively quiet, the IDF continued a strong exercise schedule and military presence in the Golan Heights.

HAMAS and Hizballah continued to finance their terrorist activities against Israel mostly through state sponsors of terrorism Iran and Syria, and through various fundraising networks in Europe, the United States, the Middle East, and to a lesser extent, elsewhere. The funds channeled to these organizations frequently passed through major international financial capitals, such as Dubai, Bahrain, Hong Kong, Zurich, London, or New York. Unlawful funding bound for terrorists that may pass through Israel's financial sector, however, was well monitored and often blocked. Israel has adopted strong measures to prevent terrorist financing through its financial sector or through the smuggling of financial instruments. Regulation and enforcement of its domestic financial industry was equivalent in scope and effect to other highly industrialized and developed nations. Israel's Counterterrorist Finance regime is administered as part of its Anti-Money Laundering program (AML/CFT).

The Israeli National Police (INP), with the advice of the security services, is charged with enforcement of counterterrorist finance laws. Regulation of and intelligence on financial crimes is coordinated by the Israel Money Laundering and Terror Financing Prohibition Authority (IMPA), in coordination with the National Security Council. The INP reported no indication of an overall increase in financial crime relative to previous years. The IMPA received approximately 17,152 suspicious transaction reports, disseminated 529 intelligence reports to law enforcement agencies and to foreign Financial Intelligence Units, and reported that approximately USD two million was frozen or forfeited in AML/CTF-related actions.

On the law enforcement front, the ISA and INP continued to cooperate with U.S. law enforcement agencies on cases involving U.S. citizens killed in terrorist attacks. On October 29, the Knesset, the Israeli parliament, voted to continue work on a biometrics bill by sending it to the Constitution, Law, and Justice Committee for further work. The bill proposed that Israel switch to "smart" identification methods such as fingerprints and digital photographs on identification cards and passports.

The Israeli government released convicted Lebanese terrorist Samir Kuntar and four Hizballah militants on July 16 in exchange for the remains of two Israeli soldiers whose capture by Hizballah sparked the 2006 War with Lebanon.

The Israeli Counterterrorism Bureau issued a warning in October in advance of the Jewish holiday season that terrorist groups may attempt to kidnap Israeli tourists in the Sinai. Terrorists held hostage and later killed four Israeli citizens at the Chabad House as part of the November 26 attacks on Mumbai, India.

West Bank and Gaza

The Palestinian Authority's (PA) counterterrorism efforts improved in 2008, with Prime Minister Salam Fayyad's government engaged in efforts to control terrorist groups, particularly HAMAS. The PA was unable to undertake counterterrorism efforts in the HAMAS-controlled Gaza Strip, however. Besides being responsible for hundreds of rocket, mortar, and small arms attacks into Israel, HAMAS and other armed groups in Gaza engaged in tunneling activity, and smuggled weapons, cash, and other contraband into the Gaza Strip. HAMAS has created its own security forces in Gaza, built around its military wing cadres, which now number at least 15,000. In the West Bank, PA security forces

(PASF) followed up on efforts to establish law and order and fight terrorist cells with security deployments to Jenin, Bethlehem, and Hebron. All observers, including Israeli security officials, credited PASF with significant security improvements across the West Bank.

Terrorist groups such as HAMAS, Palestinian Islamic Jihad (PIJ), Popular Front for the Liberation of Palestine (PFLP), and the al-Aqsa Martyrs Brigades (AAMB) remained active, but their ability to carry out attacks from the West Bank has been degraded. Extremist settler groups were also a threat in the West Bank, and have engaged in attacks against Palestinians and incitement against Palestinians and Israeli security forces.

The primary PA security forces are the National Security Forces (NSF), police, Preventive Security Organization (PSO), Presidential Guard (PG), General Intelligence (GI or Mukhabarat), and Civil Defense. All forces are under the Interior Minister's operational control and follow the Prime Minister's guidance. In the Gaza Strip, HAMAS has established separate internal intelligence, police, coastal patrol, border guard, and "Executive Force" organizations. HAMAS military-wing members were often integrated into their ranks. Militias in Gaza such as the HAMAS and PIJ military wings, the AAMB, and an assortment of clan-based armed groups also carried out attacks against Israel.

Palestinian terrorist groups, particularly PIJ and HAMAS, received substantial foreign funding and support from foreign terrorist organizations, mainly those based in Syria and Lebanon. The PA has aggressively pursued HAMAS-linked groups and institutions in the West Bank, but has not fully dismantled HAMAS or other terrorist organizations and their infrastructure in territory under its control. In March, a HAMAS cell from the southern West Bank carried out a suicide bombing in Dimona, Israel, killing an Israeli woman. In April, PIJ gunmen infiltrated the Tulkarm industrial area and killed two Israeli security guards.

The situation in and around Gaza was much worse. In April, HAMAS gunmen killed two Israeli civilians at the Nahal Oz fuel terminal after infiltrating into Israel. Over 3200 rockets and mortars were fired from Gaza into Israel in 2008, killing eight Israelis and one third-country national, and causing several injuries. HAMAS also engaged in tunneling activity and smuggled weapons, cash, and other contraband into the Gaza Strip.

No progress was made in apprehending, prosecuting, or bringing to justice the perpetrators of the October 2003 attack on a U.S. Embassy convoy in Gaza that killed three USG contractors and critically injured a fourth.

Cooperation between the PA and the Government of Israel security services improved in 2008. Nevertheless, PASF commanders have complained that the IDF did not coordinate counterterrorism efforts with them and conducted unilateral raids in towns in Palestinian areas. The PA protected and returned several Israelis, including IDF soldiers, who had inadvertently entered Palestinian cities, including Jenin, Jericho, and Bethlehem.

The United States worked with PA security commanders to assist their CT efforts, including in its deployments to Jenin, Bethlehem, and Hebron. The Antiterrorism Assistance Program provided training for over 200 PA security personnel, primarily members of the Presidential Guard.

In the West Bank, PASF's ability to counter terrorism was hindered by a lack of resources, unclear chain-of-command, and IDF-imposed restrictions on their movement, equipment, and operations. PASF officials frequently raised concerns about operational difficulties due to IDF restrictions on PASF movements. Efforts to arrest and prosecute terrorists were also impeded by a disorganized legal system and inadequate prison infrastructure. PA courts were inefficient and failed to ensure fair and expeditious trials, while most Palestinian prisons were destroyed in Israeli military operations during the second Intifada and have not been rebuilt.

President Abbas and PM Salam Fayyad have publicly and consistently supported a security program that includes disarming fugitive militants, aggressively arresting members of terrorist organizations, and gradually dismantling armed groups. PM Fayyad has condemned violence against Israelis in harsh terms and taken rapid action against those involved in attacks. Since becoming Prime Minister, Fayyad has condemned every attack against Israelis as contrary to Palestinian interests and commitments, and has ordered immediate action, including arrests and prosecutions.

The Palestinian Monetary Authority (PMA) continued building a Financial Follow-Up Unit (FFU) and developing capacity to track and deter financial transactions used to fund terrorist activity. The PA Cabinet improved efforts to counter terrorist financing, and the Finance Ministry worked with the Justice Ministry, Attorney-General, Supreme Judicial Council, and (as appropriate) Interior and Waqf Ministries to shut down illegal NGOs and charities. USAID supported the PA's financial sector reform efforts through its Modernizing Financial Institutions project. The PA enacted Anti-Money Laundering (AML) legislation in late 2007 and used its provisions to freeze suspect bank accounts, although the law does not criminalize all terrorist financing activities. The PA continued to experience substantial shortcomings in investigating and prosecuting financial crimes due to personnel shortages and limited technical expertise in law enforcement and the judiciary. The PA is also lagging in its implementation of the AML law due to limited regulatory guidance for the private sector.

Jordan

In its public statements and security measures, the Government of Jordan continued to place a high priority on its fight against violent extremism, against a backdrop of low support for terrorism among Jordanians. The Pew Research Center Global Attitudes survey of 2008 indicated that only 19 percent of Jordanian Muslims expressed confidence in Usama bin Ladin and only 25 percent believed suicide bombing was ever justified. This is approximately the same as 2007, but reflects a multi-year downward trend.

According to the same survey, however, Jordan was the only Muslim country in which most respondents had favorable opinions of HAMAS, a designated foreign terrorist organization. The demographic realities attendant to hosting a majority Palestinian population, coupled with intensifying concern in Jordan about the stalled peace process and instability in the Palestinian areas, were among the factors behind a government decision to renew contact with HAMAS. News of the meetings first surfaced in July. Jordan in recent years had maintained one of the more antagonistic policies toward HAMAS among Arab states.

The Jordanian government offered little public comment on its motivations and plans for engagement with HAMAS, saying talks were narrowly focused on security issues. According to an August poll by the Jordan Center for Strategic Studies, conducted after the first public reports of the HAMAS-Jordan meetings, the percentage of Jordanian respondents who said they viewed HAMAS as a "legitimate resistance organization" increased from 59 to 71 percent since June; the pollster attributed the rise in HAMAS' popularity in part to the HAMAS-Government of Jordan warming trend.

Even as the Jordan-HAMAS relationship thawed somewhat, the Jordanian government continued to express its staunch support for the Palestinian Authority, led by Fatah's Mahmoud Abbas, and for the peace process. Noteworthy in this regard was Jordan's ongoing training of over a thousand Palestinian security forces at the Jordan International Police Training Center (JIPTC) outside of Amman. Throughout the year, graduates were deployed in the West Bank cities of Jenin and Hebron. These forces contributed significantly to the security of these areas and helped advance peace and stability in the West Bank.

Jordan continued to reinforce the need for moderate authentic Islam worldwide. In a mid-November statement on the third anniversary of the 2005 Amman hotel bombings that killed dozens of Jordanians, King Abdullah II reiterated the need to fight terrorism and takfirism (when Muslims assert that other Muslims are not true followers of Islam, and in some cases deserving of death), and to deliver an Islamist message based on moderation and rejection of extremism. Also in November, Jordan hosted a conference entitled "Toward an Islamic Renaissance Plan." Participants called on the Arab media to "open the media, cultural, and political doors for the trends of centrism and moderation... to enable this trend to reach the large masses, which are grabbed by the trends of religious and non-religious extremism and fanaticism."

Putting such directives into practice, Jordan's Public Security Directorate (PSD) inaugurated a program in November to expose criminals in the general prison population suspected of takfiri sympathies to a select group of jurists and professors of Islamic law. It was also intended to help convince them, through dialogue, to revise their extremist thinking and thus, limit the danger that those prisoners would influence other inmates. More generally, Jordan's various security services sought to identify potential radicals before they become violent and to direct them toward a more moderate path.

Jordan's security forces remained vigilant against terrorist threats. The State Security Court (SSC), a special tribunal for terrorism and other cases that have both civilian and military judges and attorneys, maintained a heavy caseload and brought many to trial while convicting others.

Some examples:

In August, the SSC sentenced 15 men to prison for plotting to recruit people to fight Americans in Iraq, also convicting the defendants of plotting actions that would have subjected the Kingdom to hostile acts.

In June, the Court sentenced three men after they were convicted on charges of storing weapons in Jordan for HAMAS. The court sentenced Ayman Naji Hamadallah to 15 years in jail with hard labor and handed down five-year jail terms against Muhammad Ahmad Abu-Rabi and Ahmad Abu-Dhyab. The defendants were convicted on the charge of "conspiring to commit acts of terrorism."

Also in June, the SSC sentenced an al-Qa'ida (AQ) network affiliate, Awni Mansi, to life imprisonment with hard labor on charges of possessing automatic weapons with illicit intent and attempted murder during a shoot-out with police in Irbid in January 2007. According to the indictment, Mansi had been assigned by an AQ member in Syria to recruit Jordanian men for training in Syria and Lebanon before being sent to Iraq.

In May, the SSC sentenced Sattam Zawahra, Nidal Momani, and Tharwat Daraz to 15-year prison terms after convicting them of plotting to assassinate President George W. Bush during his visit to Jordan in November 2006. The tribunal first handed the defendants the death penalty but immediately commuted the sentence to 15 years because they were "still young and deserve a second chance in life."

It should also be noted that in May, Jordan's Supreme Court overturned the 10-year sentence of Muammar Ahmad Yusuf al-Jaghbir, who had been convicted for his role in the 2002 murder of USAID official Laurence Foley in Amman. The Court referred the case back to the SSC.

While the security forces and the SSC responded effectively to terrorism, some legal tools proved impotent. For example, certain multilateral conventions on counterterrorism that the Jordanians have ratified (for example, the UN Convention Against Hostage Taking, Suppression of Terrorist Bombings, Suppression of Acts of Nuclear Terrorism), were not recognized by the Ministry of Justice as able to withstand judicial scrutiny because they were never enacted by Parliament and/or published in the Gazette.

In June, the Jordanian Securities Commission Board of Commissioners issued anti-money laundering (AML) regulations for securities activities, a positive step toward defining obligated entities falling under the regulatory purview of the Commission. These regulations established requirements for creating effective internal anti-money laundering, record keeping requirements, and required specific due diligence procedures for dealing with high risk customers, including politically exposed persons. The lack of comprehensive legislation addressing terrorist financing, however, remained a gap in Jordanian efforts to impede money laundering and terrorist financing (CTF). During 2008, over 400 Jordanians in banks, the insurance commission, Jordan Customs, the Public Security Directorate, the General Intelligence Directorate, as well as judges and prosecutors, received training on the full range of AML/CTF issues.

In mid-December, the United States and Jordan signed an agreement to work cooperatively to detect, deter, and interdict illicit smuggling of nuclear material, deepening the Jordanian-U.S. partnership in the global effort to prevent nuclear terrorism and proliferation. The agreement will help Jordan expand its detection systems at various ports of entry and lead to the training of Jordanian officials on the use and maintenance of the equipment.

Kuwait

The Government of Kuwait exerted measured effort but made little progress in combating terrorism; successive parliamentary dissolutions prevented the enactment ofstronger antiterrorism and money laundering legislation, and the government continued to have difficulty prosecuting terrorists and terrorism financiers and facilitators.

Kuwait was an effective and reliable partner in providing security for U.S. military installations and convoys in Kuwait. The risk of a terrorist attack in Kuwait remained high, however, because of the government-welcomed presence of U.S. forces in the country.

Kuwait lacked legal provisions to deal with conspiracies to commit terrorist acts, a problem exacerbated by the contentious relationship between the executive branch (headed by Kuwait's ruling family) and the elected legislative body, the National Assembly, which must approve such legislation. In general, the Kuwaiti government was more likely to take action against non-Kuwaiti residents involved in terrorist facilitation, but showed reluctance to take legal or preventative action against key local Sunni extremists unless there was a perception of clear and direct danger to Kuwaiti or U.S. interests.

The Kuwait's Ministry of Awqaf (religious endowments) and Islamic Affairs' World Moderation Center offered a 45-day moderation course, which over 700 imams have completed thus far.[10] The Center also began offering this course to high school Islamic studies teachers. During the year, Kuwaiti officials visited the Kingdom of Saudi Arabia's rehabilitation center with the intent to establish a similar center in Kuwait; the Kuwaiti Prime Minister announced this initiative in a September meeting with the Secretary of State of the United States. However, as of year's end, the Rehabilitation Center had not yet been established reportedly due to legal constraints. The Amir of Kuwait made a call for tolerance and dialogue at the November UN General Assembly-sponsored Interfaith Dialogue in New York.

The Government of Kuwait increased its cooperation with NATO by conducting a six-day joint exercise in November that focused on combating terrorist attacks and piracy. Kuwait Army Commandos, Kuwait National Guards, and a Jordanian Special Forces Unit also participated in a November joint exercise on combating terrorism in residential areas.

Kuwait experienced a dramatic increase in dialogue on counterterrorism; the government engaged in numerous high-level counterterrorism talks with U.S. officials including the President, and senior civilian and military officials on issues ranging from border security, cyber security, and recidivism of terrorists. In March, Kuwait participated in an Antiterrorism Assistance (ATA) workshop designed to improve its interagency counterterrorism coordination.

The Kuwaiti government lacked sufficient enforcement mechanisms for combating money laundering and terrorist financing, thus hindering its

[10] In 2005, Kuwait's Ministry of Awqaf (religious endowments) and Islamic Affairs launched the World Moderation Center, an initiative to spread moderation and to combat extremism. In 2006, 86 Islamic Education supervisors took the same 45-day training, and in 2007, 283 senior Islamic Education teachers from the Ministry of Education and 58 instructors at the Religious Education College took the course.

effectiveness. The government implemented no cash reporting requirements for individuals leaving the country, and this was a significant vulnerability. While money laundering was a criminal offense, terrorist financing was not specifically prohibited. Kuwait had established an Anti-Money Laundering/Combating Terrorist Financing Committee, with representation from a wide range of government ministries and domestic financial institutions. Kuwait was also an active member of the Middle East and North Africa Financial Action Task Force. Although Kuwait had a Financial Intelligence Unit, it did not exercise independent authority in accordance with current international standards. A revised anti-money laundering draft law, which would criminalize terrorist financing, has been pending Council of Ministers' approval and subsequent referral to the National Assembly for passage since August. The Ministry of Social Affairs and Labor regulates charities; transfers of donated funds abroad must be approved by the ministry.

The Kuwaiti government made several arrests on terrorism-related charges, but was unable to successfully prosecute or detain for a lengthy period because of the lack of evidence and/or the lack of a clear definition of terrorism under its constitutional framework.

Significant acquittals took place during the year:

- In February, Kuwait's highest court, the Court of Cassation, acquitted two Kuwaiti former Guantanamo Bay Detention Camp detainees. The public prosecutor failed to convince the court that the defendants endangered Kuwait's ties with friendly nations by joining al-Qa'ida (AQ) and the Taliban. The Kuwaiti government later acknowledged its failure to effectively monitor the movements of these defendants when former detainee Abdullah al-Ajmi, along with another Kuwaiti citizen, participated in a March suicide attack in Mosul, Iraq.
- On April 23, the Court of Appeals overturned a seven-year sentence (in absentia) and acquitted two Peninsula Lions terrorists involved in the January 2005 confrontations with the police.

In October, the Kuwaiti Council of Ministers published an Action Plan which included and allocated USD 2.7 billion for counterterrorism initiatives to be implemented by the Ministry of Interior by 2012. Among them were:

- Counterterrorism and Radicalism programs (USD 2.6 million): These programs would focus on enforcing international security agreements related to terrorism and radicalism, countering radical thought, engaging the media to denounce radicalism, establishing preventive security measures to protect infrastructure and vital installations, censoring radical web sites, reviving the role of NGOs in combating radical thought, and protecting Kuwaiti interests all around the world.

- CCTV Surveillance System (USD 1 billion): This project aims at monitoring and securing vital installations, highways, populous areas, land borders, and islands.

Lebanon

Since 2004, there have been numerous assassinations and assassination attempts of prominent Lebanese figures, including former Prime Minister Rafiq Hariri. The attacks targeted Lebanese political and military figures and journalists, many of whom were critical of Syrian interference in Lebanon. All of these attacks remained unsolved at year's end. The UN International Independent Investigation Commission (UNIIIC) was appointed to investigate the Hariri assassination and related cases.

Terrorist violence in 2008 included the following incidents:

- On January 15, a U.S. Embassy armored vehicle was attacked with an improvised explosive device north of Beirut, injuring two embassy body guards, killing three Lebanese bystanders, and injuring 20 others, including one American citizen.
- On January 25, a car bomb in the Hazmieh suburb of Beirut killed an Internal Security Force (ISF) Intelligence officer that had been assisting with UNIIIC's investigation, along with his driver and four others.
- On August 13, a road side bomb detonated in Tripoli, killing 12 Lebanese Armed Forces (LAF) soldiers, six civilians, and wounding more than fifty.
- On September 29, a road side car bomb in Tripoli detonated, killing four LAF soldiers and two civilians.
- On September 10, a car bomb attack killed Sheikh Saleh al-Aridi, a senior member of the Lebanese Democratic Party led by Druze leader Talal Arslan. This was the first assassination since 2004 that targeted a pro-Syrian politician.

The end of former President Emile Lahoud's term in November 2007 and the subsequent vacuum in the presidency left Lebanon in a state of political turmoil. The political deadlock lasted until May 2008, when the government's designation of Hizballah's independent communications network as illegal and decision to remove the Hizballah-loyal chief of airport security sparked armed clashes between Hizballah and other groups in Beirut that quickly spread to other parts of the country. The clashes ended a few days later with the help of Arab League intervention which led to the Qatari-brokered Doha Agreement of May 21. The agreement ended the months-long political impasse and paved the way for the May 25 election of consensus candidate former LAF Commander Michel Sleiman as president. A national unity government was officially formed on July 11, including three cabinet ministers appointed by the President, 16 ministers appointed by the majority March 14 coalition, and 11 ministers appointed by the March 8 opposition (including one minister from Hizballah), as agreed in Doha.

In September, the new government selected General Jean Kahwagi as the new LAF Commander. Kahwagi is a respected commander with experience in the Nahr al-Barid Palestinian refugee camp fighting Fatah al-Islam (FAI) terrorists in an urban setting. The U.S. government has an active antiterrorism assistance program with the LAF, which includes both training and equipment.

While the Lebanese government has made progress, there were concerns about its ability to combat terrorism, especially in Lebanon's 12 Palestinian refugee camps. A porous border with Syria, weak internal camp security by Palestinian authorities and Lebanese security authorities, and reticence to enter the camps all contributed to a concern that there would be another confrontation against an armed group in one of the camps. The most widely predicted venue for such a clash is in Lebanon's most populous refugee camp, Ain al Hilweh, near the southern city of Sidon. The camp is well known for intra-Palestinian violence and is a safe haven for fugitives.[11] As of December, the Lebanese authorities were reportedly making efforts to capture Abdel al-Rahman Awad, believed to be the successor of FAI leader Shaker al-Abssi. (Abssi is a fugitive, and there is speculation that he is in Syria or that he has been killed by Syrian security authorities.)

UN Security Council Resolution (UNSCR) 1559 called for respect for the sovereignty and political independence of Lebanon, the end of foreign interference in Lebanon, and the disarming and disbanding of all Lebanese and non-Lebanese militias. Hizballah, which the United States has designated as a Foreign Terrorist Organization, is also a political party represented in Lebanon's cabinet and parliament. While the Lebanese government was committed to fulfilling the provisions of UNSCR 1559,

---

[11] Ain al Hilweh internal security relies largely on Palestinian group Fatah forces. Cooperation among the Palestinians and the government led to the establishment in 2005 of a Palestinian-Lebanese Dialogue Committee. The committee works towards establishing cooperative security arrangements and reducing the poor conditions in the camps that create a fertile environment for extremist ideology.

it maintained that implementation of Hizballah's disarmament should be accomplished through national dialogue rather than force. President Sleiman launched a new round of the National Dialogue talks in September. (The previous National Dialogue began in 2006 and was never resumed after the 2006 war.) The 14 participants in the dialogue represent the major Lebanese political parties that participated in negotiations for the May 2008 Doha Agreement. After the third round of talks in December, participants agreed to form a committee to evaluate participants, proposals for a "National Defense Strategy," which is intended to include how to deal with Hizballah's weapons.

Border security remained problematic. Even with LAF troop deployments after the 2006 war, the Government of Lebanon still does not exercise control over parts of the border in the Hizballah-dominated Bekaa Valley, in addition to the wider problem of Hizballah's military presence in the southern suburbs of Beirut, southern Lebanon, and parts of the Bekaa Valley. It was quite likely that smuggling of weapons from Syria to Hizballah and other militant groups in Lebanon continued. Reports from the UN Interim Force in Lebanon (UNIFIL) and the LAF said there was no conclusive evidence of arms smuggling to Hizballah in the area of southern Lebanon patrolled by UNIFIL (south of the Litani river). This was despite Hizballah officials' comments to the press that the organization is now more heavily armed than it was before the 2006 war with Israel.

UNSCR 1701 called upon Lebanon to secure its borders at all entry points to prevent entry of arms, weapons of mass destruction, or related material without its consent. In May 2007, the UN Secretary General dispatched a border security team to Lebanon (the Lebanon Independent Border Assessment Team or LIBAT) to assess the monitoring of Lebanon's border with Syria. In July 2008, a second assessment team (LIBAT II), responsible for assessing the implementation of the recommendations of LIBAT I, was sent to Lebanon. The overall assessment of LIBAT II was that the borders are as penetrable and insecure as they were in 2007 and concluded that the rate of implementation of LIBAT I's recommendations was insufficient. At the border crossing points and particularly along the eastern border with Syria, little progress was observed. However, some positive steps like the installation of security equipment such as scanners and computerization of passport control have been taken.

Lebanese officials played an active leadership role in the 2008 MENA-FATF (Middle East and North Africa Financial Action Task Force) and the US-MENA (Middle East and North Africa) Private Sector Dialogue. Lebanon's Financial Intelligence Unit is the Special Investigation Commission (SIC), an independent legal entity empowered to investigate suspicious financial transactions. It investigated 186 cases involving allegations of money laundering, terrorism, and terrorist financing activities. The SIC referred requests for designation or asset freeze regarding Hizballah and groups affiliated with Hizballah to the Ministry of Foreign Affairs, but does not require banks to freeze these assets, because the Lebanese government does not consider Hizballah a terrorist organization.

Lebanese authorities maintained that the amnesty for Lebanese individuals involved in acts of violence during the 1975-90 civil wars prevented the government from prosecuting terrorist cases of concern to the United States. These cases included individuals involved in the 1985 hijacking of TWA Flight 847, during which a U.S. Navy diver was murdered; the bombings of the U.S. Embassy in Beirut in 1983 and 1984; and the abduction, torture, and murder of U.S. hostages in Lebanon from 1984 to 1991. A Hizballah official suspected in several bombing attacks against U.S. citizens, Imad Mughniyeh, was killed in Damascus, Syria in February 2008. Mohammad Ali Hamadi, who spent 18 years in a German prison for his role in the TWA hijacking, was released in December 2005 and was believed to be in Lebanon. The United States continued its efforts to bring him to trial before a U.S. court and has formally requested his extradition. The United States does not have an extradition treaty with Lebanon.

Libya

The United States rescinded Libya's designation as a state sponsor of terrorism in June 2006. Libya renounced terrorism and weapons of mass destruction in 2003 and has continued to cooperate with the United States and the international community to combat terrorism and terrorist financing.

In November 2007, Egyptian cleric and al-Qa'ida (AQ) leader Ayman al-Zawahiri announced a merger between AQ and the Libyan Islamic Fighting Group (LIFG). In an audiotape, al-Zawahiri urged AQ fighters to topple the Government of Libya, describing Muammar al-Qadhafi as an "enemy of Islam" and criticizing the 2003 decision to renounce WMD and terrorism. According to press accounts, LIFG maintains a limited presence in eastern Libya and has facilitated the transfer of foreign fighters to join insurgents fighting U.S.-led forces in Iraq.

On August 14, Libya and the United States signed a comprehensive claims settlement agreement to provide compensation to claimants in both countries who allege the other country's responsibility in incidents causing injury or death. Included in the settlement agreement are claims stemming from the 1988 bombing of Pan Am flight 103 in Lockerbie, Scotland, and the 1986 bombing of the La Belle nightclub in Berlin. On October 31, the

Secretary of State certified to Congress that settlement funds had been received, paving the way for the confirmation of a U.S. Ambassador to Tripoli and the expansion of normalized relations.

Morocco

Morocco pursued a comprehensive counterterrorism approach that emphasized vigilant security measures, including international cooperation, and counter-radicalization policies. Characteristics of groups disrupted by Moroccan authorities supported previous analysis that Morocco's threat of terrorist attack continued to stem from the existence of numerous small "grassroots" extremist groups. These groups, sometimes referred to collectively as adherents to Moroccan Salafia Jihadia ideology[12], remained isolated from one another, small in size (less than 50 individuals each), and tactically limited. The existence of these relatively small groups pointed to the need for continued vigilance, but the Government of Morocco's counterterrorism efforts have done a good job of minimizing the threat.

There were reports of considerable numbers of Moroccans going to northern Mali and Algeria to receive training from AQIM elements with some returning to Morocco and others traveling to Iraq to conduct terrorist attacks. Although AQIM has been unable to support a successful terrorist attack in Morocco to date, Moroccan authorities remained concerned about the inspiration and knowledge transfer that AQIM may have provided to Moroccan extremists. AQIM repeatedly tried to incite Moroccans to commit violence against their government through website propaganda. The government remained concerned about numbers of veteran Moroccan jihadists returning from Iraq to propagate and conduct terrorist attacks at home. While overall numbers of Moroccans fighting in Iraq were difficult to confirm, some press reporting put the number at several hundred. A further cause of concern is Moroccans who were radicalized during their stays in Western Europe, such as those connected with the 2004 Madrid train bombings.

The Moroccan government pursued a comprehensive counterterrorism approach that, building on popular rejection of terrorism, emphasizes neutralizing existing terrorist cells through traditional law enforcement and preemptive security measures, and prevented terrorist recruitment through comprehensive counter-radicalization policies. Morocco aggressively targeted and dismantled terrorist cells within the Kingdom by leveraging policing techniques, coordinating and focusing the security services, and expanding and bolstering regional partnerships. These efforts resulted in

---

[12] Salafi Jihadist ideology is a catch-all term used by Moroccan authorities to describe fundamentalist teachings originally emanating from the eastern Arab world.

the neutralization of numerous Salafi Jihadi-inspired terrorist groups, the most prominent were:

- In February 2008, Moroccan authorities arrested a 36-person strong terrorist network in the cities of Nador, Rabat, Marakesh, and Casablanca. In addition to attack plotting against Moroccan and Western targets, group leader and de facto double-agent Moroccan-Belgium Abdelkader Belliraj, now in Moroccan custody, was suspected of participating in a bank robbery and half a dozen assassinations in Europe and smuggling arms into Morocco.
- In July, security services arrested, in various cities, 35 members of a terrorist network specializing in the recruitment of volunteers for Iraq.
- In August, another 15-person network calling itself Fath al-Andalus was reportedly disbanded in Laayoune, Western Sahara, and various cities in Morocco. The group was allegedly planning bombing attacks against UN peacekeeping forces in Western Sahara and tourists sites in Morocco.
- In December, authorities reportedly arrested five members of a terrorist cell in the northeastern Moroccan city of Berkane, along with nine other group members in other cities, who were allegedly preparing to rob banks in order to acquire arms for terrorist acts.

In addition to traditional security measures, Morocco's King Mohammed VI has promoted significant efforts to reduce extremism and dissuade individuals from becoming radicalized. Ordinary citizens providing tips to Moroccan security authorities have been instrumental in detecting many terrorist groups in Morocco, according to Interior Ministry sources.

After the 2003 Casablanca bombings, Morocco steadily increased attention to and focused on upgrading places of worship, modernization of the teaching of Islam, and strengthening the Ministry of Endowments and Islamic Affairs. In September 2008, Sheikh Mohamed Ben Abderrahman Al Maghraoui issued a highly inflammatory fatwa (a religious opinion on Islamic law issued by an Islamic scholar) that asserted the validity of marriage of girls, as young as nine years old. Moroccan authorities responded aggressively by discrediting the radical Sheikh and closing down approximately 60 Koranic schools under his supervision, and initiating an official inquiry into his competence. In addition, the public prosecutor's office initiated a criminal case against him for encouraging pedophilia. The Council of Ulamas, Morocco's highest religious body, was charged by the King, who is its leader, to "combat the hoaxes peddled by proponents of extremism," and to ensure the safeguarding of Morocco's tolerant Sunni Islam identity.

After this event and in a speech to the Higher Council of Ulamas in late September, the King announced his "proximity strategy," calling for the rehabilitation of 3,180 mosques, the training of 33,000 imams, and increasing the number of regional Ulama councils from 30 to 70 across Morocco, to help propagate a culture of religious tolerance and confront extremism. The pioneering experiment, begun in 2007, of training and using women as spiritual guides continued.

The Government of Morocco, and frequently the King himself, regularly and strongly condemned terrorist acts, wherever they occurred. The King has been particularly outspoken in the wake of attacks in neighboring Algeria, in expressions of sympathy for and solidarity with foreign governments and the victims.

The perceived injustice faced by the Palestinian people was cited by Moroccan officials as the single greatest radicalizing element among Moroccan extremists. Although the Moroccan Parliament remained in need of strengthening and reform, it nonetheless provided a forum for airing moderate Islamist-inspired views in a political setting, offering a counter-example to extremist rhetoric.

During the year, the Moroccan government continued to implement internal reforms aimed at ameliorating the socio-economic factors that terrorists exploit. The National Initiative for Human Development, launched by the King in 2005, is a $1.2 billion program designed to generate employment, combat poverty, and improve infrastructure, with a special focus on rural areas.

In 2008, Morocco implemented elements of a comprehensive anti-money laundering bill passed in May 2007 that provided the legal basis for the monitoring, investigation, and prosecution of illegal financial activities. The new laws allow for the freezing of suspicious accounts, permit the prosecution of terrorist finance related crimes, and call for the establishment of a Financial Intelligence Unit. U.S. and EU programs are providing Moroccan police, customs, central bank, and government financial officials with training to recognize money laundering methodologies. Morocco has a relatively effective system for disseminating U.S. government and UN Security Council Resolution terrorist freeze lists to its financial sector and legal authorities. Morocco has frozen some terrorist-related accounts.

The Government of Morocco made firm public commitments that the struggle against terrorism would not be used to deprive individuals of their rights and emphasized adherence to human rights standards and increased law enforcement transparency as part of its approach. Non-governmental organizations were granted unprecedented access to prisons where individuals convicted of terrorism-related crimes were held. Terrorist suspects and convicts were generally accorded rights and due process of law.

Moroccan laws were effective in leading to numerous convictions and the upholding of convictions of multiple terrorism-related cases:

- In January, 50 defendants in the sensational 2007 Ansar al-Mehdi terrorist conspiracy trial were convicted and sentenced to prison. Alleged mastermind Hassan al-Khattab received a 25-year sentence. Forty-nine others, including four women and several members of the security forces, received sentences of two to 10 years.
- In November, the appeals court in Sale upheld the life sentence handed down last October of would-be suicide bomber Hicham Doukkali, who was wounded in August 2007 when his booby-trapped butane canister exploded in the central city of Meknes.
- In June, a court convicted 29 men belonging to a terrorist group known as the "Tetouan Cell," after its northern Moroccan town of origin, for plotting terrorist attacks.
- An appeals court also upheld the prison sentences, ranging from two to six years, of members of the terrorist group "Jamaat al Mouslimoun al Joudoud," who were arrested in 2005 on terrorism-related charges.

In April, following the mass escape in March of eight Salafist prisoners, and concerned the Moroccan prisons were serving as a place of radical fundamentalist networking and plotting, the government created a new ministerial-level Directorate General of Prison Affairs, separate from the Ministry of Justice. By the end of the year, all but one of the escapees had been recaptured. One was arrested in and returned from Algeria, according to the press.

In mid-November, the government announced the authorization of a $27.5 million emergency program, on top of an existing $81.5 million investment budget, designed to improve prison conditions and alleviate overcrowding. In addition to providing for the construction of six new penitentiaries, the program dedicated funds toward the government strategy of making new and existing penitentiaries spaces for reeducation and social reintegration into society. In November, Moroccan law enforcement entities initiated an unprecedented series of meetings with Salafist detainees with the goal of decreasing prison conflicts and violent recidivism, and improving prisoner treatment.

Another key to Morocco's counterterrorism efforts has been its emphasis on international cooperation. Moroccan authorities continued to disrupt plots to attack Moroccan, U.S. and other Western-affiliated targets, and aggressively investigated numerous individuals associated with international terrorist groups. The Government of Morocco accepted returnees from the U.S. detention facility at Guantanamo Bay and prosecuted them under Moroccan law. In mid-November, for example, a Moroccan appeals court sentenced former Guantanamo detainee Said Boujaidia to 10 years in prison on charges of conspiracy, sabotage, financing, and participating in a criminal gang.

Morocco has also forged solid cooperative relationships with European and African partners by sharing information and conducting joint operations. Morocco is considered a Mediterranean Partner of the North Atlantic Treaty Organization and the Organization for Security and Cooperation in Europe. Morocco worked closely with African partners such as Mauritania and Senegal and is striving to improve its relationship with Algeria, a dynamic sometimes complicated by political differences. The government used army and Ministry of Interior paramilitary forces to secure its borders as best it could but faced resource constraints and a vast border area. The Moroccan government removed and prosecuted several corrupt border officers suspected this year of accepting bribes to allow AQIM members to infiltrate Morocco, according to reports.

In the wake of an AQIM attack that killed 12 Mauritanian soldiers in the region of Tourine in mid-September, the Government of Morocco sent military advisors to Mauritania to provide the government with training and advice on the protection of military bases and patrolling techniques.

Oman

Oman promoted religious moderation and tolerance and proactively implemented counterterrorism strategies and cooperated with neighboring countries to prevent terrorists from entering or moving freely throughout the Arabian Peninsula. To better coordinate efforts to prevent terrorist-related activities, the government began the formation of a national terrorism operations and analysis center. While Oman is not a major financial center and did not have a significant money laundering problem, its financial system remained vulnerable to criminal activity. The government established a Financial Intelligence Unit attached to the Directorate of Financial Crimes of the Royal Oman Police and continued to work towards finalizing a draft counterterrorism financing law. In September, a Ministerial Decree strengthened the Oman Program for Anti-Money Laundering (by requiring certain non-banking establishments and companies to verify the identity of their clients and document financial transactions.

Oman's long coastline and relatively porous borders remained vulnerable to illegal transit by migrant workers, smugglers, human trafficking victims, terrorists, and individuals involved in the traffic and sale of illegal drugs. The government was concerned about the steady flow of illegal immigrants throughout the year attempting to enter Oman, often in transit to other destinations in the Arabian Peninsula, particularly the United Arab Emirates (UAE). The majority of the illegal immigrants apprehended were from Pakistan and Afghanistan. Somalis continued to attempt to cross the border into Oman from Yemen. The Omani government actively sought training and equipment through the U.S. and British military to support its efforts to control its land and maritime borders. U.S. military assistance was used to bolster coastal patrol operations and make Oman's remote inland borders with Yemen, Saudi Arabia, and the UAE less porous and easier to observe.

Qatar

While counterterrorism cooperation between Qatar and the United States remained positive, the United States continued to strive for increased cooperation with the Qatari government on information sharing.

There has not been a terrorist attack in Qatar since the March 19, 2005, suicide vehicle-borne improvised explosive device attack at an amateur theater playhouse that killed a British citizen. Cooperation with U.S. law enforcement authorities continued to improve during and after the course of the investigation of this case. Press reports indicated that up to 19 people of various nationalities, including one Qatari, were apprehended during the ensuing investigation. There were no reports of criminal prosecution in the case; however, many of the third country nationals who were apprehended were deported subsequent to the investigation.

The Qatar Authority for Charitable Activities is responsible for overseeing all domestic and international charitable activities, including approving international fund transfers by charities and monitoring overseas charitable, development, and humanitarian projects. The Authority reports annually to Qatari government ministries on the status of their oversight and humanitarian activities.

Cooperation with U.S. authorities on counterterrorist finance continued to develop. Qatar's Financial Information Unit (FIU) resides in the Qatar Central Bank. Local banks worked with the Central Bank and the FIU on counterterrorist finance and anti-money laundering issues, and bank officials attended U.S.-sponsored conferences.

Qatar was one of two countries in the Gulf with an Attorney General independent of the Ministry of Interior or Ministry of Justice, and equivalent to a ministerial level position. The Attorney General independently controlled and oversaw public prosecutions and appointed attorneys within the Public Prosecutors Office.

The USG has provided law enforcement and counterterrorism training under various programs, including the Antiterrorism Assistance (ATA) program. The Ministry of Interior and State Security each had an officer graduate from the FBI National Academy in 2008. In addition, the FBI provided counterterrorism and investigative training to larger groups both in Qatar and the United States. The exchanges and training have had a positive effect in maintaining a good relationship with Qatari law enforcement agencies and increasing their ability to deter, disrupt, and defeat terrorist activity in Qatar. Operationally, however, this capability has yet to be fully tried, tested, or proven.

Saudi Arabia

The Saudi government continued to build its counterterrorism capacity and efforts to counter extremist ideology. In the first six months of the year, the Ministry of Interior arrested 701 militants who had allegedly been planning to attack oil fields and other vital installations. In large scale sweeps, the Kingdom confiscated weapons, ammunition, sophisticated electronics equipment, and money. As of late summer, 520 of these suspects were still being held, awaiting trial on terrorism charges. The Saudis are developing a facilities security force following an unsuccessful attack in 2006 against one of the world's largest oil processing plants in the Eastern Province.

The Government of Saudi Arabia has announced terrorism trials for 991 individuals indicted on various terrorism-related charges including terrorist finance. After deciding to not establish a specific court for terrorist trials, the Ministry of Interior determined that trials will be conducted in a Sharia court, following established court procedures, as part of a strategy to confront terrorist ideologies within the existing system. The militants were divided into two groups: those who were directly involved in attacks and those who provided refuge, transportation, and funds. The General Court of Riyadh set up a 10-member bench to look into the initial case of 70 terrorist suspects, which included Saudis and foreigners. The court sessions will be restricted to the judges, lawyers, and the accused, which has led to criticism over the lack of transparency.

The Saudi government continued to make strides in its public counterterrorism programs. In July, the Ministry of Interior issued a statement demanding citizens remain vigilant to extremist activities, even within their own families, and report deviant behavior. In response, the Grand Mufti, Shayh Abd-al-Aziz Al al-Shaykh, issued a statement in support of the state's position on terrorism and warned citizens to be smart and not fall for the lies and deception of these people [terrorists] who are pretending to be good.

In an effort to combat terrorist ideologies, the Ministry of the Interior announced the arrest of five individuals, two of whom were not Saudi, for disseminating terrorist propaganda on Internet sites in August. The five individuals were charged with seeking to recruit young people to AQ thought and mobilize them to action in Saudi Arabia or abroad. From a technical standpoint, the Ministry noted that the websites were registered outside of Saudi Arabia and that the individuals owning the websites made frequent changes to the sites in a way that made it difficult for the Saudi government to shut down.

On a more basic level, the Ministry of Islamic Affairs launched an extensive media campaign to educate young Saudis on the correct teachings of Islam in order to prevent them from becoming drawn to extremist doctrines. The campaign included messages incorporated into Friday sermons at mosques, distribution of literature and tapes, and article postings on the Internet. In 2007, the Kingdom issued identification cards to imams and religious leaders to curb instances of unauthorized persons delivering Friday sermons. In 2008, the government continued to monitor the licensed imams and looked for instances of illegal sermons.

Saudi Arabia continued to make progress in combating money laundering and terrorism finance. The Saudi Capital Authority Market stressed that financial brokerage companies be bound to the same law combating money laundering and terrorism financing when designing swap agreements with foreign investors. Banks must report suspicious transactions to the Financial Investigations Unit (FIU), which is part of the Ministry of Interior, and provide the Saudi Arabia Monetary Agency's Department of Banking Inspection and the Anti-Money Laundering Unit with a copy of the report.

In September, the Ministry of Social Affairs announced the enforcement of rules and regulations on charitable organizations aimed at preventing terrorist finance. During Ramadan in September, the Ministry of Islamic Affairs tightened controls on charitable contributions. This was in response to a 2007 incident, where seven terrorist cells were apprehended after raising 20 million Saudi Riyals from donors who thought the money was for legitimate charitable uses. The Government has stated its intent to establish a Charities Commission to ensure rigorous implementation of existing terrorist financing regulations.

The United States continued to urge the Government of Saudi Arabia to pursue and prosecute terrorist financiers more vigorously. Last year's new cash courier regulations resulted in several individuals being investigated.

Since the inception of the government-run rehabilitation program for those with extremist ideologies, a number of rehabilitated extremists have been reintegrated into Saudi society. The program incorporates scholars, intellectuals, and psychologists with the goal of helping participants overcome their extremist viewpoints. The programs generally run for three to six months, and accommodate 20 individuals at a time. According to a Ministry of Interior study, foreign fighters were not typically Sharia experts and fell victim to the extremist cause by exposure to video, film, and other material that urged them to sympathize with people in Afghanistan and Iraq.

Tunisia

The Government of Tunisia continued to place a high priority on combating extremism and terrorism. In addition to using security and law enforcement measures, the Tunisian government pursued a variety of economic and social programs aimed at addressing the underlying challenges that can contribute to the spread of extremism. The Tunisian government actively prevented the formation of terrorist groups inside Tunisia, including prohibiting the formation of religious-based political parties and groups that it believed would pose a terrorist threat.

By carefully monitoring the activities of Tunisian extremists, both in Tunisia and abroad, Tunisian law enforcement organizations challenged the ability of terrorists to organize internally. Since the passage of Tunisia's 2003 Terrorism Law, approximately 1,000,Tunisians have been detained, charged, and/or convicted on terrorism-related charges. In 2008, the Tunisian judiciary prosecuted a steady stream of such cases:

- On February 21, the Tunis Court of Appeals upheld guilty verdicts but reduced the sentences for eight of the 30 Tunisians convicted in December 2007 of involvement in the December 2006/January 2007 terrorist plot known as the "Soliman" case, in which a terrorist cell called Assad Ibn Fourat's Army had allegedly targeted domestic and foreign (including U.S. and UK) interests in Tunisia.
- On July 12, the Tunis Court of First Instance convicted five Tunisians, including two security officials, of various terrorism-related charges.
- In two separate mid-August trials, 19 Tunisians were convicted on separate terrorist-related charges.

On March 10, al-Qa'ida in the Islamic Maghreb claimed responsibility for kidnapping two Austrian tourists along the Tunisia-Algeria border. The hostages were released in Mali on October 31, reportedly in exchange for a ransom of USD 2.8 million.

Tunisian extremists were involved in terrorist activities abroad, including in France, Italy, Iraq, and Lebanon. Domestically, the government worked to improve security procedures at borders and airports. A number of

Tunisians suspected of involvement in terrorist incidents abroad were also repatriated and subsequently charged with, or convicted, of terrorist activities.

United Arab Emirates

The Government of the United Arab Emirates (UAE) repeatedly condemned terrorist acts in Iraq, Lebanon, Pakistan, and elsewhere in the region. In order to prevent extremist preaching in UAE mosques, the General Authority of Islamic Affairs and Endowments provided prescribed guidelines for all Friday sermons and monitored compliance. The UAE worked to keep its education system free of radical influences and emphasized social tolerance and moderation.

The Container Security Initiative (CSI), which became operational at Port Rashid and Jebel Ali Port in the Emirate of Dubai in 2005, has three U.S. Customs and Border Protection officers co-located with the Dubai Customs Intelligence Unit at Port Rashid. On average, CSI reviewed approximately 250 bills of lading each week, resulting in about 20 non-intrusive inspections of U.S.-bound containers; examinations were conducted jointly with Dubai Customs officers, who shared information on trans-shipments from high risk areas, including those originating in Iran. The UAE has a cyber-crime law criminalizing the use of the Internet by terrorist groups to "promote their ideologies and finance their activities." The UAE has established a National Security Council charged with formulating and implementing a national strategic plan. Cooperation on law enforcement matters was hampered by the lack of a mutual legal assistance treaty (MLAT) between the United Arab Emirates and the United States.

The UAE continued efforts to strengthen its institutional capabilities to combat terrorist financing, but challenges remain. The 2008 MENA-FATF (Middle East North Africa Financial Action Task Force) Mutual Evaluation Report for the UAE, for example, made a recommendation to amend the federal anti-money laundering law and increase dedicated resources available to the Central Bank's Financial Intelligence Unit (FIU). Although the UAE has taken important steps to address hawala remittances, further vigilance is required. The UAE Central Bank provided training programs to financial institutions on money laundering and terrorist financing. The United States has encouraged the UAE to implement additional measures to combat Bulk Cash Smuggling (BCS), in particular from countries at higher risk of terrorist finance activity. Immigration and Customs Enforcement has provided Dubai Customs with BCS training for airport interdiction of contraband currency; joint BCS operations have been proposed. The Department of Justice also provided BCS training for prosecutors in Dubai.

The Central Bank initiated memoranda of understanding with regional FIUs, and performed anti-money laundering training both locally and regionally. The Central Bank investigated financial transactions and froze accounts in response to internal investigations.

Yemen

The security situation in Yemen continued to deteriorate during 2008 and was marked by a series of attacks against both Western and Yemeni interests, culminating in the September 17 suicide bombing of the U.S. Embassy in Sanaa that killed 18. This strategy of constant offense continued despite highly publicized raids on suspected terrorist cells by Yemeni security forces. Recruitment for al-Qa'ida in Yemen (AQY) remained strong, and the use of vehicle borne improvised explosive devices (VBIEDs) and suicide vests indicated a high level of training, coordination, and sophistication by Yemen's terrorist leadership. Conversely, the government's response to the terrorist threat was intermittent and its ability to pursue and prosecute suspected terrorists remained weak due to a number of shortcomings, including stalled draft counterterrorism legislation. The government's focus on the al-Houthi rebellion in the Sada'a governorate in the North of the country and internal security concerns distracted its forces from focusing on counterterrorism activities.

The largest success for Yemen's security forces in 2008 was an August raid on an AQY cell in Tarim, in the governorate of Hadramaut. Hamza al-Qaiti was killed along with four other suspected militants. Large numbers of weapons, devices to build car bombs, and explosives, including mortars that were similar to those used in the March attack on the U.S. Embassy, were uncovered.

In spite of this, the raid did little to deter or disrupt other AQY cells. One month after the August raid, at least seven assailants dressed in Yemeni security-service uniforms attacked the U.S. Embassy using two VBIEDs and suicide vests. While unable to gain access to the Embassy itself, the attack was sophisticated and well-coordinated. Final tallies brought the death toll to 18, including one American.

A formerly unknown group calling itself Islamic Jihad in Yemen immediately claimed responsibility for the attack. The group stated the attack was motivated by the August 11 raid in Tarim, among other reasons. Initially the Yemeni government allowed an FBI investigative team full access to evidence from the attack, but cooperation has since waned. Both Yemeni and U.S. officials believe that Islamic Jihad is AQ affiliated. AQY later claimed responsibility for the attack in an online extremist magazine.

In addition to the September 17 assault, there were over half a dozen terrorist attacks in 2008:

- In January, AQY claimed responsibility for the shooting deaths of two Belgian tourists and two Yemeni drivers in the southern governorate of Hadramaut.
- On March 18, four mortars fell short of the U.S. Embassy, injuring dozens at an adjacent girls' school.
- On April 6, three mortars hit residential complex housing western workers, including several U.S. Embassy employees in Sanaa, prompting the ordered departure of non-essential U.S. Embassy staff and family members.
- On April 30, two mortars hit the Customs Administration parking lot, causing a large explosion just adjacent to the Italian Embassy, believed by many to have been the intended target.
- In May, an AQY-affiliated group claimed that it fired a mortar onto the grounds of the presidential palace in Sanaa, but no official statement was released acknowledging the incident.
- In July, AQY claimed responsibility for a suicide car bomb attack of a central security forces compound in Hadramaut that killed eight people.

Prosecuting terrorists remained a large hurdle for Yemeni courts, largely because current law, as applied to counterterrorism and the financing of terrorism, remained weak. A working group drafted new counterterrorism legislation that was sent to a committee for review, where it remained at year's end.

The absence of effective counterterrorism legislation that criminalized the activities of those engaged in planning, facilitating, or carrying out acts of terrorism, both in Yemen and abroad, contributed to Yemen's appeal as safe haven and potential base of offensive operations for terrorists. For this reason, the government was forced to apply other available laws, including fraudulent document charges, to thwart foreign fighters going to Iraq.

The Government of Yemen continued to run its surrender program for wanted terrorists that it believes it cannot apprehend. The program provides lenient requirements for completion of convictions to those who surrender. In 2008, however, 17 prior program participants were returned to custody for recidivism. In March, convicted terrorist and February 2006 prison escapee Jaber al-Banna walked into a Yemeni security court and posted bond. His sentence was later reduced from 10 to five years, supposedly for handing himself in to the authorities. The decision will need to be ratified by the Yemeni Supreme Court before it is implemented, and it remained unclear whether the time al-Banna had already served, including time he spent outside prison once he escaped, will count against the five-year sentence. Jaber al-Banna is wanted by the United States for providing material support to a terrorist organization and conspiring to provide support to AQ. Al-Banna is on the FBI's most wanted list, but the Yemeni constitution precludes extradition of Yemeni citizens, even though he also has American citizenship.

South and Central Asia Overview

We are fighting the menace and we will continue to fight. But this is the fight for the peace of the world. This is the fight for the future of generations to come. The fight against extremism is a fight for the hearts and minds of people. It can't be won only by guns and bombs. The fight must be multifaceted.

— Asif Ali Zardari, President of Pakistan
UN General Assembly, New York City
September 25, 2008

Already terrorism plagued, South and Central Asia experienced more tragedy in 2008 as terrorists expanded their operations and networks across the region and beyond. The impact of the region's terrorist problem on the United States and its citizens grew more severe as dozens of U.S. citizens were attacked, kidnapped, or killed by violent extremists. In response, the U.S. worked to increase counterterrorism cooperation with its partners in South Asia. However, continuing political unrest in the region, weak governments, and competing factions within various South Asia governments, combined with increased terrorist activities, resulted in limited progress and made South Asia even less safe for U.S. citizens and interests than it was in 2007.

Although hundreds of terrorist attacks were conducted throughout South Asia, the year was punctuated by several high-profile and immensely destructive acts of terrorism, including the July 7 bombing of the Indian embassy in Kabul, Afghanistan, the November 26 attacks in Mumbai, India and the September 20 bombing of the Marriott Hotel in Islamabad, Pakistan.

The Taliban-led insurgency in Afghanistan remained strong and resilient in the south and east. Although the insurgency absorbed heavy combat and leadership losses, its ability to recruit foot soldiers from its core base of rural Pashtuns remained undiminished.

Pakistan continued to suffer from rising militancy and extremism. The United States remained concerned that the Federally Administered Tribal Areas (FATA) of Pakistan were being used as a safe haven for al-Qa'ida (AQ) terrorists, Afghan insurgents, and other extremists.

India ranked among the world's most terrorism-afflicted countries. It was the focus of numerous attacks from both externally-based terrorist organizations and internally-based separatist or terrorist entities. Several attacks inflicted large numbers of casualties, including the most devastating attack of the year on November 26 in Mumbai. Although clearly committed to combating violent extremism, the Indian government's counterterrorism efforts remained hampered by its outdated and overburdened law enforcement and legal systems. In the wake of the Mumbai terrorist attacks, India's Parliament has introduced bills to restructure its counterterrorism laws and has proposed a new agency, the National Investigative Agency, to create national-level capability to investigate and potentially prosecute acts of terrorism. Since the Mumbai attacks, India has also greatly increased counterterrorism cooperation with the United States.

Leading up to the national elections on December 29, Bangladesh's Caretaker Government attempted to crack down on those accused of terrorism and criminality. The Awami League won a landslide electoral victory, claiming 230 of the 299 seats in Parliament. It has pledged to focus serious attention on Bangladesh's counterterrorism needs and has championed the creation of a South Asia counterterrorism task force to enable countries to work together regionally to stamp out the rise of violent extremism.

In Sri Lanka, the government continued its military campaign against the Liberation Tigers of Tamil Eelam (LTTE), a U.S.-designated foreign terrorist organization. Both sides continued to engage in any means necessary tactics to fight the war. The LTTE used suicide bombings and other terrorist attacks, some of which caused serious civilian casualties. The government has been criticized for using paramilitary organizations that rely on abduction, extra-judicial killings and other illegal tactics to combat the LTTE and their suspected sympathizers. At the end of the year, the military recaptured most of the LTTE-held territory, including Killinochchi, but the LTTE continued to fight, reverting to more asymmetrical tactics, including the continued use of suicide bombers in the capital Colombo.

In April, the Communist Party of Nepal (Maoists) won the national Constituent Assembly election, and took control of various government ministries as well as the Prime Minister's position. Despite their electoral victory, the Maoists remained a U.S.-designated terrorist entity under the Terrorism Exclusion List.

The Central Asian region's most significant terrorist organizations include the Islamic Movement of Uzbekistan (IMU) and a splinter group, the Islamic Jihad Group (IJG). However, radical extremist groups such as Hizb ut-Tahrir (HT) foment an anti-Semitic, anti-Western ideology that may indirectly generate support for terrorism. HT, an extremist political movement advocating the establishment of a borderless, theocratic Islamic state throughout the entire Muslim world, has followers in Kyrgyzstan, Kazakhstan, Tajikistan, Uzbekistan, and elsewhere. The United States has no evidence that HT has committed any acts of international terrorism, but the group's radical anti-American and anti-Semitic ideology is sympathetic to acts of violence against the United States and its allies. HT has publicly called on Muslims to travel to Iraq and Afghanistan to fight Coalition Forces.

Afghanistan

Afghanistan continued to confront the challenges of building a stable, democratic, and tolerant government in the face of an insurgency that more and more relied on vicious and increasingly sophisticated terrorist attacks by anti-Afghan forces on coalition forces, civilians, international NGOs, and other soft targets, most notably through improvised explosive devices (IEDs) and suicide bombings. Supported by the international community, the Afghan government has made suppression of such terrorist attacks and the establishment of effective law-enforcement mechanisms a high priority.

Reconciliation of members of the insurgency remained a priority, with the government undertaking a number of initiatives. Under the Disbandment of Illegal Armed Groups (DIAG) program, the follow-on to the earlier Disarmament, Demobilization, and Reintegration (DDR) program, authorities have disbanded 362 illegal armed groups and collected over 42,000 weapons in 84 districts since its inception in March 2005. In April 2007, in an effort to achieve greater local government support, DIAG began offering development assistance to qualifying districts. Forty-eight of the 84 targeted districts currently qualify for this assistance and are considered to be in compliance with DIAG disarmament regulations. DIAG operations expanded, intensifying efforts to build political will at the provincial and local levels to target the more threatening illegal armed groups. The International Security Assistance Force (ISAF) led the coalition forces' counterinsurgency campaign, using a combination of counterinsurgency means and methods, including synchronized use of combat (air and ground forces) and non-combat means (building civil governance and aiding reconstruction and development in conjunction with the UN Assistance Mission in Afghanistan (UNAMA) to fight extremism.

The Commander, U.S. Central Command, maintained command and control of U.S. counterterrorism forces operating in Afghanistan. Counterterrorism operations were coordinated with U.S. forces at Headquarters of U.S. Forces–Afghanistan (USFOR-A) and Combined

Joint Task Force 101. Special Operations Forces conducting combined operations and foreign internal defense operated under the Commander, USFOR-A. United States CT forces target insurgent leaders, and insurgent training and logistics centers, with the objective of eliminating terrorists and facilitating reconstruction and development. The Afghan National Army (ANA), and to a lesser extent, the Afghan National Police (ANP), took the lead in the majority of counterterrorism operations, in close cooperation with coalition forces. In August, the Afghan National Security Force (ANSF) assumed lead responsibility from coalition forces for Kabul City, and assumed the lead on the majority of security operations across the country. The insurgents, partly in response to their growing inability to confront coalition and ANSF forces in conventional encounters, increasingly resorted to terrorist tactics to intimidate ordinary Afghans. These tactics included greater use of IEDs along key travel arteries, assassination of lower-level Afghan government officials, and the use of suicide bombers and direct fire attacks against Afghan civilians. Integrated civilian-military counterinsurgency approaches in the east have continued to yield some successes. Nonetheless, the anti-government insurgency remained a capable, determined, and resilient threat to stability and to the expansion of government authority, particularly in the south and east. The insurgency continued to suffer heavy combat losses, including among senior leaders, but its ability to obtain al-Qa'ida (AQ) support and recruit soldiers remained undiminished. Taliban information operations were increasingly aggressive and sophisticated. Streams of Taliban financing from across the border in Pakistan, along with funds gained from narcotics trafficking and kidnapping, have allowed the insurgency to strengthen its military and technical capabilities. To address this issue, a mini-jirga between Pakistani and Afghan officials and tribal leaders was held in October. The participants also discussed other ways to end terrorism along their border, including the possibility of holding talks with the Taliban insurgents—a proposal the Taliban subsequently rejected.

Insurgents continued to target police, police recruits, government ministers, parliamentarians, civil servants, and civilians, including urban crowds, in numerous violent incidents. Terrorists, often supported by criminal gangs, also increasingly turned to kidnapping Afghans and foreigners, most notably several reporters and at least one district governor were kidnapped. Most of these kidnappings were done for ransom, presumably as a means of raising money to support their operations.

Insurgents also targeted international non-governmental organizations (NGOs), Afghan journalists, government workers, UN workers, and recipients of NGO assistance. They attacked teachers, pupils (especially girls), and schools. They also threatened and often brutally killed those who worked for religious tolerance, including ex-insurgents, tribal leaders, and moderate imams, mullahs, and religious scholars. Insurgents coupled threats and attacks against NGOs with continued targeting of Provincial Reconstruction Teams, de-mining teams, and construction crews working on roads and other infrastructure projects. The most notorious incident was an acid attack on female students outside of an all-girls school in Kandahar. That particular attack injured several students and resulted in the school being closed for a time, but the school has since re-opened.

Bangladesh

Jamaatul Mujahedin Bangladesh (JMB), the banned domestic Islamic extremist group responsible for a wave of bombings and suicide attacks in late 2005, remained a threat. During the national Parliamentary election campaign in December, authorities arrested several suspected JMB members and uncovered weapons caches that included grenades and chemicals that could be used to make explosives.

Neighboring India alleged that the United Liberation Front of Assam (ULFA) and other anti-India insurgency groups operated from Bangladesh with the knowledge of senior Bangladeshi government officials. India also blamed the terrorist group Harakat ul-Jihadi-Islami-Bangladesh (HUJI-B) for bomb attacks within India. Bangladesh strongly denied those allegations. The absence of counterterrorism cooperation between India and Bangladesh fueled mutual allegations that each country facilitated terrorism inside the borders of the other.

In April and June, the caretaker government established the Money Laundering Prevention Ordinance and the Antiterrorism Ordinance. These laws facilitated international cooperation in recovering money illegally transferred to foreign countries and mutual legal assistance in criminal investigation, trial proceedings, and extradition matters. The new ordinances are part of the effort to enable Bangladesh to enter the Egmont Group, the international body of Financial Intelligence Units (FIU) that plays a critical role in fighting terrorist financing.

U.S. and Bangladeshi law enforcement agencies cooperated well on several cases related to domestic and international terrorism. Bangladesh cooperated with the United States to further strengthen control of its borders and land, sea, and air ports of entry. The United States began human rights training for the Rapid Action Battalion, the country's premier counterterrorism law enforcement force.

India

In 2008, India ranked among the world's most terrorism-afflicted countries. On November 26 in a pivotal moment that is now called "26/11", terrorists struck at a variety of locations in Mumbai on November 26, killing at least 183 people, including 22 foreigners, six of whom were Americans and 14 members of the police and security forces. Over 300 more were injured.

The attacks in Mumbai targeted places frequented by foreigners and wealthy Indians. The attackers entered Mumbai from the sea and attacked people in two hotels, a Jewish center, the main train station, and additional locations. They also planted bombs in two taxis that later exploded in different locations in the city. The terrorists appeared to have been well-trained and took advantage of technology, such as Global Positioning System trackers. Local and state police proved to be poorly trained and equipped, and lacked central control to coordinate an effective response. This attack was the most recent in a long list of lethal terrorist incidents this year.

Among the major events:

- On May 13, Jaipur experienced serial bomb blasts at crowded market areas and at Hindu temples. At least 60 people were killed, and more than 150 injured.
- On June 29, Maoist insurgents attacked and killed 33 security forces in Malkangiri district in the eastern state of Orissa.
- On July 7, Indian interests were attacked in Afghanistan when terrorists drove a vehicle-borne IED into the outer perimeter of the Indian Embassy in Kabul on July 7. Two Indian diplomats died, and a number of Afghan citizens were wounded.
- On July 25, serial bombs were set off in Bangalore in both business and industrial areas. At least one individual died, while eight were injured.
- On July 26, in Gujarat's capital, Ahmedabad, 21 devices exploded killing 54 and injuring at least 156. These explosions took place in market areas, on buses and other vehicles, and at the hospital to which the wounded from the first serial bomb blast were being treated.
- On September 13, terrorists detonated serial bombs in New Delhi in a variety of market places and other crowded public areas. These attacks killed at least 20 individuals and wounded more than 80.
- On October 30, insurgents detonated a series of nine bomb blasts throughout the northeastern state of Assam killing approximately 110 people.

None of the perpetrators of these attacks has yet been prosecuted. The Indian government assessed that South Asian Islamic extremist groups including Lashkar-e-Tayyiba, Jaish-e-Mohammad, and Harakat-ul-Jihad-i-Islami (Bangladesh) as well as indigenous groups were behind these events. The Government of India believed these attacks were aimed at creating a break-down in India-Pakistan relations, fostering Hindu-Muslim violence within India, and harming India's commercial centers to impede India's economic resurgence.

Eastern India has a long history of Maoist (left-wing extremism), and insurgent terrorist activity that has challenged state writ and control, governance structures, and the ruling political class. In 2008, there were 50 terrorist attacks in Eastern India that killed approximately 500 individuals. No American citizens were targeted or victims of terrorism in any of these incidents.

Insurgent groups, often fighting for recognition, political, and economic rights, or independence, were also active in the Northeast. Failure to properly accommodate the competing interests of diverse ethnic groups, low levels of development, and the success of previous insurgent movements in creating new Indian states were cited as explanatory factors for the appeal of insurgent movements. In 1990, the Government of India banned one of the most active insurgent groups, the United Liberation Front of Assam (ULFA). ULFA is alleged to have been involved in several terrorist attacks this year, including the bicycle bomb blast on September 18 in Chirang district, resulting in 20 injured Indian citizens, and the October 30 serial blasts mentioned above.

The Communist Party of India (Maoists), commonly referred to as Maoist/Naxalites, were active in the states of Chhattisgarh, Andhra Pradesh, Karnataka, Orissa, Bihar, Jharkhand, and West Bengal, the so-called "Red Corridor." Companies, Indian and foreign, operating in Maoist strongholds were sometimes targets for extortion.

State governments have expressed interest in augmenting their security forces by either creating or buttressing state-level assets, or hosting central level units to address the increased terrorist threat. Chattisgarh's government has invested in counterinsurgency training for police and paramilitary forces at its Jungle Warfare Training Center. Nevertheless, there is no clear unified command structure between state and federal forces in counterinsurgency efforts, which hampers their effectiveness.

Specifically in response to the Mumbai attacks, the Indian government has proposed a new agency, the National Investigative Agency, to create national-level capability to investigate and potentially prosecute such acts. Also in response to the Mumbai attacks, the Indian government amended some existing laws to strengthen the hands of security and law enforcement agencies in fighting terrorism. Two themes have framed the public debate on the new legislation: states' rights vs. federal power, and civil liberties vs. stronger law enforcement powers.

Illicit funding sources that may have been exploited to finance terrorist operations were being closely investigated. Indian authorities believe that the Mumbai terrorists used various funding sources including credit cards, hawala, charities, and wealthy donors. In addition to the Mumbai attacks, the rise in terrorist attacks and their coordinated nature throughout India suggested the terrorists were well-funded and financially organized.

Indian officials, particularly in West Bengal and Assam, were concerned about the porous India-Bangladesh border, of which only 2500 of the 3000 km land border has been fenced (total land and water border is 4100 km). India's inability to protect its porous maritime border has been under media scrutiny since it came to light that the perpetrators of the November 26 Mumbai attacks arrived by sea. In Tamil Nadu, coast guard and police officials, as well as security analysts, all acknowledged that the government was unable to monitor sufficiently the thousands of small commercial fishing vessels that ply the waters between India and Sri Lanka.

The Indian government has implemented an advance passenger information system to receive inbound passenger information from air carriers operating in India. The system, however, is not compatible with or able to share data with the U.S. and EU equivalent systems. In addition, the Government of India and air carriers have shown an increased interest in receiving fraudulent document training from the United States and other countries.

Kazakhstan

Kazakhstan detained and prosecuted suspected terrorists and took tangible steps to cooperate and share information with the United States and international organizations. With the addition of one international terrorist organization, the Islamic Party of Turkistan, to the list of already-banned terrorist organizations, the Government of Kazakhstan now designates 16 groups as banned terrorist and extremist organizations.

In April, the Kazakhstani Committee for National Security (KNB) announced plans to submit a strict new law, *On Counteracting Terrorism*, to Parliament that would replace the current law, adopted in 1999. At the time, the KNB stated the bill was included in the government's legislative plan and would be submitted to Parliament. At year's end, however, Parliament had not yet approved the new law. Kazakhstan's Prime Minister instructed the Minister of Finance to speed up drafting a bill on combating financing of terrorism in June, but the draft law on terrorist financing remained stalled in Parliament.

Kazakhstan strengthened its engagement in international counterterrorism activities:

- In March, the Government of Kazakhstan approved a treaty with the Government of the Slovak Republic on cooperation in fighting terrorism.
- In April, President Nursultan Nazarbayev signed two draft laws on counterterrorism activities within the framework of the Shanghai Cooperation Organization.
- In June, Kazakhstan hosted the first Global Initiative to Combat Nuclear Terrorism field exercise, entitled Anti-Atom Terror, which was attended by more than 15 partner nations. Additionally, more than 900 military, intelligence, law enforcement, and security personnel from Kazakhstan took part in organizing and conducting the exercise.
- In August, the Government of Kazakhstan approved the signing of a treaty with the Government of the United Arab Emirates on cooperation in fighting terrorism.
- In September, Kazakhstan hosted a Design-Basis Threat exercise attended by seven partners from the Global Initiative to Combat Nuclear Terrorism.
- In October, Kazakhstan hosted the Common World Forum to promote intercultural and inter-religious dialogues.

Law enforcement actions against terrorists included:

- In February, a court in Stepnorgorsk sentenced two members of an extremist group to 12 years of imprisonment and six others to nine years of imprisonment for planning to commit terrorist attacks in the fall of 2006.
- In March, a court in Shymkent sentenced 15 members of a terrorist group, detained in April 2007, on charges of organizing terrorist acts against the local office of the Kazakhstani Committee for National Security (KNB), to prison terms ranging from 11 to 19 years. House searches of the convicts revealed hidden explosives, guns, ammunition, and extremist literature, along with a detailed plan of the local KNB building and a list with KNB officers' and their family members' home phone numbers and addresses.
- In November, police in the southern Zhambyl District of Almaty detained an Uzbek citizen, allegedly wanted for membership in religious extremist, separatist, and fundamentalist organizations. According to the Almaty Region's prosecutor, police placed the detainee under arrest, pending a decision on his extradition to

Uzbekistan.

Kazakhstan promoted intercultural and religious dialogues designed to prevent radicalization and supported other domestic counterterrorism initiatives. In August, the Ministry of Interior and the People's Assembly of Kazakhstan signed a memorandum on cooperation in strengthening interethnic and interfaith relations within Kazakhstani society. In December, the Ministry of Justice opened an International Center of Culture and Religions to study the positive experience of interfaith and interethnic cooperation in Kazakhstan. Kazakhstan also enacted five interagency regulatory legal acts regulating the counterterrorism activities of public bodies and conducted 149 interagency counterterrorism exercises and training programs.

Kyrgyzstan

In 2008, the Kyrgyz Republic took political, legislative, and law enforcement steps to disrupt and deter terrorism. Since 2001, Kyrgyzstan has hosted the Operation Enduring Freedom Coalition airbase at Manas International Airport near Bishkek. In November 2006, President Bakiyev signed a comprehensive law on "Counteracting Terrorist Financing and Legalization (Money Laundering) of Proceeds from Crime." The law obligates financial institutions to report any suspicious activity and bank transactions that exceed the threshold of $25,000. The law also established a Financial Intelligence Service, an administrative body charged with collecting and analyzing information related to financial transactions, developing systems to prevent and detect suspicious transactions, and submitting cases to the prosecutor's office for further action.

The Government of Kyrgyzstan, with financial support from the U.S. and other international organizations, continued efforts to improve border security throughout the country, particularly in the southern Batken region. These efforts included the construction of more modern border point facilities at several locations throughout the country, a program to create central communications between the dispersed border points and several government agencies, the installation of radiation detection equipment at select crossings, and the establishment of a tracking system to monitor the transit of certain dual-use equipment throughout the country.

Kyrgyzstan's military and internal forces worked to improve their counterterrorism capabilities and to expand cooperation with regional partners. With U.S. assistance, the Kyrgyz armed forces continued to build capacity in terms of their facilities and tactical capabilities. U.S. financial support has resulted in the training of dozens of Kyrgyz armed forces personnel, and the establishment of more modern defense facilities. Further, the Kyrgyz Ministry of Defense is in the process of reorganizing their forces to respond more efficiently to perceived threats in the southern region of Kyrgyzstan.

Kyrgyzstan's under-regulated borders, particularly in the Batken region, have allowed for people and illicit goods to move into and out of the country with a large degree of freedom. Kyrgyz law enforcement still lacked the equipment, manpower, and funding to effectively detect and deter terrorists or terrorist operations in the southern regions of Kyrgyzstan.

Hizb ut-Tahrir (HT), banned as an extremist group in Kyrgyzstan since 2003, is believed by local specialists to have approximately 15,000 members in Kyrgyzstan. These HT members are located primarily among Kyrgyzstan's ethnic Uzbek population in the south, but are reportedly achieving an increased following in the north as well. Kyrgyz officials reported growing support for and bolder public outreach by HT. Supporters of terrorist groups the Islamic Jihad Group (IJG) and the Islamic Movement of Uzbekistan (IMU) were also believed to maintain a presence in Kyrgyzstan, and Kyrgyz authorities alleged that both groups received material support from HT.

Nepal

While Nepal experienced no significant acts of international terrorism, several incidents of politically-motivated violence occurred across the country. Nepalese voters elected the Communist Party of Nepal (Maoists), a designated organization on the Terrorist Exclusion List (TEL), to lead the government. In response to continued violence by Maoist-affiliated youth, other political parties condoned the use of violence for their youth wings. Unrest in the southern Terai plains increased with the proliferation of numerous armed groups. Nevertheless, the Nepalese government made some headway in counterterrorism efforts, specifically with the passage of anti-money laundering legislation and the arrest of individuals suspected of terrorist ties. U.S. antiterrorism assistance was constrained by the presence of the Maoists within the government.

In April, the Communist Party of Nepal won a plurality of votes in the Constituent Assembly election and went on to create a new coalition government in August. Although the Maoist party ended a ten-year insurgency in 2006 and entered into the interim government in April 2007, factions of the Maoists continued to engage in violence, extortion, and abductions. The Maoist-affiliated Young Communist League, which included former members of the People's Liberation Army and grew increasingly prominent during 2007, carried on the Maoist militia's tactics of abuse, abduction, murder, intimidation, and extortion in cities and villages.

There were no indications that Nepal was a safe haven for other international terrorists; however, authorities arrested several individuals with suspected ties to Pakistani terrorist organizations using Nepal to transit between Pakistan and India. The interim Parliament passed anti-money laundering legislation in January, which led to the creation of a Financial Information Unit (FIU). Although faced with resource and staffing constraints, the FIU responded favorably to U.S. requests to freeze the assets of individuals and entities involved in the terrorist financing when or if such assets were discovered.

The United States sponsored the attendance of Nepalese security force officers at various international counterterrorism events, and hosted a regional counterterrorism seminar in Kathmandu with participants from Nepal, Sri Lanka, Bangladesh, and the Maldives.

Pakistan

International terrorist organizations, including al-Qa'ida (AQ) and its supporters, continued to operate and carry out attacks in Pakistan. Violence stemming from Sunni-Shia sectarian strife, ethnic tensions, and militant sub-nationalists claimed civilian lives. Attacks occurred with greatest frequency in the regions bordering Afghanistan: Balochistan, the North West Frontier Province (NWFP), and the adjacent Federally Administered Tribal Areas (FATA), but militant attacks continued to grow and target urban centers including Lahore, Islamabad, Peshawar, and Rawalpindi.

The coordination, sophistication, and frequency of suicide bombings that increased sharply in 2007, continued to grow in Pakistan in 2008. By November 30, there were already 57 recorded suicide attacks in Pakistan, in comparison to 45 reported attacks in 2007. These suicide attacks often resulted in large numbers of casualties, and several occurred in Islamabad, Rawalpindi, and Lahore. The attacks targeted high profile government, military, and western-related sites, such as hotels. The most prominent among the attacks this year was the September 20 suicide bombing against the Marriot Hotel in Islamabad where at least 60 people were killed and over 200 injured. Two Americans died in this sophisticated attack aimed at foreigners and Pakistan's international reputation. Other instances in which Americans were targeted included attacks on an American diplomat and the killing of a USAID contractor, both in Peshawar.

Other high profile bombings in Islamabad have targeted foreigners, including the June 2 bombing of the Danish Embassy and the March 15 bombing of an Italian restaurant where several Americans were injured. In response to these incidents, diplomatic security and police checkpoints surrounding Islamabad have increased significantly.

The majority of suicide attacks across Pakistan have targeted well-protected military and government installations. These attacks included very high profile targets and caused high casualty rates, such as the August 21 bombing of an ammunitions factory at Wah Cantonment killing over 70 people and the March 11 suicide bombings in Lahore targeting the Federal Investigation Agency. In January, the first ever female suicide bomber in Pakistan targeted a police checkpoint in NWFP. Also the newly elected civilian government has been the target of several attacks, specifically the coalition-partner Awami National Party (ANP) in the NWFP. Militants have tried unsuccessfully to kill ANP leaders across NWFP, including ANP Chairman Asfandyar Wali Khan in Charsadda and senior minister Bashir Bilour at the Inter-provincial Games in Peshawar. It is also believed that militants were responsible for the assassination of former Prime Minister Benazir Bhutto on December 27, 1007.

Extremists led by Baitullah Mehsud and other AQ-related extremists spread north throughout the FATA with an increased presence in Bajaur and Khyber. In most of the FATA, the militants continued to openly challenge the writ of the state with high levels of violence. In the bordering districts of NWFP, the militants tried to extend their influence by targeting CD shops, barber shops, police stations, and girls' schools. As the militancy seeped into the settled areas of NWFP this year, small towns such as Nowshera and Kohat saw an increase in suicide attacks.

There was a growing trend of militants garnering support by promising to fill a vacuum left by ineffective government structures. Baitullah Mehsud formed the Tehrik-i-Taliban (TTP) in Pakistan in December 2007 as a loose alliance of militants. In 2008, the TTP became the most public signal of broad local militant coordination aimed at attacking Pakistani security forces. TTP was active all over the FATA and NWFP, but specifically in Kurram, Swat, Bajaur, North Waziristan, and South Waziristan. In February, Mehsud called a unilateral ceasefire and the lull in attacks lasted until after the parliamentary elections in, but resumed shortly thereafter. In August, the Government of Pakistan officially banned the TTP and froze its bank accounts. The ban allowed Pakistani security forces to arrest anyone associated with the group. In addition, media outlets were not allowed to broadcast interviews or other interaction with the TTP. The Pakistani government also turned down the TTP's offer of a ceasefire and peace talks. Militants and related criminal elements increased their direct targeting of individual foreigners, including aid workers, journalists, diplomats, and politicians in the NWFP. Most of the victims were kidnapped for ransom whereas some of the targets were assassinated, such as American citizen and USAID worker Stefan Vance who was killed in Peshawar in November. Other significant attacks included the attempted kidnapping of the Principal Officer at the U.S.

Consulate in Peshawar, the kidnapping of the Pakistani Ambassador to Afghanistan Tariq Azizuddin, and the kidnappings of Chinese engineers and Iranian and Afghan diplomats.

Pakistani security services cooperated with the United States and other nations to fight terrorism within Pakistan and abroad. Hundreds of suspected AQ operatives have been killed or captured by Pakistani authorities since September 2001. Pakistan continued to pursue AQ and its allies through nationwide police action and military operations in the FATA and elsewhere. Despite having approximately 80,000 to 100,000 troops in the FATA, including Army and Frontier Corps (FC) units, the Government of Pakistan's authority in the area continued to be challenged. Pakistani security forces pursued major military operations in South Waziristan, Darra Adam Khel, Bajaur, Khyber, and Swat. The rise of local lashkars or tribal militias to combat militants has added some support to Pakistan Army operations.

Despite an increased number of infiltrations across the Line of Control, Pakistan-India relations were improving, with trade opened for the first time in over 60 years, until they were significantly set back by the terrorist attacks in Mumbai, India in November. These attacks were attributed to the (Pakistan-based) Kashmir terrorist group Laskhar-e-Tayyiba (LT), a designated Foreign Terrorist Organization, and to its fundraising subsidiary, the Jamaat ud-Dawa (JUD), which the Government of Pakistan banned after the UN Security Council listed the group and certain named individuals in the 1267 Sanctions Committee. In response to allegations of involvement by the LT and JUD in the Mumbai attacks, Pakistani officials cracked down on a LT camp in Muzzafarabad and arrested or detained more than 50 LT or JUD leaders in Punjab and elsewhere in Pakistan. Pakistani officials pledged to prosecute all individuals in Pakistan found to be involved in the Mumbai attacks and offered to share intelligence regarding the attacks with the Government of India. President Zardari said non-state actors (terrorists) were operating on Pakistani soil and noted his own wife (Prime Minister Benazir Bhutto assassinated on December 27, 2007) had been a victim of terrorism. The composite dialogue between Pakistan and India was frozen by the Indian government in December, however, contributing to heightened tension between the two governments.

In terrorist financing, Pakistan worked with the UNSCR 1267 Committee to freeze assets of individuals and groups identified as terrorist entities linked to LT/JUD. AQ and the Taliban, however, continued to operate in Pakistan. Despite government efforts to curb illicit financial transactions, unlicensed informal hawalas (money changers) still operated illegally in parts of the country. The informal and secretive nature of the unlicensed hawalas made it difficult for regulators to effectively combat their operations. Most illicit funds were transacted through these unlicensed operators.

The United States and Pakistan engaged in a broad range of cooperative counterterrorism efforts including border security and criminal investigations, as well as several long-term projects. Pakistan is a major recipient of U.S. military and economic assistance. [See Chapter 5, *Terrorist Safe Havens (7120 Report)* for further information on U.S. Assistance for Pakistan.*)*

Sri Lanka

The Sri Lankan government's offensive against the Liberation Tigers of Tamil Eelam (LTTE), killed more than 7,000 people and displaced many thousands more. Effective January 16, the government formally abrogated the 2002 Cease-Fire Accord (CFA) with the LTTE, and the conflict intensified during the year. The government maintained control of the Eastern Province, and captured the strategic town of Pooneryn in November, placing the entire northwestern coast under government control. The LTTE controlled a significant, although rapidly shrinking section of the north and carried out attacks throughout the country. The Sri Lankan Army remained deployed across the country in all areas it controlled to fight the insurgency. The Special Task Force (STF) police were deployed in the east, north, and in strategic locations in the west.

In 2008, there were at least 70 attacks attributed to the LTTE, including:

- The October assassination by suicide bombing of the leader of the opposition in the North Central Provincial Council retired Major General Janaka Perera, UNP organizer Dr. Raja Johnpulle, and 26 others in Anuradhapura.
- In April, a suicide bomber killed 14 people in Gampaha district including the Minister of Highways Jeyaraj Fernandopulle.
- Other major LTTE attacks included the August air strikes on the naval base in Trincomalee, a combined air-ground assault on a military base in Vavuniya in September, and the October bombings of the Thallady Army camp in Mannar and the Kelanitissa power plant in Colombo.
- The LTTE also targeted public transportation systems. In April, a parcel bomb killed 26 civilians at a bus stand in Colombo.

The government used paramilitary groups to assist its military forces in fighting the LTTE. The Tamil Makkal Viduthalai Pulikal (TMVP), led by breakaway-LTTE eastern commanders Vinayagamurthi Muralitharan aka "Karuna" and Sivanesathurai Chandrakanthen aka "Pillaiyan," operated mostly in the east. Karuna was appointed a Member of Parliament on October 7; Pillaiyan was elected as the Chief Minister of the Eastern Provincial Council. The Eelam People's Democratic Party (EPDP), led by Minister of Social Services and Social Welfare Douglas Devananda, operated in Jaffna.

In 2008, there were numerous killings of civilians by unknown actors suspected of association with the TMVP or the EPDP. The government captured the key town of Pooneryn in November. At the end of the year, government forces and the LTTE were poised to take LTTE's administrative headquarters at Kilinochchi. The LTTE maintained control of a shrinking section of the north and retained the capacity to mount attacks throughout the country.

The LTTE financed itself with contributions from the Tamil Diaspora in North America, Europe, and Australia, by imposing local "taxes" on businesses operating in the areas of Sri Lanka under its control, and reportedly by extortion in government-controlled areas. The LTTE also used Tamil charitable organizations as fronts for its fundraising. To date, the Sri Lankan Navy has sunk 10 LTTE supply ships; the most recent sinking occurred in June.

The United States has provided training for relevant Sri Lankan government agencies and the banking sector. The Government of Sri Lanka cooperated with the United States to implement both the Container Security Initiative and the Megaports program at the port of Colombo.

Tajikistan

As the poorest of the former Soviet countries, the Tajik government's main impediment to countering terrorism remained its lack of resources. The government, particularly the Border Guards, which are under the State Committee for National Security, lacked appropriate technical equipment, personnel, and training to effectively interdict illegal border crossings and to detect and analyze hazardous substances. Individual border guards and other law enforcement personnel were not motivated to interdict smugglers or traffickers due to systematic corruption, low income, conscripted service, and lack of support from senior Tajik government officials.

As a result, extremists and terrorists may exploit Tajikistan's border to travel to and from Afghanistan. To address the problem of transshipment of illicit goods across Tajikistan's borders, the United States and other donors assisted the Government of Tajikistan's efforts to secure its 1,400 kilometer porous border with Afghanistan. Assistance included a USD five million U.S. Department of Defense (DOD) radio program to improve

Border Guard communications capability. DOD held four Counter Narcoterrorism Training (formerly Joint Combined Exchange Training) events with Tajik security forces to improve their capacity to conduct counterterrorism operations.

The Defense Institute for Legal Studies conducted a Response to Terrorism course in Dushanbe that representatives from several ministries attended. Tajikistan also participated in exercise Regional Cooperation 08, sponsored by the U.S. Department of Defense and hosted by Kyrgyzstan. This exercise focused on dealing with terrorism, and strengthened cooperation between the Central Asian countries. The Tajik government also participated in regional security alliances, including the Shanghai Cooperation Organization.

Tajikistan prohibited extremist-oriented activities and closely monitored groups it listed as terrorist organizations, such as the Islamic Movement of Uzbekistan (IMU) and Hizbut-Tahrir (HT). The Government of Tajikistan believed that HT, in particular, was active in the northern part of the country. The USG believed that supporters of terrorist groups such as al-Qa'ida (AQ), the Islamic Jihad Union (IJU), and the IMU were active in the region.

Turkmenistan

The September 2008 violence in the Khitrovka region of Ashgabat forced the Government of Turkmenistan to reevaluate its counterterrorism program, training partners, and readiness. The Government of Turkmenistan cooperated with a variety of international organizations and partner countries in conducting counterterrorism training events for government personnel, including, for example, canine bomb detection and professional seminars on terrorism and security studies. While the government strictly controlled access into and passage through Turkmenistan at official border crossings and along main roads, clandestine passage was still possible due to long and porous borders that stretch across mountain and desert terrain, as well as the small size and uneven quality of Turkmenistan's border guard and customs services. Turkmenistan's law enforcement and security agencies exert stringent security control over all aspects of society, making it unlikely that Turkmenistan could easily be used as a terrorist safe haven. The government maintained a military-style counterterrorism unit said to have hostage rescue and explosives threat management capability, as well as a Department for the Prevention of Terrorism and Organized Crime in the Ministry of Internal Affairs. The government entered the names of individuals and organizations on terrorist financing lists into its banking system.

Uzbekistan

The Government of Uzbekistan worked aggressively to combat terrorists and terrorist groups. Nevertheless, widespread poverty and the government's repressive security policies created conditions that religious extremists could exploit. The government worked with international organizations and other countries to strengthen border controls in order to combat the transit of goods and people of concern across Uzbekistan's borders. The Government of Uzbekistan also said that it had conducted counterterrorism operations and government-sponsored forums, and state-controlled media warned of the dangers of terrorism and extremism. The Government of Uzbekistan pursued modest steps in resuming counterterrorism cooperation with the United States. Uzbekistan also agreed to extend overflight rights for commercial aircraft carrying non-lethal supplies contracted by the U.S. Department of Defense, and permitted such overflights of aircraft during 2008. In April, Uzbekistan joined the International Convention on the Suppression of Acts of Nuclear Terrorism. The government also participated in counterterrorism-themed UN Office of Drugs and Crime activities. Uzbekistan hosts the Shanghai Cooperation Organization's Regional Antiterrorist Structure.

Western Hemisphere Overview

Terrorism, whatever its justification or ideological motivations, has no place in the community of values that we have forged with so much difficulty. Mexico condemns it and affirms its will to cooperate on the basis of international law in order to prevent terrorist acts and to punish its authors.

— Felipe Calderon Hinojosa, President of Mexico
UN General Assembly, New York City
September 24, 2008

Regionally based Foreign Terrorist Organizations (FTOs) in Colombia, and remnants of radical leftist Andean groups were the primary perpetrators of terrorist acts in the Western Hemisphere in 2008.

In May 2008 Venezuela was re-certified as "not cooperating fully" with U.S. antiterrorism efforts under Section 40A of the Arms Export and Control Act, as amended. Cuba remained a state sponsor of terrorism.

The threat of a transnational terrorist attack remained low for most countries in the Western Hemisphere. Overall, governments took modest steps to improve their counterterrorism capabilities and tighten border security, but corruption, weak government institutions, ineffective or lack of interagency cooperation, weak or non-existent legislation, and reluctance to allocate sufficient resources limited progress. Some countries, like Argentina, Colombia, Panama, Paraguay, Mexico, and El Salvador, made serious prevention and preparedness efforts. Others lacked urgency and resolve to address counterterrorism deficiencies. Most countries began to look seriously at possible connections between transnational criminal organizations and terrorist organizations.

Colombia maintained and strengthened its Democratic Security strategy, which combines military, intelligence, police operations, efforts to demobilize combatants, and the provision of public services in rural areas previously dominated by armed groups. The Colombian military crippled the FARC's communications, destroyed major caches of weapon and supplies, and reduced the group's financial resources through counternarcotics and other security operations. Kidnappings in Colombia by both the FARC and other criminal groups have significantly decreased.

On July 2, a Colombian military operation rescued three U.S. Department of Defense contractors, former Colombian presidential candidate and Senator Ingrid Betancourt, and eleven Colombians held by the FARC. The three Americans, taken hostage in February 2003, were the longest-held U.S. hostages in the world at the time of their rescue.

After years of seeming invincibility, the FARC's Secretariat suffered several key losses in 2008. A Colombian military strike on March 1 killed Secretariat member Raúl Reyes at his camp just across the Ecuadorian border, followed less than a week later by the killing of Secretariat member Iván Ríos at the hands of one of his own security guards. Secretariat member and FARC founder Manuel Marulanda (Tirofijo) died in late March, reportedly of natural causes. Colombian security forces also captured or killed a number of mid-level FARC leaders and reduced the amount of territory where terrorists could freely operate. At least 3,027 FARC members deserted in 2008, a record number that surpassed the previous year's record number of 2,480.

The Government of Trinidad and Tobago extradited to the United States two Guyanese and one Trinidadian indicted in the United States in 2007 and accused of plotting to destroy a fuel pipeline at New York's John F. Kennedy International Airport.

Mexico and Canada were key counterterrorism partners. Cooperation with them was broad and deep, involving all levels of government and virtually all agencies, in several initiatives. Recognizing the threat from terrorist transit, the Mexican government worked with the United States to enhance aviation, border, maritime, and transportation security; to secure critical infrastructure; and to combat terrorist financing. The United States and Mexico also worked together to mitigate the threat of violence or assassination against high level officials of the Mexican Government. United States-Canadian counterterrorism cooperation took place in a number of established forums, including the terrorism subgroup of the Cross Border Crime Forum, the Shared Border Accord Coordinating

Committee, and the Bilateral Consultative Group on Counterterrorism (BCG). Each year, the BCG brings together U.S. and Canadian counterterrorism officials from over a dozen agencies to coordinate policy on bioterrorism, information sharing, and joint counterterrorism training.

The United States enjoyed solid cooperation on terrorism-related matters from most hemispheric partners, especially at the operational level, and maintained excellent intelligence, law enforcement, and legal assistance relations with most countries. The hemisphere boasts the OAS Inter-American Committee Against Terrorism, which is the only permanent regional multilateral organization focused exclusively on counterterrorism.

Tri-Border Area

The Governments of Argentina, Brazil, and Paraguay, have long been concerned with arms and drugs smuggling, document fraud, money laundering, and the manufacture and movement of contraband goods in the border region where their three countries meet. In the early 1990s, they established a mechanism to address these illicit activities. In 2002, at their invitation, the United States joined them in what became the "3+1 Group on Tri-Border Area Security" to improve the capabilities of the three to address cross-border crime and thwart money laundering and potential terrorist financing activities.

The United States remained concerned that Hizballah and HAMAS sympathizers were raising funds in the Tri-Border Area by participating in illicit activities and soliciting donations from sympathizers in the sizable Middle Eastern communities in the region. There was no corroborated information, however, that these or other Islamic extremist groups had an operational presence in the region.

Argentina

Argentina cooperated well with the United States at the operational level, and addressed many of the legal and institutional weaknesses that previously hindered its counterterrorism efforts. With U.S. support, the Government of Argentina continued to build law enforcement capacity along its eastern and its remote northern borders, dealing with challenges of drug trafficking, contraband, and other international crime. The United States government also provided equipment donations for chemical/biological/radiological/nuclear first responder operations and training to high level government officials to create more awareness about the potential threat from terrorists or terrorist organizations operating in the hemisphere. In 2007, the National Coordination Unit in the Ministry of Justice and Human Rights became fully functional, managing the government's anti-money laundering and counterterrorist finance efforts and representing Argentina to the Financial Action Task Force, Financial Action Task

Force of South America, and Group of Experts of the Inter-American Commission for the Control of the Abuse of Drugs (CICAD) of the Organization of American States' CICAD Group of Experts. The Attorney General's special prosecution unit, set up to handle money laundering and terrorism finance cases, began operations in 2007. In 2008, the Argentine Central Bank's Superintendent of Banks began specific anti-money laundering and counterterrorist finance inspections of financial entities and exchange houses. The Argentine government and Central Bank remained committed to freezing assets of terrorist groups identified by the United Nations in Argentine financial institutions.

On November 9, 2006, an Argentine judge issued arrest warrants for eight current and former Iranian government officials and one member of Hizballah, who were indicted in the July 18, 1994 terrorist bombing of the Argentine-Jewish Mutual Association (AMIA) that killed 85 and injured over 150 people.[13] Despite Iranian objections, on November 7, 2007, the INTERPOL General Assembly voted to uphold the Executive Committee's decision and the Red Notices were issued. At the 2008 UN General Assembly, President Cristina Fernández de Kirchner called on Iran to surrender the suspects to face charges in Argentina.

13 On March 13, 2007, the INTERPOL Executive Committee decided unanimously to issue international wanted notices ("Red Notices") for five of the Iranians (including the former Minister of Intelligence and Security, Ali Fallahijan, and the commanders of the Islamic Revolutionary Guard Corps and the Qods Force) and the one Lebanese national (Imad Mugniyah, recently deceased).

On December 16, 2008, at the AMIA Special Prosecutor's request, the presiding Argentine judge in a civil suit against the Iranian suspects and Hizballah ordered the attachment of six commercial properties in Argentina allegedly owned by former Iran Cultural Attaché and named suspect Mohsen Rabbani. The judge also requested that select European governments freeze up to USD one million in bank accounts allegedly belonging to former Iranian President Ali Hasehmi Rafsanjani and another Iranian accused of involvement in the attacks.

Belize

The government of Belize cooperated with the United States by sharing information and assistance to the extent of its limited resources.

[13] On March 13, 2007, the INTERPOL Executive Committee decided unanimously to issue international wanted notices ("Red Notices") for five of the Iranians (including the former Minister of Intelligence and Security, Ali Fallahijan, and the commanders of the Islamic Revolutionary Guard Corps and the Qods Force) and the one Lebanese national (Imad Mugniyah, recently deceased).

The Belize Defense Force (990 total personnel) has operated a Counterterrorism Platoon (Belize Special Assignment Group comprising 35 persons) for approximately two years to perform operations within the territory of Belize and its territorial waters in support of civil authorities. Belize's borders are extremely porous and it remained easy to change identity by purchasing stolen passports. The country is sparsely populated and has limited human and technological resources to monitor individuals and groups residing within or transiting through its borders.

Bolivia

The Bolivian government deepened its relationship with Iran, a state sponsor of terrorism, in 2008. On September 5, during an official visit to Tehran, Bolivian President Evo Morales announced that Bolivia would open a new Embassy in Iran. Morales also announced that Iran would help Bolivia develop its petrochemicals, cement fabrication, and agricultural sectors. Iranian state television agreed to provide Spanish-language programming to Bolivian state television.

On December 11, the Egmont Group announced the expulsion of Bolivia because of continued lack of adequate terrorist financing legislation. This followed Bolivia's suspension from the group in 2007. In October a working group was formed by the Bolivian Vice Ministry for Justice, the Counternarcotics Directorate, and the Financial Investigation Unit, with support from the U.S. Embassy's Narcotics Affairs Section and the Drug Enforcement Administration (DEA). It submitted legislation designed to control money laundering, including terrorist financing, to the National Council for Political and Social Economy and the Ministerial Counternarcotics Council for analysis and approval prior to submission to the Bolivian Congress. As of December, the legislation had not been forwarded to Congress.

Brazil

The Brazilian government continued to be a cooperative partner in countering terrorism, including investigating potential terrorism financing, document forgery networks, and other illicit activity. Operationally, elements of the Brazilian Government responsible for combating terrorism, such as the Federal Police, Customs, and the Brazilian Intelligence Agency, worked effectively with their U.S. counterparts and diligently pursued investigative leads provided by U.S. intelligence, law enforcement, and financial agencies regarding terrorist suspects.

Brazil's intelligence and law enforcement services were concerned that terrorists could exploit Brazilian territory to support and facilitate terrorist attacks, whether domestically or abroad, and have focused their efforts in the areas of Sao Paulo; the tri-border areas of Brazil, Argentina, and Paraguay; Brazil, Peru, and Colombia; and the Colombian and Venezuelan borders. Brazil's recognition of the potential threat from terrorism prompted a reform of the Brazilian Intelligence Agency (ABIN) that raised the profile of the issue by upgrading the counterterrorism division to the department level. ABIN hosted a multilateral conference on counterterrorism involving the security services of several South American countries. Together with the United Nations Organization for Crime and Drugs, ABIN co-hosted an international conference on terrorist financing. Brazil participated in international counterterrorism forums such as the 3+1 Mechanism on Security in the Tri-Border Area, the Working Group on Terrorism of the Common Market of the South (Mercosul), and the Sub-working Group on Financial Issues, which discusses terrorist financing and money laundering among the Mercosul countries.

Bilaterally, the USG provided a variety of training courses throughout Brazil in counterterrorism, combating money laundering, detection of travel document fraud, container security, and international organized crime. Brazil and the United States began exchanging information on critical infrastructure protection issues.

Although Brazil has no official list of terrorist groups and does not recognize the Revolutionary Armed Forces of Columbia (FARC) as a terrorist organization, President Luiz Inácio Lula da Silva has been critical of the FARC's use of violence and has publicly called on the group to desist in the armed struggle against the Colombian government. President Lula also signaled a renewed commitment to cooperate with the Colombian government that could help curtail the FARC's activities along Brazil's border. In July, Lula and Colombian President Alvaro Uribe signed bilateral accords to cooperate on combating the illicit trafficking of weapons and munitions; to enhance defense cooperation; and, together with Peru, to combat the trafficking of drugs, weapons, and munitions by increasing intelligence sharing and joint patrolling of border riverways.

Brazil was capable of monitoring domestic financial operations and effectively utilized its financial intelligence unit, the Financial Activities Oversight Council (COAF), to identify possible funding sources for terrorist groups. Through the COAF, Brazil has carried out name checks for persons and entities on the UNSCR 1267 list, but has so far not found any assets, accounts, or property in the names of persons or entities on the UNSCR 1267.

Brazil also continued to undertake steps to enhance its capabilities to combat money laundering. Since 2003, Brazil has established fifteen specialized money-laundering courts, including two in São Paulo, with each court headed by a judge who received specialized training in national money laundering legislation. In 2008, the United States and Brazil established a working group with money laundering judges to share best practices and training needs.

In 2006, Brazil adopted a national anti-money laundering strategy goal building on the success of the specialized courts by creating complementary specialized federal police financial crimes units in the same jurisdictions. In 2008, the Federal Police established such units in the Federal District (Brasilia), and the states of Rio de Janeiro and Sao Paulo. In addition, the Ministry of Justice funded the creation of technology centers to combat money laundering in the Federal District and Rio de Janeiro, the latter of which received two such centers, one embedded with the Public Ministry and one with the state Civil Police. In 2008, the Ministry signed accords to establish additional centers in Bahia, Goiás, and Rio Grande do Sul.

The Brazilian government's counterterrorism strategy consisted of deterring terrorists from using Brazilian territory to facilitate attacks or raise funds by aggressively monitoring and suppressing transnational criminal activities that could support terrorist actions. It accomplished this through effective actions between its law enforcement entities and cooperation with the United States and other partners in the region.

Brazil and the United States continued to work together through the Container Security Initiative in Santos to promote secure containerized cargo to the United States and through the establishment of a Trade Transparency Unit to detect money laundering through trade transactions. The Brazilian government achieved visible results from recent investments in border and law enforcement infrastructure that were executed with a view to gradually control the flow of goods, both legal and illegal, through the Tri-border Area (TBA). Brazilian Customs (Receita Federal) continued to take effective action to suppress the smuggling of drugs, weapons, and contraband goods along the border with Paraguay. According to Receita Federal, the agency interdicted more than $76 million in smuggled goods, including drugs, weapons, and munitions, an increase of eight percent from 2007. Because of the effective crackdown on the Friendship Bridge[14], most smuggling operations took place through the Paraná River and Lago de Itaipú and some have migrated to other sections of the border such as the towns of Guaíra and Ponta Porã. The Federal Police had Special Maritime Police Units in both Foz do Iguaçu and Guaíra that aggressively patrolled the maritime border areas.

The Brazilian government's failure to strengthen its legal counterterrorism framework significantly undermined its overall commitment to combating terrorism and the illicit activities that could be used to

---

[14] In 2007, Receita Federal completed the inspection station at the Friendship Bridge connecting Foz do Iguaçu, Brazil, and Ciudad del Este, Paraguay.

facilitate terrorism. Two key counterterrorism-related legislative initiatives continued to languish. A counterterrorism bill that would have established the crime of terrorism and other associated crimes was drafted but shelved before its introduction in Congress, and the Brazilian Congress had not approved a long-delayed anti-money laundering bill at year's end. The latter bill would have facilitated greater law enforcement access to financial and banking records during investigations, criminalized illicit enrichment, allowed administrative freezing of assets, and facilitated prosecutions of money laundering cases by amending the legal definition of money laundering, making it an autonomous offense.

Canada

In 2008, United States-Canadian counterterrorism cooperation continued in a number of established fora, including the terrorism sub-group of the Cross Border Crime Forum, the Shared Border Accord Coordinating Committee, and the Bilateral Consultative Group (BCG), which meets on an annual basis. At its January meeting, U.S. and Canadian counterterrorism officials from over a dozen agencies met to coordinate policies on terrorism and share information.

In Afghanistan, Canada's presence has grown to a 2,750-person battle group that is taking the fight to the Taliban insurgency in Kandahar province as part of the International Security Assistance Force's Regional Command South. Canada continued to provide a Provincial Reconstruction Team for stabilization and development efforts, and led a major initiative to improve cross border coordination between Afghan and Pakistani authorities, including police and military, and to enhance the capacities of the units that work to secure the border and prevent insurgent and terrorist crossings. As of December, Canada had lost 103 soldiers, one diplomat, and two aid workers in Afghanistan. It has suffered the highest proportion of casualties to troops deployed of any NATO member in country. During the October national election campaign, Prime Minister Harper re-affirmed that Canada's combat role in Afghanistan would end in 2011.

Canada helped other countries address terrorism and terrorist financing with its Counterterrorism Capacity Building Program, a USD 12 million a year program to provide training, advice, and technical assistance to counterpart agencies. Through this program, Canada provided assistance to several countries in the Caribbean to draft new counterterrorism legislation and conducted intelligence training for border officials on the Afghan-Pakistani border and financial intelligence training for officials in India. Through its Cross Cultural Roundtable and Muslim Outreach program, Canada has actively engaged its citizens in a dialogue on a broad range of national security issues, including terrorism. The Muslim Communities Working Group in the Department of Foreign Affairs and International Trade continued its efforts abroad to enhance Canada's relationships with the countries of the Muslim world, focusing on the promotion of democratic governance, pluralism, and human rights. Canada currently has two projects under the Organization of American States' (OAS) Inter-American Committee Against Terrorism: a capacity-building program on document security; and fraud prevention in El Salvador for all the countries of Central America, the Dominican Republic, and Mexico. Canada sponsors projects as part of the OAS' Hemispheric Security Group. These projects have included efforts to combat identity theft, improve port security in Jamaica, and hemisphere-wide cyber-security.

In 2008, Canada secured its first convictions under the 2001 Antiterrorism Act. In September, a Toronto court convicted a 20-year-old man for conspiring in a group plot to bomb several Canadian targets, including Parliament Hill, Royal Canadian Mounted Police headquarters, and nuclear power plants. Canada's Criminal Youth Justice Act protects his identity. The court had not set a sentencing date at year's end. The government dropped charges against seven alleged co-conspirators; ten of the accused awaited trial at year's end. The remaining individuals faced charges including participation in alleged terrorist training and terrorist financing.

In a separate trial in October, a Canadian judge convicted Momin Khawaja of five charges of financing and facilitating terrorism and two criminal code offenses related to building a remote-control device that could trigger bombs. Police arrested Khawaja in 2004, accusing him of conspiring with a British al-Qa'ida (AQ) cell in a thwarted London bomb plot in that same year. Khawaja faces a maximum of two life terms, plus a consecutive 58 years. In both cases, the judges upheld the constitutionality of Section 38 of the Canada Evidence Act, which allows Canada to protect sensitive foreign government information from public disclosure.

Police in Quebec arrested Said Namouh in September in connection with the arrest in Austria of three members of the Global Islamic Media Front, an AQ-linked propaganda and recruitment organization. Police charged Namouh with plotting a terrorist attack against an unspecified foreign country but found no direct threat to Canada. Namouh remained in custody pending a January bail hearing. In November, working in cooperation with French authorities, Canadian police arrested an Ottawa university instructor in connection with the 1980 bombing of a Paris synagogue, which killed four people. In June and October, in separate immigration cases, the Canadian Border Services Agency deported two alleged Basque Homeland and Freedom terrorists back to Spain to face criminal charges following a request from the Spanish government.

Two important pieces of legislation that the government introduced to Parliament in October 2007 met different fates during 2008. One was a bill to amend the Immigration and Refugee Protection Act to allow for continued application of security certificates, which have been in use for several decades as a way to detain, pending deportation, foreign nationals deemed to be a security threat. The bill provided for a group of cleared special advocates to challenge the evidence on behalf of the accused and for an initial judicial review of detainees in the first 48 hours of arrest and at six-month intervals. Parliament passed this bill, which entered into force on February 14. Five individuals are currently subject to security certificates. The government dropped one individual's certificate. The government released four of the certificate holders from detention subject to conditions on their movement, while one individual under a certificate remained in custody. Legal challenges to the security certificate regime continued.

The second bill was part of a mandatory review of the 2001 Antiterrorism Act. Two provisions of the Act – investigative hearings permitting police to apply for an order requiring a witness to appear before a judge and answer questions; and preventive arrest, whereby police may bring an individual before a judge in the early stages of terrorist activity to disrupt a potential terrorist attack – had sunset clauses and lapsed in February. Although the Senate passed this bill, the Commons had not done so when Governor General Michaelle Jean, on advice of Prime Minister Stephen Harper, dissolved Parliament to hold an October 14 national election. The new government of Prime Minister Harper vowed to reintroduce this legislation in the new Parliament in 2009. Other provisions of the 2001 Act remained in effect.

On December 12, Canada and the United States renewed the bilateral agreement on emergency management cooperation, updating a 1986 accord. It established the basis for mutual assistance in sending supplies, equipment, emergency personnel, and expert support in response to natural and man-made incidents, including those related to terrorism. It provided for integrated responses and relief efforts during cross-border incidents, delineated a comprehensive and harmonized approach to emergency management, and established a framework for a joint response to emergent threats.

In December, Canada renewed formal counterterrorism research and development activities with the United States by extending a 1995 Memorandum of Understanding. The agreement, between Canada's Department of Public Safety and the U.S. Department of Defense, allows the countries to pursue joint technical requirements for combating terrorism across a spectrum of activities, including chemical, biological, radiological, and nuclear countermeasures; physical security and blast mitigation; explosives detection; and countermeasures for improvised explosive devices. Canada also pursued science and technology goals with the

United States through the Public Security Technical Program, which began in 2003.

Canada significantly expanded and refined its Chemical, Biological, Radiological-Nuclear, and Explosives (CBRNE) Research and Technology Initiative (CRTI). The CRTI integrates people and knowledge from the Canadian scientific, technology, law enforcement, national security, public health, policy, and first responder communities to pursue innovative approaches to counterterrorism through CBRNE science and technology. Canadian authorities base the broad program on an annual risk assessment and priority setting process that cover areas including CBRNE detection and identification, criminal and national security investigation capabilities, emergency casualty treatment for CBRNE events, food safety, public confidence, and socio-behavioral issues.

In February, the Financial Action Task Force (FATF) released a Mutual Evaluation on Anti-Money Laundering and Combating the Financing of Terrorist Finance (AML/CFT) in Canada. According to the report, Canada has strengthened its overall AML/CFT regime since its last evaluation in 1997, but Canada's regime was generally insufficient to meet FATF recommendations. Following the FATF report, Canada amended the Proceeds of Crime (Money Laundering) and Terrorist Financing Act (PCMLTFA) in June to bring Canada more in line with international standards, including the FATF's. The PCMLTFA amendments introduced a risk-based approach as a key element of the compliance regime, allowing reporting entities to assess their own vulnerabilities, identify high-risk areas, and allocate resources appropriately. In December, the Canadian government gave Canada's financial intelligence unit the power to issue administrative fines in addition to assessing criminal penalties.

In March, Canada charged an alleged Tamil Tiger fundraiser under the country's laws against terrorist financing. Ontario resident Prapaharan Thambithurai stands accused of raising money for the World Tamil Movement. His trial is pending, and he remained free on bail at year's end. In November, the Minister of Public Safety announced that Canada had completed the mandatory two-year review of listed terrorist entities, and decided that the forty-one entities previously on the list should remain listed.

Chile

Chilean law enforcement actively cooperated in international terrorism investigations and with U.S. efforts to monitor and combat terrorist financing. Law Enforcement officials monitored possible links between extremists in Chile's Iquique Free Trade Zone and those in the Tri-Border Area, as trade links between these two areas were increasing. Chile's National Intelligence Agency remained mostly an analytical body, relying on law enforcement and investigative agencies for the vast majority of collection and operations.

The Federal Bureau of Investigation (FBI) continued to support Chile's Carabineros, the National Military Police, and Gendarmes, in a number of matters related to domestic terrorism. To promote cooperation in identifying, controlling, and more efficiently preventing violent crimes and transnational organized crime, the FBI signed memoranda of cooperation with Chile's four principal law enforcement agencies; the National Prosecutors of the Public Ministry (Fiscalía Nacional – Ministerio Público), Chilean Customs (Aduanas), the Carabineros, and the Investigative police (Policía de Investigaciones, or PDI).

The Carabineros have become members of the FBI's South America Fingerprint Exchange (SAFE) Initiative, a biometric exchange program wherein foreign governments provide and exchange biometric information on violent criminal offenders with the USG. The Department of State conducted a two-week Antiterrorism Assistance (ATA) program on Interdicting Terrorist Attack, that was attended by members of the Carabineros and the PDI.

U.S. law enforcement agencies working in the Embassy continued to monitor the Coordinadora Arauco Melleca (CAM), a violent Mapuche Indian group in southern Chile that has burned fields and attacked police while fighting for land it claims belongs to it. CAM appears to have begun to organize itself and recent incidents have demonstrated increased planning and a more professional use of weapons and tactics.

Chilean police continued monitoring for possible contacts between Mapuche groups and armed political movements in Latin America and Spain. The well trained Grupo de Operaciones Policiales Especiales, a 300-person unit of the Carabineros, served as the nation's primary counterterrorist reaction force and participates annually in Exercise Fuerzas Comando, a U.S. Special Operations Command South-sponsored special operations seminar designed to refine the tactics, techniques, and procedures used by Special Operations counterterrorism forces.

Colombia

The Government of Colombia continued vigorous law enforcement, intelligence, military, and economic measures against the Revolutionary Armed Forces of Colombia (FARC) and the National Liberation Army (ELN), along with operations against remaining elements of the United Self-Defense Forces of Colombia (AUC). Colombia increased its counterterrorism cooperation and training efforts in the region. The threat of extradition to the United States remained a strong weapon against drug traffickers and terrorists. In 2008, Colombia extradited a record 208 defendants to the United States for prosecution; most were Colombian nationals.

The administration of President Álvaro Uribe maintained its focus on defeating and demobilizing Colombia's terrorist groups through its Democratic Security policy, which combines military, intelligence, police operations, efforts to demobilize combatants, and the provision of public services in rural areas previously dominated by illegal armed groups.

On July 2, a Colombian military operation rescued three U.S. Department of Defense contractors, former Colombian presidential candidate and Senator Ingrid Betancourt, and eleven Colombians held by the FARC. The three Americans, kidnapped in February 2003, were the longest-held U.S. hostages in the world at the time of their rescue.

After years of seeming invincibility, the FARC's Secretariat suffered several key losses in 2008. On March 1, a Colombian military strike killed Secretariat member Raúl Reyes at his camp just across the Ecuadorian border, followed less than a week later by the killing of Secretariat member Iván Ríos at the hands of one of his own security guards. Secretariat member and FARC founder Manuel Marulanda (Tirofijo) died in late March, reportedly of natural causes.

In addition to the high-profile hostage rescue and the severe blows to the FARC Secretariat, Colombian security forces captured or killed a number of mid-level FARC leaders, debriefed terrorist group deserters for detailed information on their respective units, and reduced the amount of territory where terrorists could freely operate. The Colombian military crippled the FARC's communications network, destroyed major caches of weapon and supplies, and reduced the group's financial resources through counternarcotics and other security operations.

Additionally, a record number of FARC members deserted in 2008, yet another sign of the organization's deteriorating power. Desertions increased among mid-level and in some cases senior FARC leaders, such as FARC commander Nelly Ávila Moreno (Karina), who deserted in May. FARC desertions in 2008 numbered at least 3,027, surpassing the previous year's record number of 2,480.

Despite the ongoing campaign against the FARC, the group continued tactical-level terrorism, kidnapping for profit and maintained 28 political hostages including former Meta Governor Alan Jara and Valle del Cauca Assemblyman Sigifredo López. The FARC also continued narcotrafficking activities, launched several bombings against military and civilian targets in urban areas, and targeted numerous rural outposts, infrastructure targets, and political adversaries in dozens of attacks. Examples of 2008 terrorist activity attributed to the FARC included the following:

- In March, the FARC attacked electrical towers in Nariño and Cauca, cutting off power to numerous municipalities;

- In August, a bomb in Ituango, Antioquia killed seven and wounded 50;
- In August, a car bomb in front of the Justice Palace in Cali killed four and wounded 26;
- In August, two Bogota supermarkets were targeted with small incendiary devices;
- In November, guerrillas from the FARC's 49th Front in Neiva killed Caquetá council member Edinson Javier Pérez;
- In November, FARC members killed teacher Dora Liliana Saavedra and her husband Ferney Ledesma, in front of schoolchildren, for entertaining Colombian Army members at their home;
- In December, the FARC attacked a humanitarian caravan led by the Colombian Family Welfare Institute in Caquetá department with a roadside bomb, killing two health workers.

Peace talks between the government of Colombia and the ELN remained stalled throughout the year due to ELN intransigence. International and local efforts to coax the ELN back to the negotiating table—including efforts by former ELN leader Antonio Bermúdez (Francisco Galán), who announced his resignation from the group to focus on peace talks in 2008—made little progress. The ELN remained in the field, but with diminished resources, a dwindling membership of approximately 2,000 fighters, and reduced offensive capability. Still, the ELN inflicted casualties on the Colombian military through increased use of land mines. It continued to fund its operations through narcotics trafficking. The ELN and FARC clashed over territory in northeastern and southern Colombia, and the ELN continued kidnapping and extortion. Numerous ELN fronts increased their drug trafficking activities in an effort to stem losses suffered by the government of Colombia and the FARC.

The Colombian government continued to process and investigate demobilized paramilitaries under the Justice and Peace Law (JPL), which offers judicial benefits and reduced prison sentences for qualifying demobilizing terrorists. The law requires all participants to confess fully to their crimes as members of a terrorist group and to return all illicit profits. More than 32,000 rank-and-file ex-AUC members who did not commit serious crimes have demobilized, and many were receiving benefits through the government's reintegration program, including psychosocial attention, education, healthcare, and career development opportunities. Over 160,000 victims have registered under the JPL, although Colombian government efforts to create measures to provide reparations stalled. Some former paramilitaries continued to engage in criminal activities after demobilization, mostly in drug trafficking, but the AUC as a formal organization remained inactive.

In May, the Colombian government extradited 14 former top AUC leaders to the United States for prosecution for narcotrafficking offenses, and for failure to comply with their JPL obligations. Several have continued to testify about their crimes from the United States in hopes of reduced penalties in Colombia when they complete their U.S. sentences and the USG returns them to Colombia. Still, the Uribe administration suspended extraditions of several alleged AUC members who were cooperating with the paramilitary peace process under the JPL. The United States continued to seek their extraditions.

The Colombian government continued to seek the extradition of three Irish Republican Army (IRA) members. The Colombian courts first acquitted the three of charges that they trained the FARC on bomb tactics and then, following an appeal by the prosecution, sentenced them to 17 years in prison. The three fled Colombia while on bail and resurfaced in Ireland in August 2005. Colombia's extradition request remained under review before the Irish courts and the three fugitives remained at large.

Colombia kept up its close cooperation with the United States to block terrorists' assets. Financial institutions closed drug trafficking and terrorism-related accounts on Colombian government orders or in response to designation by the U.S. Treasury Department's Office of Foreign Assets Control (OFAC). Aerial and manual eradication of illicit drugs in Colombia, key to targeting terrorist group finances, covered about 225,000 hectares of illegal drug crops, thus depriving terrorist groups of potentially huge profits. OFAC carried out several designation actions against the financial assets and networks of narcotics traffickers and narcoterrorists (like the FARC) pursuant to Executive Order 12978 and the Foreign Narcotics Kingpin Designation Act. The OFAC sanctions investigations specifically targeted networks of money exchange businesses in Colombia that laundered narcotics proceeds for the FARC. The United States government continued to support the Government of Colombia in its efforts to decrease the number of kidnappings in that country and to support computer investigations and forensics units. These units were responsible for analysis of computer equipment seized during many security operations.

Colombia continued to expand its role as a regional leader in counterterrorism and provided training to several other countries, including combating terrorist financing. The Colombian government continued to seek enhanced regional counterterrorism cooperation to target terrorist safe havens in vulnerable border areas and provided counterterrorism training to officials from partner countries across the region. Colombia and Mexico significantly increased joint training and operations against narcoterrorist organizations operating in both countries, and President Uribe and Mexican President Felipe Calderón met November 10, announcing they would enhance their joint counternarcotics and counterterrorism cooperation.

In March, Ecuador suspended diplomatic relations and counterterrorism cooperation with Colombia to protest the Raúl Reyes camp attack, and the bilateral relationship remained frozen at year's end. Venezuela followed suit, but restored diplomatic relations with Colombia at the Rio Group Summit in the Dominican Republic later in March. President Uribe has called on both governments to engage against the FARC and for Nicaragua to turn over FARC members given asylum there after the attack that killed Reyes.

Dominican Republic

The Dominican Republic is considered a transit point for suspected terrorists and extremists to Europe, Africa, and within the Western Hemisphere. Despite good intentions, the Dominican government lacked the ability to control its air, land, and sea borders fully, due in part to corruption and the mismanagement of resources. While many land border, freight, and airline hubs remained permeable, some strides were taken, such as the Container Security Initiative. The United States assisted Dominican Customs in:

- Establishing criteria to use non-intrusive inspection equipment to screen high risk maritime containers that could smuggle nuclear and radioactive material into U.S. ports;
- Identification of Port Caucedo as a Megaport and its certification as part of the Customs Trade Partnership Against Terrorism initiative; and
- Creating a counterterrorism task force to counter transnational insurgents involved in narcotics trafficking.

The United States provided training and equipment to Dominican agencies involved in counterterrorism efforts. It helped introduce biometrics equipment at the Headquarters of the Dominican National Police and other key locations, which enabled U.S. and Dominican authorities to receive timely biometric data from Dominican military, law enforcement, and judicial databases. It assisted with the training and development of an elite military hostage rescue team, and the Department of State's Antiterrorism Assistance program helped train a nationally deployable Police Explosives Ordinance Unit.

Ecuador

Ecuador's greatest counterterrorism and security challenge remained the presence of Colombian narcotics and insurgent/terrorist groups in the northern border region. In order to evade Colombian military operations, these groups, principally the Revolutionary Armed Forces of Colombia (FARC), regularly used Ecuadorian territory for rest, recuperation, resupply, and training, as well as coca processing and limited planting and production, thereby involving significant numbers of Ecuadorians in direct or indirect ways. The porous 450-mile border and the lack of adequate licit employment opportunities for Ecuadorians in the region have made the area vulnerable to narcoterrorist influence and created a contraband economy. Ecuadorian officials along the border believed the FARC's economic impact allowed it to buy silence and compliance.

Ecuador stepped up its response to this threat, although it continued to face constraints on resources and limited capabilities. The Correa Administration, while maintaining the country's traditional neutrality with respect to the Colombian conflict, has stated it opposed armed encroachments of any kind across its borders. On March 1, a Colombian attack in Ecuadorian territory caused the destruction of a FARC camp and the death of FARC Secretariat member Raúl Reyes. Colombian analysis of documents contained within laptops recovered at the camp suggested elements within the Ecuadorian government had connections to the FARC. The Correa administration strongly denied ties to the FARC, claiming that the only Ecuadorian government contacts with the FARC were to negotiate the release of hostages. The government shifted troops to the border region and continued to promote a development agenda along its northern border in concert with international donors to spur economic development in the area.

Ecuador's security forces conducted operations against FARC training and logistical resupply camps along the northern border. The Ecuadorian military increased the number of operations in Ecuador's northern border region. The military's operational tempo, already higher in early 2008 than in previous years, increased further after the March 1 attack. A total of over 100 battalion-level operations along the northern border led to the discovery and destruction of 11 cocaine producing laboratories, over 130 FARC facilities (bases, houses, and resupply camps), the eradication of nine hectares of coca, and the confiscation of weapons, communications equipment, and other support equipment. These operations also netted valuable information on FARC activities and infrastructure both inside and outside of Ecuador, and resulted in the detention of 20 FARC members and the killing of one FARC member during the year. Despite increasing successes in this effort, insufficient resources, the challenging border region terrain, and a terse bilateral relationship with Colombia since the

March 1, 2008 raid made it difficult to thwart cross-border incursions.

Other groups present in Ecuador, although less active in the last couple of years, included the Popular Combatants Group, the Revolutionary Militia of the People, the Marxist-Leninist Party of Ecuador, and the Alfarista Liberation Army.

The Ecuadorian government continued to strengthen controls over money laundering through the Financial Intelligence Unit (FIU), which it established under a 2005 Money Laundering Law. The FIU cooperated closely with the Anti-Narcotics Police Directorate, the Superintendent of Banks, the courts, and the private banker association to identify suspicious transactions and develop information for the prosecution of cases.

Ecuador's judicial institutions remained weak, susceptible to corruption, and heavily backlogged with pending cases. While the military and police have made numerous arrests, the judicial system had a poor record of achieving convictions.

El Salvador

El Salvador provided valuable assistance to regional security efforts by hosting the Comalapa Cooperative Security Location (CSL), a regional Department of Defense (DOD) narcotics detection and interdiction hub. El Salvador also hosted the USG-funded International Law Enforcement Academy (ILEA), which provided instruction on counterterrorism, transnational crime, alien trafficking, and money laundering. El Salvador maintained a military contingent in Iraq in support of Coalition efforts, and worked within the Central American Regional Integration System to promote effective regional responses to transnational crime and other public security threats.

The principal Salvadoran counterterrorism entity, the National Civilian Police (PNC), worked in close cooperation with the Salvadoran Immigration Service, the Office of the Attorney General, and the Office of State Intelligence. A 2006 statute established strict criminal liability for engaging in terrorism, while other statutes outlaw money laundering and terrorist financing.

Guatemala

Guatemala continued to strengthen its anti-money laundering and terrorist financing regime since its 2004 removal from the Financial Action Task Force list of Non-Cooperative Countries. With U.S. assistance, Guatemala formed an interagency money laundering task force with representation from the Financial Intelligence Unit, the Guatemalan tax authority, and the Public Ministry (prosecutor's office). The U.S. Department of Defense continued to train the Guatemalan military's counterterrorist unit. In addition to threats posed by transnational narcotics organizations, Guatemala is a major alien smuggling route from Central and South America, which makes it a potential transit point for terrorists seeking to gain access to the United States.

Severe resource constraints, corruption, and an ineffective criminal justice system hampered efforts to combat transnational crime threats such as drug trafficking and alien smuggling, especially in remote areas of the country. Guatemala's borders lacked effective coverage by police or military personnel, and controls at its southern and eastern borders with El Salvador and Honduras have been relaxed as part of the Central American integration process. Nevertheless, Guatemalan civil aviation and port authorities cooperated with the United States in investigating potential terrorism leads.

Haiti

The Government of Haiti cooperated with the United States on counterterrorism efforts. The Financial Investigative Unit (BAFE) within the Haitian National Police and the Financial Intelligence Unit (UCREF) within the Ministry of Justice cooperated with the United States in anti-money laundering initiatives to improve the ability to detect funds acquired through criminal activity, including funds that could be acquired through terrorist networks. The Haitian government drafted Counterterrorism legislation in 2008.

Honduras

In 2008 Honduran cooperation with the United States on combating terrorist financing remained strong. The Honduran Banking and Insurance Commission, through instruction from the Ministry of Foreign Affairs, promptly sent prompt freeze orders to the entire regulated financial sector every time the United States amended Executive Order lists. Financial entities, particularly the commercial banks, promptly undertook the requested searches for accounts by terrorist entities. No terrorist-related funds have been found to date in the Honduran financial system. The Honduran Congress was considering a change to the criminal code that would criminalize terrorist financing. While terrorism is a crime, terrorist financing is not listed as a separate crime.

There was a trend in Honduras towards closer regional intelligence cooperation with neighboring countries; this cooperation was aimed principally at organized crime but it could potentially protect the country from terrorist threats. In September 2007, the Honduran government announced the adoption of a National Security Strategy, which included counterterrorism as an objective, and stressed regional and international cooperation.

The United States assisted the Honduran Armed Forces (HOAF) with its counterterrorism efforts by providing training and equipment. With U.S. assistance, the Honduran Armed Forces created a Joint Task Force.

There was no indication of terrorist groups using illegal immigration networks. Over the past five years, however, smuggling rings have been detected moving people from East Africa, the Middle East, and Southwest Asia to Honduras or through its territory. In 2008, there was an increase in the number of boats arriving on the north coast, ferrying people from all over the world seeking to enter the United States illegally via Guatemala and Mexico. Nationals of countries without Honduran visa requirements, especially Ecuador and Colombia, were involved in schemes to transit Honduras, often with the United States and Europe as their final destination. Foreign nationals have successfully obtained valid Honduran identity cards and passports under their own or false identities. The Honduran government's ability to combat transnational crime was limited by sparsely populated and isolated jungle regions, limited resources, corruption, and poor control of the north coast and eastern border. However, increased U.S. and Honduran government investment and training for members of the judicial branch, law enforcement entities, and the military have begun to decrease criminal activity and reduce the potential appeal of using the criminal infrastructure in these remote areas for the movement of terrorists and their resources.

Jamaica

Jamaica's proximity to the United States, well developed sea lanes and air links, and the transit of over two million travelers annually between the United States and Jamaica make the country a potential transit point for terrorists. In 2008, the United States and Jamaica continued their close cooperation in a variety of counterterrorism-related areas, which included the Container Security Initiative, provision of equipment and training to the Jamaica Defense Force and Constabulary Force, and law enforcement intelligence sharing. In 2007, following his imprisonment in the United Kingdom for inciting murder and for fomenting terrorism and racial hatred, British authorities deported the radical Jamaican-born cleric Sheik Abdullah El-Faisal. Jamaican and U.S. authorities remained concerned about El-Faisal's plans, intentions, and influence.

Mexico

Although no serious terrorist incidents targeting U.S. interests/ personnel have occurred on or originated from Mexican territory, violence has risen to new levels and narcotraffickers have shown a willingness to use terrorist tactics. Incidents illustrating this include the September 15 independence day grenade attack in Morelia, which claimed at least seven lives and injured scores, as well as the killing and beheading of eight military soldiers in Guerrero in mid-December. Another like incident involved a U.S. target; on October 12, unknown persons fired gunshots and tossed an undetonated grenade at the U.S. Consulate in Monterrey. Although such attacks have raised the specter of domestic terrorism, Mexico primarily represents a terrorist transit threat and bilateral efforts focused squarely on minimizing that threat.

President Calderón's Administration has demonstrated an unprecedented commitment to address national security concerns. U.S. law enforcement agencies enjoyed a much-improved relationship with Mexican security institutions across the board. Mexico worked with the United States to secure critical infrastructure, combat terrorist financing, and enhance aviation, border, maritime, and transportation security. In October 2007, Mexico and the United States announced the Mérida Initiative. The U.S. government has pledged $1.4 billion over three years to the Government of Mexico to aid in their fight against criminal elements in their country. In June 2008, Congress approved $400 million for Mexico in support of the Merida Initiative, which provides funding for equipment, vetting, and training to support law enforcement operations. It also provides technical assistance for reform and oversight of security agencies. In addition to active support for law enforcement, there are parallel efforts in the areas of judicial reform, anti-corruption, and programs to encourage participation of civil society. The Mexican government's increased commitment to national security concerns has resulted in a significant increase in violence against high level Mexican government officials. The United States government has worked closely with the Mexican government to mitigate this threat.

Mexico continued to make steady progress in the area of counterterrorism with an emphasis on border security projects targeting the smuggling of aliens who raise terrorism concerns. The government worked to professionalize federal law enforcement, restructuring and strengthening institutions responsible for fighting organized crime, and developing tools under the framework of the Security and Prosperity Partnership (SPP) to better address national security threats.

The continued exploitation of smuggling channels traversing the U.S. Mexico border, and lack of enforcement along Mexico's border with Guatemala remained strategic concerns. In 2007, Mexico passed a law against human trafficking, which will aid in pursuing criminal proceedings against traffickers and smugglers operating in the country.

One setback in United States-Mexico counterterrorism cooperation was a change in detention procedures. In 2005 and 2006, Mexico's Immigration Service (INM) maintained a policy of housing all detained aliens who may raise terrorism concerns in their detention facility near Mexico City. In March 2007, however, the INM began releasing such detainees from their point of arrest, thus hindering information sharing and the USG's ability to track the movement of these aliens. This remained a problem in 2008.

Nevertheless, cooperation between the U.S. and Mexican governments has been strong overall. The two countries exchanged information and closely cooperated in targeting alien smugglers, particularly along Mexico's northern border. The Operation Against Smugglers (and Traffickers) Initiative on Safety and Security (OASISS), which allows Mexican and U.S. law enforcement officials to share real-time information regarding ongoing alien smuggling investigations, has been particularly effective. OASISS enhances the ability of both governments to prosecute alien smugglers and human traffickers. OASISS is currently operational in the United States in all four states along the southwest border and in most of Mexico's northern border states. The program provides a model for bilateral information sharing in a variety of law enforcement and security areas. An essential next step to expand OASISS to all of Mexico's northern border states is scheduled to be completed with FY-2008 Merida Initiative funding.

The U.S.-Mexico Border Security and Public Safety Working Group, formed in March 2006, has become another important tool for bilateral cooperation, establishing protocols enabling both governments to respond cooperatively at a local level to critical incidents and emergencies. The success of the pilot sites led to the expansion and formalization of the program. These protocols are now in place along the entire U.S.-Mexico border.

Mexico coordinated with the United States on the information sharing of air passenger data and the use of its Integrated System for Migratory Operations (SIOM). In addition, the Mexican and U.S. governments agreed to share, on a case-by-case basis, biometric data for comparison to the Integrated Automated Fingerprint Identification System (IAFIS).

The United States also developed a strong working relationship with the Financial Intelligence Unit of the Attorney General's Office (PGR) and its companion unit in the Mexican Treasury (Hacienda) in combating money laundering, terrorist financing, and narcotics trafficking.

In 2007, President Calderón signed into law legislation outlawing terrorist financing and associated money laundering. The new law established international terrorism and terrorist financing as serious criminal offenses, as called for in UN resolution 1373, and provides for up to 40-year prison sentences. The measure also incorporated several non-finance related provisions including jail sentences for individuals who cover up the identities of terrorists and for those who recruit people to commit terrorist acts. While it lacked some important provisions, such as asset forfeiture measures, the law was a significant step forward. Mexico's legislature continued working on justice reform legislation, which, if enacted, will offer law enforcement officials broader authorities (including asset forfeiture) to investigate and prosecute serious criminal cases, including terrorist activity. Despite the recent legislation, money laundering remained a significant problem in Mexico.

The Mexican Navy and Army continued to expand their counterterrorism capabilities. The Mexican Navy improved control over ports of entry by deploying a newly constituted infantry force. The Navy also worked to expand its still incomplete control over Mexico's vast maritime zone by better integrating radar, patrol craft, seagoing vessels, air platforms, and land-based platforms. These enhancements to Mexico's maritime air surveillance will allow the Navy to protect key national strategic facilities, including those related to oil production in the Bay of Campeche.

Nicaragua

In 2008 Nicaragua made no substantive progress towards establishing a Financial Intelligence Unit or on a counterterrorism bill first proposed in 2004. Nicaragua's judiciary remained highly politicized, corrupt, and prone to manipulation. President Daniel Ortega's 2007 decision to grant Iranian nationals visa-free entry into Nicaragua remained in effect.

President Ortega maintained close relations with the Revolutionary Armed Forces of Colombia (FARC). On March 6, President Ortega broke diplomatic relations with Colombia for 24 hours following Colombia's March 1 military action against a FARC base in Ecuador. Nicaragua also publicly welcomed survivors of the March 1 Colombian military operation against the FARC and granted asylum to suspected FARC operatives:

- On April 19, President Ortega personally met Lucia Andrea Morett Alvarez and her parents on their arrival in Nicaragua. Morett, a Mexican university student, suffered injuries during the March 1 Colombian military operation against FARC personnel in Ecuador. According to the Nicaraguan Foreign Ministry, Morett was in Nicaragua as a tourist. She was never offered, nor did she request asylum or Nicaraguan citizenship.
- On May 11, President Ortega sent a Nicaraguan Air Force plane to Ecuador to retrieve two Colombian survivors of the March 1 operation, Doris Torres Bohórquez and Martha Pérez Gutiérrez. Nicaragua granted both asylum, and on July 19, the anniversary

of the Sandinista revolutionary victory, President Ortega officially welcomed them as survivors of state-sponsored terrorism by Colombia.

- On August 19, Nicaraguan Foreign Minister Samuel Santos, confirmed that a third Colombian, Nubia Calderón de Trujillo, also known as Esperanza, had been granted humanitarian asylum in Nicaragua. Santos stated that Nicaragua had responded to a request for assistance sent to the Nicaraguan Embassy in Ecuador by Calderón, who was also injured in the March 1 operation. On September 30, the U.S. Department of Justice Office of Foreign Asset Control (OFAC) named Calderón and seven other international representatives of the FARC as significant narcotraffickers under the Kingpin Act. The OFAC press release noted that, Nubia Calderón de Trujillo was recently granted asylum by Nicaragua, even though she is a member of an internationally recognized narcoterrorist organization. Unlike Morett and the two other Colombians, Calderón did not appear in public after arriving in Nicaragua.
- In July, the local press discovered that, in late 2007, an official of the Supreme Electoral Council (CSE) issued a Nicaraguan national identity card (cédula) to a René Alberto Gutiérrez Pastrán. Gutiérrez Pastrán was actually FARC emissary Alberto Bermúdez, aka Cojo. Bermúdez subsequently used his false identity to transit Nicaragua.

Panama

The Panamanian government approved a reform of its security forces that touched off a controversy over whether the government intended to re-militarize. The government justified these security reforms by pointing to the need to protect the Canal from possible terrorist attacks. An act of terrorism that closed off the Panama Canal would severely affect the economies of Panama, the United States, and other countries that rely heavily on the Canal for commerce.

The reforms fused the National Maritime Service (SMN) and the National Air Service (SAN) into a new, coast guard-like National Aero-Naval Service (SENAN). It also created a legal framework for the country's intelligence service, now called the National Intelligence and Security Service (SENIS). Finally, it broke off the National Frontier Directorate or the Panamanian National Police (PNP) to form a new independent security service, called the National Frontier Service (SENAFRONT). The reforms also made it possible for uniformed officers to lead all these services, something previously prohibited by law. The creation of the SENAFRONT was publicly justified by the need to keep a police force permanently deployed on the border to protect against irregulars and drug traffickers. Major investments will be required before these changes can be expected to have a serious improvement on operational capability. Some investments in improved equipment, such as new and refurbished helicopters, were underway at year's end.

Panama's highly developed commercial transport sector and shared border with Colombia made it a transshipment point for arms, drugs, and smuggling of illegal aliens. The Revolutionary Armed Forces of Colombia (FARC) continued to be active in Panama's Darien Province and Panama's Public Forces (PPF) closely monitored its activities. The PPF captured six members of the FARC in a boat off the village of Jaque in the Darien in February, after the occupants of the boat opened fire on the PPF. There were several reports of FARC members entering villages in the Darien and stealing supplies. A shoot-out occurred between the PPF and the FARC in the village of Manene in the Darien in December. The PFF wounded and captured at least one member of the FARC. The FARC was believed to have had links to several kidnappings in Panama.

Panama provided enhanced force protection for U.S. military vessels, including submarines, during "high value transits" of the Canal. U.S. officials praised Panama's level of support and security. The Ministry of Government and Justice used classroom training, tabletop exercises, and field visits to improve coordination among PPF agencies. Panama co-hosted the annual PANAMAX exercise, a multinational security training exercise tailored to the defense of the Canal. The exercise replicated real world threats to the Canal to develop appropriate responses and guarantee safe passage to the approaches to the Canal and through the waterway. Twenty nations participated, including the United States. On the margins of PANAMAX, Panama once again hosted a tabletop exercise specifically designed to examine its ability to address asymmetric threats.

Panama continued to participate in the Container Security Initiative (CSI) at two ports. CSI activities at a third port will be operational shortly, as a third scanner has just been installed in the Colón Free Trade Zone. Additionally, the Department of Energy's Megaports Radiation Portals became functional at the ports of Manzanillo and Balboa.

PPF Counterterrorism units in the police and frontier forces continued to benefit from the third year of counterterrorism training funded by United States Southern Command (SOUTHCOM) and provided by U.S. Navy Special Warfare South personnel.

Panama is an international offshore banking center. While the government has taken extensive measures to combat money laundering in the banking system, the Colón Free Trade Zone served as a vehicle for illicit finance. Panama's Foreign Ministry, Council for Public Security and

National Defense, Financial Analysis Unit, and the Superintendent of Banks were fully cooperative in reviewing terrorism finance lists.

Paraguay

A weak, politicized judicial system, a police force widely viewed as corrupt and ineffective, and a lack of strong anti-money laundering and terrorist financing legislation continued to hamper Paraguay's counterterrorism efforts. On June 25, Paraguay's Congress took the final measure to pass improved anti-money laundering legislation as part of a major overhaul of the penal code. The Congress' Legal Reform Commission also drafted a criminal procedural code reform bill that would facilitate prosecution of money laundering and terrorism and modernize Paraguay's criminal justice system. However, the procedural code reform bill has since been mothballed in the Commission for more than a year. Terrorist financing legislation will be critical to keep Paraguay current with its international obligations. Efforts to include a terrorist financing statute in the new penal code failed; however, several draft terrorist financing laws are pending in Congress. Paraguay's Secretariat for the Prevention of Money Laundering (SEPRELAD) is working on a revised draft of the terrorist financing bill to present to Congress. Using its experience in the development of a similar law, Brazil is providing technical assistance to SEPRELAD. The Egmont Group notified Paraguay about the need to comply with its international commitments regarding terrorist financing legislation. If Paraguay does not show reasonable progress in enacting such a law, it could face expulsion.

Paraguay did not exercise effective immigration or customs controls at its porous borders. Efforts to address illicit activity occurring in the Tri-Border Area were uneven due to a lack of resources and, more principally, corruption within Customs, the police, and the judicial sector. The United States continued to work closely with SEPRELAD, which made several in-roads into undermining money laundering in Paraguay, including December raids on illegal exchange houses. Paraguay fully paid its outstanding dues to the Financial Action Task Force of Latin America (GAFISUD) in mid-2008, after many years in arrears with the organization.

In October, a Paraguayan court dismissed tax evasion and money laundering charges against Kassem Hijazi, a suspected Hizballah money launderer, after significant indications of judicial and political interference with the prosecution of what had been the largest money-laundering case in Paraguay's history. A Paraguayan court convicted and sentenced suspected Hizballah fundraiser Hatem Ahmad Barakat on tax evasion charges in April 2006; during 2008, he continued to appeal his three-year sentence while on bail.

The United States assisted Paraguay with capacity building for law enforcement and training for judges, prosecutors, and police in counterterrorism awareness, as well as weapons of mass destruction response capabilities. Under the Millennium Challenge Corporation's Threshold Program, the United States assisted Paraguay with training for judges, prosecutors, and police in investigation techniques that are critical to money laundering and terrorist financing cases. Paraguay submitted a proposal for a second phase of the Threshold Program in November, which will focus in part on police corruption.

Peru

Peru's primary counterterrorism concern remained fighting remnants of the militant Maoist Sendero Luminoso (SL or Shining Path), a designated Foreign Terrorist Organization that wreaked havoc on the country in the 1980s and 1990s at a cost of more than 69,000 lives. SL remnants in the Upper Huallaga River Valley (UHV) sought to regroup and replenish their ranks following significant setbacks suffered in 2007. Separately, the SL organization in the Apurimac and Ene River Valley (VRAE) maintained its control over the area. Both groups continued to engage in drug trafficking, and during the year carried out 64 terrorist acts in remote coca-growing areas that killed at least 12 police, four civilians, and 15 members of the military. Although the Fujimori government nearly eliminated SL in the 1990s, the organization, now entwined with narcotics trafficking, remained a threat in 2008. The two SL organizations combined were thought to number several hundred armed combatants. While today's SL is shorter on revolutionary zeal than in the past, analysts believed leaders continued to use Maoist philosophy to justify their illicit activities. Involvement in drug production and trafficking provided SL with funding to conduct operations, allowing it to improve relations with local communities in remote areas and to recruit new members. While SL in the UHV worked during the year to recuperate from losses suffered in 2007, insufficient government presence in the more remote VRAE allowed the organization there to continue operating:

- On March 5, five armed attackers killed two Peruvian National Police (PNP) officers near the town of Chanchamayo in Junín department.
- On March 23, an estimated 30 SL members ambushed an anti-drug police unit near Quinua in Ayacucho department, killing one.
- On April 30, SL attackers killed two civilians who were acting as guides for military personnel, near the town of Ancoin in Ayacucho department.
- On June 27, SL members attacked troops on a counternarcotics operation near Sivia in Ayacucho department, killing one.

- On October 9, in northern Huancavelica department, SL triggered a remotely activated bomb underneath a truck returning Peruvian Army soldiers to a nearby base. The attackers then opened fire from both sides of the road, killing 14 soldiers and two civilians. Sixteen others were wounded, three of them critically. It was the deadliest SL attack since the 1992 capture of SL founder Abimael Guzmán.
- On November 16, an SL ambush killed three PNP officers in the town of Huanta in northern Ayacucho.
- On October 14, suspected SL elements attacked a PNP vehicle traveling on the highway north of Tingo María in Huánuco department, firing on it from both sides of the road. Two of the five officers inside were injured, one of whom later died.
- On November 26, suspected SL attackers ambushed a PNP convoy on the highway some 20 kilometers north of Tingo María in Huánuco department, killing five police and wounding four others.
- On December 27, SL insurgents attacked a military helicopter in Vizcatan killing one soldier and wounding two others.

In late August, the Army began an offensive called "Operation Excellence," aimed at taking control of the Vizcatán region in northern Ayacucho department. While there were unconfirmed reports of SL casualties, the military suffered losses in a number of SL attacks in response to the offensive.

Implementation of the García government's "Plan VRAE," which called for 2,000 troops and 19 counterterrorism bases operated under a central command was still evolving. Plans for new health, education, and infrastructure investment in these isolated communities where the state lacked presence were not implemented, although new Prime Minister Yehude Simon led a full cabinet delegation to the VRAE in November to evaluate the situation.

During the period June 2007 to November 2008, the "Huallaga Police Front" (an initiative begun in 2006 under then-President Toledo), prosecuted a counterterrorism campaign in the UHV and captured more than 100 alleged SL members, including one national-level leader. It also destroyed 27 SL camps, broke up an urban cell that served as an intelligence link, and seized dozens of weapons, explosives, and ammunition.

Government efforts to improve interagency cooperation, especially in intelligence, and to strengthen prosecutorial capacity were somewhat successful. Police units specializing in counterterrorism and counter-narcotics conducted some joint operations with the Peruvian Army in the UHV. President García continued reauthorizing a 60-day state of emergency in parts of Peru's five departments where SL operates, suspending some civil liberties, and giving the armed forces additional authority to maintain public order. There was no movement on President García's 2006 proposal calling for the death penalty for those convicted of acts of terrorism. The Túpac Amaru Revolutionary Movement (MRTA) has not conducted terrorist activities since the 1996 hostage taking at the Japanese Ambassador's residence in Lima. Efforts to reconstitute an organizational structure were not in evidence in 2008, though former MRTA members were working to establish a political party called the Free Fatherland Movement ("Movimiento Patria Libre") to compete in future elections. SL founder and leader Abimael Guzmán and key accomplices remained in prison serving life sentences on charges stemming from crimes committed during the 1980s and 1990s. The Revolutionary Armed Forces of Colombia (FARC) continued to use remote areas along the Colombian-Peruvian border to rest, regroup, and make arms purchases. Experts believed the FARC continued to fund coca cultivation and cocaine production among the Peruvian population in border areas.

Trinidad and Tobago

In June, the Government of Trinidad and Tobago approved the extradition of two Guyanese and one Trinidadian accused of plotting to blow up jet fuel tanks and a fuel pipeline at New York's John F. Kennedy International Airport. In a separate matter, Imam Yasin Abu Bakr of Jamaat al-Muslimeen (JAM) became the first person prosecuted under the 2005 Antiterrorism Act after delivering an allegedly seditious sermon in late 2005. Bakr challenged the validity of the Act, but a high court judge dismissed the constitutional motion. The JAM leader has filed an appeal challenging the judge's ruling. The special prosecutor for the State desired to sever the terrorism indictment so that the other charges could proceed in the interim. However, the Director of Public Prosecutions determined that the best chance for conviction was if all three charges were tried together.

In July, Trinidad and Tobago enacted the Immigration (Advance Passenger Information) Act, 2008. Under this Act, regional and international aircraft and vessels must submit Advance Passenger Information prior to arrival in and upon departure from Trinidad and Tobago. The Act makes permanent the Advance Passenger Information System measures utilized in Trinidad and Tobago and other West Indies host nations during the 2007 Cricket World Cup. The system utilizes a number of watch lists, including INTERPOL's Stolen and Lost Travel Documents database to check every passenger arriving in Trinidad and Tobago or traveling through by air or by sea. Furthermore, the government established the Trinidad and Tobago

Immigration Document Examination Laboratory at Port of Spain's Piarco International Airport. The laboratory's primary aim is to counter the fraudulent use of travel and identity documents by utilizing technical equipment and trained experts. The United States continued to support Trinidad and Tobago's counterterrorism efforts by engaging in bomb detection training and providing equipment. For its part, the Government of Trinidad and Tobago trained 16 additional tactical and bomb-sniffing dogs through its canine academy.

Trinidad and Tobago is the United States' largest supplier of liquefied natural gas (LNG) and plays an important role in Caribbean energy security. Recognizing this, the U.S. Department of Energy and the U.S. Department of Homeland Security began engaging Trinidad and Tobago, under the umbrella of the Inter-American Committee against Terrorism of the Organization of American States, to improve protection of infrastructure critical to LNG exports. Following bilateral preparatory meetings in 2007, a team of USG experts carried out a vulnerability assessment in January 2008 and prepared a report with recommendations to improve and prioritize critical infrastructure protection efforts.

Uruguay

The Government of Uruguay's cooperation and intelligence sharing on counterterrorism-related issues greatly improved in 2008, especially at the working level, where officers in law enforcement and security services recognized the importance of actively conducting investigations, sharing intelligence with the United States, and working cooperatively with regional partners. Uruguayan authorities generally cooperated with the United States and international institutions on counterterrorism efforts and have to implement a 2004 money laundering law more robustly. Uruguayan banking and law enforcement agencies have mechanisms in place to identify financial assets, individuals, and groups with links to terrorism, but to date they have discovered neither terrorist assets in Uruguayan financial institutions nor terrorist operatives in Uruguay. In October, the parliament passed legislation to create a specialized organized crime unit to prosecute crimes including terrorism and terrorist financing. The judges and prosecutors were named in December.

Uruguay is a member of the Permanent Working Group on Terrorism of the Common Market of the South (Mercosur), together with Argentina, Brazil, Chile, Paraguay, and Bolivia. The group facilitates cooperation and information sharing among countries combating terrorism. The Working Group expanded its focus from the Tri-Border Area of Argentina, Paraguay, and Brazil to the porous and insufficiently monitored Uruguayan-Brazilian border. Uruguay was also active in a range of international counterterrorism efforts, particularly in the Rio Group and the Organization of American States.

Uruguay provided the greatest number of UN peacekeepers per capita of any UN member state. Uruguayan officials believe that using its diplomatic and military resources to fight global instability served to address the conditions that terrorists exploit.

Uruguay significantly increased participation in joint military training. It hosted the Peacekeeping Operations (PKO) South in September, took second place in the Force's Commando Counter Terrorism Competition in the United States in June, and participated for the second time in the multinational training exercise, PANAMAX in August. This is a significant improvement over past reluctance to engage in security cooperation, and indicates that Uruguay is moving beyond the aftermath of its thirteen-year military dictatorship, which ended in 1985.

Venezuela

President Chávez's ideological sympathy for the FARC and the National Liberation Army (ELN) limited Venezuelan cooperation with Colombia in combating terrorism. In January, he called for, and the Venezuelan National Assembly approved, a resolution calling for international recognition of the FARC and ELN as belligerent forces, not terrorist groups. In March, he called FARC second-in-command Raúl Reyes, "a good revolutionary" and held a national moment of silence following the Colombian cross-border raid into Ecuador that killed Reyes. In March, Venezuelan authorities apprehended two FARC fighters seeking medical treatment in Venezuela. They took the injured man to a military hospital for treatment and his companion to a regional penitentiary. By May however, Venezuelan authorities declined to provide information on the whereabouts of either man. In June, President, Chávez publicly changed course, calling upon the FARC to unconditionally release all hostages, declaring that armed struggle is "out of place" in modern Latin America. In July, the Venezuelan National Guard detained FARC chief of borders and finance Gabriel Culma Ortiz and the Venezuelan government handed him over to Colombian authorities.

Venezuelan President Hugo Chávez brokered the unilateral release of six hostages from the Revolutionary Armed Forces of Colombia (FARC) in January and February 2008.

In December, a Venezuelan court sentenced two self-proclaimed Islamic extremists to 10 years each for placing a pair of pipe bombs outside the U.S. Embassy in 2006. The court convicted José Miguel Rojas Espinoza of constructing and placing the devices and found Teodoro Rafael Darnott guilty of planning the attack and instigating Rojas to conduct it.

In June, the U.S. Department of the Treasury's Office of Foreign Assets Control (OFAC) designated Venezuelan diplomat Ghazi Nasr al Din and travel impresario Fawzi Kan'an as Venezuelan Hizballah supporters. In September, OFAC designated two senior Venezuelan government officials, Hugo Armando Carvajal Barrios and Henry de Jesús Rangel Silva, and the former Justice and Interior Minister, Ramón Rodríguez Chacín, for materially assisting the narcotics trafficking activities of the FARC. Limited amounts of weapons and ammunition, some from official Venezuelan stocks and facilities, have turned up in the hands of Colombian terrorist organizations. The Venezuelan government did not systematically police the 1,400-mile Venezuelan-Colombian border to prevent the movement of groups of armed terrorists or to interdict arms or the flow of narcotics. The FARC, ELN, and remnants of the United Self-Defense Forces of Colombia (AUC) regularly crossed into Venezuelan territory to rest and regroup as well as to extort protection money and kidnap Venezuelans to finance their operations.

Iran and Venezuela continued weekly flights connecting Tehran and Damascus with Caracas. Passengers on these flights were reportedly subject to only cursory immigration and customs controls at Simon Bolivar International Airport in Caracas. Venezuelan citizenship, identity, and travel documents remained easy to obtain, making Venezuela a potentially attractive way station for terrorists. International authorities remained suspicious of the integrity of Venezuelan documents and their issuance process.

In May 2008, Venezuela was re-certified as "not cooperating fully" with U.S. antiterrorism efforts under Section 40A of the Arms Export and Control Act, as amended (the "Act"). Pursuant to this certification, defense articles and services may not be sold or licensed for export to Venezuela from October 1, 2008, to September 30, 2009.

CHAPTER – 3

State Sponsors of Terrorism

State sponsors of terrorism provide critical support to non-state terrorist groups. Without state sponsors, terrorist groups would have greater difficulty obtaining the funds, weapons, materials, and secure areas they require to plan and conduct operations. The United States will continue to insist that these countries end the support they give to terrorist groups.

Sudan continued to take significant steps towards better counterterrorism cooperation. Iran and Syria have not renounced terrorism or made efforts to act against Foreign Terrorist Organizations and routinely provided safe haven, substantial resources, and guidance to terrorist organizations. Cuba continued to publicly defend the FARC and provide safe haven to some members of terrorist organizations, though some were in Cuba in connection with peace negotiations with the Governments of Spain and Colombia.

On October 11, the United States rescinded the designation of the Democratic People's Republic of Korea (DPRK) as a state sponsor of terrorism in accordance with criteria set forth in U.S. law, including a certification that the Government of North Korea had not provided any support for international terrorism during the preceding six-month period and the provision by the government of assurances that it will not support acts of international terrorism in the future.

State Sponsor: Implications

Designating countries that repeatedly provide support for acts of international terrorism as state sponsors of terrorism imposes four main sets of U.S. Government sanctions:

1. A ban on arms-related exports and sales.
2. Controls over exports of dual-use items, requiring 30-day Congressional notification for goods or services that could significantly enhance the terrorist-list country's military capability or ability to support terrorism.
3. Prohibitions on economic assistance.
4. Imposition of miscellaneous financial and other restrictions, including:

- Requiring the United States to oppose loans by the World Bank and other international financial institutions;
- Exception from the jurisdictional immunity in U.S. courts of state sponsor countries, and all former state sponsor countries (with the exception of Iraq), with respect to claims for money damages for personal injury or death caused by certain acts of terrorism, torture, or extrajudicial killing, or the provision of material support or resources for such acts;
- Denying companies and individuals tax credits for income earned in terrorist-list countries;
- Denial of duty-free treatment of goods exported to the United States;
- Authority to prohibit any U.S. citizen from engaging in a financial transaction with a terrorist-list government without a Treasury Department license; and
- Prohibition of Defense Department contracts above $100,000 with companies in which a state sponsor government owns or controls a significant interest.

CUBA

Although Cuba no longer actively supports armed struggle in Latin America and other parts of the world, the Cuban government continued to provide safe haven to several terrorists. Members of ETA, the FARC, and the ELN remained in Cuba during 2008, some having arrived in Cuba in connection with peace negotiations with the governments of Spain and Colombia. Cuban authorities continued to publicly defend the FARC. However, on July 6, 2008, former Cuban President Fidel Castro called on the FARC to release the hostages they were holding without preconditions. He has also condemned the FARC's mistreatment of captives and of their abduction of civilian politicians who had no role in the armed conflict.

The United States has no evidence of terrorist-related money laundering or terrorist financing activities in Cuba, although Cuba has one of the world's most secretive and non-transparent national banking systems. Cuba has no financial intelligence unit. Cuba's Law 93 Against Acts of Terrorism provides the government authority to track, block, or seize terrorist assets.

The Cuban government continued to permit some U.S. fugitives—including members of U.S. militant groups such as the Boricua Popular, or *Macheteros*, and the Black Liberation Army to live legally in Cuba. In keeping with its public declaration, the government has not provided safe haven to any new U.S. fugitives wanted for terrorism since 2006.

IRAN

Iran remained the most active state sponsor of terrorism. Iran's involvement in the planning and financial support of terrorist attacks throughout the Middle East, Europe, and Central Asia had a direct impact on international efforts to promote peace, threatened economic stability in the Gulf, and undermined the growth of democracy.

The Qods Force, an elite branch of the Islamic Revolutionary Guard Corps (IRGC), is the regime's primary mechanism for cultivating and supporting terrorists abroad. The Qods Force provided aid in the form of weapons, training, and funding to HAMAS and other Palestinian terrorist groups, Lebanese Hizballah, Iraq-based militants, and Taliban fighters in Afghanistan.

Iran remained a principal supporter of groups that are implacably opposed to the Middle East Peace Process. Iran provided weapons, training, and funding to HAMAS and other Palestinian terrorist groups, including Palestine Islamic Jihad (PIJ) and the Popular Front for the Liberation of Palestine-General Command (PFLP-GC). Iran's provision of training, weapons, and money to HAMAS since the 2006 Palestinian elections has bolstered the group's ability to strike Israel. In 2008, Iran provided more than $200 million in funding to Lebanese Hizballah and trained over 3,000 Hizballah fighters at camps in Iran. Since the end of the 2006 Israeli-Hizballah conflict, Iran has assisted Hizballah in rearming, in violation of UN Security Council Resolution 1701.

Iran's IRGC Qods Force provided assistance to the Taliban in Afghanistan. The Qods Force provided training to the Taliban on small unit tactics, small arms, explosives, and indirect fire weapons. Since at least 2006, Iran has arranged arms shipments including small arms and associated ammunition, rocket propelled grenades, mortar rounds, 107mm rockets, and plastic explosives to select Taliban members.

Despite its pledge to support the stabilization of Iraq, Iranian authorities continued to provide lethal support, including weapons, training, funding, and guidance, to Iraqi militant groups that targeted Coalition and Iraqi forces and killed innocent Iraqi civilians. Iran's Qods Force continued to provide Iraqi militants with Iranian-produced advanced rockets, sniper rifles, automatic weapons, and mortars that have killed Iraqi and Coalition Forces as well as civilians. Tehran was responsible for some of the lethality of anti-Coalition attacks by providing militants with the capability to assemble improvised explosive devices (IEDs) with explosively formed projectiles (EFPs) that were specially designed to defeat armored vehicles. The Qods Force, in concert with Lebanese Hizballah, provided training both inside and outside of Iraq for Iraqi militants in the construction and use of sophisticated IED technology and other advanced weaponry.

Iran remained unwilling to bring to justice senior al-Qa'ida members it has detained, and has refused to publicly identify those senior members in its custody. Iran has repeatedly resisted numerous calls to transfer custody of its al-Qa'ida detainees to their countries of origin or third countries for trial. Iran also continued to fail to control the activities of some al-Qa'ida members who fled to Iran following the fall of the Taliban regime in Afghanistan.

Senior IRGC and Qods Force officials were indicted by the Government of Argentina for their alleged roles in the 1994 terrorist bombing of the Argentine Israel Mutual Association which, according to the Argentine State Prosecutor's report, was initially proposed by the Qods Force.

SUDAN

Sudan remained a cooperative partner in global counterterrorism efforts. During the past year, the Sudanese government continued to pursue terrorist operations directly involving threats to U.S. interests and personnel in Sudan. Sudanese officials have indicated that they view their continued cooperation with the United States as important and recognize the benefits of U.S. training and information-sharing. Though the counterterrorism relationship remained solid, some hard-line Sudanese officials continued to express resentment and distrust over actions by the USG and questioned the benefits of the bilateral cooperation. Their assessment reflected disappointment that Sudan's counterterrorism cooperation has not resulted in its removal from the State Sponsors of Terrorism list. Nonetheless, there was no indication at year's end that the Sudanese government will curtail its counterterrorism cooperation with the United States.

Al-Qa'ida (AQ)-inspired terrorist elements, and elements of both Palestine Islamic Jihad (PIJ), and HAMAS remained in Sudan. In light of the continuing hybrid UN-AU deployment to Darfur, various terrorist threats against this mission have emerged, and AQ leadership has called for jihad against UN forces in Darfur. In the early hours of January 1,

2008, attackers in Khartoum sympathetic to AQ shot and fatally wounded two U.S. Embassy staff members – an American and a Sudanese employee – both of whom worked for the U.S. Agency for International Development. Sudanese authorities cooperated closely with the USG in investigating this terrorist crime. On February 1, five alleged conspirators were arrested and put on trial for murder on August 31. Their trial was ongoing at year's end. Other extremist groups also have threatened attacks against Western interests in Sudan. The July 14 request by International Criminal Court Chief Prosecutor Moreno-Ocampo for an arrest warrant against Sudanese President Omar al-Bashir on charges related to atrocities committed in Darfur has further inflamed tensions. Therefore, the terrorist threat level remained critical in Khartoum and Darfur, and potentially other parts of Sudan. Elements of designated terrorist groups remained in Sudan. With the exception of HAMAS, whose members the Sudanese government consider to be freedom fighters rather than terrorists, the government does not appear to openly support the presence of extremist elements. We note, however, that there have been open source reports that arms were purchased in Sudan's black market and allegedly smuggled northward to HAMAS.

The Sudanese government has prevented foreign fighters from using Sudan as a logistics base and transit point for extremists going to Iraq. However, gaps remained in the Sudanese government's knowledge of and ability to identify and capture these individuals. There was evidence to suggest that individuals who were active participants in the Iraqi insurgency have returned to Sudan and were in a position to use their expertise to conduct attacks within Sudan or to pass on their knowledge. There was also evidence that Sudanese extremists continued to participate in terrorist activities in Somalia, which the Sudanese government has also attempted to disrupt.

SYRIA

Syria was designated in 1979 as a state sponsor of terrorism. Syria provided political and material support to Hizballah and allowed Iran to use Syrian territory as a transit point for assistance to Hizballah. HAMAS, Palestine Islamic Jihad (PIJ), the Popular Front for the Liberation of Palestine (PLFP), and the Popular Front for the Liberation of Palestine-General Command (PFLP-GC), among others, based their external leadership within Syria's borders. The Syrian government insisted these groups were confined to political and informational activities, but groups with leaders in Syria have claimed responsibility for deadly anti-Israeli terrorist attacks.

Over the course of the year, Syria's public support for the Palestinian groups varied, depending on Syrian national interest and international pressure. President Bashar al-Asad continued to express public support for Palestinian terrorist groups. HAMAS Politburo head and defacto leader Khalid Meshal and his deputies continued to reside in Syria. Syria provided a safe haven for Meshal and security escorts for his motorcades. Meshal's use of the Syrian Ministry of Information as the venue for press conferences this year could be taken as an endorsement of HAMAS's message. Media reports indicated HAMAS used Syrian soil to train its militant fighters. Though the Syrian government claimed periodically that it used its influence to restrain the rhetoric and activities of Palestinian groups, the Syrian government allowed a Palestinian conference organized by HAMAS, PFLP-GC, and PIJ to occur in January, and another HAMAS organized conference, reportedly funded by Iran, to take place in November.

Highlighting Syria's ties to the world's most notorious terrorists, Hizballah Operations Chief Imad Mugniyah, perished in a February 12 car bombing near Syrian Military Intelligence (SMI) headquarters in the Damascus neighborhood of Kafr Sousa. Among other atrocities, Mugniyah was wanted in connection with the 1983 bombings of the Marine barracks and the U.S. Embassy in Beirut, which killed over 350. Despite initial attempts to cover up the incident, the Syrian government reluctantly acknowledged some days later that one of the world's most wanted terrorists had been present and died on Syrian soil.

Syrian officials publicly condemned some acts of terrorism, while continuing to defend what they considered to be legitimate armed resistance by Palestinians and Hizballah against Israeli occupation of Arab territory, and by the Iraqi opposition against the "occupation of Iraq." Syria has not been directly implicated in an act of terrorism since 1986, although an ongoing UN investigation into the February 2005 assassination of former Lebanese Prime Minister Rafiq Hariri continued to investigate Syrian involvement.

Syria itself was the location of at least one major attack. On September 27, the car-bombing of a Syrian government facility reportedly injured 14 and killed at least 17 individuals, marking the first significant attack against regime institutions in nearly 20 years. Not since the Muslim Brotherhood uprising in the early 1980s had Syrian institutions been targeted by terrorists. Regional media reports indicated this bombing was directed at the Palestinian Branch of the Syrian Military Intelligence; the perpetrators remained unknown at year's end.

Throughout the year, Syria continued to strengthen ties with fellow state sponsor of terrorism, Iran. Syria's Minister of Defense visited Tehran in May and initiated a Memorandum of Understanding on defense cooperation. Syria also allowed leaders of HAMAS and other Palestinian groups to visit Tehran. President Asad repaid a 2007 visit to Damascus by Iranian President Ahmadinejad with a visit of his own to Tehran in early August, his third visit since 2005. Asad continued to be a staunch defender of Iran's policies, including Iran's "civil" nuclear ambitions.

Syria increased border monitoring activities, instituted tighter screening practices on military-age Arab males entering its borders, hosted two Border Security Working Group meetings with technical experts from the Iraqi Neighbors group, and expressed a desire to increase security cooperation with Iraq. At the same time, Syria remained a key hub for foreign fighters en route to Iraq.

The USG designated several Iraqis residing in Syria and Iraqi-owned entities, including Mishan Al-Jaburi and his satellite television channel Al-Ra'y, under Executive Order 1348 for providing financial, material, and technical support for acts of violence that threatened the peace and stability of Iraq. The United States also designated known foreign fighter facilitators based in Syria, including members of the Abu Ghadiyah network, that orchestrated the flow of terrorists, weapons, and money from Syria to al-Qa'ida in Iraq, under Executive Order 13224.

Despite acknowledged reductions in foreign fighter flows, the scope and impact of the problem remained significant. Syria continued to allow former Iraqi regime elements to operate in the country. Attacks against Coalition Forces and Iraqi citizens continued to have a destabilizing effect on Iraq's internal security. Though Syrian and Iraqi leaders met throughout the year both publicly and privately to discuss border enhancements and other measures needed to combat foreign fighter flows, there were few tangible results. While Syria has taken some positive steps, the Syrian government could do more to interdict known terrorist networks and foreign fighter facilitators operating within its borders.

Syria remained a source of concern regarding terrorist financing. The Commercial Bank of Syria remained subject to U.S. sanctions. Industry experts reported that 70 percent of all business transactions were conducted in cash and that nearly 90 percent of all Syrians did not use formal banking services. Despite Syrian governmental legislation requiring money-changers to be licensed by the end of 2007, many money-changers continued to operate illegally in Syria's vast black market, estimated to be as large as Syria's formal economy. Regional "hawala" networks remained intertwined with smuggling and trade-based money laundering, facilitated by notoriously corrupt customs and immigration officials, raising significant concerns that Syrian government and business elites are, at the very least, complicit in illicit financing schemes.

Syria's government-controlled press continued to tout Syrian regime efforts to combat terrorism. The Syrian government, using tightly-controlled press outlets, was quick to blame a Lebanon-based, al-Qa'ida-affiliated group, Fatah al-Islam, for the September 27 attack against a prominent military intelligence installation. Syrian TV broadcasted a November 7 program featuring the confessions of some 20 Fatah al-Islam members, including the daughter and son-in-law of Fatah al-Islam leader Shakr al-Absy, of their involvement.

It remained unclear why Fatah al-Islam would have launched an attack against Syrian security elements, but media reports suggested Absy's disappearance inside of Syria as a possible motive. In response to the September 27 bombing, the Syrian security services conducted at least one reported raid on an alleged terrorist cell residing in the Damascus area, killing and arresting several suspected militants and confiscating a cache of weapons and explosives.

CHAPTER – 4

The Global Challenge of WMD Terrorism

Introduction

The nexus of weapons of mass destruction (WMD) and terrorism poses one of the gravest risks to the national security of the United States and its global partners. A successful major WMD terrorist attack could result in mass casualties and produce far-reaching economic and political consequences. This chapter outlines:

- The key elements of the United States' National Strategy for Combating WMD Terrorism;
- The various types of materials terrorists may use in a WMD attack;
- The potential that resources of a state could be directed or diverted to facilitate WMD terrorism;
- The emerging WMD terrorism threat presented by non-state facilitators; and
- Transformational U.S. partnerships to combat this growing global risk.

The United States places the highest priority on working with a broad range of local governments, Federal entities, domestic emergency responders, international organizations, foreign governments, and private sector organizations to develop effective partnerships to confront the global challenge of WMD terrorism.

Diplomatic and Strategic Priorities for Combating WMD Terrorism

U.S. diplomatic priorities for combating WMD terrorism build on the comprehensive approach set forth in the National Strategy for Combating Terrorism. Specifically, the U.S. strategic approach hinges on the six objectives outlined in the National Strategy. The USG works across all objectives simultaneously to maximize its ability to eliminate the threat.

Determine terrorists' intentions, capabilities, and plans to develop or acquire WMD. Understand and assess the credibility of threat reporting and provide technical assessments of terrorists' WMD capabilities.

Deny terrorists access to the materials, expertise, and other enabling capabilities required to develop WMD, with a particular focus on weapons-usable fissile materials, dangerous pathogens, and poisonous chemicals. Denial efforts extend to the methods of transport, sources of funds, and other capabilities that could facilitate the execution of a WMD attack. In addition to building upon existing initiatives to secure materials, develop innovative approaches that blend classic counterproliferation, nonproliferation, and counterterrorism efforts.

Deter terrorists from employing WMD. A new deterrence calculus seeks to deter terrorists, facilitators, and supporters from contemplating a WMD attack and, failing that, to dissuade them from actually conducting an attack. Traditional deterrence by punishment may not work because terrorists generally show a wanton disregard for the lives of innocents and, in some cases, for their own lives. Accordingly, develop a range of deterrence strategies that are tailored to the various WMD threats and the individual actors who facilitate or enable those threats. Employ diplomatic strategies that seek to address extremism and defuse volatile conditions in order to discourage consideration of WMD as a tool to address perceived injustices.

Detect and disrupt terrorists' attempted movement of WMD-related materials, weapons, and personnel. Expand our global capability for detecting illicit materials, weapons, and personnel transiting abroad. Utilize global partnerships, international agreements, and ongoing border security and interdiction efforts to promote detection capabilities. Continue to work with countries to enact and enforce strict penalties for WMD trafficking and other suspect WMD-related activities.

Prevent a WMD-related terrorist attack and develop a response capability. Once the possibility of a WMD attack has been detected, work to contain, interdict, and eliminate the threat. Continue to develop requisite capabilities to eliminate the possibility of a WMD operation and to prevent a possible follow-on attack. Prepare ourselves for possible WMD incidents by developing capabilities to manage the range of consequences that may result from such an attack.

Define the nature and source of a terrorist-employed WMD device. Should a WMD terrorist attack occur, the rapid identification of the source and perpetrator of an attack would facilitate response efforts and may be critical in disrupting follow-on attacks. Work to maintain and improve our capability to determine responsibility for the intended or actual use of WMD via accurate attribution, using the rapid fusion of technical forensic data with intelligence and law enforcement information.

In December 2008, the Commission on the Prevention of WMD Proliferation and Terrorism released its final report to Congress. This report highlighted several key observations including the high likelihood that a WMD would be involved in a terrorist attack within the next five years. The Commission concluded that the United States, and the world, must act quickly to slow the proliferation of WMD technologies and information to avoid such an act.

As the implementation of diplomatic strategic priorities for combating WMD terrorism move forward, special care must be taken to work closely with the full range of foreign partners to prioritize and tailor capacity-building approaches to the regional and local conditions that exist worldwide.

THE MATERIAL THREATS

There are four generally accepted categories of weapons of mass destruction (WMD) that terrorists may seek to acquire and use in a WMD terrorist attack: chemical, biological, radiological, and nuclear (CBRN).

Chemical

Chemical weapons represent a potentially dangerous tool in the hands of terrorists. Effectively dispersed and in sufficient dosages, chemical agents could cause mass casualties, as was demonstrated by the use of chemical weapons during World War I and more recently during the Iran-Iraq war. Today's chemical terrorism threat ranges from the potential acquisition and use of chemical warfare agents and military delivery systems, to the production and use of toxic industrial chemicals and improvised dissemination systems, such as those used in the 1995 attack conducted by Aum Shinrikyo in the Tokyo subway system. Perpetrators of that attack used sharpened umbrellas to puncture plastic bags filled with the nerve agent sarin causing the sarin to spill out and evaporate – killing twelve and injuring thousands. Terrorists also have sought to acquire and use commercially-available materials, such as poisons and toxic industrial chemicals. The growth and sophistication of the worldwide chemical industry, including the development of complex synthetic and dual-use materials, may make the task of preventing and protecting against this threat more difficult. Preventing chemical terrorism is particularly challenging as terrorists can, with relative ease, use toxic industrial chemicals and other commonly available chemical agents and materials as low-cost alternatives to traditional chemical weapons and delivery systems, though likely with more limited effects.

Biological

Bioterrorism, another deadly threat, is the deliberate dispersal of pathogens through food, air, water, or living organisms to cause disease. The Commission on the Prevention of WMD Proliferation and Terrorism (See *The Report of the Commission on the Prevention of WMD Proliferation and Terrorism)* concluded that it is more likely that terrorists would be able to acquire and use biological agents than nuclear weapons due to the difficulty in controlling the proliferation of biotechnologies and biological agent information. If properly produced and released, biological agents can kill on a massive scale and, if terrorists use a pathogen that can be transmitted from person to person, the disease could quickly spread across oceans and continents through air travel before authorities realize their nations have been attacked.

Developing a bioterrorism capability presents some scientific and operational challenges. However, the necessary technical capabilities are not beyond the expertise of motivated scientists with university-level training. Unlike most other types of CBRN threats, the materials required to produce a biological weapon are available in laboratories worldwide, and many threat agents could be isolated from nature. International laboratories are often not safeguarded and secured up to preferred U.S. standards, making access to dual-use equipment and potentially dangerous pathogens possibly more accessible. Even the use of a badly-designed weapon can have a limited health impact but cause significant disruption. A small-scale bioterrorism attack such as the 2001 anthrax attacks in the United States, which resulted in five Americans killed and an additional 17 individuals infected, had a substantial economic impact with the costs of decontamination, medical treatment for those exposed, decreased commercial activity, social distress, and lost productivity. The terrorists can often meet their objective of creating disruption and fear without causing large numbers of casualties.

Among present-day terrorist organizations, al-Qa'ida (AQ) is believed to have made the greatest effort to acquire and develop a bioterrorism program. U.S. forces discovered a partially built biological weapons laboratory near Kandahar after expelling the Taliban from Afghanistan.

Although it was not conclusive that AQ succeeded in producing a biological weapon, the discovery demonstrated a concerted effort to acquire a biological weapons capability.

Radiological

Some terrorists seek to acquire radioactive materials for use in a radiological dispersal device (RDD) or "dirty bomb." Radioactive materials are used widely in industrial, medical, and research applications and include devices used for power supply in remote locations, cancer therapy, food and blood irradiation, and radiography. Their widespread use in nearly every country makes these materials much more accessible than the fissile materials required for nuclear weapons. Most radioactive materials lack sufficient strength to present a significant public health risk once dispersed, while the materials posing the greatest hazard would require terrorists to have the expertise to handle them without exposure to incapacitating doses of radiation or detection during transit across international borders. Public panic and economic disruption caused by setting off an explosive radiological dispersal device, however, could be substantial, even if a weak radioactive source is used.

Nuclear

Some terrorist organizations, such as al-Qa'ida, have openly stated their desire to acquire nuclear weapons. The diffusion of scientific and technical information regarding the assembly of nuclear weapons, some of which is now available on the Internet, has increased the risk that a terrorist organization in possession of sufficient fissile material could develop its own crude nuclear weapon. The complete production of a nuclear weapon strongly depends on the terrorist group's access to special nuclear materials as well as engineering and scientific expertise. Certainly with recent nuclear proliferants among less stable countries, such as North Korea, the number of potential sources of an unsecured nuclear weapon or materials is challenging world-wide efforts to control and account for nuclear materials. Terrorists may, however, seek to link up with a variety of facilitators to develop their own nuclear capability. These facilitators include black market proliferators or transnational criminal networks that may seek to profit from the sale of nuclear material, a weaponized device, or technical knowledge gathered from nuclear experts currently or formerly involved in a national nuclear program.

Dual-Use Materials, Equipment, Research, and Technologies of Concern

Reducing the risk of terrorist acquisition of, access to, and use of dual-use materials, equipment, research, and technologies remains a critical challenge. Terrorists have shown an interest in taking advantage of this trend when developing improvised devices. This challenge has only been compounded by the diffusion of dual-use information on the Internet and in academic venues. Attacks in Iraq in 2006 and 2007 involving improvised devices using chlorine cylinders, a dual-use chemical used in water treatment facilities, offered a notable example.

The United States maintains dual-use export controls based on its multilateral commitments in the export control regimes, but also maintains unilateral controls on a wide range of dual-use items predominantly for antiterrorism reasons. Effective partnerships with private sector organizations, industry, academia, and the scientific research community, as well as with local governments, will play an important role in mitigating the risk of dual-use capabilities falling into the wrong hands. Implementing the use of substitute materials in technologies is one way to limit the spread of sensitive materials around the world. For example, recent technological developments allow the use of low enriched uranium as a substitute for highly enriched uranium for production of the medical isotope Mo99.

In this era of commercial globalization, control of exports is not limited to national borders, but also extends to U.S. research universities, laboratories, and industry. The reduced domestic pool of qualified scientists and engineers has driven many U.S. companies, universities and laboratories to recruit foreign nationals in order to remain competitive. The employment of talented foreign science and engineering staff or students carries the risk of WMD technology transfers by way of *deemed exports.* A deemed export is the release of information pertaining to the design and manufacturing of dual-use technology or source code to a foreign national within the confines of the United States borders. In accordance with the Export Administration Regulations, several USG departments and agencies support a national effort to better control foreign access to sensitive dual-use technologies to prevent unauthorized transfers.

STATE SPONSORSHIP OF TERRORISM: A KEY CONCERN

A state that directs WMD resources to terrorists, or one from which enabling resources are clandestinely diverted, poses a grave WMD terrorism threat. Although terrorist organizations will continue to seek a WMD capability independent of state programs, the sophisticated WMD knowledge and resources of a state could enable a terrorist capability. State sponsors of terrorism and all nations that fail to live up to their international counterterrorism and nonproliferation obligations deserve greater scrutiny as potential facilitators of WMD terrorism.

NON-STATE FACILITATORS: AN EMERGING THREAT

State sponsors of terrorism with WMD programs represent just one facet of the overall risk of WMD terrorism. The non-state entities they use to facilitate their WMD programs have emerged as a growing WMD proliferation threat in recent years that could eventually provide terrorists with access to materials and expertise that are particularly hard to acquire. In 2003, the United States and its international partners succeeded in interdicting a shipment of WMD-related material destined for Libya's then-active nuclear weapons program. The facts surrounding this shipment revealed a transnational nuclear proliferation network reaching from Southeast Asia to Europe, developed by Pakistani nuclear scientist A.Q. Khan. This network was making available sensitive technology and WMD-related materials to nations willing to pay. There is a serious risk that such non-state facilitators and their networks could provide their services to terrorist groups.

The dismantling of the A.Q. Khan network revealed an uncomfortable truth about globalization. The very trends driving globalization, improved communications and transportation links, can enable the development of extended proliferation networks that may facilitate terrorist acquisition of WMD. Globalization requires that partner nations work together closely to prevent, detect, and disrupt linkages that may develop between terrorists and facilitators such as A.Q. Khan.

TRANSFORMATIONAL PARTNERSHIPS TO COMBAT WMD TERRORISM

Since September 11, 2001, the international community has made significant strides in responding to the threat of WMD terrorism. States are working together bilaterally and multilaterally to address these threats and protect their populations. The United States has taken concrete measures to build a layered defense against the WMD terrorism threat. In 2003, the United States announced the first National Strategy to Combat Weapons of Mass Destruction. Through a variety of multinational initiatives such as the Global Threat Reduction Initiative, the Proliferation Security Initiative (PSI), and the Global Initiative to Combat Nuclear Terrorism, the United States has taken a leadership role in reducing the threat of WMD reaching the hands of non-state actors and terrorists.

The Proliferation Security Initiative: Announced in 2003, the Proliferation Security Initiative deserves special mention as a particularly well received and effective international initiative. The PSI is a global effort that aims to stop the trafficking of WMD, its delivery systems, and related materials to and from states and non-state actors of proliferation concern worldwide. The PSI relies on voluntary actions by states, using existing legal authorities, national and international, to put an end to WMD-related trafficking. PSI partners take steps to strengthen those legal authorities as necessary. States that wish to participate in the PSI are asked to endorse its Statement of Interdiction Principles, which identifies specific measures participants commit to undertake for the interdiction of WMD and related materials. As of December 31, 2008, 94 states have endorsed the Statement. PSI participants conduct approximately seven exercises per year to improve their operational capabilities to conduct interdictions and meet periodically to share information and develop new operational concepts. The PSI has led to a number of important interdictions over the last five years and is an important tool in the overall U.S. strategy to combat WMD proliferation to state and non-state actors.

The Global Initiative to Combat Nuclear Terrorism (GICNT): President Bush and Russian Federation President Putin announced the GICNT on July 15, 2006 with the intention of expanding and accelerating the development of partnership capacity against one of the most serious threats to international security. The Global Initiative offers a comprehensive approach to strengthening all defensive layers necessary to prevent, protect against, and respond comprehensively to the nuclear terrorist threat.

- By agreeing to the Global Initiative's Statement of Principles, partner nations commit themselves to:
- Develop, if necessary, and improve accounting, control, and physical protection systems for nuclear and other radioactive materials and substances;
- Enhance security of civilian nuclear facilities;
- Improve capabilities of participants for response, mitigation, and investigation in cases of terrorist attacks involving the use of nuclear and other radioactive materials and substances, including the development of technical means to identify nuclear and other radioactive materials and substances that are, or may be, involved in the incident; and
- Promote information sharing pertaining to the suppression of acts of nuclear terrorism and their facilitation, taking appropriate measures consistent with their national laws and international obligations to protect the confidentiality of any information which they exchange in confidence.

In the beginning of 2007, the partnership consisted of 13 nations; by the end of 2008, the partnership had grown to 75 partner nations representing all regions of the world. The IAEA and the EU also participate as observers. Partner nations created a Plan of Work, committing themselves to host or co-sponsor events in furtherance of the goals in the Statement of Principles.

In 2008, nine countries conducted 11 Plan of Work activities and three exercises, implementing all eight of the principles. Additionally, the co-chairs launched the Global Initiative Exercise Planning Group (EPG), which guides and supports the development of exercises and planning scenarios to enhance the capabilities of GICNT partners to accomplish the objectives described in the GICNT Statement of Principles. The Global Initiative continued to engage the private sector and local governments, both of which have an important role to play in preventing, protecting against, and responding to acts of nuclear terrorism.

The Global Threat Reduction Initiative (GTRI): The goal of GTRI, announced by the United States on May 26, 2004, in Vienna, Austria, is to identify, secure, remove, or facilitate the disposition, as quickly and expeditiously as possible, of vulnerable nuclear and radioactive materials and equipment around the world that pose a potential threat to the international community. International partners are key participants in this initiative, and GTRI has undertaken cooperative activities in over 90 countries. In particular, GTRI seeks to facilitate globally the reduction or elimination of the use of highly enriched uranium in civilian nuclear applications and to remove or protect other vulnerable nuclear and radiological materials at civilian sites worldwide. Specific activities include the conversion of reactors used for research, testing, and medical-isotope production from the use of highly enriched uranium (HEU) fuel to low enriched uranium (LEU); repatriation of fresh and spent HEU fuel to its country of origin (the United States or Russian Federation); enhancement of physical protection at sites utilizing such materials; and removal of unwanted radiological sources and other nuclear materials not otherwise covered by the fuel-return programs.

Second Line of Defense (SLD): Under its Second Line of Defense (SLD) Program, the Department of Energy‘s National Nuclear Security Administration (DOE/NNSA) cooperates with partner countries to provide radiation detection systems and associated training to enhance host nation capabilities to deter, detect, and interdict illicit trafficking of special nuclear and other radiological materials across international borders. The SLD Program complements first line of defense threat reduction efforts which ensure that protections are in place to lock down and protect material at the source in civilian and military facilities. The second line of defense thus serves as a key component in a layered defense system, seeking to detect trafficking in material that may have been removed from these facilities as it is moved across international borders and through the maritime shipping network. The SLD Program includes two components: the Core Program and the Megaports Initiative. The Core Program focuses on providing equipment to land border crossings, feeder seaports, and international airports. This work originally began in Russia and has since expanded to include former Soviet states, the Caucasus, Eastern Europe, and other key areas. The Megaports Initiative began in 2003 and provides equipment to scan containerized cargo as it moves through the global maritime shipping network. In identifying ports of interest for engagement under the Megaports Initiative, DOE/NNSA considers a number of factors, including volume of containers and regional terrorist threat. To date, DOE/NNSA has completed deployments at over 230 sites around the world.

Global Threat Reduction (GTR): GTR programs aim to prevent proliferators and terrorists, anywhere in the world, from acquiring WMD expertise, materials and technology. GTR is actively engaged in Pakistan, Afghanistan, and other regions that are vulnerable to proliferators or that harbor terrorists who have expressed an interest in acquiring WMD. GTR programs have expanded to meet these emerging WMD proliferation threats worldwide and focus on promoting biological, chemical, and nuclear security in those countries where there is a high risk of WMD terrorism or proliferation. The programs also engage and redirect former weapons scientists in the former Soviet Union, Iraq, and Libya. By engaging biological, chemical, and nuclear scientists, and helping them to secure dangerous pathogens, improve chemical security, and adopt nuclear safety best practices, GTR seeks to keep WMD and dual-use materials, technology and expertise away from proliferators and terrorists. GTR outreach has helped at-risk facilities deter attempted thefts of dangerous pathogens, and engaged WMD scientists worldwide, among other nonproliferation successes.

Additional U.S. Efforts Supporting a Global Layered Defense: The United States has also worked with partner nations through the UN and the IAEA to reduce the threat of WMD in the hands of terrorists. The UN Security Council has passed two important resolutions related to the prevention of terrorism and the proliferation of WMD. In 2001, the Security Council adopted Resolution 1373, which requires all UN member states to refrain from providing any support, active or passive, to terrorists, and to work together to limit terrorist movement and safe haven. In 2004, the Security Council adopted Resolution 1540, which requires all UN member states to refrain from providing support to non-state actors that attempt to develop or acquire WMD and their means of delivery. The United States remains committed to full implementation of both UN Security Council Resolutions 1373 and 1540.

The Convention on the Suppression of Acts of Nuclear Terrorism (Nuclear Terrorism Convention) entered into force on July 7, 2007. On September 25, 2008, the Senate passed resolutions of advice and consent to ratification of the Nuclear Terrorism Convention to the Senate, the Amendment to the Convention on the Physical Protection of Nuclear Material, the Protocol of 2005 to the Convention on the Suppression of Unlawful Acts Against the Safety of Maritime Navigation, and the Protocol of 2005 to the Protocol for the Suppression of Unlawful Acts against the Safety of Fixed Platforms Located on the Continental Shelf. Collectively, these treaties will enhance international cooperation with regard to the prevention of WMD terrorism and proliferation of WMD, as well as the investigation and prosecution of such acts.

Conclusion

The threat of terrorists acquiring and using WMD poses one of the greatest security challenges facing the United States and the international community today. During the past year, the USG has built on a range of activities and launched new efforts to prevent, protect against, and respond to the threat or use of WMD. Together with partner nations and international organizations, the United States will continue to take the initiative to reduce the global risk of WMD terrorism.

CHAPTER – 5

Terrorist Safe Havens (7120 Report)

Terrorists operate without regard to national boundaries. To effectively counter terrorists, we are working to strengthen our regional and transnational partnerships and increasingly operate in a regional context. Denying safe haven plays a major role in undermining terrorists' capacity to operate effectively and forms a key element of U.S. counterterrorism strategy.

Terrorist safe havens are defined in this report as ungoverned, under-governed, or ill-governed areas of a country and non-physical areas where terrorists that constitute a threat to U.S. national security interests are able to organize, plan, raise funds, communicate, recruit, train, and operate in relative security because of inadequate governance capacity, political will, or both. Physical safe havens provide security for terrorist leaders, allowing them to plan acts of terrorism around the world.

Global communications and financial systems, especially those created by electronic infrastructure such as the internet, global media, and unregulated economic activity, further allow terrorists to carry out activities, particularly the dissemination of propaganda and misinformation, without the need for a physical safe haven. These "virtual" havens are highly mobile, difficult to track, difficult to control, and are not based in any particular state. This part of the report, however, will not address virtual safe havens, and will focus instead on physical safe havens.

Defeating the terrorist enemy requires a comprehensive effort executed locally, nationally, regionally, and globally. Working with partner nations, we must eliminate terrorist leadership, but incarcerating or killing terrorists will not achieve an end to terrorism. Over the last several years we've been working with partners on regional strategies to break up terrorist networks, eliminate terrorist safe havens, and disrupt those activities that support terrorists. The latter include funding, facilitation of terrorist travel, communications, and intelligence and information collection by terrorists seeking to identify potential targets. Finally, and most challenging, we must address the underlying conditions that terrorists exploit by offering a positive agenda focused on modernization and strengthening the rule of law. This includes programs based on economic liberalization, institutional reform, and democratization that would bring at-risk populations closer to the mainstream of the global system. We must continue to enlist the support and cooperation of a growing network of partners. If we are to be successful, we must all work together toward our common goal in a strategic and coordinated manner.

AFRICA

Somalia. A small number of al-Qa'ida (AQ) operatives remain in East Africa, particularly Somalia, where they pose a serious threat to U.S. and allied interests in the region. Although these elements were disrupted as a result of Ethiopian and Somali Transitional Federal Government military actions, AQ operatives continued to operate in Somalia and elsewhere in East Africa. Somalia remains a concern given the country's long, unguarded coastline, porous borders, continued political instability, and proximity to the Arabian Peninsula, all of which provide opportunities for terrorist transit and/or safe haven. AQ remains likely to make common cause with Somali extremists, most notably al-Shabaab, which has expanded its area of control during a protracted anti-Ethiopian/ Transitional Federal Government (TFG) insurgency over the past two years.

The Trans-Sahara. Remote areas of the Sahel and Maghreb regions in Africa serve as terrorist safe havens because of limited government control in sparsely populated regions. The threat to U.S. and Western interests from Islamic extremists increased in 2007 as a result of the 2006 AQ merger with the Algerian-based Salafist Group for Preaching and Combat (GSPC), which was subsequently renamed al-Qa'ida in the Islamic Maghreb (AQIM). AQIM has subsequently conducted a number of attacks, primarily on Algerian targets, but also including Western interests.

In contrast, the Libyan Islamic Fighting Group's (LIFG), November 2007 merger with AQ has yielded few successful attacks to date, reflecting the depleted capabilities of LIFG within Libya. AQIM has used the Sahel to train Islamic militants in small arms, use of explosives, and guerilla tactics for the last several years. Training appears to take place on the move or in makeshift facilities in remote areas outside government control. While Libyan extremists have trained in AQIM-run camps, a goal of their preparations was also to join anti-Coalition fighting in Iraq, particularly during 2007. AQIM taps into already existing smuggling networks in the Sahel to obtain weapons, explosives, and supplies to support its operations.

EAST ASIA AND PACIFIC

The Sulu/Sulawesi Seas Littoral. Southeast Asia includes a safe haven area composed of the Sulawesi Sea and Sulu Archipelago, which sit astride the maritime boundary between Indonesia, Malaysia, and the Philippines. The geography of the thousands of islands in the region made the area difficult for authorities to monitor. Worker migration, tourism, trade, and other non-terrorist activities, both licit and illicit, that occur in this maritime region pose another challenge to identifying and countering the terrorist threat. Although Indonesia, Malaysia, and the Philippines have improved their efforts to control their shared maritime boundaries, this expanse remains difficult to control. Surveillance is partial at best, and traditional smuggling and piracy groups provided an effective cover for terrorist activities, such as movement of personnel, equipment, and funds. The Sulu/Sulawesi Seas Littoral represents a safe haven for the Jemaah Islamiya (JI) terrorist organization and the Philippine Abu Sayyaf Group (ASG).

The Southern Philippines. The southern Philippines, specifically the Sulu archipelago and Mindanao, serve as terrorist safe havens. The government's control in this area is weak due to rugged terrain, weak rule of law, poverty, and local Muslim minority resentment of central governmental policies. In addition to a few Jemaah Islamiya (JI) fugitives and the Abu Sayyaf Group (ASG), the area hosts several terrorist and insurgent groups including the Communist Party of the Philippines/New People's Army and the Rajah Solaiman Movement.

THE MIDDLE EAST

Iraq. Iraq is not currently a terrorist safe haven, but terrorists, including Sunni groups like al-Qa'ida in Iraq (AQI), Ansar al-Islam (AI), and Ansar al-Sunna (AS), as well as Shia extremists and other groups, view Iraq as a potential safe haven. The Iraqi government, in coordination with the Coalition, made significant progress in combating AQI and affiliated terrorist organizations. The threat from AQI continued to diminish in 2008. AQI, although still dangerous, has experienced the defection of members, lost key mobilization areas, suffered disruption of support infrastructure and funding, and been forced to change targeting priorities. A number of factors have contributed to the substantial degradation of AQI. The alliance of convenience and mutual exploitation between AQI and many Sunni populations has deteriorated. The Baghdad Security Plan, initiated in February 2007, along with assistance from primarily Sunni tribal and local groups, has succeeded in reducing violence to late 2005 levels, has disrupted and diminished AQI infrastructure, and has driven some surviving AQI fighters from Baghdad and Anbar into the northern Iraqi provinces of Ninawa, Diyala, and Salah ad Din. Though AQI remained a threat, new initiatives to cooperate with tribal and local leaders in Iraq have led Sunni tribes and local citizens to reject AQI and its extremist ideology. The continued growth, professionalism, and improved capabilities of the Iraqi forces have increased their effectiveness in rooting out terrorist cells. Iraqis in Baghdad, Anbar and Diyala Provinces, and elsewhere have turned against AQI and were cooperating with the Iraqi government and Coalition Forces to defeat it.

Northern Iraq. The Kurdistan Worker's Party (PKK) maintained an active presence in northern Iraq, from which it coordinated attacks in the predominantly ethnic Kurdish areas of southeastern Turkey and provided logistical support to forces that launched attacks into Turkey, primarily against Turkish security forces, local Turkish officials, and villagers who opposed the organization. In October 2007, the Turkish Parliament overwhelmingly voted to extend the authorization for cross-border military operations against PKK encampments in northern Iraq. On November 19, 2008, Iraq, Turkey, and the United States renewed their formal trilateral security dialogue as one element of ongoing cooperative efforts to counter the PKK. Iraqi leaders, including those from the Kurdistan Regional Government, continued to publicly state that the PKK was a terrorist organization and would not be tolerated in Iraq.

Lebanon. Hizballah remained the most prominent and powerful terrorist group in Lebanon, with deep roots among Lebanon's large Shia community, especially in southern Lebanon, which comprises at least one third of Lebanon's population. The Lebanese government continued to recognize Hizballah, a U.S.-designated Foreign Terrorist Organization, as a legitimate "resistance group" and political party. Hizballah maintained offices in Beirut and military-style bases elsewhere in the country and was represented by elected deputies in parliament.

An increasing number of AQ-associated Sunni extremists are also operating within the country. AQ likely views Lebanon as an opportunity to expand its jihad into the Levant, especially after the 2006 conflict between Israel and Hizballah. The organization uses the Palestinian refugee camps as staging grounds for recruitment, training, planning, and facilitating transit of foreign fighters to and from Iraq. The camps, run by Palestinian authorities inside the camps, continue to be no-go zones for the Lebanese Armed Forces and safe havens for armed Sunni extremists. See Chapter 3, *State Sponsors of Terrorism,* for information on Iran and Syria, which provided safe haven to Hizballah and Palestinian terrorist groups and were used as safe havens by AQ-linked operatives and groups.

Yemen. The security situation in Yemen continued to deteriorate in 2008. Yemen experienced several setbacks to its counterterrorism efforts as al-Qa'ida in Yemen (AQY) carried out several attacks against tourism and U.S and Yemeni government targets. The most notable was the September 17 attack against the U.S. Embassy in Sanaa that killed 18 people. A half a dozen other attacks occurred in Yemen in 2008 including a January attack that killed two Belgian tourists and two Yemeni drivers in the southern governorate of Hadramaut. Despite an August raid on an AQY cell that resulted in the death of its leader, the Government of Yemen has been unable to disrupt other AQY cells and its response to the terrorist threat was intermittent. Yemen continued to increase its maritime security capabilities, but land border security along the extensive frontier with Saudi Arabia remained a problem, despite increased Yemeni-Saudi cooperation on bilateral security issues. The Yemeni government's focus on the al-Houthi rebellion in the Sada'a governorate in the North of the country and internal security concerns distracted its forces from adequately focusing on counterterrorism activities.

SOUTH ASIA

Afghan-Pakistan Border. Despite the efforts of both Afghan and Pakistani security forces, instability along the Pakistan-Afghanistan frontier continued to provide al-Qa'ida (AQ) with leadership mobility and the ability to conduct training and operational planning, targeting Western Europe and U.S. interests in particular. Numerous senior AQ operatives have been captured or killed, but AQ leaders continued to plot attacks and to cultivate stronger operational connections that radiated outward from Pakistan to affiliates throughout the Middle East, North Africa, and Europe.

Pakistan. AQ terrorists, foreign insurgents, and Pakistani militants have broadened and strengthened their safe havens in portions of Pakistan's Federally Administered Tribal Areas (FATA), North-West Frontier Province (NWFP) and Baluchistan in 2008. AQ and others use the FATA to launch attacks in Afghanistan, plan operations worldwide, train, recruit, and provide propaganda. Other extremists, including Taliban and traditionally Kashmir-focused organizations such as Hizb-e-Islami Gulbuddin or Hizb-e-Islami Khalis, use the area for safe haven and share short term goals of eliminating Coalition presence in Afghanistan. They exploit the local sympathetic populations to recruit, train, and conduct cross-border raids and bombings in Afghanistan. Islamist Deobandi groups and many local tribesmen in the FATA and the NWFP continue to resist the government's efforts to improve governance and administrative control at the expense of longstanding local autonomy.

Extremists led by Pakistani Taliban commander Baitullah Mehsud and other AQ-related extremists re-exerted their hold in areas of South Waziristan and captured over 200 government soldiers, who were later released after a local peace deal collapsed. Extremists have also gained footholds in the settled areas bordering the FATA, including Swat, Tank, and DI Khan. Pakistani security forces continue to fight militant leader Maulana Fazlullah in Swat, a settled area in NWFP. The Government of Pakistan maintains approximately 120,000 troops, including Army and Frontier Corps (FC) units, along the Afghanistan border. The United States plans to help modernize and increase the capacity of the FC so they can become a more effective force against extremists.

In order to increase the central government's writ in the FATA and eliminate safe havens throughout Pakistan, the Government of Pakistan seeks to implement a comprehensive approach with three prongs: political, security, and development. For the political prong, the government seeks to bolster effective governance by empowering local officials. For the security prong, Pakistan's objective is to increase the capacity and efficacy of local security forces. For the development prong, the Pakistani government has designed a comprehensive sustainable development plan for the region. The plan concentrates on four sectors – basic human services, natural resources, communication infrastructure, and economic development – and, if fully implemented, would cost $2 billion. The plan was developed with the extensive grassroots participation of all stakeholders to provide essential economic and livelihood opportunities while upgrading and expanding social services to a population at risk for recruitment by terrorist organizations.

Afghanistan. The Afghan government, in concert with ISAF/NATO forces and the international community, continued efforts to eliminate terrorist safe havens and to bring and build security on the Afghan side of the border. The border areas remained contested, however, with ongoing insurgent and terrorist attacks, including AQ activity. Attacks by the Taliban and other insurgent groups and criminal networks, along with those of extremist movements such as Hizb-e-Islami Gulbuddin (HIG) and the

Haqqani network, continued throughout Afghanistan. Criminal networks and narcotics cultivation remained particularly prevalent in the south and east of the country, constituting a source of funding for the insurgency in Afghanistan. AQ maintained its support to militants inside Afghanistan, providing funding, training, and personnel to facilitate terrorist and insurgent operations. Anti-Coalition organizations such as HIG continued to operate in coordination with AQ, Taliban, and other insurgent groups, primarily in the east.

WESTERN HEMISPHERE

Colombia Border Region. The regions adjacent to Colombia's borders with Venezuela, Ecuador, Peru, Panama, and Brazil include rough terrain and dense forest cover. These conditions, coupled with low population densities and weak government presence, create potential areas of safe haven for insurgent and terrorist groups, particularly the Revolutionary Armed Forces of Colombia (FARC). Brazil, Peru, and Panama have often adopted a tacit policy mix of containment and non-confrontation with Colombian narcoterrorist groups, although some confrontations do occur. Much depends on local decisions and cross-border relations. Ecuador increased its controls and demonstrated a willingness to militarily confront encroaching foreign narcoterrorists. The FARC has used areas in neighboring countries near Colombia's border to rest and regroup, procure supplies, and stage and train for terrorist attacks.

Venezuela. Corruption within the Venezuelan government and military; ideological ties with the FARC; and weak international counternarcotics cooperation have fueled a permissive operating environment for drug traffickers and an increase in drug transit to the United States and Europe.

The Tri-Border Area (Argentina, Brazil, and Paraguay). No corroborated information shows that Hizballah, HAMAS, or other Islamic extremist groups used the Tri-Border Area (TBA) for military-type training or planning of terrorist operations, but the United States remains concerned that these groups use the region as a safe haven to raise funds. Suspected supporters of Islamic terrorist groups, including Hizballah, take advantage of loosely regulated territory and the proximity of Ciudad del Este, Paraguay and Foz do Iguaçu, Brazil to participate in a wide range of illicit activities and to solicit donations from within the sizable Muslim communities in the region and elsewhere in Argentina, Brazil, and Paraguay. The Argentine, Brazilian, and Paraguayan governments have long been concerned with arms and drugs smuggling, document fraud, money laundering, trafficking in persons, and the manufacture and movement of contraband goods through this region. In the early years of this decade, the governments of Argentina, Brazil, and Paraguay invited the United States to participate in the Three Plus One Group on Tri-Border Area Security to focus on practical steps to strengthen financial and border controls and enhance law enforcement and intelligence sharing. The USG has been part of the 3+1 since 2002, and our law enforcement agencies are very active in the region. Despite their view that concrete evidence does not exist of terrorist financing in their countries or in the TBA, Brazil, Argentina, and Paraguay have made notable strides in launching initiatives to strengthen counterterrorist and law enforcement institutions and cooperation, including developing financial intelligence units, broadening border security cooperation, augmenting information sharing among prosecutors responsible for counterterrorism cases, and establishing trade transparency units.

STRATEGIES, TACTICS, TOOLS FOR DISRUPTING OR ELIMINATING SAFE HAVENS

The Regional Strategic Initiative. The State Department's Office of the Coordinator for Counterterrorism (S/CT) has developed the Regional Strategic Initiative (RSI) in key terrorist theaters of operation to collectively assess the threat, pool resources, and devise collaborative strategies, action plans, and policy recommendations. The RSI promotes cooperation between our counterterrorism partners, for example, between Malaysia, Indonesia, and the Philippines as they confront terrorist transit across the Sulawesi Sea; or among Mauritania, Algeria, Morocco, Niger, Chad, and Mali, to counter al-Qa'ida in the Islamic Maghreb (AQIM). Terrorists are highly adaptable. Defeating them requires both centralized coordination and field authority. Resources and responses must be applied in a rapid, flexible, and focused manner. The RSI helps achieve this coordinated approach. In 2008, RSI strategy groups were in place for South East Asia, Iraq and its neighbors, the Eastern Mediterranean, the Western Mediterranean, East Africa, the Trans-Sahara, South Asia, and Latin America.

COUNTERING TERRORISM ON THE ECONOMIC FRONT

Since the terrorist attacks of September 11, 2001, the United States has acted to block funding of terrorists and their supporters, and to promote international cooperation against them. On September 23, 2001, the President signed E.O. 13224, giving the United States a powerful tool to impede terrorist funding. This Executive Order (EO) provides a means to disrupt the financial support network for terrorists and terrorist organizations by authorizing the USG to designate and block the assets of foreign individuals and entities that commit, or pose a significant risk of committing, acts of terrorism. The EO prohibits transactions between U.S. persons and designated individuals and entities. In addition, because of the pervasiveness of the financial base of foreign terrorists, the order authorizes the USG to block the assets of individuals and entities that provide support, offer assistance to, or otherwise associate with designated terrorists and terrorist organizations. The order also covers their subsidiaries, front organizations, agents, and associates.

The Secretary of State, in consultation with the Attorney General and the Secretary of the Treasury, also has the authority to designate groups as Foreign Terrorist Organizations (FTOs) pursuant to Section 219 of the Immigration and Nationality Act, as amended. These designations play a critical role in U.S. counterterrorism efforts and are an effective means of curtailing support for terrorist activities and pressuring groups to get out of the terrorism business. As a consequence of such a designation, it is unlawful for U.S. citizens or any persons subject to the jurisdiction of the United States to provide material support or resources to a designated FTO. U.S. financial institutions are also required to freeze the funds of designated FTOs.

2008 Designations under E.O. 13224 (FTO Designations are discussed in Chapter 6): On March 11, the United States designated Harakat Ul-Jihad-i-Islami/Bangladesh (HUJI-B) under Executive Order 13224 for its support to terrorist organizations. The group seeks to establish Islamic rule in Bangladesh and was inspired by Usama bin Ladin's ideology in 1992. In April of that year several of HUJI-B's leaders addressed a press conference to demand that Bangladesh transform into an Islamic state. HUJI-B has connections to Pakistani militant groups Harakat ul-Jihadi-Islami (HUJI) and Harakat ul-Mujahidin (HUM), which have similar agendas including the integration of both Jammu and Kashmir into Pakistan. Many of HUJI-B's members reportedly both trained and fought against the former Soviet Union in Afghanistan together with the Mujahadeen. Sympathizers within Pakistan's Inter-Services Intelligence (ISI) are suspected of providing training to the group. HUJI-B is also linked to Asif Reza Commando Force (ARCF), a group that claimed responsibility for an attack on the American Center in Kolkata, the capital of West Bengal, in 2002.

On March 19, the United States designated al-Shabaab under Executive Order 13224. Founded and led by Adan Hashi Ayro, an alumnus of 1990s Afghanistan terrorist training camps, al-Shabaab is dedicated to the removal of Ethiopian forces from Somalia and the (re)-establishment of Sharia law. The group formed in 2004 as a youth movement of the Islamic Courts Union (ICU), but after the ICU lost power in 2006 to the Transitional Federal Government (TFG) and the Ethiopian military the group started recruiting jihadists to wage war against enemies of Islam. In December 2007, Ayro, the head of Somalia's Islamist movement Sheik

Hassan Dahir Aweys, and several hundred purported followers fled Mogadishu to Somalia's southern border with Kenya.

On May 27, the United States designated Zaki-ur-Rehman Lakhvi, Muhammad Saeed, Mahmoud Mohammad Ahmed Bahaziq, and Haji Muhammad Ashraf under Executive Order 13224 for providing support to and holding leadership positions in Lashkar e-Tayyiba (LT), a Pakistan-based terrorist group with links to Usama bin Ladin and the al-Qa'ida (AQ) network. LT has conducted numerous attacks against Indian military and civilian targets since 1993. The Government of India implicated LT in multiple attacks from 2001 through 2008, including the November 2008 terrorist attacks in Mumbai. In March 2002, senior AQ leader Abu Zubaydah was captured at an LT safe house in Pakistan. Despite being banned by the Government of Pakistan in January 2002, LT continues to operate in Kashmir and engage in or support terrorist activities worldwide.

- Muhammad Saeed is LT's overall leader and chief and plays a key role in LT's operational and fundraising activities worldwide. Saeed oversaw the management of a terrorist training camp in Pakistan in 2006, including funding of the camp, which prepared militants to fight against Coalition forces in Afghanistan. In 2005, he determined where graduates of an LT camp in Pakistan should be sent to fight, and personally organized the infiltration of LT militants into Iraq during a trip to Saudi Arabia. That same year, Saeed arranged for an LT operative to be sent to Europe as LT's European fundraising coordinator.
- Zaki-ur-Rehman Lakhvi is LT's chief of operations. In this capacity he directed LT military operations in Chechnya, Bosnia, Iraq, and Southeast Asia. Lakhvi instructed LT associates in 2006 to train operatives for suicide bombings. Prior to that, he instructed operatives to conduct attacks in populated areas. In 2004, Lakhvi sent operatives and funds to attack U.S. forces in Iraq. Lakhvi also directed an LT operative to travel to Iraq in 2003 to assess the terrorist situation there. In past years, Lakhvi has played an important role in LT fundraising activities, reportedly receiving AQ-affiliated donations on behalf of LT.
- Haji Muhammad Ashraf is LT's chief of finance, a position he has held since at least 2003. Ashraf traveled to the Middle East in 2003 and 2004 where he personally collected donations on behalf of LT. Ashraf assisted the Saudi Arabia-based LT leadership in 2003 in expanding its organization and increasing its fundraising activities.
- Mahmoud Mohammad Ahmed Bahaziq is a financier and is

credited with being the main financier behind the establishment of the LT and its activities in the 1980s and 1990s. He has also served as the leader of LT in Saudi Arabia. In 2003, Bahaziq coordinated LT's fundraising activities with Saudi nongovernmental organizations and Saudi businessmen, and encouraged LT operatives to continue and accelerate fundraising and organizing activities. As of mid-2005, Bahaziq played a key role in LT's propaganda and media operations.

On June 13, the United States designated the Revival of Islamic Heritage Society (RIHS) and its branches and subsidiaries under Executive Order 13224 for providing financial and material support to AQ and its affiliates. RIHS is a Kuwaiti-based non-governmental organization (NGO) that has also provided financial support for acts of terrorism. In 2002, when the United States first designated RIHS-Afghanistan and RIHS-Pakistan, there was no evidence that the Kuwait-based RIHS headquarters (RIHS-HQ) knew that the two branch offices were financing AQ. Since that time, however, evidence has mounted implicating RIHS-HQ in terrorism support activity. The USG has learned that RIHS senior leadership, who have actively managed all aspects of the organization's day-to-day operations, have been aware of both legitimate and illegitimate uses of RIHS funds. Suspected of providing support to terrorism, RIHS offices have been closed or raided by the governments of Albania, Azerbaijan, Bangladesh, Bosnia-Herzegovina, Cambodia, Kosovo, and Russia. RIHS-HQ provides significant financial and logistical support to the Pakistan-based UN-designated terrorist group Lashkar e-Tayyiba (LT) in South Asia and to Jemaah Islamiya (JI) in Southeast Asia.

On June 16, the United States designated the Rajah Solaiman Movement (RSM) under Executive Order 13224 for its support to terrorist organizations. RSM was established in 2002 and seeks to return the Philippines to an Islamic state. The group is named after Rajah Solaiman, the last king of Manila before Spanish colonization in the 1500s introduced Catholicism along with European rule to the region. The group's members have reportedly been trained, financed, and directed by both the Philippines-based Abu Sayyaf Group and the Indonesia-based JI.

On November 12, the United States designated the Union of Good under Executive Order 13224. The organization was created by HAMAS leadership to transfer funds to that terrorist organization in late 2000 shortly after the start of the second Intifada. The Union of Good facilitates the transfer of tens of millions of dollars a year to HAMAS-managed associations in the West Bank and Gaza Strip. In addition to providing cover for HAMAS financial transfers, some of the funds transferred by the Union of Good have compensated HAMAS terrorists by providing payments to the families of suicide bombers. The group's executive leadership and board of directors include HAMAS leaders and other terrorist supporters.

On November 20, the United States designated Ahmed Abdi Aw-Mohamed, Issa Osman Issa, and Mukhtar Robow under Executive Order 13224 for providing support to al-Shabaab, a terrorist group linked to AQ. The individuals include the organization's reputed leader, its spokesman, and a regional military leader. These three leaders use lethal tactics to undermine peace and civil society in Somalia and they have had direct involvement in the kidnappings and cold-blooded murders of numerous Somali officials and civilians. Al-Shabaab has used intimidation and violence to undermine the Somali government and threaten civil society activists working to bring about peace through political dialogue and reconciliation. Many of al-Shabaab's senior leaders are believed to have trained and fought with AQ in Afghanistan.

- o Ahmed Abdi aw-Mohamed is the founder and a current leader of al-Shabaab. He claimed his group was responsible for the May 2007 assassination of a judge in Beledweyne, Somalia, and in March 2007, he coordinated attacks on Ethiopian troops in Somalia. Aw-Mohamed has also served as a conduit for financing to al-Shabaab.
- o Issa Osman Issa has a leadership role in al-Shabaab and has served as a commander of al-Shabaab forces in Somalia. In late April 2007, Issa led a militia assault against Mogadishu's Basil Hotel, often frequented by Ugandan peacekeepers. He also was reportedly involved in recruiting an individual to carry out a successful April 2007 suicide attack against the Ethiopian military presence in Afgooye, Somalia. Before al-Shabaab's creation, Issa was one of the operatives who fired the surface-to-air missiles used in the failed 2002 attempt to shoot down an Israeli airliner in Mombasa, Kenya. Issa was also involved in the planning of the near-simultaneous attack in 2002 against the Paradise Hotel in Kikambala, Kenya, in which a vehicle-borne explosive device struck the hotel killing 12 and injuring 40. He is reportedly linked to 1998 bombings of U.S. Embassies in Africa.
- o Mukhtar Robow serves as al-Shabaab's spokesperson, communicating to the press and public on its behalf. He has also served as al-Shabaab's spiritual leader and as its military commander in Southern Somalia. Robow has targeted Somali Transitional Federal Government (TFG), Ethiopian, and African Union troops in Somalia. Robow and former al-Shabaab leader Aden Hashi Ayrow (deceased) were responsible for the November 2006 suicide attack against a TFG checkpoint in Baidoa, Somalia.

Rewards For Justice (RFJ) Through the RFJ program, the Secretary of State offers and pays rewards for information that prevents or successfully resolves an act of international terrorism against United States persons or property. Reward offers of up to $25 million have been authorized for information leading to the capture of Usama bin Ladin and other key terrorist leaders. Since its inception in 1984, RFJ has paid more than $82 million to over 50 people who provided credible information.

In 2008, the RFJ program added the following six terrorists to its *Most Wanted* list.

- Baitullah Mehsud, the senior leader of Tehrik-e-Taliban (Taliban Movement of Pakistan) who is regarded as the principal al-Qa'ida (AQ) leader in the Pakistani tribal areas of South Waziristan, with a reward offer of up to USD five million;
- Radullan Sahiron, a senior leader of the Abu Sayyaf Group, with a reward offer of up to USD one million;
- Abdul Basit Usman, a known terrorist responsible for bombings in the southern Philippines, with a reward offer of up to USD one million;
- Khair Mundos, an ASG member known to have funneled money from AQ to be used in bombings against Americans, with a reward offer of up to USD 500,000;
- Prominent AQ member Abu Yahya al-Libi, who has appeared in a number of propaganda videos, with a reward offer of up to USD one million; and
- RFJ added Sirajuddin Haqqani, a senior leader of the Haqqani terrorist network who maintains close ties to AQ, with a reward offer of up to USD five million.

All of these reward offerings are listed in greater detail on the www.rewardsforjustice.net website.

MULTILATERAL EFFORTS TO COMBAT TERRORISM

International cooperation remained essential to initiatives in fields ranging from intelligence and law enforcement coordination, to targeted financial sanctions, and to norms and standards of financial regulation, particularly because most funds used to support terrorism are located outside the jurisdiction of the United States.

Throughout the year, the United States worked closely with multilateral partners in numerous counterterrorist financing efforts, including the Counterterrorism Committee of the United Nations, the Egmont Group of Financial Intelligence Units, the Financial Action Task Force (FATF) and FATF-style regional bodies, the G8's Counterterrorism Action Group

(CTAG), and international financial institutions. In addition, the United States continued its regular dialogue on terrorist financing with the European Union. Since its launch in September 2004, the dialogue has served as a framework for ongoing exchanges to promote information sharing and cooperation on joint issues of concern, and on technical assistance issues.

European nations and international partners are active participants in a variety of multilateral fora that contributed to counterterrorist efforts, including the G8, NATO, the Organization for Security and Cooperation in Europe (OSCE), the Asia Pacific Economic Cooperation (APEC) forum, the ASEAN Regional Forum, and the Organization of American States. The United States and its partners worked through these organizations to establish and implement best practices, build the counterterrorism and law enforcement capabilities of "weak but willing" states, and to institutionalize global counterterrorism. The World Bank and International Monetary Fund have pledged to provide countries with training to increase their capacity to combat money laundering and terrorist financing.

The United Nations (UN). The Counter-Terrorism Committee (CTC) was established by Security Council Resolution 1373 after September 11, 2001, with the goal of enhancing the ability of UN member states to combat terrorism. The Counter-Terrorism Committee's Executive Directorate (CTED), established by Resolution 1535 in 2004, became fully operational in 2005. CTED's mandate is to enhance the Committee's ability to monitor the implementation of Resolution 1373 and to advance capacity-building work by facilitating technical assistance to member states and promoting closer cooperation and coordination with international, regional, and sub-regional organizations. It also conducts visits to member states to assess the implementation of Resolution 1373. CTED visited six states in 2008: Niger, Jamaica, Saudi Arabia, Cambodia, the Lao People's Democratic Republic, and South Africa. UN Security Council Resolution 1805 (March 20, 2008) extended CTED's mandate until December 31, 2010, and affirmed the CTC's endorsement of a revised organizational plan for CTED.

The Counterterrorism Implementation Task Force (CTITF) brought together 24 UN entities across the UN system, which work under mandates from the General Assembly, the Security Council, and various specialized agencies, funds, and programs to implement the historic Global Counterterrorism Strategy, which was agreed to by all 192 member countries in September 2006. In 2007, the Task Force developed a program of work and established working groups to carry forward a first set of initiatives to implement the Strategy. A compilation of activities undertaken by the Task Force entities in implementing the strategy was issued in a report by the Secretary General in July 2008.

The United Nations Security Council 1540 Committee on non-proliferation was established after in the adoption of Resolution 1540 that all States shall refrain from providing any form of support to non-State actors that attempt to develop, acquire, manufacture, possess, transport, transfer or use nuclear, chemical, or biological weapons and their means of delivery. The United States co-sponsored UN Security Council Resolution 1810, which extended the work of the 1540 Committee for three years until April 2011; highlighting a shift in emphasis from reporting to implementation (national action plans) and consideration of options for developing and making more effective existing funding mechanisms to enhance overall technical assistance efforts.

UN Specialized Agencies are also involved in the work of fighting terrorism. For example, the International Civil Aviation Organization (ICAO) adopted passport security standards, and the UN Office on Drugs and Crime's (UNODC's) Terrorism Prevention Branch and Global Programme Against Money Laundering continued to provide assistance to countries in the legal and related aspects of counterterrorism. UNODC's mandate in the area of counterterrorism is specifically focused on building the legal framework necessary for member states to become party to and implement the international counterterrorism conventions and protocols. The Terrorism Prevention Branch also focused on strengthening the capacity of the national criminal justice systems to apply the provisions of these instruments in compliance with the principles of rule of law and on providing substantive input on counterterrorism issues to intergovernmental bodies.

International organized crime networks and members can provide support to terrorist organizations and facilitate their activities. The UN Convention on Transnational Organized Crime (CTOC) is the main international instrument to counter international organized crime. The UNODC's implementation of the CTOC and its Protocols, specifically the Protocol on Human Smuggling, contributed to the global efforts to counter terrorism by providing technical assistance and training, and strengthening countries' legal systems and law enforcement and border control capabilities. Building the capacity of countries to control their borders helps disrupt terrorist mobility.

The International Atomic Energy Agency (IAEA) continued to implement its Nuclear Security Plan (2006-2009) for combating the threat of terrorism involving nuclear and other radioactive material. IAEA promoted its member states' ratification and implementation of international instruments relating to nuclear security, including the Amendment to the Convention on the Physical Protection of Nuclear Material, and the non-binding IAEA Code of Conduct on the Safety and Security of Radioactive Sources. The IAEA Nuclear Security Series is a framework of guidance documents designed to help states establish a coherent nuclear security infrastructure.

The United States has been working with and through the IAEA to enhance security over at-risk, vulnerable nuclear, and other radioactive materials within the IAEA's 144 Member States to reduce the risk that such materials could be used in a terrorist event.

In 2008:

The IAEA published several documents in the Nuclear Security Series, notably Nuclear Security Culture, Security in the Transport of Radioactive Material, Protective and Preventive Measures against Insider Threats, and Combating Illicit Trafficking in Nuclear and other Radioactive Material.

The IAEA continued to prioritize nuclear security training and support the development of mechanisms for nuclear security education.

More than 1500 participants from 87 countries took part in IAEA nuclear security training in a total of 68 events.

Participation in the IAEA Illicit Trafficking Database (ITDB) program expanded to 100 States. As of December 31, ITDB Participating States had reported or otherwise confirmed in total 1,340 incidents of nuclear or radiological materials outside legitimate control to the ITDB.

The IAEA continued to work with States to improve global controls for radioactive sources, particularly national regulatory infrastructures and export controls. Efforts included urging States to make political commitments to follow the non-binding IAEA Code of Conduct on the Safety and Security for Radioactive Sources and the associated Guidance on the Import and Export of Radioactive Sources, the latter of which represents the first international export control framework for radioactive sources. To date, 92 States have made a commitment to follow the Code of Conduct and 46 States to follow the import/export Guidance. In May, the IAEA held a meeting attended by experts from 88 Member States that sought to harmonize implementation of global export controls for sources, as provided in the guidance.

The IAEA continued, upon request, to assist States in developing and implementing measures to prevent incidents of nuclear terrorism at major public events. Drawing on ITDB reporting, the IAEA provided information support and advice in the areas of detection, interdiction, and response. In addition, training courses, workshops, and exercises were conducted and detection equipment purchased and supplied. In 2008, working in close cooperation with the Global Threat Reduction Initiative (GTRI), the IAEA, drawing on its successful nuclear security programs at the 2004 Olympics in Greece and at the Pan American Games in Rio de Janeiro, successfully implemented a major nuclear security program leading up to and during the 2008 Beijing Olympic Games in China.

ITDB also continued to expand its membership and now includes 100 countries. The ITDB is a voluntary program whereby states confirm incidents of illicit trafficking or other unauthorized activities involving nuclear and radioactive material. The ITDB collects authoritative information on illicit trafficking events and helps participating states better understand illicit trafficking events and trends. Additionally, the ITDB is an authoritative database for tracking nuclear and radioactive materials that have fallen outside of legitimate control and that could be used in potential actions of terrorism.

Group of Eight (G8) Counterterrorism Actions. The Group of Eight (G8), composed of Canada, France, Germany, Italy, Japan, Russia, the United Kingdom, and the United States, continued to develop and promote effective counterterrorism standards and best practices throughout the year.

Japan hosted the 2008 annual G8 Summit in Toyako Hokkaido, where G8 Leaders committed to take action on a range of counterterrorism issues, including: strengthening cooperation among the G8 and UN on capacity building for countries requiring assistance to meet international counterterrorism commitments; countering bulk cash smuggling and the exploitation of charities that finance terrorism and violent extremism; continuing to develop measures to counter and prevent radicalization leading to violence; reinforcing efforts to tackle chemical, biological, radiological, and nuclear terrorism; protecting against attacks on energy infrastructure and transportation systems; and preventing abuse of information/ communication technology.

G8 Leaders condemned all terrorist acts as criminal and unjustifiable, particularly the tactics of suicide bombings, the recruitment of the young or disadvantaged to carry out such bombings, and hostage taking. G8 Leaders also committed to economic and social development along with counterterrorism in the Afghanistan and Pakistan border regions.

Counterterrorism Action Group (CTAG). At the June 2003 Evian Summit, G8 Leaders adopted a plan to build political will and capacity to combat terrorism globally, and established the Counterterrorism Action Group (CTAG) to implement this plan. CTAG supports the UN Counter-Terrorism Committee's efforts to monitor and promote implementation of UNSCR 1373 by developing an active forum for donors to coordinate counterterrorism cooperation with, and assistance to, third countries. It promotes counterterrorism by prioritizing needs and targeting and coordinating assistance to expand counterterrorism capacity in recipient countries; and encourages all countries to meet their obligations under UNSCR 1373 and, for states party to them, the 13 international counterterrorism conventions and protocols.

Under the leadership of the rotating G8 presidency, CTAG meets two times per year with the active participation of G8 member states, the European Commission, and other donor countries and organizations. Coordination meetings hosted by the local embassy of the G8 presidency were also held among CTAG members' diplomatic missions in recipient countries, and in coordination with the UN Counterterrorism Executive Directorate's country visits.

Financial Action Task Force (FATF) and FATF-Style Regional Bodies (FSRBs). The United States continued to play a strong role in developing new initiatives within FATF as well as throughout the entire FATF network to meet evolving anti-money laundering and counterterrorism financing threats. In 2008, the United States delegation continued its contributions to the Plenary on issues of policy as well as to the Working Groups on issues of implementation. The United States continued its co-chair role, with Italy, on the International Cooperation Review Group to address jurisdictional anti-money laundering/counterterrorism financing systemic deficiencies and threats. The United States also participated in major FATF work comprising examination, negotiation, and implementation of Special Recommendation IX on cash couriers for supranational entities, examination of proliferation finance, and discussion of the inclusion of the FATF-style regional bodies in the FATF network. In 2008, additional work contributed by the United States included outreach to the private sector, public-private partnerships, development of guidance for non-financial businesses and professions, hosting mutual evaluation assessor training, and participating in FATF mutual evaluations. The United States played a similar and equally active role in the FSRBs, supporting FSRB-executed training and typologies workshops and providing technical assistance not only to members, but to the Secretariats themselves, as well as taking part in Contact Groups, mutual evaluations, and Expert Review Groups, and providing advice upon request with an eye to increasing the capacity and transparency of the Secretariats.

European Union (EU). The United States and the EU cooperated closely on combating terrorism. At the June 2008 U.S.-EU Summit, both parties recognized the need to play an active role in multilateral counterterrorism efforts at the UN and to ensure effective implementation of the UN Global Counterterrorism Strategy. The EU Counterterrorism Coordinator, Gilles de Kerchove, coordinated the counterterrorism work of the Council of the European Union, composed of representatives from all 27 EU Member States. De Kerchove participated in regular dialogues with U.S. counterterrorism officials.

The U.S. and EU have deepened cooperation in the area of domestic security, including reciprocally participating in each others' domestic response exercises. The European Council Secretariat attended the TOPOFF 4 (Top Officials) exercise to test U.S. all-hazards response capabilities. Likewise, the United States recently participated in the European Council's review of its emergency and crisis coordination arrangements. The United States and EU continued to collaborate on techniques for identifying terrorist travel. U.S. experts have met with EU counterparts on a number of occasions to exchange lessons learned on the development of passenger prescreening systems, including the use of Passenger Name Records.

In September, the European Court of Justice held that EU implementation of asset freezes required by the United Nations sanctions regime against al-Qa'ida, the Taliban, and their associates, violated procedural and property rights enshrined in European Community law. The Court annulled the regulation (insofar as it applied to the two plaintiffs), but gave the EU three months to revise it to rectify these defects. There are several other similar challenges to the EU's implementation of counterterrorism sanctions pending before the European Court of Justice. EU officials are working to remedy issues raised in the September ruling while preserving a strong counterterrorism effort that complies with UN obligations.

EU Justice and Home Affairs Ministers approved a change to the existing EU Framework Decision on Terrorism. Among other changes, the Ministers added incitement and terrorist training as criminal offences under the EU legal framework. The United States and the EU's Judicial Cooperation Unit (Eurojust) have improved cooperation and information exchange among investigators and prosecutors. Pursuant to the U.S.-Eurojust Cooperative Agreement, a U.S. National Liaison Prosecutor, resident in Brussels, assists with operational cases that include several EU member states and assists in mutual legal assistance or extradition issues involving member states. The United States and all but three EU Member States (Belgium, Greece, and Italy) have ratified the U.S.-EU Extradition and Mutual Legal Assistance Agreements; in November 2008, Eurojust hosted a seminar for law enforcement practitioners from the United States and EU Member States on implementation of the agreements.

The United States and EU have established a roadmap toward mutual recognition between the EU Authorized Economic Operator provisions and the U.S. Customs-Trade Partnership Against Terrorism, which are based on a risk management approach to cargo security. A Secure Freight Initiative pilot project in Southampton, UK was concluded in 2008 and provided valuable lessons that will assist in determining how best to execute the 9/11 Implementation Act's requirement for 100 percent scanning of maritime cargo containers.

The United States and EU organized an experts' seminar in December 2008 on enhancing the control of explosives. The forum focused on two high-priority shared challenges: improvised liquid or home-made explosives and response issues. Discussions are underway to expand existing transatlantic cooperation on research and development to include security research.

Despite this progress, EU concerns about privacy protection in the United States continue to present an operational and political obstacle to further collaboration. However, the High Level Contact Group created in 2006 to assess this problem has made considerable progress. On June 10, 2008, the EU-U.S. Summit recognized that the fight against transnational crime and terrorism requires the ability to share personal data for law enforcement purposes while fully protecting the fundamental rights and civil liberties of both sides' citizens and residents. At the December 2008 Justice and Home Affairs Ministerial, the United States and EU reaffirmed their commitment to a series of basic privacy principles and moved closer to consensus on their application in transatlantic data transfers.

The United States and the EU continued to cooperate on combating terrorist financing, including:

- Discussing implementation of specific Financial Action Task Force Special Recommendations, including Special Recommendation IX on Cash Couriers and the EU's request to be treated as a single jurisdiction for purposes of evaluation;
- Improving implementation of FATF SR III on developing effective targeted sanctions regimes;
- Improving procedures for information sharing and for working with private sector financial institutions to strengthen implementation of asset freeze measures;
- Exchanging information and best practices in expert-level discussions; and
- Holding regular senior-level meetings and practitioner workshops between the United States and EU on counterterrorist financing issues.

Organization for Security and Cooperation in Europe (OSCE). The United States worked with the OSCE through its Action against Terrorism Unit (ATU) to encourage cooperation and to address existing gaps in the capabilities and legal frameworks of the OSCE's 56 participating States. In July, the OSCE hosted an expert meeting to identify areas where the OSCE could contribute to the enhancement of protection from terrorist attacks of Critical Energy Infrastructure (CEI). The meeting highlighted various global threats to CEI, as well as potential responses, including using the OSCE as a platform to enhance information sharing, facilitate cooperation with relevant international organizations, and promote public private partnerships. In September, the OSCE organized a high-level political conference, a joint initiative of the United States and the Russian Federation, on Public-Private Partnerships (PPPs). The conference highlighted the fact that effective solutions to fighting terrorism require integrated approaches that harness the expertise of all sectors of society by bringing them together in close public-private cooperation. Over 250 participants from 54 OSCE participating states and Partners for Cooperation, and 45 civil society and business community participants, as well as representatives from 18 international organizations, discussed ways to best draw upon the capacity of businesses and civil society to help governments fight terrorism. In October, the OSCE hosted a workshop on countering violent extremism and radicalization to discuss terrorist recruitment methods. The OSCE also continued its considerable efforts to provide technical capacity-building assistance to help participating states detect and prevent the use of fraudulent and counterfeit travel documents, to make it more difficult for terrorists and other criminals to forge or counterfeit them, and to encourage the reporting of lost and stolen travel documents to INTERPOL. The OSCE Helsinki Ministerial issued a decision supporting the G8 Leaders' statement of counterterrorism principles and called upon participating states, *inter alia*, to implement the UN Global Counterterrorism strategy, promote PPPs, and enhance cooperation in countering violent extremism and radicalization, and continue to support the implementation of UNSCR 1540.

North Atlantic Treaty Organization (NATO). NATO leads International Security Assistance Force (ISAF) stability operations against radical insurgents in Afghanistan. NATO also conducts Operation Active Endeavor (OAE), a naval mission that aims to combat terrorism by monitoring Mediterranean maritime traffic. The Alliance is engaged in a far-reaching transformation of its forces and capabilities to better deter and defend against 21st Century threats, including terrorism, and is working closely with partner countries and organizations to ensure interoperability of forces, thus enhancing security and broadening cooperation.

NATO adopted its Military Concept against Terrorism in 2002, fielded a Chemical Biological Radiological and Nuclear (CBRN) defense battalion in 2004, and established a special Terrorist Threat Intelligence Unit. Efforts were underway to enhance Allied protection against the potential attempts to disrupt critical infrastructure (energy, cyber) systems. Through NATO's Defense Against Terrorism (DAT) program, the Alliance is developing 10 cutting-edge technologies to protect troops and civilians against terrorist attacks. In December 2008, NATO Foreign Ministers condemned all terrorist acts as unjustifiable and criminal and deplored tactics such as suicide bombing and hostage taking, as well as the recruitment of the young and disadvantaged to conduct terrorist activities. NATO's 26 Allies and 24 Euro-Atlantic Partnership Council Partners have all submitted initial reports as called for by UN Security Council Resolution 1540. NATO also supported a UNSCR 1540 regional implementation seminar in June in Croatia.

Trans-Sahara Counterterrorism Partnership (TSCTP). The Trans-Sahara Counterterrorism Partnership (TSCTP) is a multi-faceted, multi-year strategy to combat violent extremism and defeat terrorist organizations by strengthening individual-country and regional counterterrorism capabilities, enhancing and institutionalizing cooperation among the region's security and intelligence organizations, promoting democratic governance, and discrediting terrorist ideology. The overall goals are to enhance the indigenous capacities of governments in the pan-Sahel (Mauritania, Mali, Chad, and Niger, as well as Nigeria and Senegal) to confront the challenge posed by terrorist organizations in the trans-Sahara, and to facilitate cooperation between those countries and our Maghreb partners (Morocco, Algeria, and Tunisia). (See Chapter 2, *Country Reports, Africa,* for further information on the TSCTP.)

The African Union (AU). The African Union (AU) has several counterterrorism legal instruments including a Convention on the Prevention and Combating of Terrorism (1999), a 2002 Protocol to the Convention, and a 2004 Plan of Action. The Addis Ababa-based AU Commission provided guidance to its 53-member states and coordinated limited technical assistance to cover member states' counterterrorism capability gaps. In 2005, with Danish funding, the AU hired a consultant to draft a counterterrorism Model Law to serve as a template to assist member states in drafting language to implement counterterrorism commitments. In December 2006, an AU-sponsored group of experts drafted counterterrorism language, which was in the process of being legislated. The group of experts decided to retain options for both broad and specific laws and determined that new legislation was needed to combat money laundering and other financial crimes. In August, the AU Peace and Security Council requested the AU Commission to expedite the development of the African Anti-Terrorism Law. Some AU member states maintained that Africa's colonial legacy made it difficult to accept a definition of terrorism that excluded an exception for "freedom fighters." Nonetheless, the AU is on record strongly condemning acts of terrorism. In August 2008, the Peace and Security Council issued a statement condemning "unreservedly acts of terrorism, wherever they occur." (See Chapter 2, *Country Reports, Africa*, for further information on the AU.)

Association of Southeast Asian Nations (ASEAN) and the ASEAN Regional Forum (ARF). In January 2007, the Heads of State of the ten-member Association of Southeast Asian Nations, comprising Brunei, Burma, Cambodia, Indonesia, Laos, Malaysia, Philippines, Singapore, Thailand, and Vietnam, signed a new convention on counterterrorism cooperation. The new ASEAN treaty recognized the importance of having a global legal framework to combat terrorism, as established by the universal conventions on terrorism. The treaty further recognized that terrorism offenses such as hijacking, hostage-taking, and bombing are not political offenses, and terrorists cannot hide behind political justifications to evade justice. Under the new Convention, ASEAN members agreed to cooperate to prevent terrorist attacks, terrorist financing, and terrorist movement across national borders. They also agreed to cooperate to enhance intelligence exchanges, promote public participation in counterterrorism efforts, and strengthen preparedness for dealing with chemical, biological, and nuclear terrorism. The United States worked closely with ASEAN to enhance counterterrorism cooperation. The United States actively participated in counterterrorism-related activities of the 26-member ASEAN Regional Forum (ARF), including the annual meetings on counterterrorism and transnational crime.

Asia Pacific Economic Cooperation (APEC). The 21 member economies of APEC (Australia, Brunei, Canada, Chile, China, Hong Kong, Indonesia, Japan, Republic of Korea, Malaysia, Mexico, New Zealand, Papua New Guinea, Peru, Philippines, Russia, Singapore, Chinese Taipei, Thailand, the United States, and Vietnam), are committed to creating a safe environment for the movement of goods, services, and people throughout the region. Since 2001, APEC has worked to secure the region's economic, trade, investment, and financial systems from terrorist attack and/or abuse by proliferators. The APEC Counterterrorism Task Force (CTTF) was established in 2003 to coordinate implementation of Leaders' and Ministers' statements on counterterrorism and non-proliferation, promote information sharing, and develop counterterrorism capacity in the region. APEC also leverages its relationship with the private sector to promote public-private partnerships in counterterrorism and secure trade.

In 2008, APEC Leaders' recognized that joint counterterrorism efforts are based on a common understanding that all terrorist acts are criminal and unjustifiable, and must be unequivocally condemned, especially when they target or injure civilians, or use the abhorrent practices of suicide bombing and hostage taking. The United States continued its work within APEC to dismantle transnational terrorist groups and to eliminate the severe and growing danger posed by proliferation of weapons of mass destruction and their means of delivery. The United States also led capacity-building work to counter biological and chemical terrorism, completing a joint pilot project with Peru to implement the APEC Food Defense Principles. The United States promoted APEC efforts to counter terrorist financing and to help member economies implement the Financial Action Task Force Special Recommendations on Terrorist Financing. Lastly, the United States actively supported APEC initiatives to strengthen aviation, land, and maritime security, and support trade recovery following an attack.

OAS Inter-American Committee against Terrorism (CICTE). On March 12, 2008, at the Eighth Regular Session of CICTE in Washington DC, the Member States adopted the Declaration of Reaffirmation of the Hemispheric Commitment to Fighting Terrorism, which acknowledged that terrorism constitutes a grave threat to the lives, well-being, and fundamental freedoms of all people, threatens international peace and security, and undermines the values and principles underlying the inter-American system, democratic institutions, and the freedoms enshrined in and promoted by the Charter of the OAS, the Inter-American Democratic Charter, and other international instruments. The CICTE Ministers also reaffirmed their commitments and conclusions adopted in the Declaration of Panama on the Protection of Critical Infrastructure in the Hemisphere in the Face of Terrorism, in the Declarations adopted at the six previous regular sessions of CICTE, as well as the importance of the United Nations Global Counterterrorism Strategy, and the relevance of the implementation of these in the fight against terrorism; and the importance of the efforts of the Financial Action Task Force (FATF) and its commitment to implement and promote internationally its 40 Recommendations on Money Laundering and Nine Special Recommendations on Terrorism Financing. CICTE operates as the counterterrorism policy body for the hemisphere, with its experts representing and advising the 34 member state governments on how to meet the requirements of the international conventions and protocols relating to terrorism, UN Security Council Resolutions (especially 1373, 1267, and 1540), and the Inter-American Convention against Terrorism (IACAT).

In 2008, the Secretariat received over $4.8 million in voluntary contributions, a 300% increase over 2007. It conducted 115 activities, training courses and technical assistance missions, benefiting over 2,800 participants through nine programs in five areas: border control, critical infrastructure protection, counterterrorism legislative assistance and terrorist financing, crisis management of emerging terrorist threats, and international cooperation and partnerships. Key achievements included the development of new methodologies—workshops on best practices and crisis management exercises—and the expansion of international partnerships.

Tri-Border Area (Argentina, Brazil, and Paraguay). The Governments of the Tri-Border Area (TBA) – Argentina, Brazil, and Paraguay – have long been concerned with arms and drugs smuggling, document fraud, money laundering, trafficking in persons, and the manufacture and movement of contraband goods through this region. In the early 1990s, they established a mechanism to address these illicit activities. In 2002, at their invitation, the United States joined them in what became the "3+1 Group on Tri-Border Area Security" to improve the capabilities of the three to address cross-border crime and thwart money laundering and potential terrorist financing activities. The United States remained concerned that Hizballah and HAMAS sympathizers were raising funds in the TBA by participating in illicit activities and soliciting donations from sympathizers within the sizable Muslim communities in the region. There was no corroborated information, however, that these or other Islamic extremist groups had an operational presence in the TBA.

LONG-TERM GOALS AND PROGRAMS/ACTIONS DESIGNED TO REDUCE CONDITIONS THAT ALLOW TERRORIST SAFE HAVENS TO FORM

The **Antiterrorism Assistance Program (ATA)** provides partner countries with the training, equipment, and technology needed to increase their capabilities to find and arrest terrorists, building the kind of cooperation and interactivity between law enforcement officers that has a lasting impact. During fiscal year 2008, the State Department delivered over 280 training activities and technical consultations, and trained over 5,600 participants from 68 countries. Over the course of its 25-year existence, the ATA program has trained more than 66,500 students from 154 countries, providing programs tailored to the needs of each partner nation and to local conditions.

ATA training subjects included:

- Airport security
- Cyber terrorism
- Bomb detection
- Dignitary protection
- Border control
- Fraudulent document recognition

- Countering terrorist financing,
- Interdiction of terrorist organizations
- Crisis management and response
- Kidnap intervention
- Crisis response teams
- Hostage negotiation and rescue
- Response to incidents involving weapons of mass destruction
- Critical antiterrorism skills at the tactical, operational, and strategic levels.

All courses emphasized advanced law enforcement techniques under the rule of law. Successful ATA programs include:

Afghanistan: In April, an assassination attempt on President Karzai, by Taliban fighters in Kabul, was thwarted by the quick action of the ATA trained Presidential Protective Services (PPS) personnel. Three assassins were killed and three were arrested. Based on the elevated threat information received, the PPS were advised on the best procedures to deal with the anticipated attack. ATA continued to organize, train, equip, and mentor the 340-person Presidential Protective Service (PPS) responsible for President Karzai's safety.

Colombia: ATA continued its assistance in the development a cutting-edge anti-kidnapping training facility known by its location in Sibate, Colombia. In 2008, Colombia law enforcement began assuming full responsibility for delivering ATA-based training courses as a part of the Sibate programs. ATA training has helped Colombia's GAULA anti-kidnapping units reduce kidnappings in Colombia by 83 percent since 2002. Over the past six years, none of the ATA-trained GAULAs have lost a single hostage during rescue operations.

Indonesia: The ATA- trained and equipped tactical units of Detachment 88 (Det 88) have arrested and participated in the adjudication of over four hundred terrorist suspects. Elements of Det 88 directed the investigation that resulted in the arrest operation, and related death, of one of Southeast Asia's most wanted terrorists, Dr. Azahari bin Husin, the organizer of a nightclub bombing in Bali in 2002 that killed over 200 people. In May, ATA-trained computer forensic specialists examined the computer of an arrested terrorist, linking him to a 2005 Bali bombing revealing other terroristcells in Indonesia and connecting the suspect to another suspected bomb maker.

Kenya: In a cooperative venture with the Kenya National Steering Committee for Maritime Security, ATA completed the construction of a maritime training facility in Manda Bay, Kenya. The facility officially opened on February 28. Three eleven-week basic maritime security courses, and additional advanced courses, were conducted at the facility. ATA trained officers conducted patrols in the Port of Mombasa and at selected sites along the Kenya coastline.

Liberia: Maintaining a team of mentors/security advisors embedded in the Liberian Special Security Service, ATA continued its work to improve the personal security of Liberian President Sirleaf in 2008. Fifteen courses and consultations were offered during the year. In addition to their primary role in providing presidential protection, ATA trained SSS personnel were called upon by local Liberian police to assist with a hostage situation at the home of a former Liberian Minister. Three officers responded and safely extricated the hostages from the home.

Mexico: Due to the increasing level of violence against high-level Mexican Government officials ATA has delivered the a continuing series of VIP Protection courses in Mexico for the Office of the Attorney General, the Secretariat of Public Security, and other high level Government of Mexico Officials.

Pakistan: Using techniques based on ATA Post-Blast Investigative courses, the Federal Special Investigations Group's (SIG's) forensics laboratory developed leads gleaned from a cell phone SIM card destroyed in a bomb blast and retrieved by personnel of the Quetta Province Criminal Investigative Division. More than 33 messages were retrieved, outlining 14 bomb threats. Based on the information recovered by an ATA designed and funded SIG forensics laboratory with ATA trained staff, numerous suspects were identified and two bombs were later seized.

Palestinian Authority: The ATA program for the Palestinian Authority initially focused on providing VIP protection courses to the Presidential Guards from the West Bank. Fifteen VIP courses were delivered in less than five months, training 320 participants in VIP protection, surveillance detection, and vital installation security. Overall, the USD five million program will provide technical and leadership training, as well as operational support equipment, to enhance the VIP Protective Unit for the Palestinian Authority.

Thailand: In just one of its many successful operations this year, a Royal Thai Police (RTP) tactical team conducted a successful raid in which they arrested eight suspects and recovered—unharmed—a kidnapped American citizen. The RTP Lieutenant Colonel who led the operation, the lead investigator, and four members of the tactical entry team had completed ATA training courses in Crisis Response Team, Hostage Negotiation, Officer Survival/High-Threat Incident, and the Police Role in Crisis Management.

The **Terrorist Interdiction Program (TIP)** assisted priority countries at risk of terrorist activity to enhance their border security capabilities. TIP provided participating countries with a computerized watch listing system to identify suspect travelers at air, land, or sea ports of entry. TIP further promoted expanded cooperation, data sharing, and close liaison with host governments in the areas of rule of law, anticorruption, and law enforcement. Since 2001, the State Department has provided TIP assistance to more than 20 countries at 110 ports of entry, assistance that was instrumental in impeding and interdicting terrorist travel. High-priority countries participating in the program include Iraq, Pakistan, Afghanistan, Yemen, Thailand, and Kenya. While the primary focus of TIP is on constraining terrorist travel, thousands of individuals traveling on stolen passports in Pakistan, as well as wanted criminals, narcotics smugglers, and human traffickers have been identified and intercepted worldwide. The TIP complements other counterterrorism-related U.S. efforts to enhance aviation, border, cyber, maritime, and transportation security.

Counterterrorist Finance Training (CTFT) The State Department chaired the interagency Terrorist Finance Working Group (TFWG), which met biweekly to develop and coordinate USG CTF capacity-building efforts, and worked to expand its counterterrorist financing (CTF) capacity-building efforts in key partner nations. Although our CTF programs retained their global focus, we expanded our CTF training programs for North and West Africa in 2008. The CTF capacity-building program includes training and technical assistance in the legal, financial regulatory, financial intelligence, financial investigation, and judicial, prosecutorial, and asset forfeiture fields; as well as task force development to build interagency cooperation between the fields.

CTF 2008 programs included:

The posting of five Resident Legal Advisors (RLAs),

The development of a Regional Operational Cash Courier program and Prosecutorial and Designation Workshops,

Financial Intelligence Unit (FIU) analytical training, mentorship, and overall development,

Financial regulatory training for national and supranational supervisory authorities, and

Terrorist financing investigative, financial forensics, and analytical training on a number of levels for law enforcement authorities.

The roles and responsibilities of our five Department of Justice Resident Legal Advisors were expanded with bilateral and regional responsibilities. The RLAs have conducted training workshops, assisted with the drafting of laws and regulations, and conducted outreach to parliamentarians.

Under the auspices of the TFWG, we have worked with the Department of Homeland Security and our interagency partners to expand our bulk cash smuggling training programs. This included conducting a highly successful Regional Operational Cash Courier Training program in South East Asia and bulk cash smuggling training in a variety of countries, including Nigeria and Iraq.

Increasing Economic Development. Poverty, unemployment, weak institutions, and corruption can turn nations of great potential into recruiting grounds for terrorists. Development is central to the President's National Security Strategy and long-term U.S. economic growth. Well-conceived, targeted aid is a potential leveraging instrument that can help countries implement sound economic policies and improve the conditions that terrorists might otherwise exploit.

The Millennium Challenge Account (MCA), established by Congress in 2004, represents a new model for achieving transformational development by providing assistance to those countries that rule justly, invest in their people, and encourage economic freedom. The prospect of an MCA Compact provides a powerful incentive for the poorest countries to reform.

U.S. private sector flows to the developing world, including net trade and investment ($672 billion in 2007), dwarf our foreign aid ($21.8 billion). Unutilized capital in developing countries, owing to weak policies and poor property rights, is estimated to be as high as $9 trillion.

Debt relief for the poorest is another element of our development strategy. Our long-standing support for the Heavily Indebted Poor Countries (HIPC) initiative, as well as for the Multilateral Debt Relief Initiative (MDRI) introduced in 2006, promotes debt sustainability, reduces the likelihood of debt distress, and enables the poorest countries to devote additional resources to reducing poverty and promoting economic growth. USAID's humanitarian aid programs and its activities in the areas of economic growth, agriculture, trade, health, democracy, and conflict prevention, address the conditions that terrorists exploit for recruitment.

The Middle East Partnership Initiative (MEPI).

In 2008, MEPI provided support to reformers and civic activists to expand political participation, build education systems responsive to 21st Century challenges, assist developing economies, and empower women. Working in 16 countries and in the Palestinian territories, MEPI invested in programs ranging from broadcast media to women's entrepreneurship.

Political

MEPI supported programs to develop inclusive and representative political parties and more transparent electoral systems.

Through training and technical assistance, MEPI supported independent media outlets and efforts to advance freedom of the press.

Through numerous small grants to indigenous organizations, MEPI helped to expand civic activism and sustain efforts of activists to obtain basic rights and fundamental freedoms, including freedom of expression and association.

By supporting the G8's BMENA Initiative and the participation of civil society from across the region in the Forum for the Future and associated BMENA activities, MEPI provided rare opportunities to reformers and activists to advance their objectives directly with government officials in multilateral settings.

Economic

Provided technical and other assistance in support of free trade agreements with Bahrain, Jordan, Morocco, and Oman; and WTO accession for Yemen, Algeria, and Lebanon.

Expanded trade capacity of Arab countries with training and technical assistance; and assisted a number of Gulf and North African countries with revisions to their labor, intellectual property, and customs codes; and to their agricultural import/export standards.

Expanded efforts to strengthen indigenous labor and business organizations.

Created mechanisms to extend credit and other financial services to small- and medium-sized businesses through peer consultation and training for regional banks and financial organizations.

Supported the adoption of new corporate governance codes in Bahrain, Tunisia, and Yemen and facilitated increased awareness of corporate governance best practices in those countries.

Expanded commercial and legal reform efforts in the Gulf by working to update legal curricula at law schools in Qatar and Oman; revised commercial codes to meet international standards in Bahrain, Qatar, and Oman; and provided continuing education programs for the judiciary.

Education

Promoted critical thinking and independent reading, and prompted education reform efforts with an initiative to provide over 8.2 million high-quality Arabic-language American children's books to more than 6,770 primary schools in more than 40,620 classrooms in four Middle Eastern countries.

Provided English language study to more than 6,000 underserved youth from 13 countries in the Middle East through the English Access

Micro-scholarship Program, bringing the total number of students reached with MEPI support to more than 13,000.

Provided entrepreneurship training for more than 400 participants, almost half of them women, from 16 Middle Eastern and North African countries, with over 50 alumni going on to start or expand businesses.

Partnered with NGOs, businesses, universities, and private organizations to create five highly scalable and replicable youth education and employment programs that offer market-specific skills training, such as a Mini MBA accounting, textile management, and a workplace success training program.

Women

Strengthened the technology, business, and advocacy skills of women throughout the region.

Established the first U.S.-Middle East Partnership for Breast Cancer Awareness and Research, which enabled women across the region to join together in private-public partnerships, civic engagement, and networking.

Created business network hubs in nine countries, focusing on training, professional development, and information sharing on laws, business opportunities, skills, and the global economy.

Supported legal reform and family law initiatives in the region in order to improve gender equality and economic rights for women.

INTERNATIONAL CONVENTIONS AND PROTOCOLS

1. **Convention on Offences and Certain Other Acts Committed On Board Aircraft** Signed in Tokyo on September 14, 1963. Convention entered into force on December 4, 1969. Status: 184 Parties

2. **Convention for the Suppression of Unlawful Seizure of Aircraft** Signed in The Hague on December 16, 1970. Convention entered into force on October 14, 1971. Status: 184 Parties

3. **Convention for the Suppression of Unlawful Acts Against the Safety of Civil Aviation** Signed in Montreal on September 23, 1971. Convention entered into force on January 26, 1973. Status: 187 Parties

4. **Convention on the Prevention and Punishment of Crimes Against Internationally Protected Persons, including Diplomatic Agents** Adopted in New York on December 14, 1973. Convention entered into force on February 20, 1977. Status: 171 Parties

5. **International Convention Against the Taking of Hostages** Adopted in New York on December 17, 1979. Convention entered into force on June 3, 1983. Status: 166 Parties
6. **Convention on the Physical Protection of Nuclear Material** Signed in Vienna on October 26, 1979. Convention entered into force on February 8, 1987. Status: 139 Parties
7. **Protocol for the Suppression of Unlawful Acts of Violence at Airports Serving International Civil Aviation, Supplementary to the Convention for the Suppression of Unlawful Acts against the Safety of Civil Aviation** Signed in Montreal on February 24, 1988. Protocol entered into force on August 6, 1989. Status: 168 Parties
8. **Convention for the Suppression of Unlawful Acts Against the Safety of Maritime Navigation** Done in Rome on March 10, 1988. Convention entered into force on March 1, 1992. Status: 152 Parties
9. **Protocol for the Suppression of Unlawful Acts Against the Safety of Fixed Platforms Located on the Continental Shelf** Done in Rome on March 10, 1988. Protocol entered into force on March 1, 1992. Status: 140 Parties
10. **Convention on the Marking of Plastic Explosives for the Purpose of Detection** Done in Montreal on March 1, 1991. Convention entered into force on June 21, 1998. Status: 140 Parties
11. **International Convention for the Suppression of Terrorist Bombings** Adopted in New York on December 15, 1997. Convention entered into force on May 23, 2001. Status: 161 Parties
12. **International Convention for the Suppression of the Financing of Terrorism** Adopted in New York on December 9, 1999. Convention entered into force on April 10, 2002. Status: 167 Parties
13. **International Convention for the Suppression of Acts of Nuclear Terrorism.** Adopted in New York on April 13, 2005. Convention entered into force on July 7, 2007.

    Status: 52 Parties
14. **2005 Amendment to the Convention on the Physical Protection of Nuclear Material.** Not yet entered into force. Status: 24 States have deposited instruments of ratification, acceptance or approval with the depositary.

15. **Protocol of 2005 to the Convention for the Suppression of Unlawful Acts Against the Safety of Maritime Navigation.**

    Not yet entered into force. Status: Eight States have deposited instruments of ratification, acceptance or approval with the depositary.

16. **Protocol of 2005 to the Protocol for the Suppression of Unlawful Acts Against the Safety of Fixed Platforms Located on the Continental Shelf.**

    Not yet entered into force. Status: Six States have deposited instruments of ratification, acceptance or approval with the depositary.

Name of the country	1	2	3	4	5	6	7	8
Afghanistan	15/04/1977	29/08/1979	26/09/1984	24/09/2003	24/09/2003	12/09/2003		23/09/2003
Albania	01/12/1997	21/10/1997	21/10/1997	22/01/2002	22/01/2002	05/03/2002	29/04/2002	19/06/2002
Algeria	12/10/1995	06/10/1995	06/10/1995	07/11/2000	18/12/1996	30/04/2003	06/10/1995	11/02/1998
Andorra	17/05/2006	23/09/2004	22/05/2006	23/09/2004	23/09/2004	27/06/2006	22/05/2006	17/07/2006
Angola	24/02/1998	12/03/1998	12/03/1998				16/01/2008	
Antigua and Barbuda	19/07/19852	2/07/1985	22/07/1985	19/07/1993	06/08/1986	04/08/1993		
Argentina	23/07/1971	11/09/1972	26/11/1973	18/03/1982	18/09/1991	06/04/1989	12/02/1992	17/08/1993
Argentina	23/07/1971	11/09/1972	26/11/1973	18/03/1982	18/09/1991	06/04/1989	12/02/1992	17/08/1993
Australia	22/06/1970	09/11/1972	12/07/1973	20/06/1977	21/05/1990	22/09/1987	23/10/1990	19/02/1993
Austria	07/02/1974	11/02/1974	11/02/1974	03/08/1977	22/08/1986	22/12/1988	28/12/1989	28/12/1989
Azerbaijan	05/02/2004	03/03/2000	15/03/2000	02/04/2001	29/02/2000	19/01/2004	23/03/2000	26/01/2004
Bahamas	12/06/1975	13/08/1976	27/12/1984	22/07/1986	04/06/1981	21/05/2008	02/05/2008	25/10/2005
Bahrain	09/02/1984	20/02/1984	20/02/1984	16/09/2005	16/09/2005		12/02/1996	21/10/2005
Bangladesh	25/07/1978	28/06/1978	28/06/1978	20/05/2005	20/05/2005	11/05/2005	27/06/2005	09/06/2005
Barbados	04/04/1972	02/04/1973	06/08/1976	26/10/1979	09/03/1981		12/09/2002	06/05/1994
Belarus	03/02/1988	30/12/1971	31/01/1973	05/02/1976	01/07/1987	09/09/1993	01/05/1989	04/12/2002
Belgium	06/08/1970	24/08/1973	13/08/1976	19/05/2004	16/04/1999	06/09/1991	20/04/1999	11/04/2005
Belize	19/05/1998	10/06/1998	10/06/1998	14/11/2001	14/11/2001		10/06/1998	
Benin	30/03/2004	13/03/1972	19/04/2004	31/07/2003	31/07/2003		19/04/2004	31/08/2006
Bhutan	25/01/1989	28/12/1988	28/12/1988	16/01/1989	31/08/1981		26/08/2005	
Bolivia	05/07/1979	18/07/1979	18/07/1979	22/01/2002	07/01/2002	24/01/2002	01/02/2002	13/02/2002
Bosnia and Herzegovina	07/03/1995	15/08/1994	15/08/1994	01/09/1993	01/09/1993	30/06/1998	15/08/1994	28/07/2003
Botswana	16/01/1979	28/12/1978	28/12/1978	25/10/2000	08/09/2000	19/09/2000	30/10/2000	14/09/2000
Brazil	14/01/1970	14/01/1972	24/07/1972	07/06/1999	08/03/2000	17/10/1985	09/05/1997	25/10/2005
Brunei Darussalam	23/05/1986	16/04/1986	16/04/1986	13/11/1997	18/10/1988		20/12/2000	08/12/2003
Bulgaria	28/09/1989	19/05/1971	28/03/1973	18/07/1974	10/03/1988	10/04/1984	26/03/1991	08/07/1999
Burkina Faso	06/06/1969	19/10/1987	19/10/1987	01/10/2003	01/10/2003	13/01/2004	08/12/1998	15/01/2004
Burundi	14/07/1971		11/02/1999	17/12/1980				
Cambodia	22/10/1996	08/11/1996	08/11/1996	27/07/2006	27/07/2006	04/08/2006	08/11/1996	18/08/2006
Cameroon	24/03/1988	14/04/1988	11/07/1973	08/06/1992	09/03/1988	29/06/2004	13/03/2003	
Canada	07/11/1969	20/06/1972	19/06/1972	04/08/1976	04/12/1985	21/03/1986	02/08/1993	18/06/1993

Name of the country	9	10	11	12	13	14	15	16
Afghanistan	23/09/2003	01/10/2003	24/09/2003	24/09/2003				
Albania	19/06/2002	20/10/2004	22/01/2002	10/04/2002				
Algeria	30/06/2006	4/11/1996	08/11/2001	08/11/2001		25/04/2007		
Andorra	17/07/2006	17/05/2006	23/09/2004	22/10/2008				
Angola								
Antigua and Barbuda				11/03/2002				
Argentina	26/11/2003	08/03/1999	25/09/2003	22/08/2005				
Argentina	08/06/2005	22/07/2005	16/03/2004	16/03/2004				
Australia	19/02/1993	26/06/2007	09/08/2002	26/09/2002		17/07/2008		
Austria	28/12/1989	31/05/1999	06/09/2000	15/04/2002	14/09/2006	18/09/2006		
Azerbaijan	26/01/2004	04/07/2000	02/04/2001	26/10/2001	28/01/2009			
Bahamas	25/10/2005	21/05/2008	05/05/2008	01/11/2005				
Bahrain	21/10/2005	30/01/1996	21/09/2004	21/09/2004				
Bangladesh	09/06/2005	16/08/2005	20/05/2005	26/08/2005	07/06/2007			
Barbados	06/05/1994	12/09/2002	18/09/2002	18/09/2002				
Belarus	04/12/2002	06/02/2002	01/10/2001	06/10/2004	13/03/2007			
Belgium	11/04/2005	16/04/2007	20/05/2005	17/05/2004				
Belize			14/11/2001	01/12/2003				
Benin	31/08/2006	30/03/2004	31/07/2003	30/08/2004				
Bhutan		26/08/2005	22/03/2004					
Bolivia								
Bosnia and Herzegovina	13/02/2002	01/02/2002	22/01/2002	07/01/2002				
Botswana	28/07/2003	03/05/2004	11/08/2003	10/06/2003				
Brazil	14/09/2000	19/09/2000	08/09/2000	08/09/2000				
Brunei Darussalam	25/10/2005	04/10/2001	23/08/2002	16/09/2005				
Bulgaria	08/12/2003		14/03/2002	04/12/2002				
Burkina Faso	08/07/1999	08/09/1999	12/02/2002	15/04/2002		17/03/2006		
Burundi					24/09/2008			
Cambodia	18/08/2006		31/07/2006	12/12/2005				
Cameroon		03/06/1998	21/03/2005	06/02/2006				
Canada	18/06/1993	29/11/1996	03/04/2002	19/02/2002				

Name of the country	1	2	3	4	5	6	7	8
Cape Verde	04/10/1989	20/10/1977	20/10/1977	10/09/2002	10/09/2002	23/02/2007	12/09/2002	03/01/2003
Central African Republic	11/06/1991	01/07/1991	01/07/1991	19/02/2008	09/07/2007	20/02/2008	01/07/1991	
Chad	30/06/1970	12/07/1972	12/07/1972	01/11/2006				
Chile	24/01/1974	02/02/1972	28/02/1974	21/01/1977	12/11/1981	27/04/1994	15/08/1989	22/04/1994
China	14/11/1978	10/09/1980	10/09/1980	05/08/1987	26/01/1993	10/01/1989	05/03/1999	20/08/1991
Colombia	06/07/1973	03/07/1973	04/12/1974	16/01/1996	14/04/2005	28/03/2003	14/01/2004	
Comoros	23/05/1991	01/08/1991	01/08/1991	25/09/2003	25/09/2003	18/05/2007	10/03/2008	06/03/2008
Congo	13/11/1978	24/11/1989	19/03/1987					
Congo (Democratic Republic of the)	20/07/1977	06/07/1977	06/07/1977	25/07/1977	21/09/2004			
Cook Islands	12/04/2005	14/04/2005	14/04/2005				14/04/2005	12/03/2007
Costa Rica	24/10/1972	09/07/1971	21/09/1973	02/11/1977	24/01/2003	02/05/2003	22/04/2003	25/03/2003
Côte d'Ivoire	03/06/1970	09/01/1973	09/01/1973	13/03/2002	22/08/1989			
Croatia	05/10/1993	08/06/1993	08/06/1993	12/10/1992	23/09/2003	29/09/1992	08/06/1993	18/08/2005
Cuba	12/02/2001	27/11/2001	31/10/2001	10/06/1998	15/11/2001	26/09/1997	31/10/2001	20/11/2001
Cyprus	31/05/1972	05/07/1972	27/07/1973	24/12/1975	13/09/1991	23/07/1998	23/04/2002	02/02/2000
Czech Republic	25/03/1993	14/11/1994	14/11/1994	22/02/1993	22/02/1993	24/03/1993	25/03/1993	10/12/2004
Denmark	17/01/1967	17/10/1972	17/01/1973	01/07/1975	11/08/1987	06/09/1991	23/11/1989	23/08/1995
Djibouti	10/06/1992	24/11/1992	24/11/1992	01/06/2004	01/06/2004	22/06/2004	11/06/2004	09/06/2004
Dominica		26/07/2005	26/07/2005	24/09/2004	09/09/1986	08/11/2004	26/07/2005	31/08/2001
Dominican Republic	03/12/1970	22/06/1978	28/11/1973	08/07/1977	03/10/2007	03/07/2008		
Ecuador	03/12/1969	14/06/1971	12/01/1977	12/03/1975	02/05/1988	17/01/1996	04/03/2004	10/03/2003
Egypt	12/02/1975	28/02/1975	20/05/1975	25/06/1986	02/10/1981		25/07/2000	08/01/1993
El Salvador	13/02/1980	16/01/1973	25/09/1979	08/08/1980	12/02/1981	15/12/2006	08/04/1998	07/12/2000
Equatorial Guinea	27/02/1991	02/01/1991	02/01/1991	07/02/2003	07/02/2003	24/11/2003	14/01/2004	14/01/2004
Eritrea								
Estonia	31/12/1993	22/12/1993	22/12/1993	21/10/1991	08/03/2002	09/05/1994	22/12/1993	15/02/2002
Ethiopia	27/03/1979	26/03/1979	26/03/1979	16/04/2003	16/04/2003	15/12/1999		
Fiji	31/01/1972	27/07/1972	05/03/1973	15/05/2008	15/05/2008	23/05/2008	21/09/1992	21/05/2008
Finland	02/04/1971	15/12/1971	13/07/1973	31/10/1978	14/04/1983	22/09/1989	03/04/1998	12/11/1998
France	11/09/1970	18/09/1972	30/06/1976	26/08/2003	09/06/2000	06/09/1991	06/09/1989	02/12/1991

Name of the country	9	10	11	12	13	14	15	16
Cape Verde	03/01/2003	04/11/2002	10/05/2002	10/05/2002				
Central African Republic			19/02/2008	19/02/2008	19/02/2008			
Chad								
Chile	22/04/1994	02/08/2000	10/11/2001	10/11/2001		12/03/2009		
China	20/08/1991		13/11/2001	19/04/2006				
Colombia			14/09/2004	14/09/2004				
Comoros	06/03/2008		25/09/2003	25/09/2003	12/03/2007			
Congo				20/04/2007				
Congo (Democratic Republic of the)			27/06/2008	28/10/2005				
Cook Islands				04/03/2004			12/03/2007	
Costa Rica	25/03/2003	12/07/2005	20/09/2001	24/01/2003				
Côte d'Ivoire			13/03/2002	13/03/2002				
Croatia	18/08/2005	24/02/2005	02/06/2005	01/12/2003	30/05/2007	11/09/2006		
Cuba	20/11/2001	30/11/2001	15/11/2001	15/11/2001				
Cyprus	02/02/2000	20/09/2002	24/01/2001	30/11/2001	28/01/2008			
Czech Republic	10/12/2004	25/03/1993	06/09/2000	27/12/2005	25/07/2006			
Denmark	23/08/1995	05/10/1998	31/08/2001	27/08/2002	20/03/2007			
Djibouti	09/06/2004	11/06/2004	01/06/2004	13/03/2006				
Dominica	12/10/2004		24/09/2004	24/09/2004				
Dominican Republic			21/10/2008	04/09/2008	11/06/2008			
Ecuador	10/03/2003	15/12/1995		09/12/2003				
Egypt	08/01/1993	19/07/1993	09/08/2005	01/03/2005				
El Salvador	07/12/2000	18/02/2000	15/05/2003	15/05/2003	27/11/2006			
Equatorial Guinea	14/01/2004		07/02/2003	07/02/2003				
Eritrea		01/12/1994						
Estonia	28/01/2004	05/03/1996	10/04/2002		22/05/2002	24/02/2009	16/05/2008	16/05/2008
Ethiopia			16/04/2003					
Fiji	21/05/2008	11/07/2008	15/05/2008	15/05/2008	15/05/2008	22/06/2008	21/05/2008	21/05/2008
Finland	28/04/2000	05/12/2001	28/05/2002	28/06/2002	13/01/2009			
France	02/12/1991	21/05/1997	19/08/1999	07/01/2002				

Name of the country	1	2	3	4	5	6	7	8
Gabon	14/01/1970	14/07/1971	29/06/1976	14/10/1981	19/04/2005	19/02/2008	13/08/2003	
Gambia	04/01/1979	28/11/1978	28/11/1978				16/05/2000	01/11/1991
Georgia	16/06/1994	20/04/1994	20/04/1994	18/02/2004	18/02/2004	07/09/2006	15/02/1999	11/08/2006
Germany	16/12/1969	11/10/1974	03/02/1978	25/01/1977	15/12/1980	06/09/1991	25/04/1994	06/11/1990
Ghana	02/01/1974	12/12/1973	12/12/1973	25/04/1975	10/11/1987	16/10/2002	15/07/1997	01/11/2002
Greece	31/05/1971	20/09/1973	15/01/1974	03/07/1984	18/06/1987	06/09/1991	25/04/1991	11/06/1993
Grenada	28/08/1978	10/08/1978	10/08/1978	13/12/2001	10/12/1990	09/01/2002	15/01/2002	09/01/2002
Guatemala	17/11/1970	16/05/1979	19/10/1978	18/01/1983	11/03/1983	23/04/1985	11/10/1994	
Guinea	18/01/1994	02/05/1984	02/05/1984	22/12/2004	22/12/2004	29/11/2005	01/10/1998	01/02/2005
Guinea-Bissau	17/10/2008	20/08/1976	20/08/1976	06/08/2008	06/08/2008	08/10/2008	17/10/2008	14/10/2008
Guyana	20/12/1972	21/12/1972	21/12/1972	12/09/2007	12/09/2007	13/09/2007	19/06/2002	02/01/2003
Haiti	26/04/1984	09/05/1984	09/05/1984	25/08/1980	17/05/1989			
Holy See								
Honduras	08/04/1987	13/04/1987	13/04/1987	29/01/2003	01/06/1981	28/01/2004	20/01/2004	17/05/2005
Hungary	03/12/1970	13/08/1971	27/12/1972	26/03/1975	02/09/1987	04/05/1984	07/09/1988	09/11/1989
Iceland	16/03/1970	29/06/1973	29/06/1973	02/08/1977	06/07/1981	18/06/2002	09/05/1990	28/05/2002
India	22/07/1975	12/11/1982	12/11/1982	11/04/1978	07/09/1994	12/03/2002	22/03/1995	15/10/1999
Indonesia	07/09/1976	27/08/1976	27/08/1976			05/11/1986		
Iran (Islamic Republic of)	28/06/1976	25/01/1972	10/07/1973	12/07/1978	20/11/2006		14/02/2002	
Iraq	15/05/1974	03/12/1971	10/09/1974			28/02/1978	31/01/1990	
Ireland	14/11/1975	24/11/1975	12/10/1976	30/06/2005	30/06/2005	06/09/1991	26/07/1991	10/09/2004
Israel	19/09/1969	16/08/1971	30/06/1972	31/07/1980		22/01/2002	02/04/1993	06/01/2009
Italy	18/10/1968	19/02/1974	19/02/1974	30/08/1985	20/03/1986	06/09/1991	13/03/1990	26/01/1990
Jamaica	16/09/1983	15/09/1983	15/09/1983	21/09/1978	09/08/2005	16/08/2005	18/08/2005	17/08/2005
Japan	26/05/1970	19/04/1971	12/06/1974	08/06/1987	08/06/1987	28/10/1988	24/04/1998	24/04/1998
Jordan	03/05/1973	18/11/1971	13/02/1973	18/12/1984	19/02/1986		18/09/1992	02/07/2004
Kazakhstan	18/05/1995	04/04/1995	04/04/1995	21/02/1996	21/02/1996	02/09/2005	18/05/1995	24/11/2003
Kenya	22/06/1970	11/01/1977	11/01/1977	16/11/2001	08/12/1981	11/02/2002	05/10/1995	21/01/2002
Kiribati				15/09/2005	15/09/2005			17/11/2005
Korea (Democratic People's Republic of)	09/05/1983	28/04/1983	13/08/1980	01/12/1982	12/11/2001		19/07/1995	

Name of the country	9	10	11	12	13	14	15	16
Gabon			10/03/2005	10/03/2005	01/10/2007	20/03/2008		
Gambia		20/06/2000						
Georgia	11/08/2006	25/04/2000	18/02/2004	27/09/2002				
Germany	06/11/1990	17/12/1998	23/04/2003	17/06/2004	08/02/2008			
Ghana	01/11/2002	22/04/1998	06/09/2002	06/09/2002				
Greece	11/06/1993	30/10/1995	27/05/2003	16/04/2004				
Grenada	09/01/2002	15/01/2002	13/12/2001	13/12/2001				
Guatemala		26/11/1997	12/02/2002	12/02/2002				
Guinea	01/02/2005	23/01/2004	07/09/2000	14/07/2003				
Guinea-Bissau	14/10/2008		06/08/2008	19/09/2008	06/08/2008			
Guyana	02/01/2003	13/12/2007	12/09/2007	12/09/2007				
Haiti								
Holy See								
Honduras	17/05/2005	18/02/2004	25/03/2003	25/03/2003				
Hungary	09/11/1989	11/01/1994	13/11/2001	14/10/2002	12/04/2007	04/12/2008		
Iceland	28/05/2002	24/05/2002	15/04/2002	15/04/2002				
India	15/10/1999	16/11/1999	22/09/1999	22/04/2003	01/12/2006	19/09/2007		
Indonesia				29/06/2006	29/06/2006			
Iran (Islamic Republic of)								
Iraq								
Ireland	10/09/2004	15/07/2003	30/06/2005	30/06/2005				
Israel	06/01/2009		10/02/2003	10/02/2003				
Italy	26/01/1990	26/09/2002	16/04/2003	27/03/2003				
Jamaica	19/08/2005	18/08/2005	09/08/2005	16/09/2005				
Japan	24/04/1998	26/09/1997	16/11/2001	11/06/2002	03/08/2007			
Jordan	02/07/2004	23/05/1996	28/08/2003					
Kazakhstan	24/11/2003	18/05/1995	06/11/2002	24/02/2003	31/07/2008			
Kenya	21/01/2002	22/10/2002	16/11/2001	27/06/2003	13/04/2006	01/08/2007		
Kiribati	17/11/2005	15/09/2005	15/09/2005	26/09/2008				
Korea (Democratic People's Republic of)								

Name of the country	1	2	3	4	5	6	7	8
Korea (Republic of)	19/02/1971	18/01/1973	02/08/1973	25/05/1983	04/05/1983	07/04/1982	27/06/1990	14/05/2003
Kuwait	27/11/1979	25/05/1979	23/11/1979	01/03/1989	06/02/1989	23/04/2004	08/03/1989	30/06/2003
Kyrgyzstan	28/02/2000	25/02/2000	25/02/2000	02/10/2003	02/10/2003		28/02/2000	
Lao People's Democratic Republic	23/10/1972	06/04/1989	06/04/1989	22/08/2002	22/08/2002		07/10/2002	
Latvia	10/06/1997	23/10/1998	13/04/1997	14/04/1992	14/11/2002	06/11/2002	13/04/1997	04/12/2002
Lebanon	11/06/1974	10/08/1973	23/12/1977	03/06/1997	04/12/1997	16/12/1997	27/05/1996	16/12/1994
Lesotho	28/04/1972	27/07/1978	27/07/1978		05/11/1980			
Liberia	10/03/2003	01/02/1982	01/02/1982	30/09/1975	05/03/2003		10/03/2003	05/10/1995
Libyan Arab Jamahiriya	21/06/1972	04/10/1978	19/02/1974	25/09/2000	25/09/2000	18/10/2000	26/07/1996	08/08/2002
Liechtenstein	26/02/2001	23/02/2001	23/02/2001	28/11/1994	28/11/1994	25/11/1986	26/02/2001	08/11/2002
Lithuania	21/11/1996	04/12/1996	04/12/1996	23/10/2002	02/02/2001	07/12/1993	04/12/1996	30/01/2003
Luxembourg	21/09/1972	22/11/1978	18/05/1982	10/05/2006	29/04/1991	06/09/1991	14/11/2003	
Macedonia (The former Yugoslav Republic of)	30/08/1994	07/01/1998	04/01/1995	12/03/1998	12/03/1998	20/09/1996	04/01/1995	07/08/2007
Madagascar	02/12/1969	18/11/1986	18/11/1986	24/09/2003	24/09/2003	28/10/2003	30/03/1998	15/09/2006
Malawi	28/12/1972	21/12/1972	21/12/1972	14/03/1977	17/03/1986			
Malaysia	05/03/1985	04/05/1985	04/05/1985	24/09/2003	29/05/2007	08/09/2006		
Maldives	28/09/1987	01/09/1987	01/09/1987	21/08/1990	22/03/1999			
Mali	31/05/1971	29/09/1971	24/08/1972	12/04/2002	08/02/1990	07/05/2002	31/10/1990	29/04/2002
Malta	28/06/1991	14/06/1991	14/06/1991	11/11/2001	11/11/2001	16/10/2003	14/06/1991	20/11/2001
Marshall Islands	15/05/1989	31/05/1989	31/05/1989	27/01/2003	27/01/2003	07/02/2003	30/05/1989	29/11/1994
Mauritania	30/06/1977	01/11/1978	01/11/1978	09/02/1998	13/03/1998	29/01/2008	08/07/2003	17/01/2008
Mauritius	05/04/1983	25/04/1983	25/04/1983	24/09/2003	17/10/1980		17/08/1989	03/08/2004
Mexico	18/03/1969	19/07/1972	12/09/1974	22/04/1980	28/04/1987	04/04/1988	11/10/1990	13/05/1994
Micronesia (Federated States of)			19/03/2003	06/07/2004	06/07/2004		19/03/2003	10/02/2003
Moldova (Republic of)	20/06/1997	21/05/1997	21/05/1997	08/09/1997	10/10/2002	07/05/1998	20/06/1997	12/10/2005
Monaco	02/06/1983	03/06/1983	03/06/1983	27/11/2001	16/10/2001	09/08/1996	22/12/1993	25/01/2002
Mongolia	24/07/1990	08/10/1971	14/09/1972	08/08/1975	09/06/1992	28/05/1986	22/09/1999	22/11/2005
Montenegro	20/12/2007	20/12/2006	20/12/2006	23/10/2006	23/10/2006	21/03/2007	20/12/2006	03/06/2006
Morocco	21/10/1975	24/10/1975	24/10/1975	09/01/2002	09/05/2007	23/08/2002	15/02/2002	08/01/2002

Name of the country	9	10	11	12	13	14	15	16
Korea (Republic of)	10/06/2003	02/01/2002	17/02/2004	17/02/2004				
Kuwait	30/06/2003	18/03/1996	19/04/2004					
Kyrgyzstan		14/07/2000	01/05/2001	02/10/2003	02/10/2007			
Lao People's Democratic Republic			22/08/2002	29/09/2008				
Latvia	04/12/2002	17/08/1999	25/11/2002	14/11/2002	25/07/2006			
Lebanon	16/12/1994	26/11/1997	13/11/2006					
Lesotho			12/11/2001	12/11/2001				
Liberia	05/10/1995		05/03/2003	05/03/2003				
Libyan Arab Jamahiriya	08/08/2002	10/10/2002	22/09/2000	09/07/2002	22/12/2008	19/07/2006		
Liechtenstein	08/11/2002	04/12/2002	26/11/2002	09/07/2003				
Lithuania	30/01/2003	21/11/1996	17/03/2004	20/02/2003	19/07/2007			
Luxembourg		05/04/2007	06/02/2004	05/11/2003	02/10/2008			
Macedonia (The former Yugoslav Republic of)	07/08/2007	21/09/1998	30/08/2004	30/08/2004	19/03/2007			
Madagascar	15/09/2006	23/12/2003	24/09/2003	24/09/2003				
Malawi			11/08/2003	11/08/2003				
Malaysia		27/11/2007	24/09/2003	29/06/2007				
Maldives		22/03/1999	07/09/2000	20/04/2004				
Mali	29/04/2002	28/09/2000	28/03/2002	28/03/2002				
Malta	20/11/2001	15/11/1994	11/11/2001	11/11/2001				
Marshall Islands	16/10/1995	06/02/2003	27/01/2003	27/01/2003			09/05/2008	09/05/2008
Mauritania	17/01/2008		30/04/2003	30/04/2003	28/04/2008	28/02/2008		
Mauritius	03/08/2004		24/01/2003	14/12/2004				
Mexico	13/05/1994	09/04/1992	20/01/2003	20/01/2003	27/06/2006			
Micronesia (Federated States of)			23/09/2002	23/09/2002				
Moldova (Republic of)	12/10/2005	01/12/1997	10/10/2002	10/10/2002	18/04/2008	22/12/2008		
Monaco	25/01/2002	14/05/1998	06/09/2001	10/11/2001				
Mongolia	22/11/2005	22/09/1999	07/09/2000	25/02/2004	06/10/2006			
Montenegro	03/06/2006		23/10/2006	23/10/2006				
Morocco	08/01/2002	26/05/1999	09/05/2007	19/09/2002				

Name of the country	1	2	3	4	5	6	7	8
Mozambique	06/01/2003	16/01/2003	16/01/2003	14/01/2003	14/01/2003	03/03/2003	16/01/2003	08/01/2003
Myanmar	23/05/1996	22/05/1996	22/05/1996	04/06/2004	04/06/2004		22/05/1996	19/09/2003
Namibia	19/12/2005	04/11/2005	04/11/2005			02/10/2002	04/11/2005	20/07/2004
Nauru	17/05/1984	17/05/1984	17/05/1984	02/08/2005	02/08/2005	12/08/2005	19/08/2005	11/08/2005
Nepal	15/01/1979	11/01/1979	11/01/1979	09/03/1990	09/03/1990			
Netherlands	14/11/1969	27/08/1973	27/08/1973	06/12/1988	06/12/1988	06/09/1991	11/07/1995	05/03/1992
New Zealand	12/02/1974	12/02/1974	12/02/1974	12/11/1985	12/11/1985	19/12/2003	02/08/1999	10/06/1999
Nicaragua	24/08/1973	06/11/1973	06/11/1973	10/03/1975	24/09/2003	10/12/2004	25/04/2002	04/07/2007
Niger	27/06/1969	15/10/1971	01/09/1972	17/06/1985	26/10/2004	19/08/2004	23/12/2008	30/08/2006
Nigeria	07/04/1970	03/07/1973	03/07/1973			04/04/2007	25/03/2003	24/02/2004
Niue								
Norway	17/01/1967	23/08/1971	01/08/1973	28/04/1980	02/07/1981	15/08/1985	29/05/1990	18/04/1991
Oman	09/02/1977	02/02/1977	02/02/1977	22/03/1988	22/07/1988	11/06/2003	27/11/1992	24/09/1990
Pakistan	11/09/1973	28/11/1973	24/01/1974	29/03/1976	08/09/2000	12/09/2000	26/09/2000	20/09/2000
Palau	12/10/1995	03/08/1995	03/08/1995	14/11/2001	14/11/2001	24/04/2007	12/10/1995	04/12/2001
Panama	16/11/1970	10/03/1972	24/04/1972	17/06/1980	19/08/1982	01/04/1999	10/04/1996	03/07/2002
Papua New Guinea	15/12/1975	15/12/1975	15/12/1975	30/09/2003	30/09/2003		11/07/2002	
Paraguay	09/08/1971	04/02/1972	05/03/1974	24/11/1975	22/09/2004	06/02/1985	23/07/2002	12/11/2004
Peru	12/05/1978	28/04/1978	28/04/1978	25/04/1978	06/07/2001	11/01/1995	07/06/1989	19/07/2001
Philippines	26/11/1965	26/03/1973	26/03/1973	26/11/1976	14/10/1980	22/09/1981	17/12/2003	06/01/2004
Poland	19/03/1971	21/03/1972	28/01/1975	14/12/1982	25/05/2000	05/10/1983	12/08/2004	25/06/1991
Portugal	25/11/1964	27/11/1972	15/01/1973	11/09/1995	06/07/1984	06/09/1991	18/12/2001	05/01/1996
Qatar	06/08/1981	26/08/1981	26/08/1981	03/03/1997		09/03/2004	17/06/2003	18/09/2003
Romania	15/02/1974	10/07/1972	15/08/1975	15/08/1978	17/05/1990	23/11/1993	03/09/1998	02/06/1993
Russian Federation	03/02/1988	24/09/1971	19/02/1973	15/01/1976	11/06/1987	25/05/1983	31/03/1989	04/05/2001
Rwanda	17/05/1971	03/11/1987	03/11/1987	29/11/1977	13/05/2002	28/06/2002	16/05/2002	
Saint Kitts and Nevis		03/09/2008	10/09/2008	28/07/2008	17/01/1991	29/08/2008	03/09/2008	17/01/2002
Saint Lucia	31/10/1983	08/11/1983	08/11/1983				11/06/1990	20/05/2004
Saint Vincent and the	18/11/1991	29/11/1991	29/11/1991	12/09/2000	12/09/2000		29/11/1991	09/10/2001
Grenadines								
Samoa	09/07/1998	09/07/1998	09/07/1998				09/07/1998	18/05/2004

Name of the country	9	10	11	12	13	14	15	16
Mozambique	08/01/2003	15/03/2006	14/01/2003	14/01/2003				
Myanmar	19/09/2003	01/09/2004	12/11/2001	16/08/2006				
Namibia	07/09/2005							
Nauru	11/08/2005	03/04/2006	02/08/2005	24/05/2005				
Nepal								
Netherlands	05/03/1992	04/05/1998	07/02/2002	07/02/2002				
New Zealand	10/06/1999	19/12/2003	04/11/2002	04/11/2002				
Nicaragua	04/07/2007	10/01/2006	17/01/2003	14/11/2002	25/02/2009			
Niger	30/08/2006	06/03/2009	26/10/2004	30/09/2004	02/07/2008			
Nigeria		10/05/2002		16/06/2003		04/05/2007		
Niue								
Norway	18/04/1991	09/07/1992	20/09/1999	15/07/2002				
Oman	24/09/1990	13/12/2001						
Pakistan	20/09/2000		13/08/2002					
Palau	04/12/2001	30/11/2001	14/11/2001	14/11/2001				
Panama	03/07/2002	12/04/1996	05/03/1999	03/07/2002	21/06/2007			
Papua New Guinea			30/09/2003	30/09/2003				
Paraguay	12/11/2004	15/10/2004	22/09/2004	30/11/2004				
Peru	19/07/2001	07/02/1996	10/11/2001	10/11/2001				
Philippines	06/01/2004	17/12/2003	07/01/2004	07/01/2004				
Poland	25/06/1991	26/09/2006	03/02/2004	26/09/2003		01/06/2007		
Portugal	05/01/1996	09/10/2002	10/11/2001	18/10/2002				
Qatar	18/09/2003	09/11/1998	27/06/2008	27/06/2008				
Romania	02/06/1993	21/09/1998	29/07/2004	09/01/2003	24/01/2007	06/02/2007		
Russian Federation	04/05/2001	19/09/2007	08/05/2001	27/11/2002	20/01/2007	19/09/2008		
Rwanda			13/05/2002	13/05/2002				
Saint Kitts and Nevis		09/05/2002	16/11/2001	16/11/2001			29/03/2007	
Saint Lucia	20/05/2004							
Saint Vincent and the	09/10/2001		15/09/2005	28/03/2002				
Grenadines								
Samoa		09/07/1998		27/09/2002				

Name of the country	1	2	3	4	5	6	7	8
San Marino								
Sao Tome and Principe	04/05/2006	08/05/2006	08/05/2006	12/04/2006	23/08/2006		08/05/2006	05/05/2006
Saudi Arabia	21/11/1969	14/06/1974	14/06/1974	01/03/2004	08/01/1991	07/01/2009	21/02/1989	02/02/2006
Senegal	09/03/1972	03/02/1978	03/02/1978	07/04/2006	10/03/1987	03/11/2003	24/03/2003	09/08/2004
Serbia	06/09/2001	23/07/2001	23/07/2001	12/03/2001	12/03/2001	27/04/2002	06/09/2001	10/05/2004
Seychelles	04/01/1979	29/12/1978	29/12/1978	29/05/1980	12/11/2003	13/08/2003	21/05/2004	24/01/1989
Sierra Leone	09/11/1970	13/11/1974	20/09/1979	26/09/2003	26/09/2003			
Singapore	01/03/1971	12/04/1978	12/04/1978	02/05/2008			22/11/1996	03/02/2004
Slovakia	20/03/1995	13/12/1995	06/03/1995	28/05/1993	28/05/1993	10/02/1993	20/03/1995	08/12/2000
Slovenia	18/12/1992	27/05/1992	27/05/1992	06/07/1992	06/07/1992	07/07/1992	27/05/1992	18/07/2003
Solomon Islands	23/03/1982		13/04/1982					
Somalia								
South Africa	26/05/1972	30/05/1972	30/05/1972	23/09/2003	23/09/2003	17/09/2007	21/09/1998	08/07/2005
Spain	01/10/1969	30/10/1972	30/10/1972	08/08/1985	26/03/1984	06/09/1991	08/05/1991	07/07/1989
Sri Lanka	30/05/1978	30/05/1978	30/05/1978	27/02/1991	08/09/2000		11/02/1997	04/09/2000
Sudan	25/05/2000	18/01/1979	18/01/1979	10/10/1994	19/06/1990	18/05/2000	15/05/2000	22/05/2000
Suriname	10/09/1979	27/10/1978	27/10/1978		05/11/1981		27/03/2003	
Swaziland	15/11/1999	27/12/1999	27/12/1999	04/04/2003	04/04/2003	17/04/2003		17/04/2003
Sweden	17/01/1967	07/07/1971	10/07/1973	01/07/1975	15/01/1981	01/08/1980	26/07/1990	13/09/1990
Switzerland	21/12/1970	14/09/1971	17/01/1978	05/03/1985	05/03/1985	09/01/1987	09/10/1990	12/03/1993
Syrian Arab Republic	31/07/1980	10/07/1980	10/07/1980	25/04/1988			18/07/2002	24/03/2003
Tajikistan	20/03/1996	29/02/1996	29/02/1996	19/10/2001	06/05/2002	11/07/1996	29/02/1996	12/08/2005
Thailand	06/03/1972	16/05/1978	16/05/1978	23/02/2007	02/10/2007		14/05/1996	
Timor-Leste								
Togo	26/07/1971	09/02/1979	09/02/1979	30/12/1980	25/07/1986	07/06/2006	09/02/1990	10/03/2003
Tonga	13/02/2002	21/02/1977	21/02/1977	09/12/2002	09/12/2002	24/01/2003	10/12/2002	06/12/2002
Trinidad and Tobago	09/02/1972	31/01/1972	09/02/1972	15/06/1979	01/04/1981	25/04/2001	03/04/2001	27/07/1989
Tunisia	25/02/1975	16/11/1981	16/11/1981	21/01/1977	18/06/1997	08/04/1993	07/06/1994	06/03/1998
Turkey	17/12/1975	17/04/1973	23/12/1975	11/06/1981	15/08/1989	27/02/1985	07/07/1989	06/03/1998
Turkmenistan	30/06/1999	25/05/1999	25/05/1999	25/06/1999	25/06/1999	07/01/2005	25/05/1999	08/06/1999
Tuvalu								02/12/2005

Name of the country	9	10	11	12	13	14	15	16
San Marino			12/03/2002	12/03/2002				
Sao Tome and Principe	05/05/2006		12/04/2006	12/04/2006				
Saudi Arabia	02/02/2006	11/07/1996	31/10/2007	23/08/2007				
Senegal	09/08/2004	11/02/2004	27/10/2003	24/09/2004				
Serbia	02/03/2005	22/06/2006	31/07/2003	10/10/2002	26/09/2006			
Seychelles	24/01/1989	14/08/2003	22/08/2003	30/03/2004		09/01/2006		
Sierra Leone			26/09/2003	26/09/2003				
Singapore		20/01/2003	31/12/2007	30/12/2002				
Slovakia	08/12/2000	20/03/1995	08/12/2000	13/09/2002	23/03/2006			
Slovenia	18/07/2003	05/06/2000.	25/09/2003	23/09/2004				
Solomon Islands								
Somalia								
South Africa	08/07/2005	01/12/1999	01/05/2003	01/05/2003	09/05/2007			
Spain	07/07/1989	31/05/1994	30/04/1999	09/04/2002	22/02/2007	09/11/2007	16/04/2008	16/04/2008
Sri Lanka		11/10/2001	23/03/1999	08/09/2000	27/09/2007			
Sudan	22/05/2000	25/05/2000	08/09/2000	05/05/2003				
Suriname		27/03/2003						
Swaziland	17/04/2003	13/05/2003	04/04/2003	04/04/2003				
Sweden	13/09/1990	05/04/2007	06/09/2001	06/06/2002				
Switzerland	12/03/1993	03/04/1995	23/09/2003	23/09/2003	15/10/2008	15/10/2008	15/10/2008	15/10/2008
Syrian Arab Republic	24/03/2003	29/09/2004		24/04/2005				
Tajikistan	12/08/2005	18/07/2006	29/07/2002	16/07/2004				
Thailand		25/01/2006	12/06/2007	29/09/2004				
Timor-Leste								
Togo	10/03/2003	22/07/2003	10/03/2003	10/03/2003				
Tonga	06/12/2002	10/12/2002	09/12/2002	09/12/2002				
Trinidad and Tobago	27/07/1989	03/04/2001	02/04/2001					
Tunisia	06/03/1998	28/05/1997	22/04/2005	10/06/2003				
Turkey	06/03/1998	14/12/1994	30/05/2002	28/06/2002				
Turkmenistan	08/06/1999	14/01/2005	25/06/1999	07/01/2005	28/03/2008	22/09/2005		
Tuvalu								

Name of the country	1	2	3	4	5	6	7	8
Uganda	25/06/1982	27/03/1972	19/07/1982	05/11/2003	05/11/2003	10/12/2003	17/03/1994	11/11/2003
Ukraine	29/02/1988	21/02/1972	26/01/1973	20/01/1976	19/06/1987	06/07/1993	03/01/1990	21/04/1994
United Arab Emirates	16/04/1981	10/04/1981	10/04/1981	25/02/2003	24/09/2003	16/10/2003	09/03/1989	15/09/2005
United Kingdom	29/11/1968	22/12/1971	25/10/1973	02/05/1979	22/12/1982	06/09/1991	15/11/1990	03/05/1991
United Republic of Tanzania	12/08/1983	09/08/1983	09/08/1983	22/01/2003	24/05/2006	09/03/2004	11/05/2005	
United States of America	05/09/1969	14/09/1971	01/11/1972	26/10/1976	07/12/1984	13/12/1982	19/10/1994	06/12/1994
Uruguay	26/01/1977	12/01/1977	12/01/1977	13/06/1978	04/03/2003	24/10/2003	03/12/1998	10/08/2001
Uzbekistan	31/07/1995	07/02/1994	07/02/1994	19/01/1998	19/01/1998	09/02/1998	07/02/1994	25/09/2000
Vanuatu	31/01/1989	22/02/1989	06/11/1989				09/11/2005	18/02/1999
Venezuela (Bolivarian Republic of)	04/02/1983	07/07/1983	21/11/1983	19/04/2005	13/12/1988			
Viet Nam	10/10/1979	17/09/1979	17/09/1979	02/05/2002			25/08/1999	12/07/2002
Yemen	26/09/1986	29/09/1986	29/09/1986	09/02/1987	14/07/2000	31/05/2007	05/01/2007	30/06/2000
Zambia	14/09/1971	03/03/1987	03/03/1987					
Zimbabwe	08/03/1989	06/02/1989	06/02/1989					

Name of the country	9	10	11	12	13	14	15	16
Uganda	02/07/2004	05/11/2003	05/11/2003					
Ukraine	21/04/1994	18/03/1999	26/03/2002	06/12/2002	25/09/2007	24/12/2008		
United Arab Emirates	15/09/2005	21/12/1992	23/09/2005	23/09/2005	10/01/2008			
United Kingdom	03/05/1991	28/04/1997	07/03/2001	07/03/2001				
United Republic of Tanzania		11/02/2003	22/01/2003	22/01/2003				
United States of America	06/12/1994	09/04/1997	26/06/2002	26/06/2002				
Uruguay	10/08/2001	14/06/2001	10/11/2001	08/01/2004				
Uzbekistan	25/09/2000	09/06/1999	30/11/1998	09/07/2001	29/04/2008			
Vanuatu	18/02/1999	25/01/2006		31/10/2005			20/08/2008	20/08/2008
Venezuela (Bolivarian Republic of)			23/09/2003	23/09/2003				
Viet Nam	12/07/2002			25/09/2002				
Yemen	30/06/2000	04/07/2007	23/04/2001					
Zambia		31/05/1995						
Zimbabwe								

Support for Pakistan

The 9/11 Commission recommended the United States "make the difficult long-term commitment to the future of Pakistan" and "support Pakistan's government in its struggle against extremists with a comprehensive effort that extends from military aid to support for better education, so long as Pakistan's leaders remain willing to make difficult choices of their own."

Composition and Levels of Assistance, Including Security and other Assistance

The United States commitment to a long-term relationship with Pakistan was highlighted by President Bush's pledge to seek from Congress USD three billion in Economic Support Funds (ESF) and Foreign Military Financing (FMF) for Pakistan during the five-year period from FY-2005 through FY-2009. Since 2002, U.S. assistance to Pakistan, including security assistance and coalition support funds, totaled approximately $12.4 billion. Approximately $2.0 billion in U.S. assistance, including defense-related security assistance and reimbursements from coalition support funds, was provided to Pakistan from monies appropriated for FY-2008.

In addition to Economic Support Funds and Foreign Military Financing, the United States is also providing other forms of assistance to Pakistan, including funding for Child Survival and Health (CSH), Development Assistance (DA), International Military Education and Training (IMET), International Narcotics and Law Enforcement (INCLE), Antiterrorism Assistance (NADR-ATA), Export Control and Border Security (NADR¬EXBS), Small Arms and Light Weapons (NADR-SALW), Terrorism Interdiction Programs (NADR-TIP), Food for Peace (P.L. 480 Title I & II), Emergency Refugee and Migration Assistance (ERMA), and International Disaster and Famine Assistance (IDFA). The chart below offers a comparison of selected types of assistance and does not include security cooperation or coalition support fund requests.

Account	FY-2006	FY-2006 Supplemental	FY-2007	FY-2007 Supplemental	FY-2008	FY-2008 Supplemental
CSH	22,800	53,00	22,400		29,800	
DA	27,000	10,500	95,300		29,800	
ESF	296,600	40,500	283,700	110,000	347,200	
FMF	297,000		297,000		297,570	
IMET	2,037		1,992		2,129	
INCLE	37,620		21,350		21,800	
NADR	8,600		10,000		9,700	
P.L 480 TITLE I & II	17,700					
ERMA					5,300	
IDFA		70,000			6,500	
TOTAL	709,320	126,300	110,000	749,000		

The mix of U.S. assistance for Pakistan reflects the diverse ways the United States is cooperating with Pakistan in pursuit of critical USG policy goals. These include countering nuclear proliferation; building a stable and democratic Afghanistan; ensuring peace and stability in South Asia through the continuation of the India-Pakistan reconciliation process; supporting Pakistan's efforts to become a modern, prosperous, democratic state; and assisting it in reconstruction efforts from the October 8, 2005 earthquake.

U.S. Foreign Military Financing (FMF) funding for Pakistan supports improved border security and control along Pakistan's border with Afghanistan, improves Pakistan's counterterrorism capabilities and enhances Pakistan's force modernization through equipment acquisitions, upgrades and maintenance. FMF is helping to make Pakistan more secure so that it can more readily take the steps necessary to build a durable peace with all its neighbors, thus fostering security and stability throughout the South Asia region. FMF is being used by Pakistan to upgrade and maintain helicopters, aircraft, weapons systems, munitions, and other equipment, which have enabled Pakistan's armed forces to operate against foreign terrorists and militants in the rugged border areas along the Pakistan-Afghanistan border. Since 2001, over 2,000 Pakistani military personnel have been killed carrying out counterterrorism operations.

International Military Education and Training (IMET) assistance to Pakistan complements FMF by exposing Pakistani officers to U.S. doctrine, systems, and culture, promoting military-to-military cooperation, increased professionalism, and enhanced military interoperability between Pakistan and the United States. IMET also assists Pakistan in developing expertise to more effectively manage its defense establishment; building the military's technical skills to better operate and maintain U.S.-origin equipment; and promoting military subordination to democratic civilian rule and respect for human rights. Post is seeking sizable future increases in IMET to help bridge the gap created in U.S.-Pakistani military exchanges during the years Pakistan was sanctioned which prevented Pakistani military officials from attending training in the United States.

Measures to ensure that Assistance has the Greatest Long-Term Positive Impact on the Welfare of Pakistani People and their Ability to Counter Terrorism

Economic Support Funds, Development Assistance, and Child Survival and Health assistance were used to improve the lives of ordinary Pakistanis; lay the groundwork for the country's sustained economic growth; and strengthen social, political, and economic institutions, thus alleviating the conditions that terrorists exploit while demonstrating that United States' interests in Pakistan extends beyond counterterrorism to concern for the Pakistani people as a whole.

Pakistan's low literacy rate greatly hampers its ability to develop and expand its economic base. Literacy averages 54 percent nationwide, and in Pakistan's remote tribal areas can be as low as 0.5 percent for women. The dearth of good public schools results in thousands of youth attending madrassas, schools that teach mainly religious subjects, some of which promote a radical, violent ideology. To tackle these problems, USG-funded education programs in Pakistan are aimed at improving the quality of education in Pakistani primary and secondary schools, especially in Baluchistan, Sindh, and the Federally Administered Tribal Areas (FATA); improving early childhood education; training teachers; increasing parental and community involvement in schools; ensuring teachers have adequate classroom materials; improving access to schools, and promoting the development of a new generation of Pakistani leaders by providing scholarships for disadvantaged students to obtain a higher education. Adult and youth literacy education programs are targeting out-of-school youth and illiterate adult populations, with a focus on women and girls. In addition, post-secondary student exchanges play a large part in our education efforts, with Pakistan's Fulbright Program being the largest U.S. government-funded Fulbright Program in the world.

Democratization is another key focus of United States assistance to Pakistan. Democracy is an important tool for countering terrorism over the long term. The programs include several mutually reinforcing components: legislative training to increase the effectiveness, transparency, and accountability of Pakistan's provincial and national parliaments; political party strengthening focused on identifying and training young reformers – tomorrow's political leadership; support for increased women's political participation; independent media training for journalists; and civil society development designed to increase the capacity of indigenous nongovernmental organizations to serve as policy watchdogs and promote human rights.

Pakistan trails its South Asian neighbors in almost all key health areas: maternal and infant mortality; safe, affordable family planning; and control of infectious diseases. Child Survival and Health funds have been used to increase availability of maternal and child health services, especially in rural areas; to ensure that families who want to space births can access high quality family planning services; to help maintain Pakistan's low human immunodeficiency virus prevalence rate by increasing awareness; to eradicate polio; to support continued progress in TB diagnosis and treatment; and to increase communities' access to clean drinking water and their practice of adequate hygiene behaviors.

The United States supports Pakistan's economic growth. New programs are being developed to create jobs and increase incomes. Current programs providing microfinance and small business lending in rural and peri-urban areas will continue to enable enterprise development and smooth income streams for the poor. Programs improving the competitiveness of small and medium enterprises are assisting the growth of Pakistani exports. By generating frequent, positive coverage in the local press, these programs are helping to improve the image of U.S. government assistance.

Earthquake reconstruction efforts entered their fourth year in 2008, and continued to rebuild, furnish, and supply health and education sector infrastructure and human resource capacities; to re-establish the livelihoods of earthquake victims; to resettle displaced victims; and to train skilled and unskilled individuals in vocational training, agriculture and livestock development, asset formation, enterprise development, micro-credit, and market restoration.

Economic Support Funds and Child Survival and Health monies helped fund the government's Federally Administered Tribal Areas Sustainable Development Plan to improve governance and encourage economic development of the border area between Afghanistan and Pakistan.

International Narcotics and Law Enforcement funds for Pakistan continued to strengthen border security and enable law enforcement access to remote areas along the border between Pakistan and Afghanistan, thus enhancing the country's capability to interdict traffickers in narcotics, arms, persons, and contraband, as well as terrorists. International Narcotics and Law Enforcement funds were used to reform, strengthen, and improve cooperation between Pakistan's law enforcement agencies. International Narcotics and Law Enforcement funds supported a counternarcotics Air Wing based in Quetta, Baluchistan, operated by Pakistan's Interior Ministry. The Wing includes C-208 Caravan fixed-wing surveillance aircraft and UH-2 Huey II helicopters.

International Narcotics and Law Enforcement funds were also used to procure vehicles and communications, surveillance, and related equipment for border control and counter-narcotics activities; fund infrastructure projects to enhance roads in inaccessible parts of FATA; fund an Automated Fingerprint Identification System and National Criminal Database; and fund training and equipment to expand law enforcement investigative skills and forensic capacities.

Nonproliferation, Antiterrorism, Demining, and Related Programs/ Export Control and Related Border Security assistance strengthened Pakistan's export control system and thus prevented weapons of mass destruction and related technology transfers that raise proliferation concerns. Nonproliferation, Antiterrorism, Demining, and Related Programs/Export Control and Related Border Security funds are used for nonproliferation export control training addressing legal/regulatory reform, export licensing systems, customs enforcement, general inspection, weapons of mass destruction detection training for border control personnel, and procuring specialized radiation/chemical detection equipment.

Nonproliferation, Antiterrorism, Demining, and Related Programs/ Antiterrorism Assistance funding for Pakistan enhances the capabilities of elite national police units responsible for counterterrorism investigations and tactical operations. Nonproliferation, Antiterrorism, Demining, and Related Programs/Antiterrorism Assistance trained the Special Investigation Group and crisis response teams that were integral in making arrests after the December 2003 assassination attempts on President Musharraf and the May 2004 car bombs near the U.S Consulate in Karachi.

Nonproliferation, Antiterrorism, Demining, and Related Programs/ Terrorism Interdiction Programs funding for Pakistan is being used to support the Personal Identification Secure Comparison Evaluation System automated border control system. Funds were used to sustain ongoing program operations and expand coverage to additional Pakistani ports-of-entry.

Measures to alleviate Difficulties, Misunderstandings, and Complications in United States-Pakistani Relations

The United States and Pakistan engaged in extensive consultations to ensure that U.S. foreign assistance has the greatest long-term benefit for Pakistanis and enhances the country's ability to counter terrorism. The United States participated in the annual Pakistan Development Forum, which brought together the Government of Pakistan and bilateral and multilateral donors to discuss Pakistan's development priorities and assistance needs. The United States holds regular consultations with major donors including Great Britain, the European Union, Japan, the Asian

Development Bank, and the World Bank, to ensure that assistance to Pakistan is effectively coordinated for maximum impact.

The USAID Federally Administered Tribal Areas (FATA) Development Program supported the Government of Pakistan's FATA Sustainable Development Plan. The USAID program focused on improving health, education, access to and availability of jobs, and capacity-building of FATA institutions. In education, USAID is improving access and quality of education for students by building and furnishing 62 primary, middle, and high schools; awarding scholarships to enable 37 women from this area to attend a one-year, pre-service teacher education program; and building or restoring water and sanitation facilities at 190 girls' primary schools and in 90 villages.

In health, USAID is improving the quality of drinking water, training health practitioners, providing polio vaccines, and immunizing children. To date, the United States has conducted 13 polio eradication campaigns in the FATA. USAID is promoting competitiveness initiatives to support both the marble and granite, and gems and jewelry sectors of the local economy, as well as providing jobs, training opportunities, and access to micro loans. Finally, the program is building the capacity of the FATA Secretariat and other Government of Pakistan institutions to improve their ability to deliver services and ensure the sustainability of USAID's development efforts in the region.

USAID GLOBAL EXPORT PROMOTION PROGRAMS

The Pakistan Initiative for Strategic Development and Competitiveness (PISDAC) project aimed to increase the competitiveness of small- and medium-sized enterprises in the country. Sectors currently covered under the project are gems, jewelry, dairy, horticulture, surgical supplies, furniture, and marble granite. The project has focused on several prominent Pakistani industries and formed six strategic working groups composed of business people from the industries that develop sector-specific strategies.

USAID supported the Government of Pakistan's education reform strategy by: (1) strengthening education policy and planning; (2) improving the skills and performance of teachers and administrators; (3) increasing youth and adult literacy; (4) expanding public-private partnerships; and (5) providing school improvement grants and involving parents and communities in public schools.

Collaboration with Saudi Arabia

Steps to Institutionalize and Make More Transparent Government-to-Government Relations

The United States-Saudi Strategic Dialogue, inaugurated in November 2005, has constituted a high level institutionalized forum for coordinating

U.S. and Saudi interests. The Strategic Dialogue has consisted of six working groups focusing on human development, economy, energy, consular affairs, military cooperation, and counterterrorism. These Strategic Dialogue working groups have met periodically to address issues such as making government more accountable and participatory, human rights, visas, child custody cases, and security cooperation. Ministerial-level meetings, dealing with bilateral issues of strategic importance, have been held as part of the Strategic Dialogue.

Intelligence and Security Cooperation to Counter Terrorism

The United States and Saudi Arabia have an ongoing dialogue on a full range of counterterrorism issues, which include regular high-level discussions and close working-level collaboration. Saudi cooperation is significant, and U.S. law enforcement and intelligence agencies have benefited and continue to benefit from Saudi information and intelligence on individuals and organizations. U.S. law enforcement agencies have provided counterterrorism training to Saudi security services in both Saudi Arabia and in the United States.

Since May 2003, the Saudi government has killed or captured al-Qa'ida's (AQ's) operational Saudi-based senior leadership, as well as most of the network's key operatives and many of the Kingdom's most wanted individuals. This effort has disrupted AQ's efforts to prosecute its terrorist campaign against the Saudi government. In 2008, the Saudi government announced plans to hold trials of individuals accused of involvement in terrorist activities inside the Kingdom. Saudi security forces continued to target terrorists and their supporters, and, in 2007, the Saudi government announced the arrest of more than 400 terrorists and their supporters, including terrorist financiers and those advocating extremist ideology over the Internet. Saudi officials claimed these arrests disrupted major attacks that were planned against Saudi government and economic targets. During a July 2007 address to the Shura Council, Interior Minister Prince Nayif bin Abdulaziz Al Saud stated that more than 9,000 suspected terrorists and their supporters have been arrested since 2003 and more than 3,100 remained in custody.

Recognizing that financiers of terrorism are key actors that allow terrorist groups to operate, the Saudi government continued to target such individuals and arrested 56 terrorist financiers and prosecuted 20 in 2008. The United States continued to urge Saudi Arabia to take action against additional key terrorist financiers and facilitators in the Kingdom. While the government has not yet made operational a National Committee to oversee overseas charitable contributions, the government has prohibited

Saudi charities from sending funds abroad until the Committee is established. Saudi Arabia took action against suspected terrorist financiers by freezing their accounts and confiscating their assets. The Saudi government has frozen assets and accounts belonging to individuals designated by the 1267 committee, and also imposed the required travel ban on these individuals.

Grand Mufti Sheikh Abdulaziz al-Sheikh, Saudi Arabia's preeminent religious figure, made strong statements warning Saudis to be cautious when making charitable contributions, and the government continued to closely monitor charitable giving by Saudis. The government also implemented new customs regulations that restrict the free flow of money, precious metals, and gems across its borders.

Saudi Contributions to Stability in the Middle East and the Islamic World, including the Middle East Peace Process; Eliminating Support for Extremist Groups

Since ascending to the throne, King Abdullah has followed a more activist foreign policy, offering Saudi assistance and support in efforts to resolve regional crises in Lebanon, Sudan, and Somalia; fostering Israeli-Palestinian peace efforts; and increasing Saudi diplomatic engagement around the world. In particular, he has pursued an Interfaith Dialogue Initiative to encourage religious tolerance on a global level, which was endorsed in a November 2008 session of the UN General Assembly.

Saudi Arabia has strengthened its border controls and security and, in particular, its border with Iraq to address travel by Saudis to Iraq to join terrorist groups fighting against Coalition Forces and the travel of non-Saudis through Saudi Arabia. The Saudi government announced a project to secure its border with Iraq as part of its larger border modernization program. The project will increase physical barriers and electronic surveillance of the northern border. In the interim, the Ministry of the Interior has deployed additional forces to the border area and has been successful in interdicting illicit movement of persons and equipment across the Saudi-Iraq border. The Saudi government announced the arrest of several hundred individuals who were planning to travel to Iraq or were actually en route, and increased its security cooperation with the Government of Iraq.

Senior Saudi leaders, including King Abdullah and Interior Minister Nayif, made strong statements against Saudis traveling to Iraq to join terrorist groups. Grand Mufti Abdulaziz al-Sheikh also issued a religious edict urging Saudi youth not to travel to Iraq to join terrorist organizations. This edict was repeated by other senior Saudi religious leaders as well.

The Saudi government continued its aggressive campaign to undercut the extremist ideologies that underpin support for terrorism and terrorist groups. In 2008, the Saudi government announced plans to hold trials of terrorism suspects to publicly discredit extremist ideology. The government published a list of 85 most-wanted terrorism suspects, along with a campaign to emphasize that these individuals were practitioners of deviant ideologies. Its publicity campaign also included using print media ads, billboards, text messages, and the Internet to oppose extremist thought. The government continued to monitor speeches and writings of religious leaders closely to ensure they do not advocate extremism and to conduct re-education training for religious leaders. Those who violate government decrees and regulations were fired or reassigned. In an effort to prevent unauthorized preaching, the Saudi government has taken steps to issue identification cards to imams authorized to speak in mosques. The government has stepped up its efforts to delegitimize the extremist ideologies that glorify terrorism and undercut the so-called Islamic underpinnings of these beliefs. Senior Saudi leaders have made strong statements criticizing the extremist ideology espoused by many terrorists as evil and un-Islamic.

The government also operated a rehabilitation program designed to re-educate those arrested for supporting extremism or terrorism, including Saudis formerly held at the Guantanamo Bay detention facility. The program was designed to reintegrate individuals into society and includes educational, social, and religious components to undermine extremist messages and foster a more tolerant attitude. The program builds on family and tribal relations to reinforce the message and speed the reintegration process. Those who complete the program and show evidence of having been rehabilitated are eligible for consideration for release from custody, though not before they have served any prison sentence for their previous crimes. Employment, coupled with tribal and family reintegration, including marriage, in some cases, are important components of the post-release program, as are monitoring and follow-up by both extended families and the Saudi government. More than 1,000 Saudis have completed the program and the Saudi government states that the recidivism rate is very low. The USG is following the progress of this program closely, both to understand the program and monitor rates of recidivism, and will not hesitate to raise any concerns with the Saudi government.

The United States continued to urge the Saudis to make progress on revising their textbooks to remove hateful and intolerant references and to reform its educational system. Senior Saudi officials have acknowledged the need to combat extremism by addressing comprehensive education reform. In November 2006, the King Abdul Aziz Center for National

Dialogue held the Sixth National Dialogue Forum in Al-Jawf called Education: Reality and Promises. The Dialogue produced a road map for educational reform that included revision of textbooks, curricula, and teaching methods to promote tolerance. The Saudi government continued its National Campaign to Counter Terrorism, which includes publications, lectures, and workshops intended to educate school-age girls and boys about the evils of terrorism. Additionally, the Ministry of Education recently issued a new regulation that allows only Ministry-approved summer camps to operate.

Political and Economic Reform in Saudi Arabia and in Muslim Communities Worldwide

King Abdullah continued to pursue an incremental reform policy that aims to achieve a more tolerant society. Saudi Arabia is a conservative country and some societal elements are wary of this policy. The undercurrent against reform remains strong, albeit muted, and the government continued to move slowly in easing many social restrictions. The United States has encouraged the Government of Saudi Arabia to make legal, economic, political, and social reforms, with progress in such areas as local governance, economic reform, and religious and social freedoms.

The Saudi government has taken some steps to devolve power. In 2007, King Abdullah granted increased authority to the Majlis al-Shura, the Consultative Council, which can now offer some oversight on government actions and has the authority not only to review laws proposed by the Council of Ministers but to propose laws. King Abdullah also established an Allegiance Council to institutionalize the selection of future Crown Princes via a process to formally ratify the King's candidate for a successor. The United States will continue to urge the Government of Saudi Arabia to promote political participation, increased transparency, and accountability in government.

Recognizing the need to better prepare Saudis for the challenges of the 21st century and to address some of the root causes of extremism, King Abdullah has directed a major overhaul of the Saudi education system. Total educational spending at all levels ($33 billion) represented 25% of the entire national budget. Saudi Arabia is now in the third year of a six-year $2.4 billion program to reform its primary and secondary educational system, which includes incorporating an updated and modernized curriculum, updated teacher training, and new textbooks. It continued granting increasing independence to private schools in matters of curriculum. The government is awarding tens of thousands of scholarships for Saudi students to study in Western countries (the largest number of students are going to the United States) and expanding the numbers and striving to improve the quality of colleges and universities, both state-run and private.

While Saudi Arabia continued to have a society strictly segregated by gender. women's rights and opportunities have increased. Saudi women are joining the workforce in larger numbers and there have been efforts to rein in the Mutawwa'in (religious police) and apply official sanctions for extremist acts. Recent government initiatives to allow women to stay alone at hotels and comments about granting women the right to drive have generated resistance among religious and social conservatives, but have demonstrated the King's commitment to moving forward, albeit slowly, on women's rights.

The United States sponsors a variety of initiatives focused on increasing our engagement with Saudi society at all levels and promoting a positive view of the United States among Saudi citizens. Initiatives have included enhanced State Department educational, exchange, and outreach programs, including: reaching under-served audiences and remote areas with the International Visitor Leadership Program, English language training programs for youth (ACCESS and the Youth Exchange and Study Program), English language teacher training, leadership seminars for female university students, promotion of legal studies among women, and active collaboration with Saudi scholarship programs and individual students to promote U.S. higher education and to better prepare Saudi students for U.S. study.

Oil prices averaging $100 per barrel over the course of 2008 resulted in a budget surplus of close to $130 billion. Saudi Arabia continued to invest heavily in social development and large infrastructure projects and has supported investments to diversify the economy away from petroleum and the petrochemical industry. The Kingdom announced plans to establish six Economic Cities, including the King Abdullah Economic City, to provide regional anchors to spur economic diversification and to move into greater value-added manufacturing.

Ways to promote greater Tolerance and Respect for Cultural and Religious Diversity in Saudi Arabia and throughout Muslim Communities Worldwide

In November 2008, the Secretary of State re-designated Saudi Arabia a Country of Particular Concern pursuant to the International Religious Freedom Act. This is an important element of our bilateral dialogue with the Saudi government. The United States is working to promote religious and cultural tolerance in Saudi Arabia and to counter the spread of extremist ideology through high-level engagement and exchange programs aimed at reaching key population groups.

On April 25, 2005, following the visit of then-Crown Prince Abdullah to Crawford, Texas, the United States and Saudi Arabia issued a joint declaration noting that future relations must rest on a foundation of broad cooperation. We must work to expand dialogue, understanding, and interactions between our citizens. The declaration noted that such cooperation would include programs designed to:

- Increase the number of young Saudi students traveling and studying in the United States;
- Increase military exchange programs so that more Saudi officers visit the United States for military training and education; and
- Increase the number of Americans traveling to work and study in Saudi Arabia.

In 2005, Saudi Arabia initiated a scholarship program to increase the number of young Saudi men and women pursuing undergraduate and graduate studies in the United States. By 2008, more than 18,000 Saudis were studying in the United States on Saudi government scholarships.

Ways to assist Saudi Arabia in Reversing the Impact of Financial, Moral, Intellectual, or Other Support to Extremist Groups in Saudi Arabia and Other Countries, and to Prevent this Support from Continuing in the Future

The United States and Saudi Arabia worked closely together to combat terrorism in Saudi Arabia and abroad. The United States continued to urge the Saudi government to more vigorously pursue and prosecute terrorist financiers, and offered training to the Government of Saudi Arabia to help increase its capacity to detect and disrupt terrorist financing efforts.

While the Saudis have not yet made operational a High Commission for Charities to oversee all charities in Saudi Arabia, the government has imposed a ban on domestic charities sending money overseas except through this Commission. All international charitable work is carried out through Saudi government agencies such as the Saudi Fund for Development or the Red Crescent Society.

The United States and Saudi Arabia have worked together in the past to designate individuals and entities jointly at the UNSC 1267 Committee. To combat terrorist financing, Saudi Arabia has instituted new anti-money laundering and counterterrorism finance laws and regulations including removing charity boxes from mosques, restricting the amount of cash that can be carried into or out of the Kingdom without disclosure, and establishing a Financial Investigations Unit (FIU) in the Ministry of Interior to analyze money-laundering cases and to eventually consolidate all counterterrorism financing operations, both analysis and investigations.

Saudi Arabia needs to continue to take steps to exercise oversight of fundraising activities in the Kingdom and Saudi charitable activities abroad.

COMBATING VIOLENT EXTREMISM

The United States recognizes that the global and generational challenge of countering violent extremism requires marginalizing violent extremists and undermining their effort to exploit religion to rationalize their acts of terror. While it is important to recognize that not all extremists are Muslim, we cannot ignore the large number of extremists who have distorted Islam to promote terrorism.

Tools to Accomplish Such Goals

The United States advances these strategic objectives by:

- Amplifying credible mainstream Muslim voices.
- Engaging foreign publics to explain American policies and debunk the myths about America and Islam
- Creating networks of like-minded mainstream thinkers
- Creating organic initiatives that go to the heart of the ideological appeal. This component of Public Diplomacy is not simply trying to win the hearts and minds of Muslim communities. Our interest is in helping these communities acquire credible alternatives to the violent extremists. Thus, the key measure is not whether they like America.

Learning about the United States through experience, is important. The United States is promoting increased exchanges. The significance of people-to-people exchanges has never been more clear or compelling. The 9/11 Commission report recognized the essential contribution exchanges make to national security. The National Intelligence Reform Act of 2004 reaffirmed the importance of America's commitment to exchanges.

The United States is expanding educational opportunities, both for study in the United States and for English language training. English language programs not only provide crucial skills but also open a window to information about the United States, its people, and its values. Education USA advising centers at U.S. embassies and affiliated organizations promote U.S. higher education opportunities, including English language study, to prospective international students in the region. Americans must also better educate themselves about the world. The National Security Language Initiative is encouraging more Americans to study critical languages such as Chinese, Russian, Hindi, Persian, and Arabic.

Responding to and quickly debunking misinformation, conspiracy theories, and urban legends is crucial for success in the struggle of ideas.

That is a key objective of the State Department's Digital Outreach Team, whose members post comments on well-trafficked Arabic, Persian, and Urdu language blog sites. Additionally, State's america.gov website contains articles debunking false stories about the United States and a blog Rumors, Myths, and Fabrications is devoted to this issue.

The Internet, radio, television, and video products remain powerful tools for bringing America's foreign policy message to worldwide audiences. The State Department produces a wide array of print and electronic materials describing for foreign audiences, in their own languages, the need to counter those who have committed or wish to commit violent acts, as well as achievements made in this area.

The State Department's premier web page to explain U.S. counterterrorism policy is *Confronting Terrorism*, featured on the America.gov web site. The site is listed among the top 10 of more than 200 million sites in a Google search for the terms "terrorism U.S. At least 133 wfeaturing articles, texts, and transcripts from key policymakers, this site provides valuable links to the Electronic Journals series, the National Strategy for Combating Terrorism, the list of designated Foreign Terrorist Organizations, and the State Department's annual *Country Reports on Terrorism*.

Strengthening and empowering the voices most credible to speak out in favor of non-violence, respect for rule of law, and the compatibility of Islam and democracy, is central to our efforts. Providing Muslim youth with credible alternatives to messages coming from violent extremists is critical. We are doing this in new ways using a light U.S. government footprint.

The American people are one of public diplomacy's greatest assets. Empowerment of individuals and groups from all walks of life is a key aspect of the Department's public diplomacy efforts.

We recognize this will require a long-term effort spanning years and generations. For that reason, we are placing increased emphasis on programs directed at younger audiences, including undergraduate and, in select cases, high school students.

The U.S. government's assistance programs, administered through USAID, the Middle East Partnership Initiative, the Millennium Challenge Corporation, and other U.S. entities, advance U.S. interests in this area through programs to increase access to education, improve health care, and empower people to build better lives. Civic engagement is an important component. Assistance programs to strengthen and professionalize independent media and civic society contribute to opening the "marketplace of ideas," as well as supporting development and reform across the board. (More information on these programs can be found in this chapter.)

The Ambassador's Fund for Counterterrorism. The State Department's Office of the Coordinator for Counterterrorism has developed a strategic communication team to address the soft side of counterterrorism. The Ambassador's Fund for Counterterrorism funds innovative activities and programs that aim to shift the perceptions of target audiences, undermine the enemy's image, delegitimize extremist ideologies, and diminish support for violent extremism. In 2008, it funded 17 programs across all geographical regions (representing a total of $750,000).

Programs have included:

- Promoting Civic Engagement and Community Law Enforcement by Moroccan Youth.
- Affecting Institutional Change in Madrassa Schools in Bangladesh.
- Empowering Women against Religious Violence in India.
- Launching the Creation of a European Minority Media Network.
- Supporting De-radicalization Among Incarcerated Terrorists in Indonesia.

IRAN PROGRAMS

The United States appropriated $66 million in FY-2006 supplemental funds and almost $60 million in FY-2008 funds for civil society development, broadcasting, and exchange programs related to Iran, as well as efforts to explain U.S. policy objectives to the Iranian people.

Benchmarks for Measuring Success and Linking Resources to Accomplishments

In 2004, State established the Public Diplomacy Evaluation Office (PDEO). Its mandate was to evaluate all major public diplomacy and exchange programs individually as well as provide an overall strategic framework for public diplomacy assessment. This function was modified in July 2008 with the creation of the Evaluation and Measurement Unit (EMU) within the Office of Policy, Planning, and Resources for Public Diplomacy and Public Affairs. The Evaluation & Measurement Unit builds accountability and improves the effectiveness of U.S. mission public diplomacy activities worldwide through program evaluation that include the application of rigorous data collection methods and innovative analytical approaches. The EMU evaluates U.S. mission public diplomacy programs, products and initiatives, and educational and cultural exchange programs supported by core operating funds, primarily carried out by the Bureau of International Information Programs (IIP) and U.S. overseas missions.

Organizations as diverse as the Peace Corps, Department of Defense, the British Council, the World Bank, and non-profits in Italy, Japan, and the Netherlands have all consulted with PDEO and EMU on how to measure public diplomacy activities.

The measures of performance and accountability used by public diplomacy are based upon recognized social and behavioral science methodologies and include measuring changes in audience attitudes (knowledge, skills, perceptions, and understanding), behavior, and condition.

Examples include:

- Improved or increased understanding of the United States, its policies and values;
- Initiated or implemented "positive" change within an individual's organization (positive referring to changes that support U.S. ideals and values);
- Reduction in level of anti-American sentiment among key foreign audiences;
- Program participant (key/target audience) satisfaction scores of public diplomacy programs and public outreach activities, and

  Institutional partnerships and linkages and on-going collaboration.

Participation in International Institutions for the Promotion of Democracy and Economic Diversification

The United States is a leading participant in many international organizations, such as the United Nations and NATO. We also play a leading role in other initiatives, such as the Forum for the Future and the Community of Democracies, which stimulate cooperation with other nations to advance the agenda of freedom. For the first time since its creation in 2000 and in response to U.S. government recommendations, the Community of Democracies created regional dialogues which brought together representatives from governmental and non-governmental organizations from each region to discuss the challenges and solutions unique to their areas. We will continue to seek opportunities to build on the momentum coming out of the April ministerial, particularly in support of the Forum for the Future and the Broader Middle East and North Africa (BMENA) processes.

OUTREACH THROUGH BROADCAST MEDIA

This section is provided by the Broadcasting Board of Governors (BBG)

Broadcasting Board of Governors Initiatives: Outreach to Foreign Muslim Audiences

Overview. The Broadcasting Board of Governors (BBG) promotes freedom and democracy and seeks to enhance understanding through the broadcast of unbiased news, and information about America and the world to foreign audiences. Since September 11, this mission has become more critical among Muslim audiences and BBG programming has expanded accordingly. The result of BBG efforts, detailed below, has been to boost weekly audiences in Muslim-majority countries or regions from under 15 million a week five years ago to over 70 million today.

Four of the five broadcast entities under the supervision of the Board, the Voice of America, the Middle East Broadcasting Networks, Radio Free Europe/Radio Liberty, and Radio Free Asia, provide programming for Muslim audiences. From 24-hour broadcasting to large Muslim populations in the Middle East and South Asia, to programs heard by Muslim audiences in Indonesia, Thailand, Russia, and Russian-speaking Central Asia, BBG programs are serving Muslim audiences and promoting U.S. foreign policy goals.

A number of new or expanded broadcasts reflect the continued urgency of the broadcast priorities associated with U.S. counterterrorism efforts. For example, the programs of the Middle East Broadcasting Networks, *Radio Sawa* and *Alhurra* Television, are broadcast 24 hours a day in Arabic and reach audiences in 22 countries in the Middle East and Europe. In 2008, Persian News Network broadcast 24 hours per day into Iran, up from only eight daily broadcast hours in 2006. RFE/RL's *Radio Farda* also broadcasts 24/7, targeting a younger Iranian audience with a mix of music and information programs. The BBG's Arabic and Persian 24/7 broadcast products reach audiences in the broadcast media they prefer: radio, television, and the Internet.

To reflect the nation's critical foreign policy priorities since September 11, 2001, BBG's broadcast resources have shifted from areas of the world where the local media are increasingly free and strong to the Middle East and Central and South Asia. VOA has reduced its broadcasts to Europe, strengthening its focus on Iran, Afghanistan, Indonesia, Pakistan, and other critical nations. Eighteen of RFE/RL's broadcast languages, almost two-thirds of the total, are directed to countries or regions where the majority populations are Muslim. RFE/RL broadcasts to Iran, Iraq, Afghanistan, Azerbaijan, Bosnia, Kosovo, Kazakhstan, Kyrgyzstan, Tajikistan, Turkmenistan, and Uzbekistan; as well as the majority Muslim populations of Tatarstan, Bashkortostan, and the North Caucasus in the Russian Federation.

The BBG's research indicates that these new programs resonate with audiences and are drawing listeners and viewers, even in environments where listening or seeking access to satellite broadcasts may be illegal. Telephone surveys conducted in Iran indicate that the BBG's Persian language programming reached 29 percent of Iranians on a weekly basis.

Programming in other key areas with large Muslim populations provides relevant news and information to audiences who otherwise might not have access to unbiased reporting on key U.S. government policy statements and reporting on local or international news. VOA's Urdu language service has expanded its broadcasts to Pakistan, and Pashto language broadcasts target the Waziristan region. Both VOA and RFE/RL provide blanket news and information coverage to Afghanistan in the Dari and Pashto languages. RFE/RL is the most popular radio station for news in Afghanistan; over 56% of Afghan adults now listen to or watch one or more of BBG's various broadcasts for that country at least once a week.

The agency's broadcast strategy focuses on building program reach and impact within the Islamic world with thematic content, which includes facilitating citizen discourse, engaging the world in conversations about America, and helping audiences understand the principles of democratic societies. Technical aspects emphasize enhanced program delivery and employ modern communication techniques. The rigorous use of research about audience and broadcast environments, more frequent program review and oversight, and more compelling broadcast formats that will resonate in competitive but critical international markets and are crucial to this strategy. BBG broadcasters provide unbiased comprehensive news and information as mandated under the U.S. International Broadcasting Act.

During the past year, the agency's extensive journalistic resources reported on the regional political, military, and economic issues facing our listeners, as well as U.S. and international news. The U.S. elections provided a unique opportunity to showcase the democratic process in action, as well as the smooth transition of power from the Bush to the Obama Administration. BBG correspondents in the United States and around the world contributed to coverage available in 60 languages, providing program perspectives that were often lacking in media outlets abroad. Live, simultaneous interpretation of Congressional hearings, election debates, and Presidential speeches, such as the State of the Union, allowed Muslim audiences to hear our nation's official policies, as well as the deliberations that led to the adoption of those policies.

To deliver program content, the agency continued to make aggressive strides in using new technologies, both to combat jamming and to capture new audiences through web and other communications tools. Comprehensive Internet sites are vital tools for each BBG language service, and the use of webchats, blogsites, and other attractive Internet applications have been expanded as the Internet becomes an increasingly viable information medium in both open and closed societies. The Internet offers an exciting transmission opportunity to countries such as Iran, where the BBG's traditional broadcast technologies are jammed or blocked. Through the use of proxy sites and daily emails of news summaries, VOA Persian and Radio Farda bypass the Iranian government's censorship tools. Radio Farda's enhanced website has improved the flow of information to viewers and increased opportunities for interactivity with audiences.

In 2008, traffic to VOANews.com increased 47 percent from a year earlier to nearly 117 million visits. At least 25 percent of this traffic originated in Iran, while significant segments also came from China, Indonesia, Pakistan, India, Afghanistan, Nigeria, Turkey, and Russia.

In addition, the BBG's use of social media to distribute news and information and to engage audiences in dialogue bodes well for the future. Blogs on Iranian issues, Russian politics, U.S. politics, and African music attracted visitors to VOA content, both on VOANews.com and on other sites. New, branded pages on YouTube, Facebook, and Twitter offered another means for audiences to find VOA content. On YouTube alone, there have been more than two million views of VOA videos; much of this content was posted by VOA services targeting Muslim audiences. VOA also offers podcasts of audio and video programs on i-tunes.

VOA created a special U.S. election site that attracted traffic from more than 200 countries and resulted in many users joining an online VOA community, where they shared photos, asked questions and provided comments. Large numbers of users originated from China, India, Indonesia, Pakistan, Saudi Arabia, Nigeria, Turkey, Malaysia, Egypt, and Afghanistan.

For Arab audiences, Radio Sawa has an all-news Arabic-language website that communicated with the youthful technologically-savvy population in the Middle East. RadioSawa.com has shown tremendous growth since its inception in 2003. Some of the unique features on the website included live streaming, recorded audio programs, news update features, and continuous breaking news. Other unique features include daily interviews with important newsmakers and *Sawa Magazine*, a variety journal featuring technology, science, health, movies, and unusual events. In 2008, Alhurra increased its web presence, by streaming its programming at www.alhurra.com. In addition, Alhurra archives two months of programming on the website.

As the BBG's various Internet platforms continued to grow in popularity, however, hackers sought opportunities to exploit infrastructure and security vulnerabilities. In April, RFE/RL Internet sites in Iran, Russia, Azerbaijan, Tajikistan, Kosovo, Macedonia, Bosnia, and Belarus were targeted by a massive distributed denial of service attack (DDOS).

THE MIDDLE EAST

Arabic Broadcasting. To effectively communicate with the large, predominantly young audiences in the Middle East, the BBG launched Radio Sawa in 2002, a 24/7 network of stations specifically designed to reach the large segment of the Arabic-speaking population under the age of 35. In 2008, Radio Sawa continued to broadcast objective, authoritative, comprehensive, and timely news about the Middle East, the United States, and the world. In addition to 325 newscasts per week, Radio Sawa offered discussion and informational programs such as the popular *Sawa Chat* interactive feature and the *Free Zone*, a weekly review and discussion of democracy and freedom as they relate specifically to the Middle East. Feature programs encouraged discussion of key social and political issues in a manner very different from indigenous Arab media.

Radio Sawa broadcasts on FM in:

- Morocco (Rabat, Casablanca, Tangier, Meknes, Marrakesh, Agadir, and Fes)
- Jordan (Amman and Ajlun)
- the Palestinian Territories (Ramallah and Jenin)
- Kuwait (Kuwait City)
- Bahrain (Manama)
- Qatar (Doha),
- U.A.E. (Abu Dhabi and Dubai)
- Iraq (Baghdad, Nasiriya, Basra, Mosul, Kirkuk, Sulimaniya, Fallujah, Ramadi, Al-Hilla, Tikrit, Amara, Najaf, Samawa, and Erbil)
- Lebanon (Beirut, North Lebanon, South Lebanon, and Bekaa Valley)
- Djibouti

Radio Sawa expanded its FM coverage in Iraq by adding FM transmitters in Fallujah, Ramadi, and Tikrit. Radio Sawa also broadcasts on medium wave to Egypt, Yemen, Saudi Arabia, and throughout Sudan, and is available on Arabsat, Nilesat, and Eutelsat satellite systems.

Building on the success of Radio Sawa, the BBG launched Alhurra Television in 2004, covering 22 countries in the Middle East via the same satellites used by major indigenous Arabic channels. In the five years Alhurra has been broadcasting, it has provided in-depth coverage of historic events, such as elections in the U.S. and the Middle East and continuing developments in the Middle East peace process. Alhurra is a consistent leader in its reporting and analysis on democratic trends in the Middle East, garnering a reputation for comprehensive coverage.

In December 2008, when fighting broke out in Gaza, Alhurra broadcast live reports from correspondents in Israel and Gaza. Extensive breaking news coverage and expert analysis from Washington provided an American perspective. Through objective and accurate reporting, Alhurra has been an example of a free press to the region and has become a trusted source of news for its estimated 26 million weekly viewers.

Alhurra provided insights into life in America and the American system of government. It is the only Arabic-language network to have dedicated correspondents at the White House, State Department, Congress, and the Pentagon. During the presidential elections, Alhurra provided daily coverage of the candidates and the issues that impacted the U.S. election process, presenting a compelling platform for showcasing the political institutions of the United States.

Alhurra carried extensive live news coverage of events and speeches by U.S. senior officials. The network augments its regular news coverage of the U.S. through its current affairs programs, such as *Inside Washington,* which takes viewers behind the scenes of the political process in Washington with guests such as Supreme Court Justice Antonin Scalia, Secretary Margaret Spellings, and *New York Times* columnist Thomas Friedman. Alhurra's program on women's rights, *Musawat* (Equality), came to America to profile five influential and successful women including former Secretary Donna Shalala, American Red Cross Chairman Bonnie McElveen Hunter, and former Chairman and CEO of Hewlett-Packard, Carly Fiorina.

Alhurra also produces programs that provide a forum for discussion on sensitive issues such as women's rights and human rights. Current affairs programs, such as *Women's Views,* are unique in the region's media. Hosted by four women from different backgrounds, the program airs free discussion on social and political issues that are largely regarded as taboo in the region. Alhurra's *Eye on Democracy* focuses on democratic efforts and human rights concerns throughout the Middle East.

Throughout its five-year history, Alhurra has provided a forum for discussion of important topics by a wide variety of experts and voices of moderation. Its talk shows, roundtables, and documentaries have routinely tackled vital topics that are not addressed on many other stations in the region, including the struggle for human rights, the position of women in Arab society, religious freedom, freedom of the press, and freedom of expression.

Radio Sawa and Alhurra Television now reach a total audience of 35 million adults 15 and older, according to international research firms such as AC Nielsen. The surveys show that despite high levels of anti-American sentiment throughout the region, both Alhurra and Radio Sawa are regarded as credible sources of news and information by their audiences.

In September, the Middle East Broadcasting Networks began broadcasting a new all-news and information program to Darfur, *Afia Darfur*. The daily 30-minute program focuses on the latest news from Sudan and the plight of displaced people in Darfur and eastern Chad. Broadcasting on shortwave radio, the program includes interviews with American officials, human rights experts, Sudanese experts, and NGO representatives. *Afia Darfur* also incorporates interviews with internally displaced people living in Darfur, providing them with an opportunity to speak out about the humanitarian crisis. Additionally, the program addresses how the Western press is covering Darfur; as well as examining its rich history and cultural background.

Arabic in Europe. Since August 2006, Alhurra Europe has brought the best programs of Alhurra and Alhurra-Iraq to the Arabic-speaking population in Europe. Alhurra Europe can be seen on the Hotbird satellite system that reaches all of Europe.

Iraq

Alhurra Iraq, a dedicated television stream to Iraq containing more concentrated news and information to and about Iraq, began broadcasting in April 2004. Through satellite and terrestrial transmission, Alhurra has gained a strong foothold in one of the most competitive TV marketplaces in the world. In 2008, Alhurra-Iraq added another terrestrial channel in Tikrit (channel 33) bringing the total number of terrestrial channels in Iraq to four (including Basra, Baghdad, and Mosul.) Alhurra's goal is to help its viewers make educated and informed decisions about political, social, and economic events.

RFE/RL's **Radio Free Iraq** (RFI) continued to provide the Iraqi people with breaking news and in-depth coverage of developments in Iraq and the Middle East. Because RFI is a surrogate broadcaster, the Iraqi people see it as their radio. RFI appeals to a wide spectrum of listeners in Iraq by covering the most significant political issues in the country, including daily coverage of the activities of the Iraqi Cabinet and Parliament. RFI's extensive network of freelance reporters, based in the Baghdad bureau, risk their lives to bring objective news to their compatriots.

This past year, Radio Free Iraq focused on subjects such as efforts to secure and restore order in Basra, Iraq's second largest city; the role of U.S. forces in Iraq; relations with Iraq's neighbors, including Iran, and the U.S. presidential election and its meaning for Iraqis. RFI gave ample coverage to the Iraqi political agenda, including reform of the Al-Maliki Cabinet, the relationship between the central government and Kurdistan's Regional Government, debates on Iraqi sovereignty, reform of political institutions, and preparations in the run up to the provincial and local elections. The Service also followed Iraqi cooperation with Turkey to curb PKK activities against the Turkish military from Iraqi territory. RFI spotlighted various human rights issues such as women's rights, the fate of Iraqi prisoners in neighboring countries, and the rights of journalists. RFI broadcast interviews with numerous top Iraqi officials and politicians, including Interior Ministry Spokesman Abdel Karim Khalaf and Foreign Minister Hoshyar Zebari.

In April, RFE/RL analyst Daniel Kimmage released *The Al-Qa'ida Media Nexus*, a study on the nexus of ties and coordination between the global network of al-Qa'ida (AQ) affiliates, arguing that the marketing techniques that catapulted AQ to worldwide fame are quickly becoming obsolete as user-created content sweeps the Web. The study provided an overview of the hidden structures that disseminate AQ's claims and ideas, giving readers a conceptual vocabulary to describe this guerilla media network in order to clarify discussion on how best to counteract its influence. Fight Terror with YouTube , an op-ed by Kimmage also appeared in *The New York Times* on June 26.

VOA's Kurdish Service. Broadcasting four hours of daily radio programming, VOA's Kurdish Service remained highly popular among Kurds in Iraq. According to surveys conducted by InterMedia Research, VOA occupied a unique position among Iraqi Kurds. It is the only major international broadcaster offering programs in the two main Kurdish dialects, Kurmanji and Sorani. VOA Kurdish focused on the Iraqi scene through a network of stringers, and with special programs and call-in shows devoted to combating extremism inside the country and in the surrounding region. Special coverage highlighted the debate among Kurds on the role of Islam in the regional and national constitutions of Iraq. Some of the topics discussed in VOA Kurdish special programming included the observance of Muslim holidays in the United States, Muslim students in U.S. colleges, and the role of religion in U.S. politics.

Iran

VOA's Persian News Network. As noted above, broadcasting to Iran remained a key BBG priority. VOA's Persian News Network (PNN) has seen large audience growth, with one in four adults watching the broadcasts weekly. The seven-hour television program block opens with *Today in Washington*, a brief look at the latest news developments in Washington. Other original programming includes:

- *Today's Woman*, a one-hour program features influential women from around the world discussing social issues, medical themes, human rights, the law, sports, and business.
- *News and Views*, PNN's 2-hour flagship news program features live interviews and news coverage of the latest worldwide headlines.
- *Roundtable with You,* a talk show with expert guests who discuss current events, politics, popular culture, and global health. Viewers and listeners from Iran and around the world participate in the show via phone calls and e-mails.
- *Late Edition*, which begins with a close look at the day's top story. This program is targeted to a younger demographic and features segments on Iran's student movement, health, technology, sports, entertainment, and culture.
- *NewsTalk*, a journalists' roundtable discussion program that features an examination of the day's top stories and an in-depth look at issues relating to Iran.

PNN's achievements during 2008 included numerous high-value interviews, extensive on-the-scene coverage of the U.S. Presidential election, and an aggressive, expanding use of the PNN website to engage Iranian audiences. Key guests included U.S. Ambassador to Iraq Ryan Crocker, General David Petraeus, Nobel Peace Prize laureate Shirin Ebadi, and exiled Iranian student movement leader and human rights activist Ahmad Batebi.

PNN's reporters deployed to the sites of the U.S. Presidential debates, the Democratic and Republican conventions and to the election night camps of both the Obama and McCain campaigns in Chicago and Phoenix to provide immediate and close perspectives on the race to the White House. Following the election, PNN invited its audience to email its messages for the new President-elect. The hundreds of messages received were posted on PNN's website and shared with the new Transition Team.

Radio Farda. As of July 7, 2008, RFE/RL assumed sole managerial oversight of Radio Farda, continuing 24-hours a day broadcasting to Iran. RFE/RL and the Voice of America had jointly operated Radio Farda since its inception in December 2002. With increased funding, Radio Fardo has supported the addition of larger blocks of news and information in its tradition as a "surrogate" broadcaster, presenting news about the country to which it broadcasts. Current broadcasts include over eight hours of daily news and information programming. Radio Farda finds direct sources of information within Iran in spite of the challenging environment for journalism.

Iranians turned to Radio Farda and its website for round-the-clock breaking news on stories of global interest, such as Iran's nuclear program; Iran's economic climate and unemployment; and human rights abuses. Radio Farda devoted substantial coverage to the March 14 parliamentary elections in Iran. Before the vote, Farda broadcast a weekly program entitled *Elections Under the Magnifying Glass*. A separate program, *Fresh Glance*, provided Iranian youth with a forum to discuss the elections.

To enhance its program offerings, Radio Farda launched a new roundtable program called *Your Voice is Farda's Voice*. The program invited listeners to discuss a variety of social and political issues, with the goal of increasing interactivity by giving listeners a platform to freely express their views. During the first program, listeners from Tehran, Shiraz, and Kurdistan discussed sanctions and criticized the Iranian government for mismanaging the economy. In summer 2008, Radio Farda launched a new program devoted exclusively to women's issues. The weekly journal *The Other Voice*, investigated women's issues from theoretical and historical points of view, and analyzed current events related to women.

Radio Farda reaches significant audiences in Iran, in spite of the government's consistent jamming. Radio Farda has the highest weekly reach rate, 4.3 percent according to the January 2008 national telephone survey of Iran, of any international radio broadcaster, double that of the BBC's Persian service.

Radio Farda's website continued to show growth. The website has a variety of interactive features including Question of the Week , most popular and most emailed stories, Listeners Views , and "Farda Club for moderated discussions and blogs. It averaged close to 3 million page views each month, despite the Iranian government's efforts to block it. The regular use of online forums sparked lively discussion. Depending on the question of the week, the number of comments has exceeded 300. One of the more popular topics eliciting strong audience reaction and debate was Dutch producer Geert Wilders' disputed movie *Fitna* which is critical of Islam and the Koran. Farda received 420 audience comments in one week, mostly from inside Iran.

This year Farda also expanded its selection of popular Persian and western music, which draws in the younger audience. On a daily basis, Radio Farda receives anywhere from 50-500 messages. Many are listener comments on recent changes to Farda's music offering; some are listener comments with respect to a particular topic; and others are complaints about reception.

Afghanistan

RFE/RL's Radio Free Afghanistan has a weekly reach of 45.7 percent in the country, according to the most recent national survey conducted in August 2008, making it the number one radio station for news in Afghanistan. Afghanistan is the only country in the RFE/RL broadcast region where a U.S. government-funded broadcaster is the dominant media outlet.

Radio Free Afghanistan delivers breaking news, in-depth reporting, and analysis to the people of Afghanistan on the struggles their young democracy faces, including a resurgent Taliban. With its dual-language programming and its tone of moderation, Radio Free Afghanistan works to promote national unity and religious tolerance. In 2008, Radio Free Afghanistan covered an array of domestic, regional, and international news items, including corruption, capital punishment, increased kidnappings, ongoing reconstruction efforts, female education, the Beijing Olympics where an Afghan won the country's first Olympic medal (a bronze in Taekwondo), media freedom and government censorship; and the U.S. Presidential election and its meaning for Afghanistan.

Radio Free Afghanistan provided extensive coverage of the August 22 air strike by forces of the U.S.-led coalition in which more than 90 people in Herat province were allegedly killed. Radio Free Afghanistan was the first media outlet in the country to interview an eyewitness to the attack. Throughout October, Radio Free Afghanistan continued to cover the saga of journalist Sayed Perwiz Kambaksh, who was sentenced to death months ago for distributing an Internet article that questioned Islam's treatment of women. In November, Radio Free Afghanistan reported on an epidemic of kidnappings in the country. Taliban militants and unaffiliated armed gangs have kidnapped dozens of foreigners (as well as hundreds of Afghans) in the past five years. RFA also gained an exclusive, wide-ranging interview with Afghan President Hamid Karzai.

Radio Free Afghanistan not only maintained a close relationship and dialogue with its listeners, but it has had an impact on the country, reuniting families, providing basic health and hygiene information, and promoting change. It used the hundreds of letters it received from listeners to find stories that deserved attention.

Unfortunately, Radio Free Afghanistan faces an increasingly challenging security environment. Throughout the year, RFA journalists came under growing pressure and threats from elements most often associated with the Taliban. In fall 2008, two journalists were threatened with death and a third was kidnapped and then released.

VOA continued to rank as one of the top three international broadcasters in Afghanistan. As of September 2008, research indicated that 30.5 percent of Afghan adults were listening to or watching VOA programs at least once a week.

VOA's Afghanistan TV Broadcast *Ashna* devoted a portion of its presidential election coverage issues affecting Muslim American voters, such as the economy, the wars in Iraq and Afghanistan, and tensions in the Middle East. Correspondents interviewed Muslims at political rallies, and followed Afghan-Americans who volunteered for the Barack Obama campaign. The program also included interviews with prominent Muslim-American voices, including Representative Keith Ellison, and a profile of an Afghan-American family voting for the first time. The program also included an interview with First Lady Laura Bush on Afghanistan, and aired an original documentary on the Afghan drug trade.

VOA's Afghanistan radio focused on issues relating to Islam and human rights. Participants in live talk shows included Mawlawi Abdul Qadir and Aminudin Saeedi, leading Afghan Islamic scholars. VOA's radio programs also examined the Taliban policy of burning of schools and text books, focusing on the issue with leading Islamic scholars and Afghan analysts. Highlighted in the series were Dr. Alam Payind, head of the Middle East Department of the Ohio University and Raj Wali Khatak, a well-known Afghan author.

Pakistan

Media restrictions imposed by Musharraf in 2007 were eased and VOA Urdu Television went back on the air in April with its two private affiliates: GEO and Aaj. VOA's TV presence was further advanced when the Urdu Service joined with Pakistan's state broadcaster PTV, available to 90 percent of the population, for special live coverage of the three U.S. presidential debates.

VOA Urdu's 12/7 *Radio Aap ki Dunyaa* (*Your World*) daily program doubled its reach to Pakistan with a new, faster-paced news format.

---

16 On October 21, an Afghan court commuted the death sentence but ordered Kambaksh to spend 20 years in jail.

VOA also doubled traffic to the website: www. Urduvoa.com, which includes a polling function and runs contests to attract younger audiences.

VOA Urdu and PTV broadcast 14 hours of live TV coverage in Urdu and English on Election Night 2008, covering the historic election of Barack Obama as President. The PTV Chairman at the time said these broadcasts helped PTV dominate coverage among other private broadcasters and were well received in Pakistan's tribal areas.

A new programming venture was a new half-hour weekly television and web-based show, *Muslims'America*. The weekly 30-minute show, in English and Urdu, profiled American

Muslims in all walks of life, tackled myths and realities of American life, and focused on the subjects' positive contributions. Comments from viewers in Pakistan and elsewhere in the world were overwhelmingly positive about the first 12 episodes, which appeared on Pakistan's number one rated private cable news channel, Geo, as well as Aaj TV, VOA's Urdu website, YouTube, and Facebook.

In 2008, VOA Urdu attracted new audiences by creating an Urdu Service YouTube channel, providing content on Facebook, Veoh, and a blog for university-aged students in Pakistan. The blog is linked to a popular VOA Urdu TV. segment called *Campus*, which follows the experience of four VOA Urdu reporters who are also attending college in the United States.

The Pakistan/Afghanistan Border Region

VOA's Deewa Radio (Light), a broadcast stream aimed at the more than 40 million Pashto-speaking people living in the volatile Afghanistan-Pakistan border region, offered local, regional, U.S., and international news, as well as features on politics, illegal drug and narcotics trafficking, the economy, health, education, and sports. With a network of more than 20 stringers in the target region, the service covered the fast-moving developments on the ground, including recent military operations in the volatile Swat region and in North and South Waziristan.

Radio Deewa's two daily, live call-in shows attract about 300 calls a day, scores of e-mails, and voice messages. Program topics included suicide bombings, school burnings, and discussions of religious moderation. In addition, Deewa has interviewed current federal ministers, provincial ministers, NWFP officials, party leaders, members of parliament, and experts on regional politics such as Nawaz Sharif, the former prime minister. Deewa's audiences benefited from wide-ranging interviews with Islamic scholars, human rights activists, members of the U.S. Congress, State Department officials, and regional experts.

India. VOA Hindi TV, with a broadcast affiliation with India's Zee TV, reached the country's large Muslim population of nearly 150 million. The Hindi Service presented discussions about events in Pakistan and Kashmir, India-Pakistan peace initiatives, Iran's nuclear ambitions, developments in Afghanistan, and the Iraq war. Hindi TV broadcast five days a week via Zee TV, offering exclusive interviews with U.S. government senior officials, Muslim-American leaders and scholars, and provided extensive coverage of the Mumbai attacks, other major developments in the region, and India's relations with Iran, Pakistan, and the United States. VOA's Hindi radio broadcasts ended on September 30, 2008.

Bangladesh. Bangladesh has one of the largest Muslim populations in the world. During the past year, VOA Bangla produced numerous radio and television features on Muslim youth, Islamic centers in the United States, and other topics of interest. In addition, the Service broadcast call-in shows on Muslim celebrations in the U.S at the end of the fast of Ramadan. VOA Bangla Service also conducted many interviews with U.S. officials and experts, and provided comprehensive coverage of elections in the U.S. and Bangladesh.

Turkish. Throughout 2008, VOA's Turkish Service focused on the role of Islam in politics under the strictly secular Turkish constitution. Coverage included Turkey's mediation efforts between Syria and Israel and relations with the United States and Iran. Interviews included U.S. and Turkish officials, President Abdullah Gul, members of the United States Congress, and other experts. In addition to its extensive multimedia coverage of the U.S. presidential elections, VOA Turkish prepared programs and reports on the role of religion in the U.S. for radio, television, and the Internet.

This year, VOA Turkish expanded its TV affiliation in Turkey by launching daily, live webcam reports for the TGRT News TV network. TGRT News, a 24-hour nationwide news network with a weekly audience share of over 30 percent of Turkey's estimated 25 million regular viewers, carried a live 15-minute VOA Turkish news and current affairs program three times a week, in addition to a weekly VOA 30-minute news and magazine program. At the request of TGRT, VOA also produced a number of live and special programs on the U.S. presidential elections.

Indonesia. VOA's weekly audience in Indonesia increased in 2008 to 17.5 percent, or more than 25 million people, because of the placement of short program segments on popular local television stations. VOA Indonesian TV products can now be regularly seen on seven of Indonesia's 11 national TV stations, in addition to more than 20 local and regional stations. During the fasting month of Ramadan, VOA produced a special series of 12 stories on Islam in the United States, which were carried by national stations. VOA Indonesian also produced eight hours daily of original radio programming for a network of more than 230 affiliate FM and medium wave stations across the country. Radio programming included five-minute *Headline News* reports, which were aired 32 times a day, seven days a week.

Central Asia

BBG's programming to Central Asia–RFE/RL to Uzbekistan, Turkmenistan, Tajikistan, Kazakhstan, and Kyrgyzstan; VOA to Uzbekistan–continued despite increased harassment and repression against its correspondents and editors and new challenges to delivering programs to audiences.

Uzbekistan. Uzbek authorities stepped up its attacks on RFE/RL's Uzbek Service in June when state-owned television accused RFE/RL journalists of "anti-state activities" and broadcast personal information about them, including the names of their children and other family members, photographs, passport information, addresses, and places of work. Operating in conditions reminiscent of the Soviet era, RFE/RL's Uzbek Service continued to provide news coverage and democracy promotion.

VOA's daily 30-minute radio broadcasts were carried on shortwave and medium wave from Tajikistan. In 2008, under pressure from the government of Uzbekistan, the Kyrgyz government banned two FM stations in Osh and Jalalabad, Kyrgyzstan, from rebroadcasting VOA Uzbek programs. Under similar pressures, Ayna TV, the VOA Uzbek affiliate in neighboring Afghanistan stopped broadcasting the weekly VOA Uzbek TV program, *Exploring America.* Currently, this program is carried by Keremet TV in Osh, Kyrgyzstan, where a large ethnic Uzbek community lives. Some viewers in Uzbekistan's Ferghana Valley region were able to watch this broadcast. VOA Uzbek featured interviews with various U.S. and international sources discussing critical issues, such as the fight against terrorism, religious extremism, and U.S.-Uzbek relations. Interviews with Members of Congress and key officials provided a unique perspective on U.S. policymaking. The Service also featured reporting on Muslim life in the United States and served as a window into religious tolerance and understanding in America. In order to expand VOA's reach, the Uzbek Service launched *uzmobil.com,* distributing VOA news to mobile phone subscribers in Uzbekistan, the largest Muslim country in former Soviet Central Asia.

Tajikistan. In Tajikistan, RFE/RL's Tajik-language Service Radio Ozodi is the largest independent media outlet in the country and top international broadcaster. The Tajik government has repeatedly expressed its dissatisfaction with RFE/RL's coverage of local political, economic, and social issues. The Service's website has become one of the best content-oriented Tajik-language sites. Ozodi forum and Ozodi polling were popular among users and attracted hundreds of comments.

Kyrgyzstan. RFE/RL's popular Kyrgyz-language Service was dealt a major setback when state authorities pulled the plug on RFE/RL radio and TV programming in October 2008. Kyrgyz authorities have stated that RFE/RL's Kyrgyz Service will not be restored to the airwaves unless its programs are submitted to the government for prior approval. According to the most recent national survey, the Service's unduplicated weekly reach on radio and TV was 33.8% of the population.

Kazakhstan. As of September 1, 2008, RFE/RL's Kazakh Service transitioned to an Internet platform, continuing radio programming for one hour in the evening and one hour repeat in the morning. The Kazakh Service launched a bilingual (Kazakh and Russian) site in summer 2008. Within the first month, visits increased by 270 %; page views were up by 540% and average time spent on site grew by almost 300%. The Service received two national Internet awards from Award.kz for best Kazakh-language site and best new media site. The competition was independent and involved over 1,000 websites.

Turkmenistan. RFE/RL, which is barred from having a bureau and accredited domestic correspondents, reported on government harassment of civil society and independent journalists in the run up to the country's Parliamentary election.

Balkans and Caucasus

Bosnia and Herzegovina. VOA broadcasts to Bosnia and Herzegovina included programming targeted to the half of the population that are Bosnian Muslims. VOA's Bosnian Service broadcasts a 30-minute live, daily news and current affairs television show, which is tailored to address concerns of the Muslim population in Bosnia and provides exclusive interviews with Bosnian politicians and moderate Muslim religious leaders. VOA Bosnian programs explain U.S. policy on topics such as counterterrorism, and focus on a variety of Bosnian issues, including the dangers radical Islamic groups pose to the country. In addition, the Service produces a weekly interactive TV program that airs Sundays during a prime time news program on BHT1, Bosnia's public broadcaster. The Sarajevo-based BHT1 network is internationally funded and is the only station that reaches audiences in both the Bosnian-Croat Federation and Republika Srpska. VOA's programs are also aired by 15 television affiliate stations throughout Bosnia, and are available via satellite. The Bosnian Service is also working to significantly enhance the content, functionality, and design of its website to complement its popular TV broadcasts.

RFE/RL's South Slàvic and Albanian Languages Service continued to fulfill a unique role in the Balkans with its regional programming. With bureaus in Belgrade and Pristina, the Service provided extensive coverage of events and analysis surrounding Kosovo independence and its impact in the region and beyond. Programming stressing the bonds among the peoples of the former Yugoslavia regularly reached Muslim listeners in Kosovo and Bosnia and Herzegovina. The Service broadcast two popular thirty-minute television programs in Bosnia, *TV Liberty* and *Open Parliament*.

Azerbaijan. VOA's Azerbaijani Service provided extensive coverage on Muslims in America, including special programs on the occasion of Muslim holidays, with messages of congratulation by the President of the United States, Administration officials, and Congressional leaders. The Azerbaijani broadcasts of VOA and RFE/RL reached radio audiences in and around Baku, the capital, via a local 24/7 dedicated FM frequency.

The Russian Federation

Tatarstan/Bashkortostan. RFE/RL's Radio Azatliq is the only major international broadcaster in the Tatar and Bashkir languages, providing listeners with objective news and information not available from Russian media. The Service's newly designed website, launched in November 2007, has shown steady growth. Since May 2008, page views increased by 70 percent.

North Caucasus. The North Caucasus remained politically unstable. Thus, the media environments were limited, with few sources of independent news and information available in the region, regardless of language. RFE/RL remained the only international broadcaster providing content targeted at the region in three local languages, Avar, Chechen, and Circassian.

Africa

Nigeria. VOA has strong audiences in Nigeria, Africa's most populous nation with about 73 million Muslims. The Hausa and the English-to-Africa services have a weekly audience of 21 million. Some 47 percent of the Hausa-speaking population of Nigeria listen to VOA at least once a week. The Hausa service, aimed primarily at the country's Northern region, covered violent clashes between Muslims and Christians in the northern state of Jos that broke out after local elections in late November 2008. VOA's coverage included on-the-scene stringer reports, and interviews with witnesses, victims, and Nigerian government and security officials. The Service provided extensive analysis of the sectarian conflict, interviewed religious and ethnic leaders who appealed for calm, interviewed the governor, and organized a panel discussion with members of opposing factions.

In October 2008, VOA staff traveled to northern Nigeria to organize and cover Town Hall meetings in Kaduna and Bauch, which attracted more than 4,000 people. The meetings, which focused on health issues, were covered by, among others, the Nigerian Television Authority's national network, BBC, Deutsche Welle, Radio France International, and four Nigerian national dailies.

Somalia. In its second year of broadcasting, VOA's Somali Service covered the continuing conflict in Somalia and efforts to find a negotiated peace agreement between the transitional government and an Islamic insurgency. Research in 2008 showed that more than 66 percent of adults in Mogadishu listened to VOA. The service also covered the growing threat of piracy off the coast of Somalia. The VOA Somali Service spoke with all protagonists of a political crisis that resulted in the resignation of Somali President Abdullahi Yusuf on December 29. Interviews included Mr. Yusuf; Prime Minister Nur Hassan Hussein, who had opposed the president over the naming of a cabinet; Sheikh Sharif Sheikh Ahmed, head of the Somali opposition group Alliance of Re-Liberation of Somalia (ARS); and House Speaker Sheikh Aden Mohamed Nur, Somalia's current Acting President. The Service also spoke with Senator Russ Feingold, Chairman of the Senate Foreign Relations Subcommittee on African Affairs, during the lawmaker's visit to Djibouti on December 13.

Ethiopia and Eritrea. VOA's Horn of Africa Service broadcasts 17 hours a week in the evenings in three languages: seven 60-minute broadcasts in Amharic, five 30-minute broadcasts in Tigrigna and five 30-minute broadcasts in Afan Oromo. These VOA broadcasts provided uncensored reporting of ethnic clashes and conflict resolution.

Swahili. VOA's Swahili Service has strong listenership in Tanzania and Kenya. VOA's audience is more than 23 percent of adults in Tanzania. On March 16, 2008, VOA Swahili expanded its broadcasts to two hours each weekday, and one hour on Saturdays and Sundays. In 2008, there was a huge demand for news and information about the U.S. election.

French to Africa. VOA's French to Africa Service broadcasts 23 hours weekly on radio via shortwave and to an array of affiliates across the region to the 250 million French speakers in Africa, many of whom live in predominantly Muslim countries such as Senegal, Mali, Burkina Faso, Niger, and Chad. It also broadcasts a 30-minute weekly television program.

China

Radio Free Asia (RFA) provided service to Muslim audiences through its Uyghur language service launched in December 1998. It is the only international radio service providing impartial news and information in the Uyghur language to the potential audience of more than 16 million Uyghur Muslims in Western China and Central Eurasia. The Xinjiang Uyghur Autonomous Region (XUAR) alone comprises roughly one-sixth of China's territory and is estimated to have more than 10 million Uyghur speakers.

Consistent with RFA's mandate, the Uyghur service acts as a substitute for indigenous media reporting on local events in the region. The service broadcasts two hours daily, seven days a week, often breaking stories that go unreported by China's state-run media or foreign news organizations. RFA provided a forum for a variety of opinions and voices from within the XUAR with its programs that included breaking news, analysis, interviews, commentary, a hotline call-in show, a weekly news review, and feature stories.

The Uyghur Service news and stories featured important interviews with various U.S. and international sources, including officials, scholars, scientists, artists, historians, educators, and human rights activists, as well as Chinese and Uyghur dissidents from all over the world. Programs addressed pressing issues like China's relationship with Central Asian countries, democratic development in Central Asia, Uyghur history, literature, the arts, human rights, religious freedom, labor issues, official corruption, the environment, Internet control in China, and AIDS and other health issues. Additionally, RFA brings U.S. policy, debate, and Congressional resolutions on China to its listeners via interviews with members of Congress and other policymakers. This past year, the RFA Uyghur service was the first to report on the executions of two Uyghurs accused of terrorism, broke the news of an impending forced abortion in Gulja, and chronicled the systematic tightening of Uyghur political and religious activities in the lead up to the 2008 Beijing Olympics. These stories, among many more, were picked up by the *New York Times, Time Magazine*, ABC News, AP, Reuters, and other international media outlets.

RFA's Uyghur service website, launched in September 2004, provides continuously updated news in all three writing systems used to convey the Uyghur language: Arabic, Latin, and Cyrillic. RFA's site is the only non-Chinese Uyghur news website and the only Unicode Uyghur news website. The site streams the daily RFA broadcast in Uyghur and offers ongoing coverage of events in the XUAR in text, image, and video. The archived audio files can be retrieved on a special page or downloaded via podcast. RSS feeds are also available, making it possible for people to automatically update their news readers or web pages with RFA news content.

RFA continued to be confronted with continuous jamming of broadcasts and blocking of its website. RFA confronts Chinese censorship by broadcasting on multiple short-wave frequencies and by regularly e-mailing instructions on accessing the banned www.rfa.org through proxy web servers. Despite Chinese censorship, research indicates that Uyghur listeners and web users consider RFA a lifeline in a controlled media environment, a station offering unique content worth taking risks to access. The Uyghur Service received the 2005 Edward R. Murrow Regional Award for outstanding achievements in electronic journalism.

Transmission. Since September 11, 2001, the Broadcasting Board of Governors (BBG) has modernized its transmission capabilities, continuing its move from a predominantly shortwave environment to one that uses AM, FM, satellite, and Internet capabilities to reach its audience. By bolstering transmission capabilities to the Muslim world, BBG has improved opportunities to deliver news and information clearly, reliably, and effectively. New transmission capabilities have been added, and assets reallocated from regions of lesser geopolitical importance and from technologies of declining effectiveness. The BBG has worked to ensure that programming is delivered in the media that are most effective in reaching local populations. In the past year, shortwave transmission facilities in Morocco were closed to shift available resources to more effective delivery media. An emergency back-up power system was installed at the Kabul medium wave transmitting facility to overcome erratic local electricity supply problems and to ensure more reliable delivery of BBG medium wave programs to audiences in Afghanistan. Backup generators were also being installed at BBG FM stations in Afghanistan. In the past year, a new BBG TV transmitter and two new BBG FM transmitter systems came on the air in cities in Iraq. Arrangements were being made to establish FM transmitters in Somalia at Hargeysa and on cell phone towers at other key locations in the country. Shortwave transmissions were added to support a new half hour news and information program in Arabic for audiences in Sudan. Arrangements were being made with the Government of Kuwait to share shortwave transmitters, and ongoing meetings with the Directors General of various other international broadcasters are leading to other economical arrangements to share transmission resources. At year's end, the BBG was supporting the construction of a number of additional FM transmitters in various locations and two high power medium wave radio transmitters that should come on the air in the coming year: one medium wave transmitter for Pashto programming in Afghanistan was nearing completion, and one for Radio Farda programs to Iran was under construction.

Any recommendations the President may have for additional funding and legislation necessary to achieve the objectives of the strategy?

The President's budget request for FY-2009 includes funding for a number of initiatives that support outreach to Muslim audiences. These initiatives include a signature three-hour daily program to provide additional information about American policies, people, institutions, and perspectives to its audiences across 22 countries in the Middle East; increasing Alhurra's newscast capability to 24 hours a day (from the current 16 hour capability), and enhancing Radio Sawa's coverage of the region. The FY-2009 budget also continues VOA's Somalia three hour program stream, maintains program strength in Iran, Afghanistan, and Pakistan, launches a new RFE/RL Azerbaijani to Iran broadcast, and supports significant enhancement to Internet efforts in several key languages, including Russian and Persian. These initiatives are critical to the continued outreach to Muslim audiences.

Further, the BBG's current authority for personal services contracting (PSC) for up to 60 PSCs at any given time, has assisted the agency in staffing broadcast services experiencing a surge in broadcast requirements, or which are operated pursuant to a grant from USAID. This authority has been extended by the Congress on an annual basis.

Presenting the United States Point of View through Indigenous Broadcast Media

At the Department of State, the Bureau of Public Affairs, Office of Broadcast Services uses television and video products as strategic tools for bringing America's foreign policy message to Middle East and worldwide audiences. A state-of-the-art digital broadcast television facility enables the Department to deliver messages instantly, using the same technology as commercial broadcast television networks. Public Affairs facilitates live and taped interviews with the Secretary of State and other State Department principals to all the major Arab networks such as Middle East Broadcasting Corporation (MBC), Al Arabiya, Al Iraqiya, Abu Dhabi TV, Dubai Television, Arab Radio and Television Network (ART), Alhurra, Kuwait TV, Egyptian TV (ETV), and the Lebanese Broadcasting Corporation (LBC). This investment in people and technology was developed to give senior USG officials an opportunity to engage and inform the largest audiences possible about our foreign policy and public diplomacy objectives.

The Bureau of Public Affairs Office of Broadcast Services also works with broadcast industry recognized, internet-based news clip service providers to extend the reach and placement of U.S. government officials. These vendors, thenewsmarket.com and Pathfire, have thousands of servers in newsrooms all over the world, that enable broadcasters to quickly receive and re-purpose video footage of State Department ceremonies and remarks by officials presenting foreign policy positions and representing democratic principles.

To enhance the capacity of the U.S. Embassy in Iraq, the Department of State operates a television studio inside the Embassy. This fully-functioning studio allows senior U.S. government officials to conduct live interviews via satellite with national and international media on a range of topics related to the current situation and future of Iraq, as well as America's role in the broader Middle East.

The Bureau of Near Eastern Affairs, Press & Public Diplomacy Office, through its Middle Eastern Press Unit, has significantly expanded the Department's outreach to Arabic, Hebrew, and Persian media outlets (print, broadcast, and Internet) through a strategy of proactive engagement. Since its creation, it has recorded an ever-increasing number of interviews with Arab and regional media outlets. In 2008, the Middle Eastern Press Unit, together with NEA posts, gave over 1,500 interviews, up 25% from 2007. Many of the broadcasts aired multiple times and were picked up by other regional media outlets and wire services. The outreach to new media has also increased in an effort to reach regional audiences directly. The Arabic language web chats have continued allowing Arab audiences to interact directly with USG policy makers on topics such as, What is a Provincial Reconstruction Team (PRT), Muslims and Political Participation in the United States, and Solving the Western Sahara Dilemma.

This capacity was further enhanced by the Office of the Under Secretary for Public Diplomacy and Public Affairs' creation of Regional Media Hubs in London, Brussels, and Dubai. In these key media markets, spokesmen advocate U.S. policies and actively encourage and facilitate a growing number of USG officials to appear on important Arabic, European, and other international media. For example, between November 2007 and November 2008, the Dubai Hub Director and Deputy Director participated in 273 on-air interviews, talk shows, and panel discussions (most in Arabic) with Arab broadcast media, including Al Jazeera, Al Arabiya, MBC 1, LBC, Al Hurra, Sharqiyya, Nile TV, BBC Arabic, Radio Sawa, Sawt al Arab, and a number of smaller local and regional stations. Major engagements included the Annapolis Conference on Middle East Peace in November 2007, where the Dubai Hub Director was live on-air all day with various pan-Arab outlets; the March 2008 fifth anniversary of the war in Iraq, with USG officials conducting 49 interviews with Arab outlets that month on that topic; and the November 2008 U.S. elections, with 62 interviews by various USG officials on Arab outlets that month. The

London Hub and domestic office have also increased efforts this year to reach Iranian audiences through increased engagement with BBC Persian, VOA Persian, and Radio Farda. The London Hub also continued to produce a weekday morning report on the pan-Arab media for readers throughout the USG, matched by the Brussels' Hub morning report on key European media.

The State Department's Rapid Response Unit (RRU) monitors all major stories in world media, with additional focus on Arabic electronic and internet media, in real time. It produces a daily, early morning report for internal U.S. government use that analyses opinion trends on foreign policy issues of key importance to the U.S. and provides appropriate messaging that explains U.S. positions on those issues. The report is delivered by LISTSERV to U.S. officials, including cabinet secretaries, ambassadors, heads of military commands, public affairs officers, and others. The RRU provides other analysis and regional media compilations for U.S. officials.

Presenting the U.S. Point of View through Internet-based Media

The Department of State directly engages participants in online discussion forums on the Internet through the Digital Outreach Team. The Team participates in discussions of policy issues and related developments on websites in Arabic, Persian, and Urdu. Openly representing the State Department, but using the more informal language of the discussion forums, the Team seeks to ensure that the U.S. perspective is heard in cyberspace, providing a counterpoint to anti-U.S. rhetoric and misinformation. Other public diplomacy efforts of the Department of State and other agencies targeted at countering extremist use of the Internet are coordinated with the Global Strategic Engagement Center, an interagency organization that is staffed with personnel from the State Department, the Department of Defense, the National Counterterrorism Council, and the Intelligence Community and that is housed at the State Department in order to support the Under Secretary for Public Diplomacy and Public Affairs with interagency coordination and subject matter expertise.

The Department has expanded its web presence via the State.gov website and the America.gov website in English, Arabic, Russian, Persian, French, and Spanish.

The introduction of multimedia interactive products such as ads, videos, podcasts, web chats, blogging, and other interactive elements widen audience participation. Country-specific websites run by our Embassies overseas provide a wide range of information and advocate U.S. policies to foreign audiences.

In the absence of a U.S. embassy in Iran, the Bureau of International Information Programs manages a Persian-language website directing policy and general information into Iran. The website supports active engagement via web chats, webcasts, and listservs to connect U.S. policymakers and subject-matter experts with Iranian citizens. IIP's Arabic-language website provides information about U.S. policies, society, and values directly to audiences in the Middle East.

Presenting the U.S. Point of View through U.S. Missions in the Field

The Strategic Speakers Initiative (SSI) identifies, recruits, and programs prominent U.S. experts to engage foreign opinion leaders on key strategic themes such as Islam in America, democracy and Islam, rule of law, violent extremism and security, energy, the environment, and trade and development. The Citizen Dialogue Program, allows Muslim-American citizens from different fields to share their personal stories in strategically important countries. Many audiences are not aware of the strength and diversity of Islam in America. Strategic Speaker participants are often part of a bigger public diplomacy package that includes web chats, direct video conferences, and other outreach.

IIP's INFOCENTRAL website provides guidance and background information on U.S. policy priorities to U.S. embassies and military commands worldwide.

Major Themes of Biased or False Media Coverage of the United States in Foreign Countries and Actions Taken to Address this Type of Media Coverage.

The Department of State is taking a leading role to counter misinformation and falsehoods about the United States and its policies or intentions. The Department of State's actions to address these false allegations include:

- The Department of State's America.gov webpage entitled "Identifying Misinformation," which appears in English and Arabic, provides truthful information and analysis to the public to debunk false allegations about Iraq and other issues.
- The Department has instructed spokespeople in Washington and Public Affairs Officers at our embassies around the world to use information on the website to counter false stories in the local media, or to contact the Department's Counter-Misinformation Officer, who can rapidly provide research and guidance.

Potential incentives for and costs associated with encouraging U.S. broadcasters to dub or subtitle into Arabic and other relevant languages their news and public affairs programs broadcast to Muslim communities in order to present those programs to a much broader Muslim audience than is currently reached.

The single greatest incentive for U.S. broadcasters to dub or subtitle their news and public affairs programs would be evidence that there is adequate demand for the programming among the targeted foreign publics. The Office of the Under Secretary for Public Diplomacy and Public Affairs is working with the Bureau of Public Affairs and other elements within the Department to explore avenues to demonstrate that a potentially profitable market exists for this programming. If data emerges that indicates that this translation makes sense from a business standpoint, we will present this data to broadcasters in an effort to encourage this activity.

VISAS FOR PARTICIPANTS IN U.S. GOVERNMENT PROGRAMS

According to the State Department's Bureau of Consular Affairs, current visa processing guidelines are sufficient to meet any requirements for the issuance of appropriate visas to individuals from predominantly Muslim nations to participate in any new exchange program, as envisioned by the Intelligence Reform and Terrorism Protection Act of 2004.

The Bureau of Consular Affairs' policy is to expedite all student and exchange visitor applications, with the goal of giving every student and exchange visitor applicant the opportunity to meet their program start date in the United States, providing the individual is admissible. This policy is in place at every embassy and consulate worldwide. In countries with a significant waiting period for a visa appointment due to high demand, this policy reduces the wait time for students and exchange visitors from weeks to mere days. In all cases requiring a separate administrative processing, the average processing time is now about 60 to 90 days. Processing can take longer, however, and applicants should allow additional time. Administrative processing can only be expedited when circumstances involve significant USG interests or life and death situations.

The most important factor in expediting visa applications is for the applicants, in conjunction with their program sponsors, to initiate their visa applications well in advance of their planned travel. New exchange programs should be planned far enough in advance to allow the necessary time for visa processing. Candidates should be advised to obtain passports immediately, visit embassy websites for instructions on applying for U.S. visas, and ensure they follow instructions concerning required documents and procedures, as well as for information on how to complete a visa application and how to arrange an appointment.

Economic Reform

High unemployment and underemployment, often a result of slow economic growth, are among the most critical issues in predominantly Muslim countries. U.S. assistance programs attempt to address this issue with reforms to improve the investment climate. Such reforms could include business registration, dispute settlement, financial sector and agricultural reforms, combined with education, job training, and health programs.

The U.S. strategy of Total Economic Engagement pursues economic reform, rule of law, and global economic integration, in countries with predominantly Muslim populations. Total Economic Engagement includes:

- Regular bilateral discussions on these topics with host government officials, with both U.S. Embassy officials and officials from a wide range of U.S. agencies participating;
- Formal structured dialogues, high-level Economic Dialogues, and Trade and Investment Framework Agreement (TIFA) Councils;
- U.S. bilateral and multilateral assistance programs for economic reform, trade capacity-building, and rule of law managed chiefly through USAID, the Millennium Challenge Corporation (MCC), and the State Department's Middle East Partnership Initiative (MEPI). Programs are often complemented with technical assistance provided by specialized U.S. agencies and offices;
- Coordinated multilateral policies and assistance strategies to advance reform goals by working with such international organizations as the International Monetary Fund, the World Bank, the World Trade Organization, and OECD (MENA-OECD Investment), and other multilateral donors; and
- Working with NGOs, such as Transparency International, and U.S. and foreign business associations, such as American Chambers of Commerce and Business Councils, to advance reform issues of mutual concern.

Integrating Predominantly Muslim Countries into the Global Trading System

There are a number of U.S. government-funded programs to promote predominantly Muslim countries' integration into the global trading system. The following table lists U.S. government funding for trade and capacity-building programs in these countries.

USG Funding for Trade and Capacity-building[17]	
Country	USG FY-2008 Funding
Afghanistan	12,621,961
Bangladesh	773,297
Egypt	17,229,944
Indonesia	13,442,029
Iraq	6,935,264
Jordan	11,271,667
Lebanon	0
Morocco	534,925,762[18]
Pakistan	836,400
West Bank/Gaza	18,267,194
Yemen	3,955,000

World Trade Organization (WTO) Awareness and Accession. USAID programs with components dealing with WTO awareness, accession, and compliance are being implemented in the following countries:

- **Afghanistan.** Since 2003, USAID has been contributing to a thriving and growing economy through private sector strengthening activities and the creation of an enabling environment for trade and business.
  - o The Economic Growth and Private Sector Strengthening Project supports the development of sound economic governance across economic ministries and agencies of the Government of Afghanistan.
  - o In the area of **customs administration reform**, USAID supported the development and implementation of a modern Customs code, refurbishment of Customs facilities at key border crossings, and Afghanistan's observer status in the World Customs Organization (WCO).
  - o In the area of **trade development**, USAID has trained government officials in trade policy. In August, it supported

[17]For further information, see the Trade Capacity Building Database at: http://qesdb.usaid.gov/tcb/

[18]Figure includes $532 million of the $697.5 million (total) Millennium Challenge Compact, which will be spent over a five year period beginning in FY2009.

Afghanistan to participate in negotiations to sign onto the South Asia Free Trade Agreement (SAFTA). It also supported public education on free trade and provided assistance to draft Afghanistan's Memorandum of Foreign Trade Regime (MFTR), to be submitted to the WTO in the coming months as a first step toward WTO accession.

- **Indonesia.** The Trade Assistance Project focuses on legal support, economic research, public outreach, organizational development, information technology, and WTO awareness and agreements. The objective is to improve the Ministry of Trade's capacity to analyze and implement trade reforms that will lead to increased exports and a more attractive investment climate.
- **Iraq.** The Trade Policy and Market Access Support Project provides technical assistance to the Government of Iraq on legal, procedural, and practical matters pertaining to Iraq's bid to join the WTO. This includes technical assistance in completing key accession-relation documentation, in particular agriculture, sanitary and phyto-sanitary, technical barriers to trade, intellectual property, and modifications and updates as WTO-related regulatory reforms progress.
- **Jordan:** WTO Accession in 2000 set off numerous successful trade reforms and market liberalization efforts. Current compliance issues are being addressed with a focus on Intellectual Property Rights.
- **Lebanon:** Since 2000, the USG has been funding technical assistance to the Government of Lebanon to help it achieve full integration into the world economy and the multilateral trading system through securing membership in the World Trade Organization (WTO). As part of the U.S. government effort, Lebanon is working to meet WTO accession requirements. Working directly with the Lebanese Ministry of Economy and Trade USAID/Middle East Partnership Initiative (MEPI) has provided the necessary technical assistance, guidance, and structure to facilitate the advancement of Lebanon through the accession process. This assistance has also brought in the private sector into the dialogue creating a firmer basis for economic development and stability. With 12 years being the average length of accession, Lebanon is well on track and within the normal range to achieve membership. During a time of civil strife, this process has remained on track despite the numerous political challenges.

- **Yemen:** In conjunction with funding from the USAID Mission in Yemen and additional support from the Middle East Partnership Initiative (MEPI), the FASTrade project has been active in supporting a number of customs reform efforts, working primarily with the Yemen Customs Authority (YCA). In 2005, a comprehensive initiative to assist YCA with the implementation of the WTO Valuation Agreement and related reforms was initiated. Over several months time, legal assistance was provided to prepare and recommend a valuation law that would be fully compliant with the WTO Agreement on Customs Valuation. In addition, training on WTO valuation procedures was provided to Customs officials at each of three principal field offices and in the Headquarters in Yemen's capital, Sanaa. Yemen's periodic security situation resulted in numerous delays with the provision of further technical assistance. However, by 2007, a team of FASTrade advisors were mobilized to Yemen to carry out extensive training for YCA officials on risk management issues. Extensive preparatory work of appropriate training materials was carried out in the United States after which the team traveled to Yemen to provide both classroom and field training on risk management techniques to enable Yemen to meet best international practices for applying risk management principles in a customs administration. These best practices are consistent with the WCO SAFE Standards and also utilize the application of the Automated System for Customs Data Selectivity Module to target shipments at risk for high revenue loss or otherwise incorrect declarations.

USAID Global Export Promotion Programs. USAID global export promotion programs include Afghanistan, Bangladesh, Indonesia, and Pakistan:

- **Afghanistan.** The Afghanistan Small Medium Enterprise Development (ASMED) Project supports the development of the Afghan private sector by addressing non-governmental barriers to enterprise development. Key activities include improving access to market information through market-sector studies, strengthening internal capacity of business associations to lay the groundwork for future advocacy, a youth internship placement program, an innovative grants program to support global development alliances, technical assistance, market-place development in post-kinetic areas, value chain improvements, participation in trade fair and trade missions, and training for firms and business service providers.

- **Bangladesh.** The Shrimp Quality Support Project focuses on improving the quality and quantity of shrimp exports by Bangladesh in socially and environmentally acceptable ways by transferring appropriate applied research to farmers.
- **Indonesia.** The Enterprise and Agribusiness Development Activity supports the competitiveness of labor-intensive manufacturing industries, including footwear, furniture, auto parts, garments, home accessories, and information and communications technology. Competitiveness is strengthened by strengthening industry value chains, improving business skills, such as export readiness; and developing new industry-based standards to improve product quality and access to markets.
- **Pakistan.** The Initiative for Strategic Development and Competitiveness provides technical assistance and training to increase the competitiveness of Pakistani small and medium-sized enterprises. The project works with a number of sectors, including gems, jewelry, dairy, marble, horticulture, and furniture to improve their capacity to market and export their products. The project has formed six strategic working groups to develop sector-specific strategies aimed at upgrading production and improving marketing and trade.

Customs Reforms. Customs reforms are supported by USAID programs in Egypt and Afghanistan.

USAID Africa Bureau Programs. Programs managed within the USAID Africa Bureau include Sub-Saharan integration into the global trading system, the driving forces of which are the African Growth and Opportunity Act and the African Global Competitiveness Initiative. Program efforts are focused on helping countries build a sound enabling environment including policies, laws, and regulations governing business and trade; improving infrastructure to facilitate trade; strengthening financial services to small and medium-sized enterprises and other businesses; and developing the energy sector to meet the needs of growing African economies.

USAID Asia Bureau Programs:

Central Asia Region. The Regional Trade Liberalization and Customs Project has been operating in Kazakhstan, the Kyrgyz Republic, and Tajikistan since July 2007. The project seeks to help host governments and the private sector capitalize on the advantages of greater regional and global economic integration, by providing assistance and training to improve conditions for international and cross-border trade and transit. Support includes advice on: simplification of tariffs, preferences, and pre-export barriers; World Trade Organization accession or improved compliance with obligations; customs procedures to reduce delays and costs to traders; efficiency of transport and transit for goods and traders; and private sector access to market information.

The Business Environment Improvement Project was launched for Kazakhstan, the Kyrgyz Republic, and Tajikistan in October 2006. This program supports the streamlining of legal and regulatory processes and facilitates multi-party engagement to improve the business, trade, and legal environment.

The Central Asia Infrastructure Integration Initiative, under the Regional Electricity Market Assistance Project, helps to establish a transparent and competitive regional electricity market to increase regional electricity trade, stimulate economic growth, and provide market-based solutions for regional disputes related to hydro facilities and reservoirs.

USAID supports the U.S.-Central Asia Republics Trade and Investment Framework Agreement to help foster increased regional trade through reduced transaction costs for businesses through streamlining of border-crossing procedures and increasing information.

Kazakhstan. The Regional Trade Liberalization and Customs Project provides analysis and recommendations on World Trade Organization (WTO)-compliant laws and regulations, including technical regulations, amendments to the Customs Code, veterinary, food safety and phyto-sanitary controls; and copyright, trademarks, patents, and trade-related intellectual property rights. Training is provided for WTO-compliant implementation for proposed food safety reforms; implementation of the Customs Valuation Agreement; and calculation of aggregate measures of support in agriculture. Support to Customs modernization includes analysis of Integrated Border Management issues, assessing status and capacity building on risk management. Activities to improve trade and transit include legal analysis and advice on recommendations for a Single Window system for pre-customs clearance, which is designed to streamline required paperwork and reform the import and export licensing system. The Kazakhstan Small Business Development Project, funded in October 2006, aims to promote the development of small business.

Kyrgyz Republic. The Regional Trade Liberalization and Customs Project provides support to the World Trade Organization (WTO) Department within the Kyrgyz Ministry of Economic Development and Trade (MEDT). Among its goals are to strengthen MEDT's technical capacity in legal and regulatory processes to meet outstanding WTO compliance obligations, including technical regulations and protection of trade-related intellectual property rights. Training is conducted on requirements of accession to the WTO Government Procurement Agreement and on improved implementation of the Customs Valuation Agreement. Assistance on trade facilitation includes assessment of the Customs risk management system, developing draft instructions on the interaction of state control bodies for border-crossing points, and expert advice on simplification of export and import procedures and documentation.

Tajikistan. The Regional Trade Liberalization and Customs Project works directly with the Tajik government to prepare it to meet its World Trade Organization (WTO) commitments by revising and updating legislation to bring trade-related legislation into conformity with the provisions of WTO Agreements, currently focusing on sanitary and phyto-sanitary standards, veterinary surveillance, technical regulations, trade related intellectual property rights protection, and customs valuation. Trade facilitation work focuses on improving customs procedures and border transit management, including assessment and recommendations for the Customs risk management system, advising on amendments to the Customs Code to bring it fully in line with the Customs Valuation Agreement; providing expert recommendations on simplification of export and import procedures and documentation; and on measures to increase efficiency of trade management, such as bonded warehouses and expedited border-crossing procedures. Fiscal reform projects focus on reducing regional disparities by increasing the effectiveness of local tax administration and increasing the capacity of local governments to develop and execute budgets.

Turkmenistan. USAID works to foster trade advisory services and implement International Financial Reporting Standards in Turkmenistan.

USAID Europe and Eurasia Bureau Programs

Albania. The objective in Albania is to strengthen its integration into the Euro-Atlantic community and promote its contribution to integration of ethnic groups in the region. USAID worked with the Albanian government to improve the business climate for private sector growth and investment, and to improve private sector competitiveness to meet international export requirements. The Albanian Center for International Trade, founded in 2003, assists the Government of Albania to improve the quality of its trade policies. The Enterprise Development and Export Market Services Project, which ran through September 2008, promoted the competitiveness of small and medium Albanian enterprises in domestic and foreign markets, and accelerated the entry of Albanian exports into global markets.

Azerbaijan. Azerbaijan's program emphasizes economic growth and reform, with a focus on developing the non-oil sectors of the economy.

Bosnia and Herzegovina (BiH). The program in BiH supports progress towards full integration into the EU. USAID/BiH worked to integrate the energy sector into the regional European framework and supported the development and implementation of a coherent regionally competitive direct taxation system. USAID's competitiveness projects promote trade and investment in agribusiness, wood processing, and tourism by improving the competitiveness of the firms, industries, and training firms to meet EU standards.

Kosovo. The objective in Kosovo is to strengthen its economic ties in the region and promote its integration into Euro-Atlantic institutions. USAID's goal is to help Kosovo make the transition from international administration to self-governance in an effective and peaceful manner. USAID provides training and expert counsel to build capacity in the fiscal and economic policy sectors, private enterprise development, and energy management. One such program is the Kosovo Private Enterprise Program, which assists businesses in targeted sectors (including agriculture, road construction, and forestry and wood processing) by promoting improved productivity, improving the business operating environment, providing workforce training to improve job skills in targeted areas, and identifying trade, marketing, and import-substitution opportunities.

The Regional Cooperation Council (RCC). The RCC was officially launched in February 2008 as the successor to the Stability Pact for South Central Europe. Since Kosovo's declaration of independence on February 17, 2008, the RCC has encountered difficulties in arranging meetings that involve both Serbia and Kosovo. The RCC has several relevant programs related to global trade that affect parts of the region with significant Muslim populations, including Albania, Bosnia and Herzegovina, and Kosovo. The RCC's Trade Working Group has encouraged the negotiation, ratification, and implementation of a network of bilateral free trade agreements among the members of the RCC and supports negotiation of a single regional trade agreement to harmonize bilateral trade agreements to encompass all RCC members. The United States supports this process by providing technical assistance to lower non-tariff barriers within the region, consistent with World Trade Organization principles.

Under RCC auspices, the Organization of European Cooperation and Development Investment Compact for Southeastern Europe aims to improve the region's investment conditions, by setting out commitments for policy reform and to encourage increasing local and foreign direct investment. Signatories include Albania and Bosnia and Herzegovina.

Possible Actions to Promote Intraregional Trade and Rule of Law in the Region

Intraregional Trade

- The vision of a Middle East Free Trade Area (MEFTA) by 2013, linking countries in the region with each other and the United States, is the centerpiece of our effort to promote intraregional trade. Our strategy for attaining MEFTA includes:
  - o Negotiating Free Trade Agreements (FTAs) with countries ready for that step. The United States has concluded FTAs with Israel, Jordan, Morocco, Bahrain, and Oman;
  - o Working with additional countries through the TIFA process to advance readiness for FTA negotiations; and
  - o Assisting reform-minded Middle East countries that are not yet in the World Trade Organization (WTO) accession process.
- The MEPI, MCC, and USAID Missions in the Middle East provide support for the MEFTA initiative through a variety of programs in trade capacity-building. MEPI and USAID missions in the Middle East are supporting the WTO accession efforts of Iraq, Yemen, and Lebanon. U.S. government assistance programs assist FTA partners Jordan, Morocco, Bahrain, and Oman with free trade implementation with the United States.
- USAID/Jordan's Business Development Center supports implementation of the FTA between the United States and Jordan, and assists small and medium-sized firms to modernize and improve their competitiveness so they can move into higher value sectors and take advantage of FTA export opportunities.
- USAID/Morocco's New Business Opportunities (NBO) Program helps export-oriented Moroccan firms to take advantage of new opportunities for entry and expansion into the United States created by the Morocco-U.S. Free Trade Agreement. NBO includes business development services that help exporting firms to identify new market opportunities, and then work to improve their marketing and promotion to turn these opportunities into exports to the United States.

The Rule of Law

- **The Middle East Partnership Initiative** (MEPI) will continue to support rule of law activities aimed at strengthening the capacity of regional governments to enact and implement commercial laws conducive to promoting economic growth. By working with legislators, judges, lawyers, and business persons, improvements in the commercial legal and regulatory environment focused on international best practices should lead to increased investment and employment across the region.

- **Egypt**. USAID's Administration of Justice Support II project promotes the rule of law by reforming and modernizing the commercial court system and improving the access to quality legal services.
- **Indonesia**. USAID's Financial Crime Prevention Project (FCPP), which ended in June 2008, was designed to strengthen Indonesia's ability to combat financial crimes. FCPP provided technical assistance to the FIU (PPATK), Supreme Audit Commission, Attorney General's Office, Corruption Eradication Commission, and Ministry of Finance-Inspector General Office. FCPP's work aided Indonesia's own efforts to build a more modern legal and institutional framework to detect and prosecute corruption and financial crime. The USG will continue to provide assistance to the Indonesian government to strengthen its capacity to combat financial crime.

USAID's Judicial Reform Support Program assists Indonesia's Attorney General's Office (AGO) to implement reforms in the public prosecution system including development of a database to track prosecutors and profiles, development of a code of conduct, continuing legal education for prosecutors, and bureaucratic reform to improve human resources. This support is helping to reduce the backlog of civilian complaints and establish more objective assessment criteria for evaluating performance of prosecutors and work units. Assistance is also being extended to the Supreme Court under this program.

The Millennium Challenge Corporation (MCC). The MCC provides assistance for transformational development in countries that perform well on 17 independent, transparent policy indicators in the areas of ruling justly, investing in people, and economic freedom. Besides the financial support provided by MCC programs, the selection criteria creates an incentive for candidate countries to adopt related legal, policy, regulatory, and institutional reforms.

Summary of Millennium Challenge Corporation (MCC) Activities in Predominantly Muslim Countries

Compact-Eligible Countries. Based on their good performance on the 17 policy indicators mentioned above, Compact-Eligible countries are invited to apply for substantial grants from MCC for programs that they design and implement through a "Compact."

Mali. Mali signed a five-year, $460.8 million Compact with MCC in November 2006 that entered into force in September 2007. It aims to reduce rural poverty and to help achieve national food security through a sustainable increase in the economic performance of the agricultural sector, and to spur economic growth and reduce poverty by increasing the competitiveness of light industry and increasing the value-added of exports and tourism. These objectives will be met through investments that increase farmers' productivity, enhance agricultural supply chains, reduce transport costs, and create a platform for industry. The Compact focuses on improved infrastructure at the Bamako Airport, a key gateway for trade, and along the Niger River for irrigated agriculture.

Burkina Faso. Burkina Faso signed a five-year, $480.9 million Compact with MCC in July 2008. It aims to promote economic growth in the rural sector by fostering land tenure security; investing in irrigation and watershed management infrastructure for agricultural purposes; constructing national roads, feeder roads, and market infrastructure; and improving existing agro-industrial supply chains.

Morocco. Morocco signed a five-year, $697.5 million Compact with MCC in August 2007 which entered into force in September 2008. The Compact focuses on relieving constraints to growth in the agriculture, fishing, artisan, and small enterprise finance sectors.

Threshold Programs are designed to assist countries that have demonstrated significant commitment to improving their performance on MCC selection criteria, but do not yet pass more than half the indicators in each of the three selection categories of ruling justly, investing in people, and encouraging economic freedom. A Threshold Program provides financial assistance to help improve a low score on at least one of MCC's policy indicators.

Albania. Reducing corruption was the primary focus of the $13.9 million Albanian program signed in April 2006. The MCC program funded projects designed to reform tax administration, public procurement, and business administration and helped to reduce the extensive red tape and below-board payments needed to start a business while increasing the national tax base. Albania signed a second Threshold program with MCC in October 2008, which builds on the success of the first program and seeks to institutionalize reforms in public administration and judicial capacity building to support further anticorruption activities.

Burkina Faso. Burkina Faso's $12.9 million program, signed in July 2005, officially ended on September 30, 2008. The program sought to improve performance on girls' primary education completion rates. Specific interventions included the construction of 132 "girl-friendly" schools, teacher training, provision of take-home dry rations to girls who maintain a 90 percent school attendance rate, and literacy training for mothers.

Indonesia. Indonesia's $55 million program, signed in November 2006, seeks to immunize at least 80 percent of children under the age of one for diphtheria, tetanus, and pertussis, and 90 percent of all children for measles. The Threshold Program also has a component aimed at curbing public corruption by reforming the judiciary and strengthening government institutions that fight corruption. Indonesia is also eligible for Compact assistance.

Jordan. Jordan's $25 million Jordanian program, signed in October 2006, aims to strengthen democratic institutions by supporting Jordan's efforts to broaden public participation in the political and electoral process, increasing government transparency and accountability, and enhancing the efficiency and effectiveness of customs administration. The Threshold Program is also a part of Jordan's reform efforts focused on improvements in public administration, civil liberties, infrastructure, and the economy. Jordan is also eligible for Compact assistance.

Kyrgyz Republic. The Kyrgyz Republic's $16 million Threshold Program was signed in March 2008 to help the Kyrgyz government fight corruption and improve the rule of law through judicial, criminal justice, and law enforcement reforms.

Basic Education in Muslim Countries

The United States continued to support an increased focus on education in predominantly Muslim countries and those with significant Muslim populations. The U.S. government approach stressed mobilizing public and private resources as partners to improve the access, quality, and relevance of education, with a specific emphasis on youth and on developing civic-mindedness in young people. In many Muslim-majority countries, such as Afghanistan and Yemen, the challenge was to increase country capacity to provide universal access to primary education and literacy. Countries faced increasing enrollments and low education quality in the classroom while struggling with limited budgets.

In the Middle East, USAID and the Department of State's Middle East Partnership Initiative (MEPI) continued responding to these needs by working to improve policy, learning outcomes, teacher training, education finance/governance, and community participation. These efforts complement investments of partner countries and other donors. MEPI funding for projects in basic education totaled approximately 53.2 million (FY-2002-08).

USAID/Asia and Middle East Bureaus' total education assistance for the region was approximately $463.7 million, of which $451.4 million was targeted in predominantly Muslim countries: Afghanistan, Bangladesh, Egypt, Indonesia, Jordan, Lebanon, Morocco, Pakistan, Philippines (Mindanao), West Bank/Gaza, and Yemen. Out of the $467.1 million total, approximately $385 million went towards basic education programs.

In 2008, USAID/Africa Bureau's total education assistance for the region was approximately $76 million in basic education (including the Africa Education Initiative); approximately $30 million benefit Muslim populations in Chad, Djibouti, Ethiopia, Kenya, Mali, Mauritania, Niger, Nigeria, Senegal, Somalia, Tanzania, and Uganda.

The U.S. Strategy to Meet Challenges in Education

To promote transformational diplomacy and development, the Department of State and USAID have articulated a common Foreign Assistance Framework. In the "Investing in People" objective, education is a major element with basic education as an important sub-element. This strategy is applied to programs worldwide.

Basic Education: USAID has an Agency-wide *Basic Education Strategy* (2005) that targeted underserved populations and promoted access to quality universal basic education. The goal was to help learners gain the general skills and relevant knowledge needed to function effectively in life. Basic education programs focused on three areas:

- **Increasing Access:** Targeting groups that have been marginalized in the education system such as minority, rural, out-of-school youth, girls, and young adults; and those who have been impacted by conflict or disaster, thus helping ensure equitable access to education.
- **Improving Quality:** Improving the quality of education is pivotal for ensuring attendance and learning outcomes of basic education. Attention was focused on curriculum reform and measuring learning outcomes.
- **Improving Relevance:** Education programs that develop human capacities and livelihood skills, and aimed to link learning with skill development and employment opportunities, particularly in areas with high youth unemployment.

In designing and implementing basic education programs throughout the world, USAID worked closely with host-country governments (national and local), non-governmental organizations, communities, and the private sector to maximize program impact and sustainability.

Working with the International Community. The U.S. government continued to be an active member of several international bodies and activities to achieve universal primary education, including the International Working Group on Education, which originally proposed the "Education for All" initiative begun in the late 1980s.

Coordination of the International Effort. USAID provided technical guidance to the EFA effort through the UNESCO-aligned International Institute for Educational Planning. The U.S. Director of Foreign Assistance represented the U.S. at the annual High Level Group meeting for "Education for All," and the USAID Office of Education participated in the annual EFA Working Group meeting.

In engaging the G8 and governments for Broader Middle East and North Africa (BMENA) initiatives, USAID collaborated closely with the State Department and other U.S. government agencies, especially on literacy. At the Sea Island Summit, the G8 launched the Broader Middle East and North Africa (BMENA) Literacy Initiative aimed at halving illiteracy rates in the region by 2015. This initiative launched a series of Literacy Working Group and Education Ministerial Dialogues in the BMENA region. Education Ministers from the BMENA region and the G8 have met annually since 2005; they met in Oman in November 2008.

In 2008, USAID contributed $2.5 million to the UNESCO Literacy Trust Fund, supported literacy assessments in the BMENA region, and developed the BMENA Literacy Hub' database of global best practices in promoting literacy. The BMENA Literacy Hub' was transferred to the Afghanistan Ministry of Education in October 2008.

Leveraging other Donors. USAID coordinated closely with multilateral (e.g. World Bank and the Asian Development Bank) and other bilateral donors in each country. In Indonesia, for example, the Australian bilateral aid agency, AusAID, used a USAID pilot education program 's methodology for supporting local government management of education and for promoting active learning in classrooms. Collaboration with AusAID, as well as other donors such as UNICEF, continued during implementation in the form of jointly-prepared training materials and activities in communities to avoid duplication as well as combined approaches in working with local and national officials. This coordinated approach has extended donor program coverage in Indonesia in the education sector.

In Tajikistan, USAID-developed training modules on interactive learning and teaching methods and teacher trainers support the Government of Tajikistan's implementation of the "Education for All" Fast Track Initiative, leveraging funds of approximately $1.6 million. This basic education project also complemented World Bank and Asia Development Bank (ADB) projects in the area of education finance, curriculum revision, teacher training, and strengthening capacity of teacher training institutes. In Kyrgyzstan, USAID-supported independent testing organization won a World Bank tender to implement the Program for International Student Assessment (PISA); USAID-developed teacher standards were used in revision of the teacher incentive system. The basic education project collaborated with the ADB project by providing training for textbook authors.

Leveraging Contributions from the Private Sector and Civil Society Organizations. The U.S. government used development assistance to leverage other resources for education by developing alliances or partnerships with the private sector and non-governmental organizations (NGOs). USAID's Global Development Alliances (GDAs), also known as public-private partnerships, were tailored to country-specific needs and the private sector partners' interests. In 2008, the USG succeeded in getting public-private partnership support to education on the agenda for the annual World Economic Forum meeting. USAID received on average a greater than a two-to-one match for education alliances in the Asia and Middle East region, of which the total life of project value is $271 million. Below are several examples of ongoing and new country-specific partnerships in the region:

In Western and Central Mindanao, and the Autonomous Region of Muslim Mindanao in the Philippines, there are currently six GDA partnerships to increase educational opportunities for children by ensuring access to quality education; to improve the capacity of teachers, and raise math, science and English skills among elementary school beneficiaries; to increase employment opportunities and engage young leaders; and, to provide business and skills training for out-of-school youth; and, to provide opportunity for school drop-outs and out-of-school youths to rejoin formal schooling through an accreditation and equivalency mechanism.

In Indonesia, public private partnerships were used to expand the reach of USAID activities and to respond in natural disaster situations. A partnership with British Petroleum was helping improve education quality in Papua, one of the most underserved and isolated areas of Indonesia. An alliance with ConocoPhillips is helping restore education services in communities affected by the May 2006 earthquake that struck Yogyakarta and Central Java, and an alliance with Intel was helping teachers effectively use technology in classrooms. A partnership with Chevron has expanded vocational and technical education opportunities for youth in Aceh.

In India, USAID has supported Quality Education and Skills Training (Quest), in an alliance with leading non-government organizations, and global corporations to promote the effective use of technologies to improve basic education and skills training. Through various pilot initiatives and advocacy efforts, the alliance has established its credibility in the field of education technology.

In Morocco and Jordan, a USAID information technology partnership with CISCO, UNIFEM, and the Governments of Morocco and Jordan, has introduced CISCO Certified Network Associate and job-readiness training to eleven Moroccan institutions (900 students, 49 percent women) and just over 1,700 students in Jordan. Seven CISCO Networking Academies were established in Jordan. In both countries, there was a focus on job skills and placement for women. Fifty percent of the first student cohort who completed the program found jobs within six months after graduation.

USAID's Office of Middle East Affairs implemented a GDA that engaged and supported emerging youth leaders in Egypt, Jordan, Lebanon, West Bank, Gaza, and Yemen. Partnering with the Ford Foundation and Save the Children International, it has created a youth development tool kit. It linked emerging young leaders to a network of youth development workers and institutions that assist young people with building leadership capacity and exercising positive, moderate leadership behaviors within a community development context.

In cooperation with the Department of State's Middle East Partnership Initiative (MEPI) in the Bureau of Near Eastern Affairs, Scholastic Inc. is providing 8.2 million Arabic-language classroom libraries to more than 40,620 classrooms in more than 6,770 primary schools in the Middle East and North Africa. Scholastic's substantive contribution allows MEPI to leverage its $12 million investment in this critical-thinking and independent reading skills development program. In another example, MEPI's partnership with the CISCO Learning Institute developed on-line English language curricular materials to complement the efforts of the private sector-based World Economic Forum-sponsored Jordan Education Initiative.

USG Coordination to Reduce Duplication and Waste. The Department of State and USAID coordinated their Foreign Assistance Framework, which included education, and a joint Operational Plan process, to reduce duplication of effort and/or waste.

To minimize any potential duplication of efforts and investments, USAID collaborated with the Department of State/Middle East Partnership Initiative (MEPI) to promote education within the Near East region, with a focus on civic education. The MEPI education pillar supported education systems that enabled all people, especially girls, to acquire the knowledge and skills necessary to compete in today's economy, participate actively and effectively in the civic arena, and improve the quality of their lives.

Training and Exchange Programs. Bridging both basic and higher education, USAID and the State Department Bureau of Education and Cultural Affairs (ECA) coordinated in the area of providing training and exchanges for students from Muslim-majority countries to the United States. In Egypt, ECA has also financed awards for teachers/administrators to enhance the Ministry's technical college instructor capacity.

Scholarship Programs. MEPI has launched two pilot scholarship programs, the basic-education based MEPI Scholarship Program, and the higher-education based Tomorrow's Leaders program. The MEPI Scholarship Program provides disadvantaged youth with the opportunity of receiving a democratic based education (grades 7–12) at American-sponsored schools abroad. The program was launched with the September 2007 school year and has been enthusiastically received by teachers, parents, students, and the communities in Oman, Egypt, Morocco, and Jordan. The Tomorrow's Leaders scholarship recipients will be selected from among the underserved in the Middle East and North Africa, and the scholarship will provide a four-year academic and internship/study-abroad opportunity with specialized curricula through which to develop their civic engagement, entrepreneurial, and leadership skills. The first cohort of Tomorrow's Leaders began the program in September 2008.

For younger students, there are some programs, such as the **English Microscholarship Access Program**, which provides English classes for deserving high school students from non-elite sectors. The program delivers language instruction in a civic education context, and helps students compete for future job and educational opportunities. U.S. embassies selected schools in 45 countries to enroll approximately 10,000 students in the program. In addition to teaching English, the program provides an American classroom experience using U.S. materials and emphasizes active learning.

The State Department's **Youth Exchange and Study Program (YES)** and **Future Leaders Exchange Program (FLEX)** bring high school students from Muslim countries to live with American host families and attend American public high schools for an academic year. The FLEX students also receive special training in civic education and work as volunteers.

Student Leaders/Study of the United States Institutes provide young people with intensive training in civic engagement and leadership skills in both U.S. and regionally-based settings.

The State Department's **International Leaders in Education Program** brings secondary school teachers of English, social studies, math, and science from South and Southeast Asia, the Near East, and North and Sub-Saharan Africa, and the Western Hemisphere to U.S. universities for a semester to develop their teaching skills, to increase their subject-matter expertise, and to pursue coursework and practical teaching experiences in U.S. high schools. U.S. teachers may then apply to participate in a reciprocal exchange program in several of the participating countries.

The **Teaching Excellence and Achievement Program** (TEA) provides secondary school teachers from Eurasia, South Asia, and Southeast Asia with unique opportunities to enhance their teaching skills and increase their knowledge about the United States. The participants participate in a professional teacher development program in the United States. The six-week program, based at a U.S. university's school of education, also includes a three-week internship at a secondary school where participants actively engage with American teachers and students. The TEA program provides follow-on grants to the international teachers to purchase essential materials for their schools, to offer follow-on training for other teachers, and to conduct other activities that will build on the exchange visits.

USAID's **Training Future Leaders** initiative highlights the importance of U.S. trained scholars and their unique role in developing their nations upon returning home. There are currently 13 scholars now enrolled in Masters degree programs in the United States.

USAID's **Office of Middle East Partnerships (OMEP)** program also supports a **Peace Scholars** program. This program supports 30 young people annually from the Middle East and North Africa who have demonstrated a commitment to their communities with undergraduate level scholarships to study for one year in the United States. These programs complement ongoing efforts carried out by State/ECA and MEPI.

Funds Needed to Achieve Universal Basic Education

The UN Educational, Scientific, and Cultural Organization (UNESCO) estimates that $5.6 billion are needed per year to achieve "Education for All" by 2015. Globally UNESCO estimates that 72 million children are enrolled in school, but many of those in school are not there regularly, and many more do not receive a quality education. For the countries in the Muslim world, this figure is estimated to be around 40 million. Estimating that it costs roughly $50 per year per child to complete six years of schooling, it would cost $2.2 billion per year in Muslim countries as a whole to achieve education for all children to that level.

Efforts to Encourage Development and Implementation of a National Education Plan

In countries with predominantly Muslim populations, the effectiveness of basic education systems is at the crux of their development future. The United States encourages countries to develop and implement national education plans by offering assistance to support education reform developments and program funding once reforms have moved into the implementation phase. For example, funding for the International Expanding Education Initiative supports countries which have national education plans approved by the Fast Track Initiative. The United States has influenced national education plans and reform by way of pilot programs that model best practices in education. These positive experiences galvanize support for broader change and can impact the education system beyond the pilots programs' localities. Model programs also potentially have an impact outside of targeted interventions.

Closing the Digital Divide and Expanding Vocational/Business Skills

To "close the digital divide" and expand vocational/business skills, USAID, the Department of State, and other agencies implement public-private partnerships, information technology in the classroom, school-to-work and workforce training programs, improved quality of basic and secondary education programs, and scholarships and exchanges. A few programs are highlighted below.

USAID/Asia and Middle East Bureaus' **Education and Employment Alliance** promotes private sector participation in Egypt, Morocco, Pakistan, India, Indonesia, and the Philippines to enhance skills and improve education and employment opportunities among over one million underserved youth. In addition to local profit and non-profit partners, corporate partners include Chevron/Unocal, GE, Ink Media, Lucent, Microsoft, Nike, and Oracle.

The State Department's **Global Connections and Exchange Program** seeks to promote mutual understanding and civic education in countries with significant Muslim populations by bringing together more than 1,000 schools from 16 countries for online collaborative projects that focus on professional development, media literacy, and civic education. Teachers also develop skills needed to participate in collaborative activities with U.S. schools, and teachers and students are offered opportunities to travel to their partner schools as a way to strengthen mutual understanding and solidify virtual relationships through in-person meetings.

MEPI is partnering with the Education for Employment Foundation (EFE) and with businesses, universities, and private organizations to create four highly scalable and replicable youth education and employment programs that offer real employment to 80 percent of all graduates. The programs are as follows: in Egypt, both a Mini MBA accounting training and a textile management and workplace for success training program; in Morocco, sales force training; in Jordan, vocational scholarships and workplace for success training; and in Yemen, information technology training. EFE will also create an affiliate foundation in Yemen that will partner with business, universities, and civil society leaders that are dedicated to youth education and employment to develop employer-driven education and training linked to jobs. This initiative also supports broader education goals articulated under the Broader Middle East and North Africa initiative.

USAID/India's Technology Tools for Teaching and Training (T4) employs educational technologies to educate poor and disadvantaged children studying in public schools in the states of Karnataka, Chhattisgarh, Madhya Pradesh, Jharkhand, and Bihar and will soon operate in Delhi and Rajasthan. Combining technology tools with sound pedagogy and effective teacher training, USAID and its partners are developing high-quality, interactive radio, video, and computer programs that simplify the teaching of difficult concepts in various subjects, including language, math, science, and social studies. T4 currently reaches more than 22 million children. In addition, USAID/India's Youth Skill Development Initiative provides education in basic life and employability skills to deprived out-of-school youth, effectively linking their education to the skills demanded by the new economy. The program provides training to these youth in market-oriented skills such as computer usage, spoken English, communication, and customer relations to make them more employable. Over 14,000 youth have been trained in the three Indian states of Delhi, Jharkhand, and Maharashtra; 76% of the trainees have received employment and many have opted for further studies. Designed as a public-private initiative, 50% of the program costs come from non-USAID sources.

USAID/Central Asian Republics also supports Junior Achievement (JA) programs which provide training for secondary school students in basic entrepreneurship skills. In 2008, JA reached more than 15,000 students in Kazakhstan and more than 3,500 students in Turkmenistan. JA organized student fairs across the region for thousands of Junior Achievement program participants to showcase their school companies which provided an opportunity for students to gain practical experience in entrepreneurship by organizing and operating a model' business enterprise. Students learned to produce and sell products and services to their communities and the fair provided an additional opportunity to market student products to organizations from other regions that attend the fair.

USAID continued working with the private sector to strengthen their support of JA to ensure sustainability of the programs.

USAID/Cambodia supports an in-school effort aimed at making education more relevant to Cambodia's needs, particularly for Cham and rural areas; and also supported the development of a new national curriculum which reinforces math, science, and language skills, and includes a life skills component focused on agriculture, pre-vocational skills, and health education in primary schools.

The **USAID Internet Access Training Program** (IATP), administered by the International Research and Exchanges Board (IREX) since 1995, provides free internet access and training in 11 countries throughout Central Asia, the Caucasus, and Western Eurasia. From major cities to small communities, IATP encourages information sharing, network building, and collaboration among U.S. government exchange alumni and other targeted audiences. IATP staff train alumni and other targeted audiences in the effective use of the Internet and sponsor the development of local language web sites. The centers also conduct training in basic civics, entrepreneurship, and English.

USAID and the Intel Corporation signed Memorandum of Understanding in December 2006 to broaden access and usage of information and communications technologies (ICT) in developing communities worldwide. This alliance envisions collaboration and partnership in enabling "last mile" internet connectivity and locally relevant applications; supporting ICT usage and deployment by small and medium-sized enterprises to enhance economic development; and increasing the use of ICTs to support education and health. Intel's prior experience in the education sector includes software development and teacher training programs for K-12.

Countries Eligible for Assistance. USAID has education programs in Muslim-majority countries and countries with large Muslim populations that potentially overlap those which might be targeted by the President under an International Youth Opportunity Fund [section 7114(b)]. Below is a list, though not exhaustive, of programs in the Asia Near East, Africa, Europe, and Eurasia regions.

The Asia and Middle East regions contain several Muslim-majority countries with significant education needs. Basic education program highlights include, in alphabetical order by country:

Afghanistan. Because Afghans lost years of formal schooling under the Taliban, many students are not at their appropriate grade level. USAID created an accelerated learning program that compresses two years of study into a single year through innovative teaching techniques. This program trained an estimated 10,500 teachers in teaching methodologies for accelerated learning and enrolled nearly 170,000 students, over half of them girls. In addition, the Community Schools Program supports 50,000 students annually, and has trained over 65,000 teachers across all provinces through daily radio broadcasts. Since 2002, over 60 million textbooks were printed and distributed nationwide in Dari and Pashto for grades one through 12, in part in collaboration with the Danish International Development Agency. To strengthen the Ministries of Education and Higher Education, USAID provides advisors to help develop and implement education policy; supports the International School of Kabul, an English language high school with an enrollment of approximately 260 students from more than 20 countries, the majority of whom are Afghans; and works with 16 Afghan universities to upgrade teacher training. USAID supports the American University of Afghanistan, and has refurbished the Women's Dormitory at Kabul University to house over 1,000 women, mainly from rural areas.

In **Bangladesh**, USAID's Early Learning for School Success Program (SUCCEED), has become the model program for support of early learning activities in the country. SUCCEED is carried out in 1,800 preschools in 600 communities, which prepares children ages five to 13, including children with disabilities, to achieve greater success in school. The program provides extra-curricular educational activities to increase learning skills, strengthen community involvement in school management, and model successful teaching methodologies to primary school teachers. SUCCEED has facilitated 1,800 small peer support groups that discuss local health, environment and social issues, and work together to initiate positive changes in these areas. The program has established an innovative after-school program using educational toys and games that stimulate learning for more than 53,274 primary school children. This program helps children to utilize their free time to improve their critical thinking, reading, and social skills. The SUCCEED program has also developed a Reading Buddy and Mentoring program, which couples struggling students with their progressing peers. USAID-sponsored preschools encourage the enrollment of children with mild disabilities, which currently comprise approximately five percent of the total enrolment.

USAID also supports the extremely successfully television program, Sisimpur (Sesame Street), which is the most widely viewed children's television show in Bangladesh. It is estimated to reach 7.5 million young children weekly, nearly half of all three to six year olds. The television episodes aim to improve skills such as literacy, numeracy, and critical thinking, as well as hygiene practices such as hand washing and dental hygiene. The TV program also portrays positive socio-emotional and cultural knowledge, values, and skills; appreciation of diversity; illustrates the capacity of children with disabilities; depicts successful women across professions; and demonstrates self-respect and respect for others. Combined, the two programs have helped to combat traditionally low achievement and high dropout rates in the lower primary grades.

In **Central Asia,** USAID supports a regional basic education project in the Kyrgyz Republic, Tajikistan, and Turkmenistan, the Quality Learning Project (QLP). Awarded in October 2007, QLP is a five-year $12 million dollar project with a focus on expanding access to quality basic education. QLP activities continued to build on the achievements and lessons learned on the previous USAID-funded basic education project, including support to the governments of the Kyrgyz Republic and Tajikistan in implementing their national education strategies and Education for All Fast Track Initiative grants. QLP activities will result in: (1) improved quality of teacher training in student-centered methodologies; (2) introduction and application of modern skill-based student assessment methodologies; (3) greater involvement of teachers in curriculum development; and (4) use of transparent and efficient school finance and management systems.

- **Kyrgyz Republic.** The Quality Learning Project (QLP) has encountered unanticipated delays in signing the MOU with the Ministry of Education and Science (MES) that led to delays in project implementation. The MOU was signed in November and stipulates support for implementation of the Kyrgyz National education strategies and the Fast Track Initiative Catalytic Grant. Despite the delays, the project has established cooperation with the Kyrgyz Academy of Education and its Center for Teacher Training and Retraining – the two institutions critical for achieving improved teacher training. In order to ensure sustainability of in-service teacher training activities within the legislative framework, QLP developed recommendations to the draft law on general secondary education and teacher training for the KR Parliament Committee on Education, Science, Information, and Culture, and participated in elaboration of the Education Development Strategy for 2010-2020 for the MOES. In October 2008, USAID signed the Loan Portfolio Guarantee Agreements for tuition financing with two Kyrgyz financial institutions to increase access to higher and vocational education. This initiative aims to create a replicable, private sector tuition financing model that would provide students with more choice as to which education institutions they could attend. Over the next seven years USAID will guarantee up to $1.5 million in student loans and up to 50% of losses. USG continues to provide support to the American University–Central

Asia through a joint USAID/State Department grant that supports activities toward achieving accreditation from a U.S. accrediting body.

- **Tajikistan.** To address improvement of teacher training, the Quality Learning Project (QLP), in collaboration with the Ministry of Education (MOE), established a Teacher Training Working Group and signed a memorandum of understanding with the Republican Teacher Training Institute (RTTI) to collaborate on training of module developers and revisions of training modules under the FTI grant. Under the Formative Student Assessment component, the project trained 25 MOE and RTTI staff and eight local module developers in formative assessment approaches. As a result of the training, key elements of formative assessment were incorporated into the revised training modules developed as part of FTI. The QLP team closely collaborates with the newly-established Education Finance Working Group and implementation of the new education finance policy.
- **Turkmenistan.** The overall strategy for project implementation in Turkmenistan is to work under the umbrella of a formal agreement with the Ministry of Education (MOE). While awaiting the signing of the memorandum of understanding, the Quality Learning Project organized a three-day seminar for MOE staff to familiarize them with the proposed activities of the project.

USAID/**Egypt** supports the Government of Egypt in sustaining improvements in learning outcomes in grades K-12. The program focuses on improving teaching and learning, increasing equitable access to education, and strengthening management and governance in seven governorates. Activities include in-service teacher training, school libraries, information technology, and some school construction in remote and densely populated areas. USAID assistance strengthens school governance and management through leadership training for school principals; the development of nationwide management information systems; and, the training of school Boards of Trustees. The current education strategy runs through September 2009. To date, USAID has also provided 25 million books for libraries and classrooms in all 39,000 public primary, preparatory, and secondary schools in Egypt. Books range from non-fiction to reference materials to novels. Libraries are 80% in Arabic and 20% in English language. Over 39,000 students now have access to computer technology. USAID has built 70 new girls schools serving almost 40,000 students. Nearly 100,000 girls' scholarships have been provided to date. USAID supported the development of the Egyptian Sesame Street, which reaches over 85 percent of all children under age eight, helping them acquire early literacy and numeracy skills.

The U.S. **Indonesia** Education Initiative program works with over 100 districts (25 percent of the nation) providing training and technical assistance to school officials, communities, and local governments on education management and finance. This Presidential initiative also includes in-service teacher training, mentoring, and teacher resource centers to improve the quality of classroom instruction. Approximately 24,000 educators have been trained to improve the quality of teaching and learning and over 1,050,000 students are reaping the benefits. Over 245,000 junior secondary students and out-of-school youth are learning employment-related life skills while working toward school completion or its equivalency. USAID is supporting the creation of an Indonesian *Sesame Street, Jalan Sesame,* which debuted in late 2007. Through direct assistance and dissemination of best practices, education programs are expected to reach 9,000 public and private schools, 2.5 million students, 90,000 educators, and one million out-of-school youth by 2010.

In July 2003, the Government of **Jordan** launched the Education Reform for the Knowledge Economy (ERfKE) initiative, a five-year, $380 million program developed with USAID assistance. The goal of this initiative, one of the most ambitious education reform programs in the Arab region, l is to re-orient education policy, restructure education programs and practices, improve physical learning environments, and promote learning readiness through improved and more accessible early childhood education. USAID, in coordination with Jordan and eight other donor nations and multi-lateral organizations, will provide $80 million in support of reform efforts through ERfKE. USAID's efforts under this initiative (1) assist the Government of Jordan's early child care initiative, with the creation of 100 public kindergartens, field-test curriculum, and the development of an accreditation system; (2) develop school-to-work programs and an IT curriculum stream for high school students; (3) connect 100 Discovery' schools to broadband and test e-learning modules for all subject; (4) expand youth and life skills programs to secondary schools in new underserved areas in Jordan; and (5) construct up to 28 new schools and rehabilitate another 100 schools to create the appropriate learning environment that supports the reform efforts and accommodates the recent influx of refugees from the region. In 2006, the sector reform activities were expanded into the Southern governorates of Aqaba, Ma'an and Tafileh to work with all the public schools.

In **Lebanon,** in response to the 2006 conflict, USAID worked to repair and upgrade schools throughout the country. The work was finished in time for the start of the 2007 school year and continued in 2008. Other program components included providing equipment for laboratories, supplies and books, awareness programs on health, nutrition and social awareness for a better learning environment; and extracurricular activities to enhance students' skills and learning experiences. The program benefits over 200 public primary, intermediary, and secondary schools and over 80,000 students. Over the past two years, USAID provided over 560 students with scholarship assistance at the American Community School and the International College (secondary schools); and also provided about 3,100 students with scholarship assistance at the American University of Beirut and the Lebanese American University.

In **Morocco,** Improved Education and Training for Employment aims to assist Morocco's basic education and vocational training systems in preparing young graduates to meet Morocco's entry-level workforce needs. While pursuing partnerships to institutionalize programs for longer-term impact, USAID works within existing structures, emphasizing the relevance of content and the ability of instructors to deliver this content effectively, in four of Morocco's 16 regions, in collaboration with the Moroccan government. Over 200,000 children (45% girls) and 1,600 teachers (23% women) from some 337 participating schools are benefiting from USAID's Advancing Learning and Employability for a Better Future (ALEF) program, which assists the Government of Morocco in improving the quality and relevance of basic education. Teachers and children demonstrated tremendous creativity and innovativeness in information technology, entrepreneurship, and other initiatives.

Middle East Partnership Initiative (MEPI) funds for the development of learner-friendly literacy materials based on the Family Code have benefited over 9,600 rural women. Grants have been awarded to 30 non-governmental organizations who implement literacy programs not only in classical Arabic but in the rural women's mother tongue (Moroccan dialect and Amazigh), a breakthrough for Morocco. MEPI funds supported 215 rural girls with scholarships to attend middle school while living in supervised boarding facilities.

In **Pakistan,** USAID-funded programs benefit more than 600,000 children and 60,000 teachers. Since 2006, 3,770 teachers and supervisors have been trained in interactive teaching and learning skills. Nearly 2,400 classrooms of 327 primary, middle, and high schools; and model colleges have been equipped with new learning materials. More than 4,500 parents have learned basic literacy and math skills. Links to Learning (ED-LINKS), with the objective of improving the quality and sustainability of teacher education and student performance, is located in Sindh, Balochistan, Islamabad Capital Territory (ICT), and the Federally Administered Tribal Area (FATA). The ED-LINKS program has three basic components: 1)

Teacher Education and Professional Development; 2) Student Learning and Achievement; and 3) Governance of Teaching and Learning. The program will contribute to better quality education in approximately 22 districts and 6,000 middle and high schools, affecting 600,000 students and 60,000 teachers.

Focusing on early childhood and primary education, the Interactive Teaching and Learning Program brings child-centered teaching into public and private classrooms. As a result, 399 schools have begun to move away from rote learning and repetitive memorization toward interactive learning that emphasizes critical-thinking skills. The program also encourages family members to participate in the schools.

USAID is enhancing professional development and teacher education across Pakistan by assisting the Ministry of Education in the formulation of a strategic framework for teacher certification and accreditation. The Strengthening Teacher Education in Pakistan (STEP) initiative transforms teacher education through the development of national standards for teacher certification and accreditation and improves networking among government teacher training institutions. Under the FATA School Rehabilitation and Construction Program, USAID has supported the rehabilitation and furnishing of 58 public schools and two Government Colleges of Elementary Teachers (GCETs) in the FATA. The schools have been completed and handed over to FATA authorities.

In the **Philippines**, in Mindanao province, USAID is training teachers and providing computers, textbooks, and other materials to schools. To reduce instability in conflict-prone areas in Mindanao, tens of thousands of out-of-school youth are being prepared to return to the formal education system, and thousands of others have been provided with employable skills. A matching grants program for school improvements encourages greater participation by parents and communities in the education of their children. The U.S. government is partnering with local private sector firms to increase the quality of basic education and provide training to educators to improve the teaching of English, science, and math. USAID's education program is providing more than two million textbooks and other learning materials to elementary school students and out-of-school youth through a partnership with the U.S. military, which delivers the donated materials to remote communities. Computer and internet education has been introduced into schools in Mindanao.

USAID/**West Bank and Gaza** improved the quality of and increased access to primary and secondary education through the construction and rehabilitation of schools and kindergartens. To date, 773 classrooms have been built or rehabilitated, generating more than 150,780 person-days of short-term employment for unemployed Palestinians. The American

Scholarship Fund Program awards approximately 7,500 disadvantaged students with scholarships to pay tuition fees at private schools per year. The assistance will also make it possible for private schools to maintain basic educational services. Since September 2007, USAID has supported a Model Schools Network program and a Vocational Training and Education Development Program. The Model School program develops innovative concepts and pedagogical approaches in cooperation with the Palestinian Ministry of Education and Higher Education through a network of 20 private schools. The Vocational Training program aims to increase the relevance of non-governmental technical and vocational education and training to meet labor market needs. The Palestinian Faculty Development Program increases the capacity of the higher education sector. Finally, the Ruwwad Youth Empowerment program provides Palestinian youth with opportunities to gain leadership skills and serve their communities through youth-led initiatives.

To assist the government of **Yemen** in reforming its education system, USAID has developed programs to improve the teaching of reading, writing, and mathematics, and offers adult literacy and life-skills classes. In-service training for teachers and Parent Councils was conducted and schools were renovated and expanded. The government's decentralization goals in the education sector were supported with officials at the governorate and district levels training in data collection, data management and using data for informed decision making. A catalogue of Ministry of Education approved teaching aids has been developed to assist headmasters and teachers in acquiring educational aids through ministry channels as well as help other donors intending to support schools in Yemen. A Renovation Risk Management System was developed for 77 school renovations and all were assessed, and a mobile repair team supports self-help efforts to maintain facilities, furniture, and equipment. To date, 2,577 teachers and school administrators were trained in student-centered and active learning techniques. The impact of the teacher training at 23 schools indicates that 64% of third graders taught by USAID-trained teachers performed math problems at their grade level or above, and 74.6% read and wrote Arabic at their grade level or above.

The Asia Near East region also contains countries with significant Muslim populations though not in the majority, such as India (second largest Muslim population in the world).

USAID/India's madrassa intervention began as a pilot project with eleven madrassas in Hyderabad, Andra Pradesh in 2004. The goal of the pilot was to demonstrate an effective and scalable model for introducing formal curriculum into these religious schools. The program worked with Muslim community leaders and madrassa administrators to introduce formal curricula, enroll and retain out-of-school children, improve the quality of education, and prepare madrassas to meet government standards. The pilot program has now been extended to 586 madrassas covering 48,000 children. Resources such as honorarium, technical support and training to teachers; and textbooks and meals to students are leveraged from the government. A similar initiative is being launched in the state of West Bengal.

The **sub-Saharan Africa region** contains a number of important Muslim and Muslim majority countries, in which support to basic education activities and improved learning opportunities for in-school and out-of-school youth figure prominently. The Bureau for Africa's Office of Sustainable Development has re-evaluated the role of education and taken a more strategic approach to address the concerns of a post-9/11 society. USAID partners with Muslim communities to ensure that children in these communities are receiving the best and broadest education possible.

In support of President Bush's East Africa Counterterrorism Initiative (EACTI), programs were initiated in 2003 in East Africa that provided basic education opportunities in marginalized Muslim communities. The targeted countries include Kenya, Uganda, Tanzania, and Ethiopia.[19] A summary of these programs include:

- **USAID/Ethiopia** implemented various activities in Muslim-dominated areas particularly in Somali, Afar, and Oromia regions. The activities included support to pre-service and in-service teacher training to improve the quality of primary education; building the capacity of primary school principals to improve the management of schools; provision of capacity building training for Parent Teacher Associations (PTAs) and community members to increase parent and community involvement in school management; building the capacity of education officers to improve the planning and management of the education system; and establishment and expansion of alternative basic education centers to provide non-formal primary education to children, especially girls; and adult literacy classes for illiterate men and women.
- **USAID/Kenya's** basic education program, Education for Marginalized Children in Kenya, is concentrated in the North Eastern and Coast Provinces. Both Provinces have predominantly Muslim populations and the lowest education statistics in the country. This activity began in 2004 with supplemental funding specifically targeted at Muslim communities and continued as a part of the mission's portfolio. Over 125,000 children have been

[19]Eritrea had been part of the original list, but was eliminated during the USAID/Eritrea closeout.

reached in the Coast Province, with over 250 Early Childhood Development Centers supported and more than 3,200 teachers trained in child-centered teaching methods. The School Infrastructure Program has successfully built 107 classrooms, three dining halls, eight dormitories, and supplied desks along with bunk-beds with mattresses. In 2007, Kenya instituted a program to strengthen the management of education and its resources at the local levels, thereby beginning to address the need for more effective and higher quality basic education. In 2008, USAID launched a Higher Education Scholarship Program in collaboration with the Ministry of Education and civil society. A full four-year scholarship for undergraduate study at public university in Kenya was offered. The geographic focus was on the predominantly Muslim North Eastern province that shares a border with Somalia.

- **USAID/Tanzania's** program focused on strengthening primary school students' performances in general, and secondary math and science over the next four years with an emphasis on basic education activities for under-served children (especially girls in Muslim and rural areas). The basic education initiative provided training and materials to teachers and students; thousands of students' textbooks written in Kiswahili; and girls' scholarships. U.S. resources over the next four years will enable two programs to increase the number of girls receiving preschool, primary, and secondary education; improve primary and secondary skills in math and science; and provide specialized training for teachers in math, science, English, and the needs of children with disabilities. USAID worked with Muslim and pastoralist populations in geographic areas where there was little or no other donor support. Service delivery in Zanzibar was enhanced, in addition to two pilot districts (Lindi Urban and Mtwara Urban) on the southern Tanzanian mainland. Over 90,000 secondary, 49,000 primary, and 7,000 pre-primary school students will benefit from U.S. support targeting education delivery systems at local, district, and regional levels. In addition, an innovative radio instruction activity focused on pre-primary and primary-level education. The radio instruction activity will continue to establish 100 informal learning centers in Tanzania mainland, 125 Play and Learn Clubs in Zanzibar, and pilot radio instruction in 60 formal primary-school classrooms in Zanzibar. By the end of 2008, the program had provided equitable access to quality education for 14,700 children in Kiswahili, English, mathematics, social studies, science, and life skills.
- **USAID/Uganda** supported Madrassa Early Childhood Development (ECD), which targets poor communities and builds

on existing non-formal and informal early child education at selected community mosques and madrassas. Through the Madrassa Resource Center activity, communities are supported to establish and manage their own pre-schools by using intensive community participation methods. The project seeks to provide access to high quality, value-based, culturally relevant and affordable early childhood education and development in order to increase the chances of children from underprivileged communities entering and succeeding in the formal education system. The project has mobilized 15 community schools to participate in the program; supported 13 community schools under post graduation continuous support to ensure the long-term sustainability of the pre-schools; supported over 1,200 children in new schools and other schools; trained approximately 300 Schools' Management Committee members on how to manage their schools and 120 ECD teachers in ECD methodologies; and close to 2000 parents have been mobilized to send their children to the community schools. In addition, the Project hosted the first of its kind ECD Stakeholder Conference with the Islamic leadership and 100 participants to assist them to collectively and effectively manage the schools.

In support of the Trans-Sahara Counterterrorism Partnership

- **USAID/Mali** includes a focus on supporting moderate Islamic schools (medersas) as part of a broader strategy to improve access to quality basic education for all Malian boys and girls. Approximately 1,600 medersas will take part in USAID's "Road to Reading" program, which will use a combination of teacher training and materials development to improve the quality of French language instruction in Mali's public, community-owned, and medersa schools. A cornerstone of the "Road to Reading" program will be the development and broadcast of Interactive Radio Instruction (IRI) programs for Grades 1-6. These IRI programs will build medersa teachers' and students' ability to make the transition from Arabic into French, thus expanding students' educational and employment opportunities. To gauge the quality of instruction and impact of USAID programming in medersas, the "Road to Reading" program will implement Early Grade Reading Assessments in Arabic and French. USAID/Mali's strategy will ensure that medersas benefit from the same programs intended for public and community-owned schools. In addition, to orient USAID's and USG interventions, a comprehensive study will be conducted that will lead to recommendations for how to best support medersas in Mali.

- **USAID/Senegal's** program aimed at improving basic education in Koranic schools and benefits approximately 5,000 vulnerable children living and studying in these schools. The pilot activity, launched in late 2005, supported improvements in the living, health, nutrition, and learning conditions of children in Koranic schools. It accomplished this through the provision of hot meals; basic learning materials such as pens, books, and notebooks; and first aid kits. The program also provides training to teachers in how to effectively teach languages, math, life skills, and health education. Vocational training was offered in the areas of carpentry, sewing, masonry, and tannery. The leaders of these schools have begun to incorporating secular education in their curriculum and in promoting better nutrition and hygiene among their students.
- The President's Africa Education Initiative (AEI) in **Niger, Chad, and Mauritania** complemented the TSCTP's efforts to counter terrorism. The AEI's Ambassador Girls' Scholarship Program has enabled more girls to attend schools, and engaged parents and communities in the north of Mali and throughout Niger, Chad, and Mauritania.

While not part of EACTI or TSCTP, other countries have benefited from USAID's Bureau for Africa's efforts to reach out to Muslim populations, including Somalia, Sudan, and Djibouti.

USAID/Somalia recently increased its support for education programs that will contribute to peace building, stabilization, and counterterrorism. The USAID/Somalia education portfolio includes an innovative education program that uses radio to deliver high-quality, interactive instructional programs to marginalized children. The radio programs are broadcast throughout Somalia, including in Mogadishu, and have provided quality education to more than 200,000 school children. USAID/Somalia is also renovating 500 classrooms, improving water and sanitation facilities and strengthening communities to support local schools. A new higher education partnership between the University of Hargeisa and Eastern Mennonite University is establishing the first ever higher education program for conflict mitigation in Somalia. USAID/Somalia is also supporting a new youth education and training program that will provide 1,500 Somalia youth with viable employment opportunities.

USAID/Sudan continued to implement programs to enhance inter-religious peace-building through improving education access. Formal and non-formal programs focused on primary and girls' education, teacher training and institutional development, targeting out-of-school youth, women girls, returnees, and other vulnerable groups. The U.S. government expedited the provision of primary education and adult literacy through radio-based instruction, providing a high standard of learning for students and teachers. Conflict resolution, recovery, and prevention were integrated into the broadcasts to support the peace process.

Since 2003, **USAID/Djibouti** has supported Djibouti's education reform program to increase access to Basic Education through school rehabilitation, renovating/building water and sanitation facilities, the provision of textbooks, equipment and kits, community participation through the establishment and training of PTAs, the provision of scholarships to 1,000 girls and 338 boys, and non-formal education programs to increase girls' education. The program improved quality through teacher training, development of teachers and school principals' guides, provision of English Language learning materials, teaching and teacher training for secondary levels, and construction and equipment of pedagogic resources centers. The Ministry of Education's strategic planning and decision making system is being strengthened through the development of a planning framework using selected norms as a basis for resource allocations, and the establishment and training of a national strategic planning team to enforce its policy for decentralized planning, improved data quality, management, and use. Finally, the program provides opportunities for out-of-school youth, especially girls, through job search training, upgrading youth vocational skills, and designing and implementing partnership mechanisms to provide employment opportunities for out-of-school youth. On this and other activities, USAID collaborates with the U.S. Embassy and the Combined Joint Task Force/Horn of Africa.

Key components of **USAID/Nigeria** in FY-2008 included strengthening teachers' instructional skills in English literacy and numeracy; fostering increased enrollment, attendance and retention of girls in primary school; increasing community and civil society involvement in schools' management; promoting child-focused classroom instructional methods; and improving local and state government skills in school-based data collection and use. Approximately one-fourth of participating schools are Islamic schools, integrating secular and religious instruction, while three-quarters are public schools. The current program integrates health and education activities, provides pre- and in-service teacher training, implements interactive radio instruction, and addresses school health and nutrition issues.

CHAPTER – 6

Terrorist Organizations

Foreign Terrorist Organizations

Foreign Terrorist Organizations (FTOs) are foreign organizations that are designated by the Secretary of State in accordance with section 219 of the Immigration and Nationality Act (INA), as amended. FTO designations play a critical role in our fight against terrorism and are an effective means of curtailing support for terrorist activities and pressuring groups to get out of the terrorism business.

Identification

The Department of State continually monitors the activities of terrorist groups active around the world to identify potential targets for designation. When reviewing potential targets, the Department looks not only at the actual terrorist attacks that a group has carried out, but also at whether the group has engaged in planning and preparations for possible future acts of terrorism or retains the capability and intent to carry out such acts.

Designation

Once a target is identified, a detailed "administrative record" is prepared demonstrating that the statutory criteria for designation have been satisfied. If the Secretary of State, in consultation with the Attorney General and the Secretary of the Treasury, decides to make the designation,

Congress is notified of the Secretary's intent to designate the organization and given seven days to review the designation, as required by the Immigration and Nationality Act (INA). Upon the expiration of the seven-day waiting period and in the absence of Congressional action to block the designation, notice of the designation is published in the *Federal Register*, at which point the designation takes effect. By law an organization designated as an FTO may seek judicial review of the designation in the United States Court of Appeals for the District of Columbia Circuit not later than 30 days after the designation is published in the *Federal Register*.

Until recently the INA provided that FTOs must be redesignated every two years or the designation would lapse. Under the Intelligence Reform and Terrorism Prevention Act of 2004 (IRTPA), however, the redesignation requirement was replaced by certain review and revocation procedures. IRTPA provides that an FTO may file a petition for revocation two years after its designation date (or in the case of redesignated FTOs, its most recent redesignation date) or two years after the determination date on its most recent petition for revocation. In order to provide a basis for revocation, the petitioning FTO must provide evidence that the circumstances forming the basis for the designation are sufficiently different as to warrant revocation. If no such review has been conducted during a five year period with respect to a designation, then the Secretary of State is required to review the designation to determine whether revocation would be appropriate. In addition, the Secretary of State may at any time revoke a designation upon a finding that the circumstances forming the basis for the designation have changed in such a manner as to warrant revocation, or that the national security of the United States warrants a revocation. The same procedural requirements apply to revocations made by the Secretary of State as apply to designations. A designation may be revoked by an Act of Congress, or set aside by a Court order.

Legal Criteria for Designation under Section 219 of the INA as amended

1. It must be a *foreign organization*.
2. The organization must *engage in terrorist activity*, as defined in section 212 (a)(3)(B) of the INA (8 U.S.C. § 1182(a)(3)(B)), or *terrorism*, as defined in section 140(d)(2) of the Foreign Relations Authorization Act, Fiscal Years 1988 and 1989 (22 U.S.C. § 2656f(d)(2)), *or retain the capability and intent to engage in terrorist activity or terrorism*.
3. The organization's terrorist activity or terrorism must threaten the security of U.S. nationals *or* the national security (national defense, foreign relations, *or* the economic interests) of the United States.

U.S. Government Designated Foreign Terrorist Organizations

Abu Nidal Organization (ANO)

Abu Sayyaf Group (ASG)

Al-Aqsa Martyrs Brigade

Al-Shabaab

Ansar al-Islam

Armed Islamic Group

Asbat al-Ansar

Aum Shinrikyo

Basque Fatherland and Liberty (ETA)

Communist Party of Philippines/New People's Army

Continuity Irish Republican Army (CIRA)

Gama'a al-Islamiyya

HAMAS

Harakat ul-Jihad-i-Islami/Bangladesh (HUJI-B)

Harakat ul-Mujahideen

Hizballah Islamic Jihad Union (IJU)

Islamic Movement of Uzbekistan

Jaish-e-Mohammed

Jemaah Islamiya (JI)

Al-Jihad

Kahane Chai (Kach)

Kurdistan Workers' Party (PKK)

Lashkar e-Tayyiba (LT)

Lashkar i Jhangvi (LJ)

Liberation Tigers of Tamil Eelam (LTTE)

Libyan Islamic Fighting Group

Moroccan Islamic Combatant Group

Mujahadin-e Khalq Organization

National Liberation Army (ELN)

Palestine Liberation Front – Abu Abbas Faction

Palestinian Islamic Jihad – Shaqaqi Faction

Popular Front for the Liberation of Palestine

Popular Front for the Liberation of Palestine-General Command

Al-Qa'ida

Al-Qa'ida in Iraq (Tanzim Qa'idat al-Jihad fi Bilad al-Rafidayn)

Al-Qa'ida in the Islamic Maghreb (AQIM)

Real IRA

Revolutionary Armed Forces of Colombia

Revolutionary Nuclei

Revolutionary Organization 17 November

Revolutionary People's Liberation Party/Front

Shining Path

United Self-Defense Forces of Colombia

ABU NIDAL ORGANIZATION

a.k.a. ANO; Arab Revolutionary Brigades; Arab Revolutionary Council; Black September; Fatah Revolutionary Council; Revolutionary Organization of Socialist Muslims

Description: The Abu Nidal Organization (ANO was designated as a Foreign Terrorist Organization on October 8, 1997. The ANO, an international terrorist organization, was founded by Sabri al-Banna (a.k.a. Abu Nidal) after splitting from the Palestine Liberation Organization (PLO) in 1974. The group's previous known structure consisted of various functional committees, including political, military, and financial. In August 2002, Abu Nidal died in Baghdad, probably at the hands of Iraqi security officials. Present leadership of the organization remains unclear.

Activities: The ANO has carried out terrorist attacks in 20 countries, killing or injuring almost 900 persons. The group has not staged a major attack against Western targets since the late 1980s. Major attacks included the Rome and Vienna airports in 1985, the Neve Shalom synagogue in Istanbul, the hijacking of Pan Am Flight 73 in Karachi in 1986, and the City of Poros day-excursion ship attack in Greece in 1988. The ANO is suspected of assassinating PLO Deputy Chief Abu Iyad and PLO Security Chief Abu Hul in Tunis in 1991. In 2008, a Jordanian official reported the apprehension of an ANO member who planned to carry out attacks in Jordan. The ANO did not successfully carry out attacks in 2008.

Strength: Current strength is unknown.

Location/Area of Operation: The group is largely considered inactive, although former and possibly current ANO associates might be in Iraq and Lebanon.

External Aid: The ANO's current access to resources is unclear, but it is likely that the decline in state support has had a severe impact on its capabilities.

ABU SAYYAF GROUP

a.k.a. al Harakat al Islamiyya

Description: The Abu Sayyaf Group (ASG) was designated as a Foreign Terrorist Organization on October 8, 1997. The ASG is a terrorist group operating in the southern Philippines. Some ASG leaders allegedly fought in Afghanistan during the Soviet invasion and are students and proponents of radical Islamic teachings. The group split from the much larger Moro National Liberation Front in the early 1990s under the leadership of Abdurajak Abubakar Janjalani, who was killed in a clash with Philippine police in December 1998. His younger brother, Khadaffy Janjalani, replaced him as the nominal leader of the group. In September 2006, Janjalani was killed in a gun battle with the Armed Forces of the Philippines. Radullah Sahiron is assumed to be the new ASG leader.

Activities: The ASG engages in kidnappings for ransom, bombings, beheadings, assassinations, and extortion. The group's stated goal is to promote an independent Islamic state in western Mindanao and the Sulu Archipelago, areas in the southern Philippines heavily populated by Muslims, but the ASG primarily has used terrorist for financial profit. Recent bombings may herald a return to a more radical, politicized agenda, at least among certain factions. In 2006, the Armed Forces of the Philippines began "Operation Ultimatum," a sustained campaign that disrupted ASG forces in safe havens on Jolo Island in the Sulu archipelago, and resulted in the killing of ASG leader Khadaffy Janjalani in September 2006 and his deputy, Abu Solaiman in January 2007. In July 2007, the ASG, and Moro Islamic Liberation Front (MILF) engaged a force of Philippine marines on Basilan Island, killing fourteen, ten of which were beheaded.

The group's first large-scale action was a raid on the town of Ipil in Mindanao in April 1995. In April 2000, an ASG faction kidnapped 21 persons, including ten Western tourists, from a resort in Malaysia. In May 2001, the ASG kidnapped three U.S. citizens and 17 Filipinos from a tourist resort in Palawan, Philippines. Several of the hostages, including U.S. citizen Guillermo Sobero, were murdered. A Philippine military hostage rescue operation in June 2002 freed U.S. hostage Gracia Burnham, but her husband Martin Burnham, also a U.S. national, and Filipina Deborah Yap were killed.

U.S. and Philippine authorities blamed the ASG for a bomb near a Philippine military base in Zamboanga in October 2002 that killed a U.S.

serviceman. In February 2004, Khadaffy Janjalani's faction bombed SuperFerry 14 in Manila Bay, killing 132. In March 2004, Philippine authorities arrested an ASG cell whose bombing targets included the U.S. Embassy in Manila. The ASG also claimed responsibility for the 2005 Valentine's Day bombings in Manila, Davao City, and General Santos City, which killed eight and injured more than 150. In November 2007, a motorcycle bomb exploded outside the Philippines Congress, killing a congressman and three staff members. While there was no definitive claim of responsibility, three suspected ASG members were arrested during a subsequent raid on a safe house.

Strength: ASG is estimated to have 200 to 500 members.

Location/Area of Operation: The ASG was founded in Basilan Province and operates primarily in the provinces of the Sulu Archipelago, namely Basilan, Sulu, and Tawi-Tawi. The group also operates on the Zamboanga peninsula, and members occasionally travel to Manila. In mid-2003, the group started operating in Mindanao's city of Cotobato and on the provincial coast of Sultan Kudarat, Mindanao. The ASG was expelled from Mindanao proper by the Moro Islamic Liberation Front in mid-2005. The group expanded its operational reach to Malaysia in 2000 with the abduction of foreigners from a tourist resort there.

External Aid: The ASG is funded through acts of ransom and extortion, and receives funding from both regional terrorist groups such as Jemaah Islamiya (JI), which is based mainly in Indonesia, and Middle Eastern Islamic extremists. In October 2007, the ASG appealed for funds and recruits on *YouTube* by featuring a video of the Janjalani brothers before they were killed.

AL-AQSA MARTYRS BRIGADE

a.k.a. al-Aqsa Martyrs Battalion

Description: The al-Aqsa Martyrs Brigade was designated as a Foreign Terrorist Organization on March 27, 2002. The al-Aqsa Martyrs Brigade consists of loose cells of Palestinian militants loyal to, but not under the direct control of, the secular-nationalist Fatah movement. Al-Aqsa emerged at the outset of the 2000 Palestinian al-Aqsa intifada as a militant offshoot of the Fatah party, attacking Israeli military targets and settlers with the aim of driving Israel from the West Bank and Gaza and establishing a Palestinian state. Al-Aqsa has no central leadership; the cells operate with autonomy, although they remained ideologically loyal to Palestinian Authority (PA) President and Fatah party head Yassir Arafat until his death in November 2004.

Activities: Al-Aqsa initially focused on small arms attacks against Israeli military personnel and settlers in the West Bank. In 2002, however, the group began to conduct suicide bombings against Israeli civilians. Al-Aqsa suspended most anti-Israel attacks as part of the broader unilateral Palestinian ceasefire agreement during 2004 but resumed them following HAMAS's January 2006 victory in Palestinian Legislative Council elections. Al-Aqsa members continued the anti-Israeli and intra-Palestinian violence that contributed to the overall chaotic security environment in the Palestinian territories. In 2008, the majority of al-Aqsa attacks were rocket and mortar attacks into southern Israel from HAMAS-ruled Gaza. Israel agreed to extend a conditional pardon to 300 West Bank al-Aqsa members, but did not expand the program to the rest of the organization. Al-Aqsa has not targeted U.S. interests as a policy, although its anti-Israeli attacks have killed some dual U.S.-Israeli citizens.

Strength: Current strength is unknown, but most likely numbers a few hundred.

Location/Area of Operation: Al-Aqsa operates mainly in the West Bank and Gaza Strip and has conducted attacks inside Israel and Gaza. The group also has members in Palestinian refugee camps in Lebanon.

External Aid: Iran has exploited al-Aqsa's lack of resources and formal leadership by providing funds and other aid, mostly through Hizballah facilitators.

AL-SHABAAB

a.k.a. The Harakat Shabaab al-Mujahidin, al-Shabab, Shabaab, the Youth, Mujahidin al-Shabaab Movement, Mujahideen Youth Movement, Mujahidin Youth Movement

Description: Al-Shabaab was designated as a Foreign Terrorist Organization on February 29, 2008. Al-Shabaab is the militant wing of the former Somali Islamic Courts Council that took over most of southern Somalia in the second half of 2006. In December 2006 and January 2007, Somali government and Ethiopian forces routed the Islamic Court militias in a two-week war. Since the end of 2006, al-Shabaab and disparate clan militias led a violent insurgency, using guerrilla warfare and terrorist tactics against the Ethiopian presence in Somalia and the Transitional Federal Government of Somalia, and the African Union Mission in Somalia (AMISOM) peacekeepers.

Activities: Al-Shabaab has used intimidation and violence to undermine the Somali government and regularly kills activists working to bring about peace through political dialogue and reconciliation. The group has claimed responsibility for several high profile bombings and shootings in Mogadishu targeting Ethiopian troops and Somali government officials. It has been responsible for the assassination of numerous civil society figures, government officials, and journalists. Al-Shabaab fighters or those who have claimed allegiance to the group have also conducted violent attacks and targeted assassinations against international aid workers and nongovernmental aid organizations.

Location/Area of Operation: The majority of Ethiopian troops left Somalia in late January and the subsequent security vacuum in parts of central and southern Somalia has led divergent factions to oppose al-Shabaab and its extremist ideology. However, hardcore al-Shabaab fighters and allied militias continue to conduct brazen attacks in Mogadishu and outlying environs, primarily in lower-Somalia. After al-Shabaab's leaders publicly ordered their fighters to attack African Union (AU) peace-keeping troops based in Mogadishu, a suicide vehicle bomber detonated near an AU base in the capital on January 24, 2008, killing an estimated 13 people.

Strength: Precise numbers are unknown, however some of al-Shabaab's senior leaders are affiliated with al-Qa'ida (AQ) operatives, and it is believed that specific al-Shabaab members have previously trained and fought with AQ in Afghanistan. Al-Shabaab has issued statements praising Usama Bin Ladin and linking Somalia jihadists to AQ's global ideology.

External Aid: Al-Shabaab receives significant donations from the global Somali diaspora. It also raises funds in Somalia.

ANSAR AL-ISLAM

a.k.a. Ansar al-Sunna; Ansar al-Sunna Army; Devotees of Islam; Followers of Islam in Kurdistan; Helpers of Islam; Jaish Ansar al-Sunna; Jund al-Islam; Kurdish Taliban; Kurdistan Supporters of Islam; Partisans of Islam; Soldiers of God; Soldiers of Islam; Supporters of Islam in Kurdistan

Description: Ansar al-Islam (AI) is a Salafi terrorist group whose goals include expelling the U.S.-led Coalition from Iraq and establishing an independent Iraqi state based on Sharia law. AI was established in 2001 in Iraqi Kurdistan with the merger of two Kurdish extremist factions that traced their roots to the Islamic Movement of Kurdistan. In a probable effort to appeal to the broader Sunni jihad and expand its support base, AI changed its name to Ansar al-Sunna in 2003, in a bid to unite Iraq-based extremists under the new name. In December 2007, it changed its name back to Ansar al-Islam. AI has ties to the al-Qa'ida (AQ) central leadership and to al-Qa'ida in Iraq (AQI). Although AI did not join the

AQI-dominated "Islamic State of Iraq", relations between AI and AQI have greatly improved and efforts to merge the groups are ongoing. Some members of AI trained in AQ camps in Afghanistan, and the group provided safe haven to affiliated terrorists before Operation Iraqi Freedom (OIF). Since OIF, AI has become the second-most prominent group engaged in anti-Coalition attacks in Iraq behind AQI and has maintained a strong propaganda campaign.

Activities: AI continued to conduct attacks against a wide range of targets including Coalition Forces, the Iraqi government and security forces, and Kurdish and Shia figures. AI has claimed responsibility for many high profile attacks in 2007, including the execution-style killing of nearly two dozen Yazidi civilians in Mosul in reprisal for the stoning death of a Muslim convert in April, the car-bombing of a police convoy in Kirkuk in July, the suicide bombing of Kurdistan Democratic Party offices in Khursbat in October, and numerous kidnappings, executions, and assassinations.

Strength: Precise numbers are unknown. AI is one of the largest Sunni terrorist groups in Iraq.

Location/Area of Operation: Primarily northern Iraq, but maintains a presence in western and central Iraq.

External Aid: AI receives assistance from a loose network of associates in Europe and the Middle East.

ARMED ISLAMIC GROUP

a.k.a. GIA, al-Jama'ah al-Islamiyah al-Musallah, Groupement Islamique Arme

Description: The Armed Islamic Group (GIA) aims to overthrow the Algerian regime and replace it with a state governed by Sharia law. The GIA began its violent activity in 1992 after the military government suspended legislative elections in anticipation of an overwhelming victory by the Islamic Salvation Front, the largest Algerian Islamic opposition party.

Activities: The GIA engaged in attacks against civilians and government workers. The group began conducting a terrorist campaign of civilian massacres in 1992, sometimes wiping out entire villages and killing tens of thousands of Algerians, alienating itself from the Algerian populace. Since announcing its campaign against foreigners living in Algeria in 1992, the GIA killed more than 100 expatriate men and women, mostly Europeans, in the country. Almost all of the GIA's members have now joined other Islamist groups or have been killed or captured by the Algerian government. The Algerian government's September 2005 reconciliation program led to an increase in the number of GIA terrorist suspects who surrendered to security forces. Algerian press continues to report attacks local people attribute to the GIA, but the most recent significant attacks known to be perpetrated by the GIA occurred in August 2001. After the arrest of the GIA's last known emir and subsequent counterterrorism operations, the Algerian government declared that the GIA network was almost entirely broken up.

Strength: Precise numbers are unknown, but the group continues to decline.

Location/Area of Operation: Algeria

External Aid: Unknown.

ASBAT AL-ANSAR

Description: Asbat al-Ansar was designated as a Foreign Terrorist Organization on March 27, 2002. Asbat al-Ansar is a Lebanon-based Sunni extremist group composed primarily of Palestinians with links to the al-Qa'ida (AQ) organization and other Sunni extremist groups. Some of the group's goals include thwarting perceived anti-Islamic and pro-Western influences in the country.

Activities: Asbat al-Ansar maintains close ties with the AQ network. Its base of operations is located in the Ain al-Hilwah Palestinian refugee camp near Sidon. Asbat al-Ansar has recently been reluctant to involve itself in operations in Lebanon due in part to concerns over losing its safe haven in Ain al-Hilwah. Various extremist web forums criticized Asbat al-Ansar for its failure to support fellow Sunni extremist group Fatah al-Islam (FAI) during the Lebanese Armed Forces campaign in summer 2007. That campaign forced FAI out of Nahr al-Barid refugee camp in northern Lebanon, and severely damaged the group.

Members of Asbat al-Ansar were believed responsible for a Katyusha rocket attack on the Galilee region of Israel in December 2005. Asbat al-Ansar operatives have been involved in fighting Coalition Forces in Iraq since at least 2005 and several members of the group have been killed in anti-Coalition operations. Al-Sa'di was working in cooperation with Abu Muhammad al-Masri, the head of AQ at the Ain al-Hilwah refugee camp, where fighting has occurred between Asbat al-Ansar and Fatah elements. In 2007, Asbat al-Ansar remained focused on supporting jihad in Iraq and planning attacks against UNIFIL, Lebanese security forces, and U.S. and Western interests. Asbat al-Ansar-associated elements were implicated in the June 17, 2007 Katyusha rocket attack against northern Israel.

Asbat al-Ansar first emerged in the early 1990s. In the mid-1990s the group assassinated Lebanese religious leaders and bombed nightclubs, theaters, and liquor stores. It was involved in clashes in northern Lebanon in December 1999, and carried out a rocket-propelled grenade attack on the Russian Embassy in Beirut in January 2000. Asbat al-Ansar's leader, Ahmad Abd al-Karim al-Sa'di, a.k.a. Abu Muhjin, remains at large despite being sentenced to death in absentia for the 1994 murder of a Muslim cleric. In September 2004, operatives with links to the group were allegedly involved in planning terrorist operations targeting the Italian Embassy, the Ukrainian Consulate General, and Lebanese government offices. In October 2004, Mahir al-Sa'di, a member of Asbat al-Ansar, was sentenced in absentia to life imprisonment for his 2000 plot to assassinate then U.S. Ambassador to Lebanon, David Satterfield.

Strength: The group commands between 100 and 300 fighters in Lebanon. Its named leader is Ahmad Abd al-Karim al-Sa'di.

Location/Area of Operation: The group's primary base of operations is the Ain al-Hilwah Palestinian refugee camp near Sidon in southern Lebanon.

External Aid: It is likely the group receives money through international Sunni extremist networks.

AUM SHINRIKYO

a.k.a. A.I.C. Comprehensive Research Institute; A.I.C. Sogo Kenkyusho; Aleph; Aum Supreme Truth.

Description: Aum Shinrikyo was designated as a Foreign Terrorist Organization on October 8, 1997. Shoko Asahara established Aum Shinrikyo (Aum) in 1987, and the cult received legal status as a religious entity in 1989. Initially, Aum aimed to take over Japan and then the world, but over time it began to emphasize the imminence of the end of the world. Asahara predicted 1996, and 1999 to 2003, as likely dates and said that the United States would initiate Armageddon by starting World War III with Japan. The Japanese government revoked its recognition of Aum as a religious organization following Aum's deadly sarin gas attack in Tokyo in March 1995. In 1997, however, a government panel decided not to invoke the Operations Control Law to outlaw the group. A 1999 law authorized the Japanese government to maintain police surveillance over the group because of concerns that Aum might launch future terrorist attacks. In January 2000, under the leadership of Fumihiro Joyu, the chief of Aum's once thriving Moscow operation, Aum changed its name to Aleph and tried to distance itself from the violent and apocalyptic teachings of its founder. In late 2003, however, Joyu stepped down under pressure from members who wanted to return fully to the worship of Asahara. A growing divide between members supporting Joyu and Asahara emerged. In 2007, Joyu officially split and in May established a splinter group called

Hikari No Wa, which is translated as Circle of Light or Ring of Light. Japanese authorities continued to monitor both Aum (now called Aleph) and Hikari No Wa.

Activities: In March 1995, Aum members simultaneously released the chemical nerve agent sarin on several Tokyo subway trains, killing 12 persons and causing up to 6,000 to seek medical treatment. Subsequent investigations by the Japanese government revealed the group was responsible for other mysterious chemical incidents in Japan in 1994, including a sarin gas attack on a residential neighborhood in Matsumoto that killed seven and hospitalized approximately 500. Japanese police arrested Asahara in May 1995, and in February 2004 authorities sentenced him to death for his role in the 1995 attacks. In September 2006, Asahara lost his final appeal against the death penalty.

Since 1997, the cult has recruited new members, engaged in commercial enterprises, and acquired property, although it scaled back these activities significantly in 2001 in response to a public outcry. In July 2001, Russian authorities arrested a group of Russian Aum followers who had planned to set off bombs near the Imperial Palace in Tokyo as part of an operation to free Asahara from jail and smuggle him to Russia.

Although Aum has not conducted a terrorist attack since 1995, concerns remain regarding their continued adherence to the violent teachings of founder Asahara that led them to perpetrate the sarin gas attack in Tokyo.

Strength: According to a study by the Japanese government issued in December 2008, current Aum Shinrikyo/Aleph membership in Japan is approximately 1,500 as well as approximately 200 in Russia, in addition to maintaining 30 facilities in 15 Prefectures, to include Tokyo and a few in Russia. At the time of the Tokyo subway attack, the group claimed to have as many as 40,000 members worldwide, including 9,000 in Japan and 30,000 members in Russia.

Location/Area of Operation: Aum's principal membership is located in Japan while a residual branch of about 300 followers live in Russia.

External Aid: None.

BASQUE FATHERLAND AND LIBERTY (ETA)

a.k.a. ETA, Askatasuna; Batasuna; Ekin; Euskal Herritarrok; Euzkadi Ta Askatasuna; Herri Batasuna; Jarrai-Haika-Segi; K.A.S.; XAKI

Description: Basque Fatherland and Liberty (ETA) was designated as a Foreign Terrorist Organization on October 8, 1997. Basque Fatherland and Liberty (ETA) was founded in 1959 with the aim of establishing an independent homeland based on Marxist principles encompassing the

Spanish Basque provinces of Vizcaya, Guipuzcoa, and Alava, the autonomous region of Navarra, and the southwestern French territories of Labourd, Basse-Navarre, and Soule. Spain and the EU both have listed ETA as a terrorist organization; in 2002 the Spanish Parliament banned the political party Batasuna, ETA's political wing, charging its members with providing material support to the terrorist group. In September 2008, Spanish courts in September also banned two other Basque independence parties with reported links to Batasuna.

Spanish and French prisons together are estimated to hold a total of more than 750 ETA members. In March 2006, days after claiming responsibility for a spate of roadside blasts in northern Spain that caused no injuries, ETA announced that it would implement a "permanent" cease-fire. On December 30, 2006, however, ETA exploded a massive car bomb that destroyed much of the covered parking garage outside the new Terminal Four of Madrid's Barajas International Airport. Two individuals killed in the blast became ETA's first fatalities in more than three years. The Spanish Government suspended talks with ETA and government officials later said political negotiations with the group had ended.

Activities: ETA primarily conducts bombings and assassinations. Targets are typically Spanish government officials, security and military forces, politicians, and judicial figures, but the group also has targeted journalists and tourist areas. The group is responsible for killing more than 800 and injuring thousands more since it began its lethal attacks in the late 1960s. Security service scrutiny and a public outcry after the Islamic extremist train bombings in Madrid in March 2004 have limited ETA's capability and willingness to inflict casualties. In February 2005, ETA detonated a car bomb in Madrid at a convention center where Spanish King Juan Carlos and then Mexican President Vicente Fox were scheduled to appear, wounding more than 20 people. ETA also detonated an explosive device at a stadium constructed as part of Madrid's bid to host the 2012 Olympic Games. There were no injuries in that attack. ETA's late 2006 attack at Madrid's airport was the group's first fatal attack since March 2003.

ETA formally renounced its permanent cease-fire in June 2007 and three months later threatened a wave of attacks throughout Spain. By mid-2007, there were indications that the group may have expanded its logistical operations, such as renting vehicles, into Portugal. In October 2007, Spain and Portugal agreed to intensify their cooperation against ETA by establishing a joint counterterrorism team based in Lisbon.

In 2008, ETA continued to perpetrate attacks which resulted in casualties. In March 2008, just days before the national election, ETA fatally shot a former Spanish politician, Isaias Carrasco, outside his home in northern Spain. In May, a car bomb exploded outside a Civil Guard barracks in Legutiano, killing one policeman and wounding four others. In July, Eta was responsible for five bomb explosions in northern Spain, including four at popular seaside resorts. In September, a an ETA car bomb killed an army officer and injured several other people in the northern town of Santona. In October, ETA members conducted a car bomb attack at a university in Pamplona that injured more than one dozen people. The group also claimed responsibility for the December killing of Ignacio Uria, a leading Basque businessman, for failing to pay extortion money to ETA and for his construction company's involvement in the building of high-speed train links in the Basque Country, which ETA opposes.

In 2008, French authorities apprehended ETA's top three leaders, beginning in May with the arrest of Francisco Javier Lopez Pena (a.k.a. Thierry). In November, French police arrested Garikoitz Aspiazu (a.k.a. Txeroki), who is suspected of ordering a December 2006 car bombing at the Madrid airport. One month later, French police captured his alleged replacement, Aitzol Iriondo Yarza (a.k.a. Gurbitz).

Strength: ETA's current strength is unknown as a result of the arrest of 365 ETA members in 2007 and 2008.

Location/Area of Operation: ETA operates primarily in the Basque autonomous regions of northern Spain and southwestern France, but has attacked Spanish and French interests elsewhere.

External Aid: ETA finances its activities primarily through bribery and extortion of Basque businesses. It has received training at various times in the past in Libya, Lebanon, and Nicaragua. Some ETA members have allegedly fled to Cuba and Mexico, while others reside in South America. ETA members have operated and been arrested in other European countries, including France, Belgium, the Netherlands, the UK, Germany, and Portugal.

COMMUNIST PARTY OF PHILIPPINES/NEW PEOPLE'S ARMY

a.k.a. CPP/NPA; Communist Party of the Philippines; the CPP; New People's Army; the NPA.

Description: The Communist Party of the Philippines (CPP/NPA) was designated as a Foreign Terrorist Organization on August 9, 2002. The military wing of the Communist Party of the Philippines (CPP), the New People's Army (NPA), is a Maoist group formed in March 1969 with the aim of overthrowing the government through protracted guerrilla warfare. Jose Maria Sison, the chairman of the CPP's Central Committee and the NPA's founder, reportedly directs CPP and NPA activity from the Netherlands, where he lives in self-imposed exile. Luis Jalandoni, a fellow Central Committee member and director of the CPP's overt political wing, the National Democratic Front (NDF), also lives in the Netherlands and has become a Dutch citizen. Although primarily a rural-based guerrilla group, the NPA has an active urban infrastructure to support its terrorist activities and at times uses city-based assassination squads.

In September 2007, Sison was briefly arrested in the Netherlands, but was released on a judge's order a few days later. In November 2007, the Armed Forces of the Philippines announced the capture of Elizabeth Principe, a suspected member of the Central Committee of the Communist Party of the Philippines.

Activities: The NPA primarily targets Philippine security forces, government officials, local infrastructure, and businesses that refuse to pay extortion, or "revolutionary taxes." The NPA charges politicians running for office in NPA-influenced areas for "campaign permits." The group opposes any U.S. military presence in the Philippines and has attacked U.S. military interests; it killed several U.S. service personnel before the U.S. base closures in 1992. The NPA claimed responsibility for the assassination of two congressmen, one from Quezon in May 2001 and one from Cagayan in June 2001, among other killings. Periodic peace talks with the Philippine government stalled after these incidents. In December 2005, the NPA publicly expressed its intent to target U.S. personnel if they were discovered in NPA operating areas.

Strength: Estimated at less than 9,000, a number significantly lower than its peak strength of approximately 25,000 in the 1980s.

Location/Area of Operations: The NPA operates in rural Luzon, Visayas, and parts of northern and eastern Mindanao. There are cells in Manila and other metropolitan centers.

External Aid: Unknown.

CONTINUITY IRISH REPUBLICAN ARMY (CIRA)

a.k.a. Continuity Army Council; Continuity IRA; Republican Sinn Fein

Description: The Continuity Irish Republican Army (CIRA) was designated as a Foreign Terrorist Organization on July 13, 2004. CIRA is a terrorist splinter group formed in 1994 as the clandestine armed wing of Republican Sinn Fein, which split from Sinn Fein in 1986. "Continuity" refers to the group's belief that it is carrying on the original Irish Republican Army's (IRA) goal of forcing the British out of Northern Ireland. CIRA's aliases, Continuity Army Council and Republican Sinn Fein, are included in its FTO designation. CIRA cooperates with the larger Real IRA (RIRA).

Activities: CIRA has been active in Belfast and the border areas of Northern Ireland, where it has carried out bombings, assassinations, kidnappings, hijackings, extortion, and robberies. On occasion, it has provided advance warning to police of its attacks. Targets have included the British military, Northern Ireland security forces, and Loyalist paramilitary groups. CIRA did not join the Provisional IRA in the September 2005 decommissioning and remains capable of effective, if sporadic, terrorist attacks. In early 2006, the Independent Monitoring Commission reported that two splinter organizations, Óglaigh na hÉireann and Saoirse na hÉireann, were formed as a result of internal disputes within CIRA. In late 2006, CIRA members issued a list of up to 20 individuals they were targeting for paramilitary attacks, several of whom were wounded in subsequent shootings. Around the same time, CIRA claimed the firebomb attacks of B&Q home-supply stores, although RIRA also claimed such attacks. CIRA activity has largely decreased from previous levels seen in 2005.

By 2007, the group had become increasingly active in criminal activity in Northern Ireland and Ireland. In April 2007, following the discovery of an improvised mortar (direct-fire mode) adjacent to the railway line in Lurgan, three CIRA members were arrested and charged with conspiracy to murder, possession of explosives with intent to endanger life, and possession of articles for use in terrorism. The Independent Monitoring Commission, which was established to oversee the peace process, assessed that CIRA was responsible for both the June 2008 command detonated explosive device against a police patrol car and an August 2008 attempted rocket attack in Lisnaskea. In November 2008, CIRA publicly threatened to murder any Belfast Catholic community workers found to be cooperating with the police.

Strength: Membership is small, with possibly fewer than 50 hard-core activists. Police counterterrorist operations have reduced the group's strength.

Location/Area of Operation: Northern Ireland and the Irish Republic. CIRA does not have an established presence in Great Britain.

External Aid: Suspected of receiving funds and arms from sympathizers in the United States. CIRA may have acquired arms and materiel from the Balkans, in cooperation with the Real IRA.

GAMA'A AL-ISLAMIYYA

a.k.a. al-Gama'at; Egyptian al-Gama'at al-Islamiyya; GI, Islamic Gama'at, IG; Islamic Group, Egyptian Islamic Group.

Description: Gama'a al-Islamiyya (IG) was designated as a Foreign Terrorist Organization on October 8, 1997. Gama'a al-Islamiyya, once Egypt's largest militant groups, was active in the late 1970s, but is now a loosely organized network. Many of its members have renounced terrorism, although some have begun to work with or have joined al-Qa ida (AQ). The external wing, composed of mainly exiled members in several countries, maintains that its primary goal is to overthrow the Egyptian government and replace it with an Islamic state, though most of the group's leadership have renounced violence as a means to do so. The IG announced a cease-fire in 1997 that led to a split into two factions: one, led by Mustafa Hamza, supported the cease-fire; the other, led by Rifa'i Taha Musa, called for a return to armed operations. The IG announced another ceasefire in March 1999, but its spiritual leader, Sheik Umar Abd al-Rahman, sentenced to life in prison in January 1996 for his involvement in the 1993 World Trade Center bombing and incarcerated in the United States, rescinded his support for the cease-fire in June 2000. IG has not conducted an attack inside Egypt since the 1997 Luxor attack, which killed 58 tourists and four Egyptians, and wounded dozens more. In February 1998, a senior member signed Usama bin Ladin's fatwa call for attacks against the United States.

In early 2001, Taha Musa published a book in which he attempted to justify terrorist attacks that cause mass casualties. Musa disappeared several months afterward and the United States has no information about his whereabouts. In March 2002, members of the group's historic leadership in Egypt declared the use of violence misguided and renounced its future use, prompting denunciations from much of the leadership abroad. The Egyptian government continued to release IG members from prison; approximately 900 were released in 2003 and most of the 700 persons released in 2004 at the end of the Muslim holy month of Ramadan were IG members. In August 2006, Ayman al-Zawahiri announced that IG had merged with AQ, but the group's Egypt-based leadership quickly denied this claim which ran counter to their reconciliation efforts.

Activities: Before the 1997 cease-fire, IG conducted armed attacks against Egyptian security and other government officials, Coptic Christians, and Egyptian opponents of Islamic extremism. After the cease-fire, the faction led by Taha Musa launched attacks on tourists in Egypt, most notably the 1997 Luxor attack. IG claimed responsibility for the June 1995 assassination attempt on Egyptian President Hosni Mubarak in Addis Ababa, Ethiopia. IG was dormant in 2008.

Strength: At its peak, IG probably commanded several thousand hardcore members and a similar number of supporters. Security crackdowns following the 1997 attack in Luxor, the 1999 cease-fire, and post-September 11 security measures and defections to AQ have probably resulted in a substantial decrease in what is left of an organized group and its ability to conduct attacks.

Location/Area of Operation: The IG maintains an external presence in Afghanistan, Yemen, Iran, the United Kingdom, Germany, and France. IG terrorist presence in Egypt is minimal due to the reconciliation efforts of former local members.

External Aid: AQ and Afghan militant groups provide support to members of the organization to carry out support on behalf of AQ. IG also may obtain some funding through various Islamic non-governmental organizations.

HAMAS

a.k.a. the Islamic Resistance Movement, Harakat al-Muqawama al-Islamiya; Izz al-Din al Qassam Battalions; Izz al-Din al Qassam Brigades; Izz al-Din al Qassam Forces; Students of Ayyash; Student of the Engineer; Yahya Ayyash Units; Izz al-Din al-Qassim Brigades; Izz al-Din al-Qassim Forces; Izz al-Din al-Qassim Battalions

Description: HAMAS was designated as a Foreign Terrorist Organization on October 8, 1997. HAMAS includes military and political wings and was formed in late 1987 at the onset of the first Palestinian uprising, or Intifada, as an outgrowth of the Palestinian branch of the Muslim Brotherhood. The armed element, called the Izz al-Din al-Qassam Brigades, conducts anti-Israeli attacks, including suicide bombings against civilian targets inside Israel. HAMAS also manages a broad, mostly Gaza-based network of "Dawa" or ministry activities that include charities, schools, clinics, youth camps, fund-raising, and political activities. A Shura council based in Damascus, Syria, sets overall policy. After winning Palestinian Legislative Council elections in January 2006, HAMAS seized control of significant Palestinian Authority (PA) ministries, including the Ministry of Interior. HAMAS subsequently formed an expanded, overt militia called the Executive Force, subordinate to the Ministry. This force and other HAMAS cadres took control of Gaza in a military-style coup in June 2007, forcing Fatah forces to either leave Gaza or go underground.

Activities: Prior to 2005, HAMAS conducted numerous anti-Israeli attacks, including suicide bombings, rocket launches, improvised-explosive device (IED) attacks, and shootings. HAMAS has not directly targeted U.S. interests, though the group makes little or no effort to avoid soft targets frequented by foreigners. The group curtailed terrorist attacks in February 2005 after agreeing to a temporary period of calm brokered by the PA, and ceased most violence after winning control of the PA legislature and cabinet in January 2006. After HAMAS staged a June 2006 attack on IDF soldiers near Kerem Shalom that resulted in two deaths and the abduction of Corporal Gilad Shalit, Israel took steps that severely limited the operation of the Rafah crossing. In June 2007, HAMAS took control of Gaza from the PA and Fatah in a military-style coup, leading to an international boycott and closure of Gaza borders. HAMAS has since dedicated the majority of its activity in Gaza to solidifying its control, hardening its defenses, tightening security, and conducting limited operations against Israeli military forces.

HAMAS fired rockets from Gaza into Israel in 2008 but focused more on mortar attacks targeting Israeli incursions. Additionally, other terrorist groups in Gaza fired rockets into Israel, most, presumably, with HAMAS support or acquiescence. Following the June 2007 takeover of the Gaza Strip the majority of HAMAS activity has been directed at solidifying its control, including providing security and enforcing law and order. In June 2008, HAMAS agreed to a six-month cease-fire with Israel and temporarily halted all rocket attacks emanating from the Gaza Strip by arresting Palestinian militants and violators of the agreement. HAMAS fought a 23-day war with Israel from late December 2008 to January 2009, in an effort to break an international blockade on the Gaza Strip and force the openings of the international crossings. HAMAS' failure to end its international isolation and open the borders could lead to future violent actions, but HAMAS appears, for now, to be focusing on a diplomatic solution.

Strength: HAMAS probably has several thousand operatives with varying degrees of skills in its armed wing, the al-Qassam Brigades, along with its reported 9,000-man Executive Force and tens of thousands of supporters and sympathizers.

Location/Area of Operation: HAMAS has an operational presence in every major city in the Palestinian territories and currently focuses its anti-Israeli attacks on targets in the West Bank and within Israel. HAMAS could potentially activate operations in Lebanon or resume terrorist operations in Israel. The group retains a cadre of leaders and facilitators that conducts diplomatic, fundraising, and arms-smuggling activities in Lebanon, Syria, and other states. HAMAS is also increasing its presence in the Palestinian refugee camps in Lebanon, probably with the mid-term goal of eclipsing Fatah's long-time dominance of the camps and long-term goal of seizing control of the Palestinian Liberation Organization.

External Aid: HAMAS receives some funding, weapons, and training from Iran. In addition, fundraising takes place in the Persian Gulf countries, but the group also receives donations from Palestinian expatriates around the world and private benefactors in Arab states. Some fundraising and propaganda activity takes place in Western Europe and North America.

HARAKAT UL-JIHAD-I-ISLAMI/BANGLADESH (HUJI-B)

a.k.a. Harakat ul Jihad e Islami Bangladesh; Harkatul Jihad al Islam; Harkatul Jihad; Harakat ul Jihad al Islami; Harkat ul Jihad al Islami; Harkat-ul-Jehad-al-Islami; Harakat ul Jihad Islami Bangladesh; Islami Dawat-e-Kafela; IDEK

Description: Harakat ul-Jihad-i-Islami/Bangladesh (HUJI-B) was designated as a Foreign Terrorist Organization on March 5, 2008. HUJI-B was formed in April 1992 by a group of former Bangladeshi Afghan veterans to establish an Islamic social system based on the Medina Charter. The group was banned by Bangladeshi authorities in October 2005. In May 2008, HUJI-B members formed a new organization, the Islamic Democratic Party (IDP). In November, government authorities rejected their application for registering as a party that could participate in elections. HUJI-B has connections to the Pakistani militant groups Harakat ul-Jihad-Islami (HUJI) and Harakat ul-Mujahedin (HUM), which advocate similar objectives in Pakistan, Jammu, and Kashmir. The leaders of HUJI-B and HUM both signed the February 1998 fatwa sponsored by Usama bin Ladin that declared American civilians to be legitimate targets for attack.

Activities: HUJI-B may be responsible for numerous terrorist attacks in India, including an October 2008 attack in a shopping area in Agartala, Tripura that killed three and wounded over 100 people. The Agartala attack may have been conducted jointly with a local Indian separatist group. HUJI-B has trained and fielded operatives in Burma to fight on behalf of the Rohingya, an Islamic minority group. Three HUJI-B members were convicted in December 2008 for the grenade attack on the British High Commissioner in May 2004 in Sylhet, Bangladesh. Bangladeshi courts issued warrants in December 2008 for the arrest of eight HUJI-B members for the bombing at a festival in April 2001 that killed 10 and injured scores of people. In May, Indian police arrested HUJI-B militant Mohammad Iqbal, a.k.a. Abdur Rehman, who was charged with plotting attacks in Delhi, India. HUJI-B and its detained leader, Mufti Hannan, are also suspected in a 2000 assassination attempt on Bangladeshi Prime Minister Sheikh Hasina.

Strength: HUJI-B leaders have claimed up to 400 members are Afghan war veterans, but its total membership is unknown.

Location/Area of Operation: The group operates primarily in Bangladesh, India, and Burma. HUJI-B has a network of madrassas and conducts trainings in Bangladesh.

External Aid: HUJI-B funding comes from a variety of sources. Several international Islamic NGOs such as the South African-based Servants of Suffering Humanity may have funneled money to HUJI-B and other Bangladeshi militant groups. HUJI-B also can draw funding from local militant madrassa leaders and teachers.

HARAKAT UL-MUJAHIDEEN (HUM)

a.k.a. HUM; Harakat ul-Ansar; HUA; Jamiat ul-Ansar.

Description: Harakat ul-Mujahideen (HUM) was designated as a Foreign Terrorist Organization on October 8, 1997. HUM, an Islamic militant group based in Pakistan, is politically aligned with the political party Jamiat Ulema-i-Islam's Fazlur Rehman faction (JUI-F), and operates primarily in Kashmir. Reportedly under pressure from the Government of Pakistan, HUM's long-time leader Fazlur Rehman Khalil stepped down and was replaced by Dr. Badr Munir as the head of HUM in January 2005. Khalil has been linked to Usama bin Ladin, and his signature was found on Bin Ladin's fatwa in February 1998, calling for attacks on U.S. and Western interests. HUM operated terrorist training camps in eastern Afghanistan until Coalition air strikes destroyed them in autumn 2001. Khalil was detained by Pakistani authorities in mid-2004 and subsequently released in late December of the same year. In 2003, HUM began using the name Jamiat ul-Ansar (JUA). Pakistan banned JUA in November 2003.

Activities: HUM has conducted a number of operations against Indian troops and civilian targets in Kashmir. It is linked to the Kashmiri militant group al-Faran that kidnapped five Western tourists in Kashmir in July 1995; the five reportedly were killed later that year. HUM was responsible for the hijacking of an Indian airliner in December 1999 that resulted in the release of Masood Azhar, an important leader in the former Harakat ul-Ansar, who was imprisoned by India in 1994 and then founded Jaish-e-Mohammed (JEM) after his release. Ahmed Omar Sheik also was released in 1999 and was later convicted of the abduction and murder in 2002 of U.S. journalist Daniel Pearl.

Strength: HUM has several hundred armed supporters located in Azad Kashmir, Pakistan; India's southern Kashmir and Doda regions; and in the Kashmir valley. Supporters are mostly Pakistanis and Kashmiris, but also include Afghans and Arab veterans of the Afghan war. HUM uses light and heavy machine guns, assault rifles, mortars, explosives, and rockets. When JEM was founded in 2000, HUM lost a significant share of its membership in defections to the JEM.

Location/Area of Operation: Based in Muzaffarabad, Rawalpindi, and several other cities in Pakistan, HUM conducts insurgent and terrorist

JAISH-E-MOHAMMED

a.k.a. the Army of Mohammed; Mohammed's Army; Tehrik ul-Furqaan; Khuddam-ul-Islam; Khuddamul Islam; Kuddam-e-Islami

Description: Jaish-e-Mohammed (JEM) was designated as a Foreign Terrorist Organization on December 26, 2001. JEM is an Islamic extremist group based in Pakistan that was founded in early 2000 by Masood Azhar, a former senior leader of Harakat ul-Ansar, upon his release from prison in India. The group's aim is to unite Kashmir with Pakistan and it has openly declared war against the United States. It is politically aligned with the radical political party Jamiat Ulema-i-Islam's Fazlur Rehman faction (JUI-F). Pakistan outlawed JEM in 2002. By 2003, JEM had splintered into Khuddam ul-Islam (KUI), headed by Azhar, and Jamaat ul-Furqan (JUF), led by Abdul Jabbar, who was released from Pakistani custody in August 2004. Pakistan banned KUI and JUF in November 2003.

Activities: JEM continued to operate openly in parts of Pakistan despite then President Musharraf's 2002 ban on its activities. The group was well-funded and was said to have tens of thousands of followers who supported attacks against Indian targets, the Pakistani government, and sectarian minorities. Since Masood Azhar's 1999 release from Indian custody in exchange for 155 hijacked Indian Airlines hostages, JEM has conducted many fatal terrorist attacks in the area.

JEM continued to claim responsibility for several suicide car bombings in Kashmir, including an October 2001 suicide attack on the Jammu and Kashmir legislative assembly building in Srinagar that killed more than 30 people. The Indian government has publicly implicated JEM, along with Lashkar e-Tayyiba (LT), for the December 2001 attack on the Indian Parliament that killed nine and injured 18. Pakistani authorities suspect that JEM members may have been involved in the 2002 anti-Christian attacks in Islamabad, Murree, and Taxila that killed two Americans. In December 2003, Pakistan implicated elements of JEM in the two assassination attempts against President Musharraf. In July 2004, Pakistani authorities arrested a JEM member wanted in connection with the 2002 abduction and murder of U.S. journalist Daniel Pearl. In 2006, JEM claimed responsibility for a number of attacks, including the killing of several Indian police officials in the Indian-administered Kashmir capital of Srinagar.

Strength: JEM has at least several hundred armed supporters, including a large cadre of former HUM members, located in Pakistan, in India's southern Kashmir and Doda regions, and in the Kashmir Valley. Supporters are mostly Pakistanis and Kashmiris, but also include Afghans and Arab veterans of the Afghan war. The group uses light and heavy machine guns, assault rifles, mortars, improvised explosive devices, and rocket-propelled grenades.

Location/Area of Operation: Pakistan and Kashmir. Prior to autumn 2001, JEM maintained training camps in Afghanistan.

External Aid: Most of JEM's cadre and material resources have been drawn from the Pakistani militant groups Harakat ul-Jihad-i-Islami (HUJI-B) and the Harakat ul-Mujahadin (HUM). In anticipation of asset seizures by the Pakistani government, JEM withdrew funds from bank accounts and invested in legal businesses, such as commodity trading, real estate, and production of consumer goods. In addition, JEM collects funds through donation requests in magazines and pamphlets, and allegedly from al-Qa'ida.

JEMAAH ISLAMIYA (JI)

Description: Jemaah Islamiya (JI) was designated as a Foreign Terrorist Organization on October 23, 2002. Southeast Asia-based JI is a terrorist group that seeks the establishment of an Islamic caliphate spanning Indonesia, Malaysia, southern Thailand, Singapore, Brunei, and the southern Philippines. More than 300 JI operatives, including operations chief Hambali, have been captured since 2002, although many of these were subsequently released after serving short sentences, including former JI emir Abu Bakar Bashir. Abu Bakar was released from prison in 2006 after serving a 25-month sentence for his involvement in the 2002 Bali bombings. Indonesia's Supreme Court later that year acquitted him of the charges. The death of top JI bomb maker Azahari bin Husain in 2005 and a series of high-profile arrests between 2005 and 2008, in combination with additional efforts by the Government of Indonesia, likely disrupted JI's anti-Western attacks that occurred annually from 2002-2005. These included the 2006 arrests of several close associates of senior JI operative Noordin Mat Top, the 2007 arrests of former acting JI emir Muhammad Naim (a.k.a. Zarkasih) and JI military commander Abu Dujana, the 2008 arrests of two senior JI operatives in Malaysia, and the mid-2008 arrest of a JI-linked cell in Sumatra.

Activities: The group's most recent high-profile attack occurred in Bali on October 1, 2005, which left 25 persons dead, including the three suicide bombers. Other major JI attacks included the September 2004 bombing outside the Australian Embassy in Jakarta, the August 2003 bombing of the J. W. Marriott Hotel in Jakarta, and the October 2002 Bali bombing. The 2002 Bali attack, which killed more than 200, was one of the deadliest terrorist attacks since 9/11. In December 2001, Singaporean authorities uncovered a JI plot to attack the U.S. and Israeli Embassies, and British and Australian diplomatic buildings in Singapore. In December 2000, JI coordinated bombings of numerous Christian churches in Indonesia and was involved in the bombings of several targets in Manila. In February 2004, JI facilitated attacks in Manila, Davao, and General Santos City. JI associates in the Philippines provide operational support and training for indigenous Philippine Muslim violent extremists.

Strength: Exact numbers currently are unknown. Estimates of total JI members vary from the hundreds to one thousand.

Location/Area of Operation: JI is based in Indonesia and is believed to have cells in Indonesia, Malaysia, and the Philippines.

External Aid: Investigations indicate that JI is fully capable of its own fundraising, although it also has received financial, ideological, and logistical support from Middle Eastern contacts and non-governmental organizations.

AL-JIHAD

a.k.a. Egyptian Islamic Jihad; Egyptian al-Jihad; New Jihad; Jihad Group.

Description: In 2001, this Egyptian Islamic extremist group merged with al-Qa'ida (AQ). Usama bin Ladin's deputy, Ayman al-Zawahiri, was the former head of Al-Jihad (AJ). Active since the 1970s, AJ's primary goal has been the overthrow of the Egyptian government and the establishment of an Islamic state. The group's targets, historically, have been high-level Egyptian government officials as well as U.S. and Israeli interests in Egypt and abroad. Regular Egyptian crackdowns on extremists and Cairo's deradicalization measures, such as its very successful reconciliation program aimed at imprisoned AJ members have greatly reduced AJ's capabilities in Egypt.

Activities: The original AJ was responsible for the 1981 assassination of Egyptian President Anwar Sadat. It claimed responsibility for the attempted assassinations in 1993 of Interior Minister Hassan al-Alfi and Prime Minister Atef Sedky. AJ has not conducted an attack inside Egypt since 1993 and has never successfully targeted foreign tourists there. The group was responsible for the Egyptian Embassy bombing in Islamabad in 1995 and a disrupted plot against the U.S. Embassy in Albania in 1998. AJ has not committed independent acts of terrorism since its merger with AQ in 2001.

Strength: Believed to have an indeterminate number of hard-core members outside Egypt.

Location/Area of Operation: Most AJ members today are outside Egypt in countries such as Afghanistan, Pakistan, Lebanon, the United Kingdom, and Yemen. AJ activities have been centered outside Egypt for several years under the auspices of AQ.

KAHANE CHAI (KACH)

a.k.a. American Friends of the United Yeshiva; American Friends of Yeshivat Rav Meir; Committee for the Safety of the Roads; Dikuy Bogdim; DOV; Forefront of the Idea; Friends of the Jewish Idea Yeshiva; Jewish Legion; Judea Police; Judean Congress; Kach; Kahane; Kahane Lives; Kahane Tzadak; Kahane.org; Kahanetzadak.com; Kfar Tapuah Fund; Koach; Meir's Youth; New Kach Movement; Newkach.org; No'ar Meir; Repression of Traitors; State of Judea; Sword of David; The Committee Against Racism and Discrimination (CARD); The Hatikva Jewish Identity Center; The International Kahane Movement; The Jewish Idea Yeshiva; The Judean Legion; The Judean Voice; The Qomemiyut Movement; The Rabbi Meir David Kahane Memorial Fund; The Voice of Judea; The Way of the Torah; The Yeshiva of the Jewish Idea; Yeshivat Harav Meir

Description: Kahane Chai's (Kach) stated goal was to restore the biblical state of Israel. Kach was founded by radical Israeli-American rabbi Meir Kahane. Its offshoot, Kahane Chai, (translation: "Kahane Lives") was founded by Meir Kahane's son Binyamin following his father's 1990 assassination in the United States. Both Kach and Kahane Chai were declared terrorist organizations in 1994 by the Israeli Cabinet under its 1948 Terrorism Law. This designation followed the groups' statements in support of Dr. Baruch Goldstein's attack in February 1994 on the Ibrahimi Mosque and their verbal attacks on the Israeli government. Palestinian gunmen killed Binyamin Kahane and his wife in a drive-by shooting in December 2000 in the West Bank. The group has attempted to gain seats in the Israeli Knesset over the past several decades, but has won only one seat, in 1984.

Activities: Kach has harassed and threatened Arabs, Palestinians, and Israeli government officials, and has vowed revenge for the death of Binyamin Kahane and his wife. Kach is suspected of involvement in a number of low-level attacks since the start of the al-Aqsa Intifada in 2000.

Strength: Unknown.

Location/Area of Operation: Israel and West Bank settlements, particularly Qiryat Arba' in Hebron.

External Aid: Receives support from sympathizers in the United States and Europe.

KURDISTAN WORKERS' PARTY (PKK)

a.k.a. the Kurdistan Freedom and Democracy Congress; the Freedom and Democracy Congress of Kurdistan; KADEK; the Kurdistan Workers' Party; Partiya Karkeran Kurdistan; the People's Defense Force; Halu Mesru Savunma Kuvveti (HSK); Kurdistan People's Congress (KHK); People's Congress of Kurdistan; KONGRA-GEL.

Description: The Kurdistan Workers' Party (PKK) was designated as a Foreign Terrorist Organization on October 8, 1997. The PKK was founded by Abdullah Ocalan in 1978 as a Marxist-Leninist separatist organization. The group, composed primarily of Turkish Kurds, launched a campaign of violence in 1984. The PKK aspired to establish an independent Kurdish state in southeastern Turkey, but in recent years has spoken more often about autonomy within a Turkish state that guaranteed Kurdish cultural and linguistic rights.

In the early 1990s, the PKK moved beyond rural-based insurgent activities to include urban terrorism. In the 1990s, southeastern Anatolia was the scene of significant violence; some estimates place casualties at approximately 30,000 persons. Following his capture in 1999, Ocalan announced a "peace initiative," ordering members to refrain from violence and requesting dialogue with Ankara on Kurdish issues. Ocalan's death-sentence was commuted to life-imprisonment; he remains the symbolic leader of the group. The group foreswore violence until June 2004, when the group's hard-line militant wing took control and renounced the self-imposed cease-fire of the previous five years. Striking over the border from bases within Iraq the PKK engaged in terrorist attacks in eastern and western Turkey.

Activities: Primary targets have been Turkish government security forces, local Turkish officials, and villagers who oppose the organization in Turkey. The PKK's reputed military wing, the People's Defense Force (HPG), has been responsible mainly for attacks against military and paramilitary targets in the southeastern area of Turkey. The PKK's reported urban terrorist arm, the Kurdistan Freedom Hawks (TAK) has attacked primarily tourist areas in Western Turkey, and in late February 2008, announced a new wave of terrorist actions against Turkey.

In an attempt to damage Turkey's tourist industry, the PKK has bombed tourist sites and hotels and kidnapped foreign tourists. In July, PKK operatives kidnapped three German tourists on Mount Ararat in eastern Turkey in retaliation for Germany's tough stance against the group. On October 3, PKK militants killed 15 Turkish soldiers at the Aktutun outpost on the Turkish-Iraqi border, and five days later the group killed several police officers and wounded 19 in an attack in the southeastern province of Diyarbakir.

Strength: Approximately 4,000 to 5,000; 3,000 to 3,500 are located in northern Iraq.

Location/Area of Operation: Operates primarily in Turkey, Iraq, Europe, and the Middle East.

External Aid: In the past, the PKK received safe haven and modest aid from Syria, Iraq, and Iran. Since 1999, Syria and Iran have cooperated in a limited fashion with Turkey against the PKK. In 2008, Turkey and Iraq began cooperating to fight the PKK. The group maintains a large extortion, fundraising, and propaganda network in Europe.

LASHKAR E-TAYYIBA (LT)

a.k.a. al Mansooreen; Al Mansoorian; Army of the Pure; Army of the Pure and Righteous; Army of the Righteous; Lashkar e-Toiba; Lashkar-i-Taiba; Paasban-e-Ahle-Hadis; Paasban-e-Kashmir; Paasban-i-Ahle-Hadith; Pasban-e-Ahle-Hadith; Pasban-e-Kashmir; Jamaat-ud-Dawa, JUD; Jama'at al-Dawa; Jamaat ud-Daawa; Jamaat ul-Dawah; Jamaat-ul-Dawa; Jama'at-i-Dawat; Jamaiat-ud-Dawa; Jama'at-ud-Da'awah; Jama'at-ud-Da'awa; Jamaati-ud-Dawa; Idara Khidmat-e-Khalq.

Description: Lashkar e-Tayyiba (LT) was designated as a Foreign Terrorist Organization on December 26, 2001. The group remains the prime suspect for the November 26 Mumbai attacks. LT is one of the largest and most proficient of the traditionally Kashmiri-focused militant groups. LT formed in the late 1980s or early 1990s as the militant wing of the Islamic extremist organization Markaz Dawa ul-Irshad (MDI), a Pakistan-based Islamic fundamentalist mission organization and charity founded to oppose the Soviet presence in Afghanistan. LT, which is not connected to any political party, is led by Hafiz Muhammad Saeed. Shortly after LT was designated as an FTO, Saeed changed the name to Jamaat-ud-Dawa (JUD) and began humanitarian projects to avoid restrictions. LT functions and disseminates its message through JUD's media outlets. Elements of LT and Jaish-e-Muhammad (JEM) combined with other groups to mount attacks as "The Save Kashmir Movement. The Pakistani government banned the group and froze its assets in January 2002. LT and its leader, Hafiz Muhammad Saeed, continued to spread ideology advocating terrorism, as well as virulent rhetoric condemning the United States, India, Israel, and other perceived enemies.

Activities: LT has conducted a number of operations against Indian troops and civilian targets in Jammu and Kashmir since 1993, as well as several high profile attacks inside India itself. LT claimed responsibility for numerous attacks in 2001, including an attack in January on Srinagar airport that killed five Indians; an attack on a police station in Srinagar that killed at least eight officers and wounded several others; and an attack in April 2007 against Indian border security forces that left at least four dead. The Indian government publicly implicated LT, along with JEM, for the December 2001 attack on the Indian Parliament building, although concrete evidence was lacking. LT is also suspected of involvement in the May 2002 attack on an Indian Army base in Kaluchak that left 36 dead. India blamed LT for an October 2005 attack in New Delhi and a December 2005 Bangalore attack. Senior al-Qa'ida (AQ) lieutenant Abu Zubaydah was captured at an LT safe house in Faisalabad in March 2002, which suggested that some members were facilitating the movement of AQ members in Pakistan. Indian governmental officials hold LT responsible for the July 11, 2006 train attack in Mumbai and several attacks since then in Hyderabad. In 2008, the Indian government assessed that LT was behind the November 26-28 attacks in Mumbai against luxury hotels, a Jewish center, a prominent train station, and a popular café that killed at least 183, including 22 foreigners, and injured over 300.

Strength: The actual size of the group is unknown but LT has several thousand members in Azad Kashmir, Pakistan, in the southern Jammu and Kashmir and Doda regions, and in the Kashmir Valley. Most LT members are Pakistanis or Afghanis and/or veterans of the Afghan wars, though the group is alleged to augment its strength through collaboration with terrorist groups comprised of non-Pakistanis. The group uses assault rifles, light and heavy machine guns, mortars, explosives, and rocket-propelled grenades.

Location/Area of Operation: Based in Muridke (near Lahore) and Muzaffarabad, Pakistan; maintains a number of facilities, including training camps, schools, and medical clinics.

External Aid: Collects donations from the Pakistani expatriate communities in the Middle East and the United Kingdom, Islamic NGOs, and Pakistani and other Kashmiri business people. LT coordinates its charitable activities through its front organization Jamaat ud-Daawa (JUD), which spearheaded humanitarian relief to the victims of the October 2005 earthquake in Kashmir. The precise amount of LT funding is unknown.

LASHKAR I JHANGVI (LJ)

Description: Lashkar I Jhangvi (LJ) was designated as a Foreign Terrorist Organization on January 30, 2003. LJ is the militant offshoot of the Sunni Deobandi sectarian group Sipah-i-Sahaba Pakistan. LJ focuses primarily on anti-Shia attacks and was banned by then Pakistani President Musharraf in August 2001 as part of an effort to rein in sectarian violence.

Many of its members then sought refuge in Afghanistan with the Taliban, with whom they had existing ties. After the collapse of the Taliban, LJ members became active in aiding other terrorists with safe houses, false identities, and protection in Pakistani cities, including Karachi, Peshawar, and Rawalpindi.

Activities: LJ specializes in armed attacks and bombings and has admitted responsibility for numerous killings of Shia religious and community leaders in Pakistan. In January, the Interior Ministry ordered the arrest of three LJ militants suspected of being involved in a suicide bombing at a Shia religious procession in Peshawar that killed 15 people. In February, police arrested 20 LJ militants wanted for various terrorism attacks in the Punjab and Sindh provinces. In June, Sindh authorities issued a statement attributing the April 2006 Mishtar Parking bombing in Karachi to a militant with ties to LJ. The Government of Pakistan claimed that the group was involved in the April 2006 assassination attempt and the July 2006 assassination of Allama Turabi, an influential Shia leader. In October 2008, Afghan security forces claimed to have arrested four Pakistani suicide bombers in Kandahar who asserted that they belonged to LJ.

In May 2006, Pakistani police arrested two LJ militants suspected of involvement in the March bombing outside the U.S. Consulate in Karachi that killed one U.S. official. Pakistani authorities have publicly linked LJ members to the 2002 abduction and murder of U.S. journalist Daniel Pearl. Media reports linked LJ to attacks on Christian targets in Pakistan, including a March 2002 grenade assault on the Protestant International Church in Islamabad that killed two U.S. citizens, but no formal charges were filed. Pakistani authorities believe LJ was responsible for the July 2003 bombing of a Shia mosque in Quetta, Pakistan. Authorities also implicated LJ in several sectarian incidents in 2004, including the May and June bombings of two Shia mosques in Karachi that killed more than 40 people. In January 1999, the group attempted to assassinate former Prime Minister Nawaz Sharif and his brother Shabaz Sharif, Chief Minister of Punjab Province.

Strength: Probably fewer than 100.

Location/Area of Operation: LJ is active primarily in Punjab and Karachi. Some members travel between Pakistan and Afghanistan.

External Aid: Unknown.

LIBERATION TIGERS OF TAMIL EELAM (LTTE)

a.k.a. Ellalan Force; Tamil Tigers.

Description: The Liberation Tigers of Tamil Eelam (LTTE) was designated as a Foreign Terrorist Organization on October 8, 1997. Founded in 1976, the LTTE is a powerful Tamil secessionist group in Sri Lanka.

The LTTE wants to establish an independent Tamil state in the island's north and east. Since the beginning of its insurgency against the Sri Lankan government in 1983, it has evolved its capability from terrorist and guerilla tactics to conventional warfare. Although the LTTE nominally committed to a 2002 cease-fire agreement with the Sri Lankan government, it continued terrorist attacks against government leaders and dissident Tamils.

Activities: LTTE has integrated a battlefield insurgent strategy with a terrorist program that targets key personnel in the countryside and senior Sri Lankan political and military leaders in Colombo and other urban centers. It has conducted a sustained campaign targeting rival Tamil groups and figures, and assassinated Prime Minister Rajiv Gandhi of India in 1991, and President Ranasinghe Premadasa of Sri Lanka in 1993. Although most notorious for its cadre of suicide bombers, the Black Tigers, the organization also features an amphibious force, the Sea Tigers; and a nascent air wing, the Air Tigers. Fighting between the LTTE and the Sri Lanka government escalated in 2006 and continued through 2008. Open source reporting asserts the LTTE is believed to have detonated a claymore mine on a crowded bus near Colombo on June 6, 2008, killing 22 civilians and wounding more than 50 others. Political assassinations and bombings were commonplace tactics prior to the cease-fire and have increased again since mid-2005. Most LTTE attacks targeted Sri Lankan military and official personnel but, as illustrated by the June 6, 2008 bombing, the LTTE appears to continue to target civilians on occasion.

Strength: Exact strength is unknown, but LTTE is estimated to have 8,000 to 10,000 armed combatants in Sri Lanka, with an elite cadre of 5,000 to 7,000. LTTE also has a significant overseas support structure for fundraising, weapons procurement, and propaganda activities.

Location/Area of Operations: In June 2008, Sri Lankan government forces increased military operations against the LTTE capturing the Jaffna Peninsula and Kilinochchi, LTTE's administrative center of operations, reducing LTTE's control in Sri Lanka to a region around the northeastern town of Mullaitivu.

External Aid: The LTTE uses its international contacts and the large Tamil Diaspora in North America, Europe, and Asia to procure weapons, communications, funding, and other needed supplies. The group employs charities as fronts to collect and divert funds for their activities.

LIBYAN ISLAMIC FIGHTING GROUP

a.k.a. LIFG.

Description: The Libyan Islamic Fighting Group (LIFG) was designated as a Foreign Terrorist Organization on December 17, 2004. In the early 1990s, LIFG emerged from the group of Libyans who had fought Soviet forces in Afghanistan and the Qadhafi regime in Libya, and declared Libyan President Muammar Qadhafi un-Islamic and pledged to overthrow him. In the years following, some members maintained a strictly anti-Qadhafi focus and targeted Libyan government interests. Others, such as Abu al-Faraj al-Libi, who in 2005 was arrested in Pakistan, aligned with Usama bin Ladin, and are believed to be part of the al-Qa'ida (AQ) leadership structure or active in the international terrorist network. On November 3, 2007, senior AQ leaders announced that LIFG had officially joined AQ.

Activities: Libyans associated with LIFG are part of the broader international terrorist movement. LIFG is one of the groups believed to have planned the Casablanca suicide bombings in May 2003. LIFG continued to target Libyan interests, and attempted to assassinate Qadhafi four times; the last attempt was in 1998. The LIFG engaged Libyan security forces in armed clashes during the 1990s. However, the LIFG has been largely operationally inactive in Libya since the late 1990s when members fled predominately to Europe and the Middle East because of tightened Libyan security measures. To date, the November 3, 2007 merger with AQ has not resulted in a significant increase in LIFG activities within Libya.

Strength: The LIFG probably has several hundred active members or supporters, mostly in the Middle East or Europe.

Location/Area of Operation: Since the late 1990s, many members have fled to various Asian, Arabian Gulf, African, and European countries, particularly the UK. It is likely that LIFG maintains a limited presence in eastern Libya.

External Aid: Unknown. The LIFG has used Islamic charitable organizations as cover for fundraising and transferring money and documents; it may have also financed operations with criminal activity.

MOROCCAN ISLAMIC COMBATANT GROUP

a.k.a. Groupe Islamique Combattant Marocain (GICM).

Description: The Moroccan Islamic Combatant Group (GICM) was designated as a Foreign Terrorist Organization on September 11, 2005. The GICM is a clandestine transnational terrorist group centered in the Moroccan Diaspora communities of Western Europe. Its goals include establishing an Islamic state in Morocco and supporting al-Qa'ida's (AQ 's) war against the West by assisting in the assimilation of AQ operatives into Moroccan and European society. The group emerged in the 1990s and is composed of Moroccan recruits who trained in armed camps in Afghanistan, including some who fought in the Soviet Afghan war. GICM members interact with other North African extremists, particularly in Europe.

Activities: GICM members were among those responsible for the 2004 Madrid bombing, and Moroccans associated with the GICM are part of the broader international terrorist movement. GICM members were implicated in the recruitment network of individuals for Iraq, and at least one GICM member carried out a suicide attack against Coalition Forces in Iraq. GICM individuals are believed to have been involved in the 2003 Casablanca attacks.

Strength: Much of the GICM's leadership in Morocco and Europe has been killed, imprisoned, or are awaiting trial. Alleged leader Mohamed al-Guerbouzi was convicted in absentia by the Moroccan government for his role in the Casablanca attacks but remains free in exile in the UK.

Location/Area of Operation: Morocco, Western Europe, Afghanistan, and Canada.

External Aid: The GICM has been involved in narcotics trafficking in North Africa and Europe to fund its operations. Moroccan security officials believe money from drug trafficking largely financed the 2003 Casablanca attacks. The Madrid attacks were financed mainly by the narcotics trafficking of Moroccan terrorist Jamal Ahmidan.

MUJAHADIN-E KHALQ ORGANIZATION

a.k.a. MEK; MKO; Mujahadin-e Khalq (Iranian government name for group); Muslim Iranian Students' Society; National Council of Resistance; NCR; Organization of the People's Holy Warriors of Iran; the National Liberation Army of Iran; NLA; People's Mujahadin Organization of Iran; PMOI; National Council of Resistance of Iran; NCRI; Sazeman-e Mujahadin-e Khalq-e Iran.

Description: The Mujahadin-e Khalq Organization (MEK) advocates the violent overthrow of the Iranian government and was responsible for the assassination of several U.S. military personnel and civilians in the 1970s. The MEK's armed wing is known as the National Liberation Army of Iran (NLA). In December 2008, the European Court of First Instance annulled the European Union's designation of the MEK as a terrorist organization.

The MEK emerged in the 1960s as one of the more violent political movements opposed to the Pahlavi dynasty and its close relationship with the United States. MEK ideology has gone through several iterations and blends elements of Marxism, Islam, and feminism. The group has planned and executed terrorist operations against the Iranian government for nearly three decades from its European and Iraqi bases of operations. Additionally, it has expanded its fundraising base, further developed its paramilitary skills, and aggressively worked to expand its European ranks. In addition to its terrorist credentials, the MEK has also displayed cult-like characteristics.

Upon entry into the group, new members are indoctrinated in MEK ideology and revisionist Iranian history. Members are also required to undertake a vow of "eternal divorce" and participate in weekly "ideological cleansings." Additionally, children are reportedly separated from parents at a young age. MEK leader Maryam Rajavi has established a "cult of personality." She claims to emulate the Prophet Muhammad and is viewed by members as the "Iranian President in exile."

Activities: The group's worldwide campaign against the Iranian government uses propaganda and terrorism to achieve its objectives and has been supported by reprehensible regimes, including that of Saddam Hussein. During the 1970s, the MEK assassinated several U.S. military personnel and U.S. civilians working on defense projects in Tehran and supported the violent takeover in 1979 of the U.S. Embassy in Tehran.

In 1981, MEK leadership attempted to overthrow the newly installed Islamic regime; Iranian security forces subsequently initiated a crackdown on the group. The MEK instigated a bombing campaign, including an attack against the head office of the Islamic Republic Party and the Prime Minister's office, which killed some 70 high-ranking Iranian officials, including Chief Justice Ayatollah Mohammad Beheshti, President Mohammad-Ali Rajaei, and Prime Minister Mohammad-Javad Bahonar. These attacks resulted in a popular uprising against the MEK and an expanded Iranian government crackdown which forced MEK leaders to flee to France. For five years, the MEK continued to wage its terrorist campaign from its Paris headquarters. Expelled by France in 1986, MEK leaders turned to Saddam Hussein's regime for basing, financial support, and training. Near the end of the 1980-1988 Iran-Iraq War, Baghdad armed the MEK with heavy military equipment and deployed thousands of MEK fighters in suicidal, mass wave attacks against Iranian forces.

The MEK's relationship with the former Iraqi regime continued through the 1990s. In 1991, the group reportedly assisted the Iraqi Republican Guard's bloody crackdown on Iraqi Shia and Kurds who rose up against Saddam Hussein's regime. In April 1992, the MEK conducted near-simultaneous attacks on Iranian embassies and installations in 13 countries, demonstrating the group's ability to mount large-scale operations overseas. In April 1999, the MEK targeted key Iranian military officers and assassinated the deputy chief of the Iranian Armed Forces General Staff, Brigadier General Ali Sayyaad Shirazi.

In April 2000, the MEK attempted to assassinate the commander of the Nasr Headquarters, Tehran's interagency board responsible for coordinating policies on Iraq. The pace of anti-Iranian operations increased during "Operation Great Bahman" in February 2000, when the group launched a dozen attacks against Iran. One attack included a mortar attack against a major Iranian leadership complex in Tehran that housed the offices of the Supreme Leader and the President. In 2000 and 2001, the MEK was involved in regular mortar attacks and hit-and-run raids against Iranian military and law enforcement personnel, as well as government buildings near the Iran-Iraq border. Also in 2001, the FBI arrested seven Iranians in the United States who funneled $400,000 to an MEK-affiliated organization in the UAE, which used the funds to purchase weapons. Following an initial Coalition bombardment of the MEK's facilities in Iraq at the outset of Operation Iraqi Freedom, MEK leadership negotiated a cease-fire with Coalition Forces and voluntarily surrendered their heavy-arms to Coalition control. Since 2003, roughly 3,400 MEK members have been encamped at Ashraf in Iraq.

In 2003, French authorities arrested 160 MEK members at operational bases they believed the MEK was using to coordinate financing and planning for terrorist attacks. Upon the arrest of MEK leader Maryam Rajavi, MEK members took to Paris' streets and engaged in self-immolation. French authorities eventually released Rajavi. Although currently in hiding, Rajavi has made motivational appearances via video-satellite to MEK-sponsored conferences across the globe.

According to evidence which became available after the fall of Saddam Hussein, the MEK received millions of dollars in Oil-for-Food program subsidies from Saddam Hussein from 1999 through 2003. In addition to discovering 13 lists of recipients of such vouchers on which the MEK appeared, evidence linking the MEK to the former Iraqi regime includes lists, as well as video footage of both Saddam Hussein handing over suitcases of money to known MEK leaders, and of MEK operatives receiving training from the Iraqi military.

Strength: Estimates place MEK's worldwide membership at between 5,000 and 10,000 members, with large pockets in Paris and other major European capitals. In Iraq, roughly 3,400 MEK members are gathered at Camp Ashraf, the MEK's main compound north of Baghdad. As a condition of the 2003 cease-fire agreement, the MEK relinquished more than 2,000 tanks, armored personnel carriers, and heavy artillery. Between 2003–2006, a significant number of MEK personnel have voluntarily left Ashraf, and an additional several hundred individuals have renounced ties to the MEK and been voluntarily repatriated to Iran.

Location/Area of Operation: The MEK maintains its main headquarters in Paris and has concentrations of members across Europe, in addition to the large concentration of MEK located at Camp Ashraf in Iraq. The MEK's global support structure remains in place, with associates and supporters scattered throughout Europe and North America. Operations target Iranian government elements across the globe, including in Europe and Iran. MEK's political arm, the National Council of Resistance of Iran (NCRI), has a global support network with active lobbying and propaganda efforts in major Western capitals. NCRI also has a well-developed media communications strategy.

External Aid: Before Operation Iraqi Freedom began in 2003, the MEK received all of its military assistance and most of its financial support from Saddam Hussein. The fall of Saddam's regime has led MEK increasingly to rely on front organizations to solicit contributions from expatriate Iranian communities.

NATIONAL LIBERATION ARMY (ELN)

a.k.a. Ejercito de Liberacion Nacional.

Description: The National Liberation Army (ELN) was designated as a Foreign Terrorist Organization on October 8, 1997. The National Liberation Army (ELN) is a Colombian Marxist-Leninist terrorist group formed in 1964 by urban intellectuals inspired by Fidel Castro and Che Guevara. It is primarily rural-based, although it also has several urban units. Peace talks between the ELN and the Colombian government began in Cuba in December 2005 and continued as recently as August 2007. To date, Bogota and the ELN have yet to agree on a formal framework for peace negotiations and talks have been indefinitely suspended. Suspensions have occurred before with talks subsequently resuming.

Activities: The ELN engages in kidnappings, hijackings, bombings, drug trafficking, and extortion activities. It has minimal conventional military capabilities. The group conducts kidnappings for ransom, often targeting foreign employees of large corporations, especially in the petroleum industry. On February 17, 2008, ELN rebels kidnapped a Radio Delfin journalist near Dibuya. It attacks energy infrastructure and has inflicted major damage on oil and natural gas pipelines and the electrical distribution network, but has lost much of its capacity to carry out these types of attacks in recent years. The ELN derives some revenue from taxation of the illegal narcotics industry, and its involvement may be increasing.

Strength: Approximately 2,000 armed combatants and an unknown number of active supporters.

Location/Area of Operation: Mostly in rural and mountainous areas of northern, northeastern, and southwestern Colombia, as well as Venezuelan border regions.

External Aid: Cuba provides some medical care and political consultation. In spite of this, Cuba appears to encourage the Colombian government and the ELN to reach an agreement.

PALESTINE LIBERATION FRONT- ABU ABBAS FACTION

a.k.a. PLF; PLF-Abu Abbas; Palestine Liberation Front.

Description: The Palestinian Liberation Front – Abu Abbas Faction (PLF) was designated as a Foreign Terrorist Organization on October 8, 1997. In the late 1970s the Palestine Liberation Front (PLF) splintered from the Popular Front for the Liberation of Palestine-General Command (PFLP-GC), and later split into pro-PLO, pro-Syrian, and pro-Libyan factions. The pro-PLO faction was led by Muhammad Zaydan (a.k.a. Abu Abbas) and was based in Baghdad prior to Operation Iraqi Freedom.

Activities: Abbas's group was responsible for the 1985 attack on the Italian cruise ship *Achille Lauro* and the murder of U.S. citizen Leon Klinghoffer. In 1993, the PLF officially renounced terrorism when it acknowledged the Oslo accords, although it was suspected of supporting terrorism against Israel by other Palestinian groups into the 1990s. In April 2004, Abu Abbas died of natural causes while in U.S. custody in Iraq. Current leadership and membership of the relatively small PLF appears to be based in Lebanon and the Palestinian territories. The PLF took part in the 2006 Palestinian parliamentarian elections but did not win a seat. In 2008, as part of a prisoner exchange between Israel and Hizballah, Samir Kantar, a PLF member and purportedly the longest serving Arab prisoner in Israeli custody was released from an Israeli prison. After going approximately 16 years without claiming responsibility for an attack, PLF claimed responsibility for two attacks against Israeli targets on March 14, 2008, according to media reports. One attack was against an Israeli military bus in Huwarah, West Bank, and the other involved a PLF brigade firing at an Israeli settler south of the Hebron Mountain, seriously wounding him. On March 28, 2008, shortly after the attacks, a PLF Central Committee member reaffirmed PLF's commitment to using all possible means to restore its previous glory and to adhering to its role in the Palestinian struggle and resistance, through its military.

Strength: Estimates have placed membership between 50 and 500.

Location/Area of Operation: Based in Iraq from 1990 until 2003. The group currently is based in Lebanon and Syria.

External Aid: Unknown.

PALESTINE ISLAMIC JIHAD - SHAQAQI FACTION

a.k.a. PIJ; Palestine Islamic Jihad; PIJ-Shaqaqi Faction; PIJ-Shallah Faction; Islamic Jihad of Palestine; Islamic Jihad in Palestine; Abu Ghunaym Squad of the Hizballah Bayt Al-Maqdis; Al-Quds Squads; Al-Quds Brigades; Saraya Al-Quds; Al-Awdah Brigades.

Description: The Palestine Islamic Jihad (PIJ) was designated as a Foreign Terrorist Organization on October 8, 1997. Formed by militant Palestinians in Gaza during the 1970s, PIJ is committed to both the creation of an Islamic state in all of historic Palestine, including present day Israel, and the destruction of Israel through attacks against Israeli military and civilian targets.

Activities: PIJ terrorists have conducted numerous attacks, including large-scale suicide bombings against Israeli civilian and military targets. PIJ continues to plan and direct attacks against Israelis both inside Israel and in the Palestinian territories. Although U.S. citizens have died in PIJ mounted attacks, the group has not directly targeted U.S. interests. PIJ attacks in 2008 have primarily been rocket attacks aimed at southern Israeli cities. In April 2008, alone, PIJ fired 216 rockets and mortar shells at various Israeli towns. In March 2008, two IDF soldiers died as a result of an explosive device detonated near their jeep while patrolling the security fence in the central Gaza Strip, near Kissufim. HAMAS and PIJ claimed responsibility for the attack.

Strength: Unknown.

Location/Area of Operation: Primarily Israel, the West Bank, and Gaza. The group's senior leadership resides in Syria. Other leadership elements reside in Lebanon and official representatives are scattered throughout the Middle East.

External Aid: Receives financial assistance and training primarily from Iran. Syria provides the group with safe haven.

POPULAR FRONT FOR THE LIBERATION OF PALESTINE

a.k.a. PFLP; Halhul Gang; Halhul Squad; Palestinian Popular Resistance Forces; PPRF; Red Eagle Gang; Red Eagle Group; Red Eagles; Martyr Abu-Ali Mustafa Battalion.

Description: The Popular Front for the Liberation of Palestine (PFLP) was designated as a Foreign Terrorist Organization on October 8, 1997. The PFLP, a Marxist-Leninist group founded by George Habash, broke away from the Arab Nationalist Movement in 1967. The PFLP views the Palestinian struggle not as religious, but as a broader revolution against Western imperialism. The group earned a reputation for spectacular international attacks in the 1960s and 1970s, including airline hijackings that killed at least 20 U.S. citizens. A leading faction within the PLO, the PFLP has long accepted the concept of a two-state solution but has opposed specific provisions of various peace initiatives.

Activities: The PFLP stepped up its operational activity during the al-Aqsa intifada. This was highlighted by at least two suicide bombings since 2003, multiple joint operations with other Palestinian terrorist groups, and the assassination of Israeli Tourism Minister Rehavam Ze'evi in 2001 to avenge Israel's killing of the PFLP Secretary General earlier that year. In March 2006, the PFLP's current Secretary General, Ahmed Sa'adat, then imprisoned by the Palestinian Authority for his involvement in the Ze'evi assassination, was seized from the Jericho prison compound by Israeli forces and sentenced to 30 years in prison by an Israeli military court in December 2008. The PFLP was involved in several rocket attacks against Israel in 2008.

Strength: Unknown.

Location/Area of Operation: Syria, Lebanon, Israel, the West Bank, and Gaza.

External Aid: Receives safe haven and some logistical assistance from Syria.

POPULAR FRONT FOR THE LIBERATION OF PALESTINE - GENERAL COMMAND

a.k.a. PFLP-GC.

Description: The Popular Front for the Liberation of Palestine - General Command (PFLP-GC) was designated as a Foreign Terrorist Organization on October 8, 1997. The PFLP-GC split from the PFLP in 1968, claiming it wanted to focus more on resistance and less on politics. Originally, the group was violently opposed to the Arafat-led PLO. Ahmad Jibril, a former captain in the Syrian Army whose son, Jihad, was killed by a car bomb in May 2002, has led the PFLP-GC since its founding. The PFLP-GC is closely tied to both Syria and Iran.

Activities: The PFLP-GC carried out dozens of attacks in Europe and the Middle East during the 1970s and 1980s. The organization was known for cross-border terrorist attacks into Israel using unusual means, such as hot-air balloons and motorized hang gliders. The group's primary focus is now on supporting Hizballah's attacks against Israel, training members of other Palestinian terrorist groups, and smuggling weapons. The PFLP-GC maintains an armed presence in several Palestinian refugee camps and at its own military bases in Lebanon and along the Lebanon-Syria border. The PFLP-GC has been implicated by Lebanese security officials in several rocket attacks against Israel in 2008. In May 2008, the

PFLP-GC claimed responsibility for a rocket attack on a shopping center in Ashkelon, wounding at least ten people. A health clinic took the brunt of the attack.

Strength: Several hundred to several thousand.

Location/Area of Operation: Headquartered in Damascus with bases in southern Lebanon and a presence in the Palestinian refugee camps in Lebanon and Syria.

External Aid: Receives logistical and military support from Syria and financial support from Iran.

AL QA'IDA

Variant spelling al-Qa'ida; translation "The Base;" Qa'idat al-Jihad (The Base for Jihad); formerly Qa'idat Ansar Allah (The Base of the Supporters of God).

a.k.a. al Qaeda; the Islamic Army; Islamic Salvation Foundation; the Base; The Group for the Preservation of the Holy Sites; The Islamic Army for the Liberation of the Holy Places; the World Islamic Front for Jihad Against Jews and Crusaders; the Usama Bin Laden Network; the Usama Bin Laden Organization; al-Jihad; the Jihad Group; Egyptian al-Jihad; Egyptian Islamic Jihad; New Jihad

Description: Al-Qa'ida (AQ) was established by Usama bin Ladin in 1988 with Arabs who fought in Afghanistan against the Soviet Union. The group helped finance, recruit, transport, and train Sunni Islamic extremists for the Afghan resistance. AQ's near-term goal is uniting Muslims to fight the United States and its allies, overthrowing regimes it deems "non-Islamic," and expelling Westerners and non-Muslims from Muslim countries. Its ultimate goal is the establishment of a pan-Islamic caliphate throughout the world. AQ leaders issued a statement in February 1998 under the banner of "The World Islamic Front for Jihad against the Jews and Crusaders" saying it was the duty of all Muslims to kill U.S. citizens, civilian and military, and their allies everywhere. AQ merged with al-Jihad (Egyptian Islamic Jihad) in June 2001, renaming itself Qa'idat al-Jihad.

Activities: Even as AQ's top leaders continue to plot and direct terrorist attacks worldwide, terrorists affiliated with, but not necessarily controlled by AQ, have increasingly carried out high-profile attacks. AQ, its affiliates, and those inspired by the group were involved in anti-U.S. and anti-Coalition attacks in Africa, Europe, the Middle East, Afghanistan, Pakistan, and Iraq, including suicide bombings and vehicle-borne improvised explosive devices.

Although bin Ladin remains the group's ideological figurehead, Zawahiri has emerged as AQ's strategic and operational planner.

AQ is assessed to be the top terrorist threat to the United States and is developing stronger operational relationships with affiliates in the Middle East, North Africa, and Europe. AQ remains committed to attacking the United States and focuses its planning on targets that would produce mass casualties, dramatic visual destruction, and economic dislocation.

In January 2008, militants attacked a convoy of Belgian tourists in Hadhramout, Yemen, killing two Belgian women and two Yemeni drivers. AQ claimed responsibility for the attack. In June 2008, a suicide car bomber attacked the Danish Embassy in Islamabad, killing six people, including a Danish citizen. The blast was so powerful that it damaged windowpanes of buildings in a four kilometer radius and left a three-foot crater at impact. In a press interview, an AQ commander in Afghanistan claimed responsibility for the attack, on behalf of AQ.

The Government of Pakistan accused AQ, along with the Taliban, of being responsible for the October 2007 suicide bombing attempt against former Pakistani Prime Minister Benazir Bhutto that killed at least 144 people in Karachi, Pakistan. On December 27, 2007, the Government of Pakistan stated that Baitullah Mahsud, a leading Pakistani Taliban commander with close ties to AQ, was responsible for the assassination of Benazir Bhutto.

Bin Ladin's deputy Ayman al-Zawahiri claimed responsibility on behalf of AQ for multiple attacks on July 7, 2005 against the London public transportation system. The extent of senior leadership involvement in planning the July 2005 attacks was unclear. Some suspects in the attacks included homegrown UK-based extremists who were inspired by AQ.

In 2003 and 2004, Saudi-based AQ operatives and associated extremists launched more than a dozen attacks, killing at least 90 people, including 14 Americans in Saudi Arabia. AQ may have been connected to the suicide bombers and planners of the November 2003 attacks in Istanbul that targeted two synagogues, the British Consulate, and the HSBC Bank, and resulted in the deaths of more than 60 people. Former Pakistani President Musharraf blamed AQ for two attempts on his life in December 2003. In October 2002, AQ directed a suicide attack on the French tanker MV Limburg off the coast of Yemen that killed one and injured four. The group also carried out the November 2002 suicide bombing of a hotel in Mombasa, Kenya that killed 15. AQ probably provided financing for the October 2002 Bali bombings by Jemaah Islamiya that killed more than 200.

On September 11, 2001, 19 AQ members hijacked and crashed four U.S. commercial jets – two into the World Trade Center in New York City, one into the Pentagon near Washington, DC, and a fourth into a field in Shanksville, Pennsylvania – leaving nearly 3,000 individuals dead or missing. In October 2000, AQ conducted a suicide attack on the USS Cole in the port of Aden, Yemen, with an explosive-laden boat, killing 17 U.S. Navy sailors and injuring 39. AQ also carried out the August 1998 bombings of the U.S. Embassies in Nairobi and Dar es Salaam killing at least 301 individuals and injuring more than 5,000 others. AQ and its supporters claim to have shot down U.S. helicopters and killed U.S. servicemen in Somalia in 1993, and to have conducted three bombings that targeted U.S. troops in Aden in December 1992.

Strength: AQ's organizational strength is difficult to determine in the aftermath of extensive counterterrorist efforts since 9/11. The arrests and deaths of mid-level and senior AQ operatives have disrupted some communication, financial, and facilitation nodes and disrupted some terrorist plots. Additionally, supporters and associates worldwide who are inspired by the group's ideology may be operating without direction from AQ central leadership; it is impossible to estimate their numbers. AQ serves as a focal point of inspiration for a worldwide network that is comprised of many Sunni Islamic extremist groups, including some members of the Gama'at al-Islamiyya, the Islamic Movement of Uzbekistan, the Islamic Jihad Group, Lashkar i Jhangvi, Harakat ul-Mujahadin, Ansar al-Sunnah, the Taliban, and Jemaah Islamiya.

Location/Area of Operation: AQ worldwide networks are augmented by ties to local Sunni extremists. The group was based in Afghanistan until Coalition Forces removed the Taliban from power in late 2001. While the largest concentration of senior AQ members now resides in Pakistan's Federally Administered Tribal Areas, the network incorporates members of al-Qa'ida in Iraq and other associates throughout the Middle East, Southeast Asia, Africa, Europe, and Central Asia.

External Aid: AQ primarily depends on donations from like-minded supporters and individuals who believe that their money is supporting a humanitarian or other cause. Some funds are diverted from Islamic charitable organizations. In addition, parts of the organization raise funds through criminal activities; for example, al-Qa'ida in Iraq raises funds through hostage-taking for ransom, and members in Europe have engaged in credit card fraud. U.S. and international efforts to block AQ funding have hampered the group's ability to raise money.

AL-QA'IDA IN IRAQ (TANZIM QA'IDAT AL-JIHAD FI BILAD AL-RAFIDAYN)

a.k.a. al-Qa'ida Group of Jihad in Iraq; al-Qa'ida Group of Jihad in the Land of the Two Rivers; al-Qa'ida in Mesopotamia; al-Qa'ida in the Land of the Two Rivers; al-Qa'ida of Jihad in Iraq; al-Qa'ida of Jihad Organization in the Land of The Two Rivers; al-Qa'ida of the Jihad in the Land of the Two Rivers; al-Tawhid; Jam'at al-Tawhid Wa'al-Jihad; Tanzeem Qa'idat al Jihad/Bilad al Raafidaini; Tanzim Qa'idat al-Jihad fi Bilad al-Rafidayn; The Monotheism and Jihad Group; The Organization Base of Jihad/Country of the Two Rivers; The Organization Base of Jihad/Mesopotamia; The Organization of al-Jihad's Base in Iraq; The Organization of al-Jihad's Base in the Land of the Two Rivers; The Organization of al-Jihad's Base of Operations in Iraq; The Organization of al-Jihad's Base of Operations in the Land of the Two Rivers; The Organization of Jihad's Base in the Country of the Two Rivers; al-Zarqawi Network

Description: In January 2006, in an attempt to unify Sunni extremists in Iraq, al-Qa'ida in Iraq (AQI) created the Mujahidin Shura Council (MSC), an umbrella organization meant to encompass the various Sunni terrorist groups in Iraq. AQI claimed its attacks under the MSC until mid-October, when Abu Mus'ab al-Zarqawi's successor, Abu Ayyub al-Masri, took the first step toward al-Qa'ida's goal of establishing a caliphate in the region by declaring the "Islamic State of Iraq" (ISI), under which AQI now claims its attacks. Although Iraqis compose at least 90 percent of the group's membership, it is probable that the majority of AQI's senior leadership is foreign-born. In an attempt to give AQI a more Iraqi persona, the AQI-led ISI was created and headed by Abu Umar al-Baghdadi.

Abu Ayyub al-Masri, Zarqawi's successor, issued a statement pledging to continue what Zarqawi began, and AQI has continued its strategy of targeting Coalition Forces, Iraqi government groups, anti-AQI Sunni tribal and security elements, and Shia civilians to provoke violence and undermine perceptions that the Iraqi central government can effectively govern.

AQI has claimed joint attacks with both Ansar al-Islam (AI) and the Islamic Army in Iraq (IAI); however, ideological differences have prevented these groups from merging. More recently, IAI and the 1920 Revolution Brigades cooperated with Coalition Forces in targeting AQI. (See Chapter 2, *Country Reports, Middle East and North Africa, for further information on U.S. efforts to counter AQI.)*

Activities: The threat from AQI continued to diminish in 2008. AQI, although still dangerous, has experienced the defection of members, lost key mobilization areas, suffered disruption of support infrastructure and funding, and been forced to change targeting priorities. Indeed, the pace of suicide bombing countryside, which we consider one indicator of AQI's operational capability, fell significantly during last year.

High-profile attacks in 2007 included the suicide car-bombing attack of a mosque in Al Habbaniyah in February, the multiple suicide bombing attack of Shia pilgrims in Al Hillah in March, several chlorine gas canister bombings from January through June, an orchestrated bridge bombing campaign throughout Iraq aimed at isolating Baghdad Shia population concentrations and disrupting ground transportation from January through October, the suicide truck bombing of a market in Tall Afar in March, the suicide truck bombings of a market and Patriotic Union of Kurdistan (PUK) party offices in Amurli and Kirkuk in July, and the single deadliest attack of the Iraq war, the multiple suicide truck bombings of two Yazidi villages near Sinjar in August.

In August 2003, Zarqawi's group carried out major terrorist attacks in Iraq when it bombed the Jordanian Embassy in Baghdad, which was followed 12 days later by a suicide vehicle-borne improvised explosive device (VBIED) attack against the UN Headquarters in Baghdad that killed 23, including the Secretary-General's Special Representative for Iraq, Sergio Vieira de Mello. That same month the group conducted a VBIED attack against Shia worshippers outside the Imam Ali Mosque in al Najaf, killing 85, including the leader of the Supreme Council for the Islamic Revolution in Iraq (SCIRI). The group kept up its attack pace throughout 2003, striking numerous Iraqi, Coalition, and relief agency targets such as the Red Cross. Zarqawi's group conducted VBIED attacks against U.S. military personnel and Iraqi infrastructure throughout 2004, including suicide attacks inside the Green Zone perimeter in Baghdad. The group successfully penetrated the Green Zone in the October 2004 bombing of a popular café and market. It also claimed responsibility for the videotaped execution by beheading of Americans Nicholas Berg (May 11, 2004), Jack Armstrong (September 22, 2004), and Jack Hensley (September 21, 2004). AQI was likely involved in other hostage incidents as well. In 2005, AQI largely focused on conducting multiple high-profile, coordinated suicide attacks. AQI claimed numerous attacks primarily aimed against civilians, the Iraqi government, and security forces, such as the coordinated attacks against polling sites during the January elections and the coordinated VBIED attacks outside the Sheraton and Palestine hotels in Baghdad on October 24. The group also continued assassinations against Shia leaders and members of the Shia militia groups Jaysh al-Mahdi and Badr Corps.

AQI increased its external operations in 2005 by claiming credit for three attacks: suicide bomber attacks against three hotels in Amman on November 9; a rocket attack against U.S. Navy ships in the port of Aqaba in August, which resulted in limited damage in Jordan and in Eilat,

Israel; and the firing of several rockets into Israel from Lebanon in December. In August 2005, an AQI operative was arrested in Turkey while planning an operation targeting Israeli cruise ships. Prior to 2005, Zarqawi planned and conducted limited attacks in Jordan, including the assassination of USAID official Laurence Foley in 2002. In October 2006, AQI declared the ISI would become a platform from which AQI would launch terrorist attacks throughout the world. Following the announcement, AQI members marched through cities they considered to be part of their new state as a show of force. AQI attack claims, which the group released under the auspices of the Mujahidin Shura Council and now the ISI, increased in 2006 but decreased significantly starting in late 2007.

AQI was implicated in the February 2006 Samarra' al-Askari Mosque bombing that precipitated the escalation in sectarian violence.

AQI senior leaders in Iraq may have had advance knowledge of terrorist attacks in Iraq that incorporated chlorine into VBIEDs. However, the use of chlorine in suicide attacks probably represents an opportunistic evolution of conventional VBIED attacks.

Strength: Membership is estimated at 2,000-4,000, making it the largest, most potent Sunni extremist group in Iraq. AQI perpetrates the majority of suicide and mass casualty bombings in Iraq, using both foreign and Iraqi operatives. The selection of civilian targets, particularly in large urban areas, generates widespread media coverage, but garners public backlash against the group.

Location/Area of Operation: AQI's operations are predominately Iraq-based, but it has perpetrated attacks in Jordan. The group maintains an extensive logistical network throughout the Middle East, North Africa, Iran, South Asia, and Europe. In Iraq, AQI currently conducts the majority of its operations in Ninawa, Diyala, Salah ad Din, and Baghdad provinces and to a lesser extent Al Anbar.

External Aid: AQI probably receives funds from donors in the Middle East and Europe, local sympathizers in Iraq, from a variety of businesses and criminal activities, and other international extremists throughout the world. In many cases, AQI's donors are probably motivated to support terrorism rather than an attachment to any specific terrorist group.

AL-QA'IDA IN THE ISLAMIC MAGHREB

a.k.a. AQIM, formerly known as Group for Call and Combat; GSPC; Le Groupe Salafiste Pour La Predication Et Le Combat; Salafist Group for Preaching and Combat.

Description: Al-Qa'ida in the Islamic Maghreb (AQIM) was designated as a Foreign Terrorist Organization on March 27, 2002. The Salafist Group for Preaching and Combat (GSPC) officially merged with al-Qa'ida (AQ) in September 2006 and subsequently changed its name to al-Qa'ida in the Islamic Maghreb (AQIM). The GSPC formed in 1998 when its members left the Armed Islamic Group (GIA) over disagreements about leadership, tactics, and indiscriminant targeting of Algerian civilians. In contrast to the GIA, it has pledged to avoid attacks on civilians inside Algeria. Nevertheless, civilians have died in numerous GSPC/AQIM attacks. The GSPC retained GIA's mission of overthrowing the Algerian government and installing an Islamic regime. AQIM is the most effective and largest armed group inside Algeria. AQIM and AQ have used the merger extensively in their propaganda.

Activities: AQIM employed sophisticated suicide tactics for the first time on April 11, 2007. The near-simultaneous bombings of multiple targets inside Algiers, including the office of Algeria's prime minister, claimed more than 30 lives. Shortly thereafter, AQIM vowed to continue to use suicide tactics, and proceeded to carry out five additional suicide attacks in Algeria in 2007. On December 11, AQIM carried out two near-simultaneous suicide vehicle-borne improvised explosive device (VBIED) attacks that struck two UN offices and the headquarters of Algeria's Constitutional Council, killing 41 people, (including 17 UN employees), and wounding at least 170 others. AQIM had previously attacked vehicles belonging to foreign corporations several times during the year, beginning in December 2006 with an attack in Algiers on a bus belonging to a U.S.-Algeria joint venture and carrying several expatriate workers. There was a rise in terrorist attacks claimed by AQIM during the month of August 2008, with at least 79 people killed in various incidents across northeastern Algeria

Outside Algeria, in December 2007, multiple AQIM-linked attacks in Mauritania were the first terrorist incidents since 2005, when the GSPC had claimed responsibility for an attack on a remote Mauritanian military outpost that killed 15; this appeared to indicate an AQIM shift towards a more regional terrorist campaign. Also during 2007, police in France, Italy, and Spain arrested several individuals from Algeria and other Maghreb countries suspected of providing support to AQIM. French officials announced that AQIM had issued an Internet call-to-action against France, declaring France "public enemy number one."

AQIM maintains a safe haven in northern Mali. This safe haven functions as a training area and logistics-facilitation hub for AQIM operations in Algeria and Mauritania. AQIM hostages are generally held in this area.

Strength: AQIM has an estimated several hundred fighters operating in Algeria with a smaller number in the Sahel. Abdelmalek Droukdel, a.k.a. Abu Mus'ab Abd al-Wadoud, is the leader of the group.

Location/Area of Operation: Algeria and the Sahel, with affiliates and logistics/fundraisers in Western Europe.

External Aid: Algerian expatriates and AQIM members abroad, many residing in Western Europe, provide financial and logistical support. AQIM members also engage in hostage-taking for ransom and criminal activity to finance their operations.

REAL IRA

a.k.a. RIRA; Real Irish Republican Army, 32 County Sovereignty Committee; 32 County Sovereignty Movement; Irish Republican Prisoners Welfare Association; Real Oglaigh Na Heireann.

Description: The Real IRA (RIRA) was designated as a Foreign Terrorist Organization on May 16, 2001. RIRA was formed in 1997 as the clandestine armed wing of the 32 County Sovereignty Movement, a "political pressure group" dedicated to removing British forces from Northern Ireland and unifying Ireland. RIRA also seeks to disrupt the Northern Ireland peace process and did not participate in the September 2005 weapons decommissioning. The 32 County Sovereignty Movement opposed Sinn Fein's adoption in September 1997 of the Mitchell principles of democracy and non-violence; it also opposed the amendment in December 1999 of Articles 2 and 3 of the Irish Constitution that laid claim to Northern Ireland. Despite internal rifts and calls by some jailed members, including the group's founder Michael "Mickey" McKevitt, for a cease-fire and disbandment, RIRA has pledged additional violence and continues to conduct attacks.

Activities: Many RIRA members are former Provisional Irish Republican Army members who left the organization after it renewed its cease-fire in 1997. These members brought a wealth of experience in terrorist tactics and bomb-making to RIRA. Targets have included civilians (most notoriously in the Omagh bombing in August 1998), British security forces, police in Northern Ireland, and local Protestant communities. RIRA's most recent fatal attack was in August 2002 at a London army base, killing a construction worker. The organization wants to improve its intelligence-gathering ability, engineering capacity, and access to weaponry; it also trains members in the use of guns and explosives. RIRA continued to attract new members, and its senior members were committed to launching attacks on security forces. Three suspected RIRA members that engaged in cigarette smuggling were arrested in Spain in 2006. From 2006 to November 2007, terrorist activity in the form of successful and attempted attacks by RIRA only slightly decreased. Notably, between August and November 2006, throughout Northern Ireland, RIRA targeted B&Q home-supply stores and other retail businesses in successful and attempted fire bombings, although a handful of these attacks were also claimed by the Continuity Irish Republican Army (CIRA). In November 2007, RIRA claimed two armed attacks that wounded two Police Service of Northern Ireland (PSNI) officers that same month. RIRA claimed responsibility for a May 2008 improvised explosive device that injured a PSNI officer in Belfast and the firebombing of two stores. The Independent Monitoring Commission, which was established to oversee the peace process, assesses that RIRA members were likely responsible for the majority of the shootings and assaults that occurred in Northern Ireland in 2008. In November 2008, Lithuania arrested a RIRA member for attempting to arrange a shipment of weapons to Northern Ireland.

Strength: According to the Irish government, RIRA has approximately 100 active members. The organization may receive limited support from IRA hardliners and Republican sympathizers who are dissatisfied with the IRA's continuing cease-fire and with Sinn Fein's involvement in the peace process. Approximately 40 RIRA members are in Irish jails.

Location/Area of Operation: Northern Ireland, Great Britain, and the Irish Republic.

External Aid: RIRA is suspected of receiving funds from sympathizers in the United States and of attempting to buy weapons from U.S. gun dealers. RIRA also is reported to have purchased sophisticated weapons from the Balkans.

REVOLUTIONARY ARMED FORCES OF COLOMBIA

a.k.a. FARC; Fuerzas Armadas Revolucionarias de Colombia.

Description: The Revolutionary Armed Forces of Colombia (FARC) was designated as a Foreign Terrorist Organization on October 8, 1997. The Revolutionary Armed Forces of Colombia (FARC) is Latin America's oldest, largest, most capable, and best-equipped insurgency, and remains so in spite of recent losses at the hands of the Colombian government. It began in the early 1960s as an outgrowth of the Liberal Party-based peasant self-defense leagues, but took on Marxist ideology. Today, it only nominally fights in support of Marxist goals. The FARC is governed by a general secretariat led by new Supreme Commander Guillermo Leon Saenz (a.k.a. Alfonso Cano) and six others, including senior military commander Victor Suarez (a.k.a. Jorge Briceno or "Mono Jojoy"). The FARC is organized along military lines and includes some specialized urban fighting units. In 2008, the FARC experienced several significant setbacks. A robust and continuing Colombian military offensive targeting key FARC units and leaders succeeded in capturing or killing a number of FARC senior and mid-level commanders. Colombian military operations on March 1 resulted in the death of Luis Devia Silva (a.k.a. Raul Reyes), the FARC's second-in-command at the time. In early March the FARC lost another secretariat member, Manuel Jesus Munoz Ortiz (a.k.a. Ivan Rios) when he was killed by one of his own security guards, and the FARC's co-founder and Supreme Leader Antonio Marin (a.k.a. Manuel Marulanda or Tirofijo) died in late March, reportedly from heart failure. In July, the Colombian military pulled off a dramatic rescue of 15 high-value FARC hostages including three U.S. Department of Defense contractors and former Colombian presidential candidate Ingrid Betancourt.

Activities: The FARC has carried out bombings, murder, mortar attacks, kidnapping, extortion, and hijacking, as well as guerrilla and conventional military action against Colombian political, military, and economic targets. Foreign citizens were often targets of abductions that the FARC carried out to obtain ransom and political leverage. The FARC has well-documented ties to the full range of narcotics trafficking activities, including taxation, cultivation, and distribution.

Strength: Approximately 9,000 to 12,000 combatants and several thousand more supporters.

Location/Area of Operation: Primarily in Colombia with some activities, such as extortion, kidnapping, weapons sourcing, and logistics in neighboring countries.

External Aid: Cuba provided some medical care, safe haven, and political consultation. Venezuela supplied some logistical, financial, and lethal aid to the FARC, although this may be a result of individual corruption rather than official policy; available information is not conclusive. The FARC often used the Colombia/Venezuela, Colombia/Panama, and Colombia/Ecuador border areas for incursions into Colombia and also used Venezuelan and Ecuadorian territory for safe haven, although the degree of government acquiescence was not clear and may vary depending on localized cross-border relations.

REVOLUTIONARY NUCLEI

a.k.a. Revolutionary Cells; ELA; Epanastatiki Pirines; Epanastatikos Laikos Agonas; June 78; Liberation Struggle; Organization of Revolutionary Internationalist Solidarity; Popular Revolutionary Struggle; Revolutionary People's Struggle; Revolutionary Popular Struggle.

Description: Revolutionary Nuclei (RN) was designated as a Foreign Terrorist Organization on October 8, 1997. RN emerged from a broad range of anti-establishment and anti-U.S./NATO/EU leftist groups active in Greece between 1995 and 1998. The group is believed to be the successor to or offshoot of Greece's most prolific terrorist group, Revolutionary People's Struggle (ELA), which has not claimed an attack since January 1995. Indeed, RN appeared to fill the void left by ELA, particularly as lesser groups faded from the scene. RN's few communiqués show strong similarities in rhetoric, tone, and theme to ELA proclamations.

Activities: Since it began operations in January 1995, the group has claimed responsibility for some two dozen arson attacks and low-level bombings against a range of U.S., Greek, and other European targets in Greece. In its most infamous and lethal attack to date, the group claimed responsibility for a bomb it detonated at the Intercontinental Hotel in April 1999 that resulted in the death of a Greek woman and injury of a Greek man. RN's modus operandi includes warning calls of impending attacks, attacks targeting property instead of individuals, use of rudimentary timing devices, and strikes during the late evening to early morning hours. RN's last confirmed attacks against U.S. interests in Greece occurred in November 2000, with two separate bombings against the Athens offices of Citigroup and the studio of a Greek-American sculptor. Greek targets have included judicial and other government office buildings, private vehicles, and the offices of Greek firms involved in NATO-related defense contracts in Greece. Similarly, the group has attacked European interests in Athens.

Strength: Group membership is unknown.

Location/Area of Operation: Unknown, but historically RN's area of operation was Athens.

External Aid: Unknown but believed to be self-sustaining.

REVOLUTIONARY ORGANIZATION 17 NOVEMBER

a.k.a. Epanastatiki Organosi 17 Noemvri; 17 November.

Description: The Revolutionary Organization 17 November (17N) was designated as a Foreign Terrorist Organization on October 8, 1997. Revolutionary Organization 17 November (17N) is a radical leftist group established in 1975 and named for the student uprising in Greece in November 1973 that protested the ruling military junta. 17N is an anti-Greece, anti-U.S., anti-Turkey, and anti-NATO group that seeks the ouster of U.S. bases from Greece, the removal of Turkish military forces from Cyprus, and the severing of Greece's ties to NATO and the European Union (EU).

Activities: Initial attacks consisted of assassinations of senior U.S. officials and Greek public figures. Five U.S. Embassy employees have been murdered since 17N began its terrorist activities in 1975. The group began using bombings in the 1980s. In 1990, 17N expanded its targets to include Turkish diplomats, EU facilities, and foreign firms investing in Greece, and added improvised rocket attacks to its methods. The group supported itself largely through bank robberies. A failed 17N bombing attempt in June 2002 at the port of Piraeus in Athens, coupled with robust detective work,. led to the arrest of 19 members, the first 17N operatives ever arrested, including a key leader of the organization. In December 2003, a Greek court convicted 15 members, five of whom were given multiple life terms. Four other alleged members were acquitted for lack of evidence. In May 2007, two of these 15 members were acquitted on appeal due to doubts surrounding the charges against them. The convictions of the other 13 were upheld on appeal.

Strength: Unknown but presumed to be small.

Location/Area of Operation: Athens, Greece.

External Aid: Unknown.

REVOLUTIONARY PEOPLE'S LIBERATION PARTY/FRONT

a.k.a. DHKP/C; Dev Sol; Dev Sol Armed Revolutionary Units; Dev Sol Silahli Devrimci Birlikleri; Dev Sol SDB; Devrimci Halk Kurtulus Partisi-Cephesi; Devrimci Sol; Revolutionary Left.

Description: The Revolutionary People's Liberation Party/Front (DHKP/C) was designated as a Foreign Terrorist Organization on October 8, 1997. The DHKP/C originally formed in 1978 as Devrimci Sol, or Dev Sol, a splinter faction of Dev Genc (Revolutionary Youth). It was renamed in 1994, after factional infighting. "Party" refers to the group's political activities, while "Front" is a reference to the group's militant operations. The group espouses a Marxist-Leninist ideology and is vehemently an anti-U.S., anti-NATO, and anti-Turkey establishment. Its goals are the establishment of a socialist state and the abolition of F-type prisons, which contain one to three-man prison cells. DHKP/C finances its activities chiefly through donations and extortion.

Activities: Since the late 1980s, the group has primarily targeted current and retired Turkish security and military officials. It began a new campaign against foreign interests in 1990, which included attacks against U.S. military and diplomatic personnel and facilities. In order to protest perceived U.S. imperialism during the Gulf War, Dev Sol assassinated two U.S. military contractors, wounded an Air Force officer, and bombed more than 20 U.S. and NATO military, commercial, and cultural facilities.

In its first significant terrorist act as DHKP/C in 1996, the group assassinated a prominent Turkish businessman and two others; the perpetrators fled to Belgium, where legal cases continue. DHKP/C added suicide bombings to its repertoire in 2001, with successful attacks against Turkish police in January and September. Since the end of 2001, DHKP/C has typically used improvised explosive devices against official Turkish targets and soft U.S. targets of opportunity. Attacks against U.S. targets beginning in 2003 were probably a response to Operation Iraqi Freedom.

Operations and arrests against the group have weakened its capabilities. In late June 2004, the group was suspected of a bus bombing at Istanbul University, which killed four civilians and 21 other people. In July 2005, in Ankara, police intercepted and killed a suicide bomber who attempted to attack the Ministry of Justice. In June 2006, the group fired upon and killed a police officer in Istanbul; four members of the group were arrested the next month for the attack.

The DKHP/C was dealt a major ideological blow when Dursun Karatas, leader of the group, died in August 2008 in the Netherlands. Throughout 2008, several DHKP/C members were arrested in Turkey and Europe, and several members stood trial for previous terrorist activity. In early March, Turkish Authorities arrested three DHKP/C members preparing bombings. German authorities in late July indicted a DKHP/C senior leader, and in November German authorities arrested several individuals suspected of serving as high-ranking DHKP/C functionaries. In addition, Belgian authorities reviewed the acquittal of several DHKP/C members and began retrial to reach final judgment.

Strength: Probably several dozen terrorist operatives inside Turkey, with a limited support network throughout Europe.

Location/Area of Operation: Turkey, primarily Istanbul, Ankara, Izmir, and Adana.

External Aid: Widely believed to have training facilities or offices in Lebanon and Syria. DHKP/C raises funds in Europe.

SHINING PATH

a.k.a. SL; Sendero Luminoso; Ejercito Guerrillero Popular (People's Guerrilla Army); EGP; Ejercito Popular de Liberacion (People's Liberation Army); EPL; Partido Comunista del Peru (Communist Party of Peru); PCP; Partido Comunista del Peru en el Sendero Luminoso de Jose Carlos Mariategui (Communist Party of Peru on the Shining Path of Jose Carlos Mariategui); Socorro Popular del Peru (People's Aid of Peru); SPP.

Description: Shining Path (SL) was designated as a Foreign Terrorist Organization on October 8, 1997. Former university professor

Abimael Guzman formed the Shining Path (SL) in Peru in the late 1960s; his teachings created the foundation of SL's militant Maoist doctrine. In the 1980s, SL became one of the most ruthless terrorist groups in the Western Hemisphere. The Peruvian government made dramatic gains against SL during the 1990s, capturing Guzman in 1992 and killing a large number of militants. SL's stated goal is to destroy existing Peruvian institutions and replace them with a communist peasant revolutionary regime. It also opposes any influence by foreign governments. More recently, SL members have attempted to influence the local populace through indoctrination as opposed to violence.

Activities: In the past, SL has conducted indiscriminate bombing campaigns, ambushes, and selective assassinations. Remnants of SL now focus on drug-trafficking and production activities to obtain funds to carry out attacks.

A recent increase in SL attacks against Peruvian security forces and counter-narcotics personnel during fall 2008 underscored that the SL remained a threat. In response to SL's bloody attacks, Peruvian authorities stepped up counterterrorism efforts against the group and have since kept the SL remnants largely on the defensive.

Strength: Unknown but estimated to be between 200 and 300 armed militants.

Location/Area of Operation: Peru, with most activity in rural areas, specifically the Huallaga Valley, the Ene River, and the Apurimac Valley of central Peru.

External Aid: None.

UNITED SELF-DEFENSE FORCES OF COLOMBIA

a.k.a. AUC; Autodefensas Unidas de Colombia.

Description: The United Self-Defense Forces of Colombia (AUC) was designated as a Foreign Terrorist Organization on September 10, 2001. The United Self-Defense Forces of Colombia (AUC), commonly referred to as the paramilitaries, was an umbrella group formed in April 1997 to organize loosely affiliated illegal paramilitary groups that had emerged to retaliate against leftist guerillas fighting the Colombian government and the landed establishment. The AUC increasingly discarded its counter-guerilla activities, electing instead to involve itself in the illegal drug trade. By 2007, as the result of a large demobilization process, most of the AUC's centralized military structure had been dismantled, and all of the top paramilitary chiefs had stepped down with the majority being held in a maximum security facility. More than 31,000 paramilitary members and support personnel demobilized bloc by bloc from 2003 to 2006. Colombia now faces criminal gangs composed of some demobilized paramilitaries and other individuals, and one minor paramilitary group that refused to disarm. Unlike the AUC, the new criminal groups make little claim of fighting insurgents. They are more clearly criminal enterprises focused primarily on drug trafficking, other lucrative illicit activities, and influencing local politics to facilitate their criminal ventures. These new criminal groups are not a reconstituted AUC, but they recruit from the pool of former AUC members. Some of the various groups' leadership appears to be former mid-level paramilitary commanders who did not participate in demobilization.

Activities: Prior to the 2006 demobilization, the AUC engaged in terrorist activity through a variety of activities including political killings and kidnappings of human rights workers, journalists, teachers, and trade unionists, among others. As much as 70 percent of the paramilitary operational costs were financed with drug-related earnings. The emerging criminal groups include some remnants of the AUC, and their members continued to engage heavily in criminal activities.

Strength: With the exception of a few paramilitary fronts who refused to participate in the demobilization process, the AUC's organizational structure no longer exists. According to Colombian government figures, approximately 10 to 15 percent of the 3,000 to 4,000 members of these criminal groups are former members of paramilitary groups, including the AUC.

Location/Areas of Operation: Paramilitary forces were strongest in northwest Colombia in Antioquia, Cordoba, Sucre, Atlantico, Magdelena, Cesar, La Guajira, and Bolivar Departments, with affiliate groups in the coffee region, Valle del Cauca, and Meta Department.

External Aid: None.

Notes

Notes